ANCIENT CHRISTIAN TEXTS

COMMENTARY ON JEREMIAH

Jerome

TRANSLATED WITH AN
INTRODUCTION AND NOTES BY

MICHAEL GRAVES

EDITED BY

CHRISTOPHER A. HALL

SERIES EDITORS

THOMAS C. ODEN AND GERALD L. BRAY

IVP Academic

An imprint of InterVarsity Press
Downers Grove, Illinois

InterVarsity Press
P.O. Box 1400, Downers Grove, IL 60515-1426
World Wide Web: www.ivpress.com
E-mail: email@ivpress.com

InterVarsity Press® is the book-publishing division of InterVarsity Christian Fellowship/USA®, a movement of students and faculty active on campus at hundreds of universities, colleges and schools of nursing in the United States of America, and a member movement of the International Fellowship of Evangelical Students. For information about local and regional activities, write Public Relations Dept., InterVarsity Christian Fellowship/USA, 6400 Schroeder Rd., P.O. Box 7895, Madison, WI 53707-7895, or visit the IVCF website at <www.intervarsity.org>.

Design: Cindy Kiple
Images: Saints Peter and Paul by Carlo Crivelli at Accademia, Venice/Art Resource, NY
Monogrammatic cross: Early Christian monogrammatic cross from Monastero, at Kunsthistorisches Museum, Vienna, Austria. Erich Lessing/Art Resource, NY

ISBN 978-0-8308-2910-1

Printed in the United States of America ∞

Library of Congress Cataloging-in-Publication Data

Jerome, Saint, d. 419 or 20.
   [Commentariorum in Jeremiam. English]
   Commentary on Jeremiah/Jerome; translated with an introduction
and notes by Michael Graves; edited by Christopher A. Hall.
      p. cm.—(Ancient Christian texts)
   Includes bibliographical references (p.   ) and indexes.
   ISBN 978-0-8308-2910-1 (hardcover: alk. paper)
   1. Bible. O.T. Jeremiah—Commentaries.   I. Graves, Michael, 1973-
II. Hall, Christopher A. (Christopher Alan), 1950- III. Title.
   BS1525.J4714 2011
   224'.207—dc23

2011047307

P	24	23	22	21	20	19	18	17	16	15	14	13	12	11	10	9	8	7	6	5	4	3	2	1
Y	31	30	29	28	27	26	25	24	23	22	21	20	19	18	17	16	15	14	13	12	11			

CONTENTS

GENERAL INTRODUCTION

The Ancient Christian Texts series (hereafter ACT) presents the full text of ancient Christian commentaries on Scripture that have remained so unnoticed that they have not yet been translated into English.

The patristic period (A.D. 95-750) is the time of the fathers of the church, when the exegesis of Scripture texts was in its primitive formation. This period spans from Clement of Rome to John of Damascus, embracing seven centuries of biblical interpretation, from the end of the New Testament to the mid-eighth century, including the Venerable Bede.

This series extends but does not reduplicate texts of the Ancient Christian Commentary on Scripture (ACCS). It presents full-length translations of texts that appear only as brief extracts in the ACCS. The ACCS began years ago authorizing full-length translations of key patristic texts on Scripture in order to provide fresh sources of valuable commentary that previously was not available in English. It is from these translations that the ACT Series has emerged.

A multiyear project such as this requires a well-defined objective. The task is straightforward: *to introduce full-length translations of key texts of early Christian teaching, homilies and commentaries on a particular book of Scripture.* These are seminal documents that have decisively shaped the entire subsequent history of biblical exegesis, but in our time have been largely ignored.

To carry out this mission the Ancient Christian Texts series has four aspirations:

1. To show the approach of one of the early Christian writers in dealing with the problems of understanding, reading and conveying the meaning of a particular book of Scripture.

2. To make more fully available the whole argument of the ancient Christian interpreter of Scripture to all who wish to think with the early church about a particular canonical text.

3. To broaden the base of biblical studies, Christian teaching and preaching to include classical Christian exegesis.

4. To stimulate Christian historical, biblical, theological and pastoral scholarship toward deeper inquiry into early classic practitioners of scriptural interpretation.

For Whom Is This Series Designed?

We have selected and translated these texts primarily for general and nonprofessional use by an audience of persons who study the Bible regularly.

In varied cultural settings around the world, contemporary readers are asking how they might grasp the meaning of sacred texts under the instruction of the great minds of the ancient church. They often study books of the Bible verse by verse, book by book, in groups and workshops, sometimes with a modern commentary in hand. But many who study the Bible intensively hunger to have available to them as well the thoughts of some reliable classic Christian commentator on this same text. This series will give the modern commentators a classical text for comparison and amplification. Readers will judge for themselves as to how valuable or complementary are their insights and guidance.

The classic texts we are translating were originally written for anyone (lay or clergy, believers and seekers) who would wish to reflect and meditate with the great minds of the early church. They sought to illuminate the plain sense, theological wisdom, and moral and spiritual meaning of an individual book of Scripture. They were not written for an academic audience, but for a community of faith shaped by the sacred text.

Yet in serving this general audience, the editors remain determined not to neglect the rigorous requirements and needs of academic readers who until recently have had few full translations available to them in the history of exegesis. So this series is designed also to serve public libraries, universities, academic classes, homiletic preparation and historical interests worldwide in Christian scholarship and interpretation.

Hence our expected audience is not limited to the highly technical and specialized scholarly field of patristic studies, with its strong bent toward detailed word studies and explorations of cultural contexts. Though all of our editors and translators are patristic and linguistic scholars, they also are scholars who search for the meanings and implications of the texts. The audience is not primarily the university scholar concentrating on the study of the history of the transmission of the text or those with highly focused interests in textual morphology or historical-critical issues. If we succeed in serving our wider readers practically and well, we hope to serve as well college and seminary courses in Bible, church history, historical theology, hermeneutics and homiletics. These texts have not until now been available to these classes.

Readiness for Classic Spiritual Formation

Today global Christians are being steadily drawn toward these biblical and patristic sources for daily meditation and spiritual formation. They are on the outlook for primary classic sources of spiritual formation and biblical interpretation, presented in accessible form and grounded in reliable scholarship.

These crucial texts have had an extended epoch of sustained influence on Scripture interpretation, but virtually no influence in the modern period. They also deserve a hearing among modern readers and scholars. There is a growing awareness of the speculative excesses and spiritual and homiletic limitations of much post-Enlightenment criticism. Meanwhile the motifs, methods and approaches of ancient exegetes have remained unfamiliar not only to historians but to otherwise highly literate biblical scholars, trained exhaustively in the methods of historical and scientific criticism.

It is ironic that our times, which claim to be so fully furnished with historical insight and research methods, have neglected these texts more than scholars in previous centuries who could read them in their original languages.

This series provides indisputable evidence of the modern neglect of classic Christian exegesis: it remains a fact that extensive and once authoritative classic commentaries on Scripture still remain untranslated into any modern language. Even in China such a high level of neglect has not befallen classic Buddhist, Taoist and Confucian commentaries.

Ecumenical Scholarship

This series, like its two companion series, the ACCS and Ancient Christian Doctrine (ACD), are expressions of unceasing ecumenical efforts that have enjoyed the wide cooperation of distinguished scholars of many differing academic communities. Under this classic textual umbrella, it has brought together in common spirit Christians who have long distanced themselves from each other by competing church memories. But all of these traditions have an equal right to appeal to the early history of Christian exegesis. All of these traditions can, without a sacrifice of principle or intellect, come together to study texts common to them all. This is its ecumenical significance.

This series of translations is respectful of a distinctively theological reading of Scripture that cannot be reduced to historical, philosophical, scientific, or sociological insights or methods alone. It takes seriously the venerable tradition of ecumenical reflection concerning the premises of revelation, providence, apostolicity, canon and consensuality. A high respect is here granted, despite modern assumptions, to uniquely Christian theological forms of reasoning, such as classical consensual christological and triune reasoning, as distinguishing premises of classic Christian textual interpretation. These cannot be acquired by empirical methods alone. This approach does not pit theology against critical theory; instead, it incorporates critical historical methods and brings them into coordinate accountability within its larger purpose of listening to Scripture.

The internationally diverse character of our editors and translators corresponds with the global range of our audience, which bridges many major communions of Christianity. We have sought to bring together a distinguished international network of Protestant, Catholic and Orthodox scholars, editors, and translators of the highest quality and reputation to accomplish this design.

But why just now at this historical moment is this need for patristic wisdom felt particularly by so many readers of Scripture? Part of the reason is that these readers have been long deprived of significant contact with many of these vital sources of classic Christian exegesis.

The Ancient Commentary Tradition

This series focuses on texts that comment on Scripture and teach its meaning. We define a commentary in its plain-sense definition as a series of illustrative or explanatory notes on any work of enduring significance. The word *commentary* is an Anglicized form of the Latin *commentarius* (or "annotation" or "memorandum" on a subject or text or series of events). In its theological meaning it is a work that explains, analyzes or expounds a biblical book or portion of Scripture. Tertullian, Origen, John Chrysostom, Jerome, Augustine and Clement of Alexandria all revealed their familiarity with both the secular and religious commentators available to them as they unpacked the meanings of the sacred text at hand.

The commentary in ancient times typically began with a general introduction covering such questions as authorship, date, purpose and audience. It commented as needed on grammatical or lexical problems in the text and provided explanations of difficulties in the text. It typically moved verse by verse through a Scripture text, seeking to make its meaning clear and its import understood.

The general western literary genre of commentary has been definitively shaped by the history of early Christian commentaries on Scripture. It is from Origen, Hilary, the *Opus imperfectum in Matthaeum*, John Chrysostom and Cyril of Alexandria that we learn what a commentary is—far more so than in the case of classic medical, philosophical or poetic commentaries. It leaves too much unsaid simply to assume that the Christian biblical commentary took a previously extant literary genre and reshaped it for Christian texts. Rather it is more accurate to say that *the Western literary genre of the commentary (and especially the biblical commentary) has patristic commentaries as its decisive pattern and prototype.*

It is only in the last two centuries, since the development of modern historicist methods of criticism, that modern writers have sought more strictly to delimit the definition of a commentary so as to include only certain limited interests focusing largely on historical-critical method, philological and grammatical observations, literary analysis, and socio-political or economic circumstances impinging on the text. While respecting all these approaches, the ACT editors do not hesitate to use the classic word *commentary* to define more broadly the genre of this series. These are commentaries in their classic sense.

The ACT editors freely take the assumption that the Christian canon is to be respected as the church's sacred text. The reading and preaching of Scripture are vital to religious life. The central hope of this endeavor is that it might contribute in some small way to the revitalization of religious faith and community through a renewed discovery of the earliest readings of the church's Scriptures.

An Appeal to Allow the Text to Speak for Itself

This prompts two appeals:

1. For those who begin by assuming as normative for a commentary only the norms considered typical for modern expressions of what a commentary is, we ask: Please allow the ancient commentators to define *commentarius* according to their own lights. Those who assume the preemptive authority and truthfulness of modern critical methods alone will always tend to view the classic Christian exegetes as dated, quaint, premodern, hence inadequate, and in some instances comic or even mean-spirited, prejudiced, unjust and oppressive. So in the interest of hermeneutical fairness, it is recommended that the modern reader not impose on ancient Christian exegetes modern assumptions about valid readings of Scripture. The ancient Christian writers constantly challenge these unspoken, hidden and indeed often camouflaged assumptions that have become commonplace in our time.

We leave it to others to discuss the merits of ancient versus modern methods of exegesis. But even this cannot be done honestly without a serious examination of the texts of ancient exegesis. Ancient commentaries may be disqualified as commentaries by modern standards. But they remain commentaries by the standards of those who anteceded and formed the basis of the modern commentary.

The attempt to read a Scripture text while ruling out all theological and moral assumptions—as well as ecclesial, sacramental and dogmatic assumptions that have prevailed generally in the community of faith out of which it emerged—is a very thin enterprise indeed. Those who tendentiously may read a single page of patristic exegesis, gasp and toss it away because it does not conform adequately to the canons of modern exegesis and historicist commentary are surely not exhibiting a valid model for critical inquiry today.

2. In ancient Christian exegesis, chains of biblical references were often very important in thinking about the text in relation to the whole testimony of sacred Scripture, by the analogy of faith, comparing text with text, on the premise that *scripturam ex scriptura explicandam esse.* When ancient exegesis weaves many Scriptures together, it does not limit its focus to a single text as much modern exegesis prefers, but constantly relates it to other texts, by analogy, intensively using typological reasoning, as did the rabbinic tradition.

Since the principle prevails in ancient Christian exegesis that each text is illumined by other texts and by the whole narrative of the history of revelation, we find in patristic comments on a given text many other subtexts interwoven in order to illumine that text. In these ways the models of exegesis often do not correspond with modern commentary assumptions, which tend to resist or rule out chains of scriptural reference. We implore the reader not to force the assumptions of twenty-first-century hermeneutics on the ancient Christian writers, who themselves knew nothing of what we now call hermeneutics.

The Complementarity of Research Methods in this Series

The Ancient Christian Texts series will employ several interrelated methods of research, which the editors and translators seek to bring together in a working integration. Principal among these methods are the following:

1. The editors, translators and annotators will bring to bear the best resources of *textual criticism* in preparation for their volumes. This series is not intended to produce a new critical edition of the original-language text. The best Urtext in the original language will be used. Significant variants in the earliest manuscript sources of the text may be commented on as needed in the annotations. But it will be assumed that the editors and translators will be familiar with the textual ambiguities of a particular text and be able to state their conclusions about significant differences among scholars. Since we are working with ancient texts that have, in some cases, problematic or ambiguous passages, we are obliged to employ all methods of historical, philological and textual inquiry appropriate to the study of ancient texts. To that end, we will appeal to the most reliable text-critical scholarship of both biblical and patristic studies. We will assume that our editors and translators have reviewed the international literature of textual critics regarding their text so as to provide the reader with a translation of the most authoritative and reliable form of the ancient text. We will leave it to the volume editors and translators, under the supervision of the general editors, to make these assessments. This will include the challenge of considering which variants within the biblical text itself might impinge on the patristic text, and which forms or stemma of the biblical text the patristic writer was employing. The annotator will supply explanatory footnotes where these textual challenges may raise potential confusions for the reader.

2. Our editors and translators will seek to understand the *historical context* (including socioeconomic, political and psychological aspects as needed) of the text. These understandings are often vital to right discernment of the writer's intention. Yet we do not see our primary mission as that of discussing in detail these contexts. They are to be factored into the translation and commented on as needed in the annotations, but are not to become the primary focus of this series. Our central interest is less in the social location of the text or the philological history of particular words than in authorial intent and accurate translation. Assuming a proper social-historical contextualization of the text, the main focus of this series will be on a dispassionate and fair translation and analysis of the text itself.

3. The main task is to set forth the meaning of the biblical text itself as understood by the patristic writer. The intention of our volume editors and translators is to help the reader see clearly into the meanings which patristic commentators have discovered in the biblical text. *Exegesis* in its classic sense implies an effort to explain, interpret and comment on a text, its meaning, its sources and its connections with other texts. It implies a close reading of the text, utilizing whatever linguistic, historical, literary or theological resources are available to explain the text. It is contrasted with *eisegesis*, which implies that interpreters have imposed their own personal opinions or assumptions on the text. The patristic writers actively practiced intratextual exegesis, which seeks to define and identify the exact wording of the text, its grammatical structure and the interconnectedness of its parts. They also practiced extratextual exegesis, seeking to discern the geographical, historical or cultural context in which the text was written. Our editors and annotators will also be attentive as needed to the ways in which the ancient Christian writer described his own interpreting process or hermeneutic assumptions.

4. The underlying philosophy of translation that we employ in this series, like that of the Ancient Christian Commentary on Scripture, is termed *dynamic equivalency*. We wish to avoid the pitfalls of either too loose a paraphrase or too rigid a literal translation. We seek language that is literary but not purely literal. Whenever possible we have opted for the metaphors and terms that are normally in use in everyday English-speaking culture. Our purpose is to allow the ancient Christian writers to speak for themselves to ordinary readers in the present generation. We want to make it easier for the Bible reader to gain ready access to the deepest reflection of the ancient Christian community of faith on a particular book of Scripture. We seek a thought-for-thought translation rather than a formal equivalence or word-for-word style. This requires the words to be first translated accurately and then rendered in understandable idiom. We seek to present the same thoughts, feelings, connotations and effects of the original text in everyday English language. We have used vocabulary and language structures commonly used by the average person. We do not leave the quality of translation only to the primary translator, but pass it through several levels of editorial review before confirming it.

The Function of the ACT Introductions, Annotations and Translations

In writing the introduction for a particular volume of the ACT series, the translator or volume editor will discuss, where possible, the opinion of the writer regarding authorship of the text, the importance of the biblical book for other patristic interpreters, the availability or paucity of patristic comment, any salient points of debate between the Fathers, and any special challenges involved in translating and editing the particular volume. The introduction affords the opportunity to frame the entire commentary in a manner that will help the general reader understand the nature and significance of patristic comment on the biblical texts under consideration and to help readers find their critical bearings so as to read and use the commentary in an informed way.

The footnotes will assist the reader with obscurities and potential confusions. In the annotations the volume editors have identified Scripture allusions and historical references embedded within the texts. Their purpose is to help the reader move easily from passage to passage without losing a sense of the whole.

The ACT general editors seek to be circumspect and meticulous in commissioning volume editors and translators. We strive for a high level of consistency and literary quality throughout the course of this series. We have sought out as volume editors and translators those patristic and biblical scholars who are thoroughly familiar with their original language sources, who are informed historically, and who are sympathetic to the needs of ordinary nonprofessional readers who may not have professional language skills.

Thomas C. Oden and Gerald L. Bray, Series Editors

ABBREVIATIONS

For the transliteration of ancient languages, I have followed as closely as possible the *SBL Handbook of Style* (Peabody, MA: Hendrickson, 1999). Abbreviations used are given below.

General

b.	Babylonian Talmud
bk.	book
ca.	*circa*, about, approximately
Gk	Greek
Heb	Hebrew
Ketiv	the form as written (as indicated in Masoretic manuscripts)
Lat	Latin
lit.	literal, literally
MS, MSS	manuscript, manuscripts
p.	Palestinian Talmud
pref.	preface
prol., prols.	prologue, prologues
Qere	the form to be read (as indicated in Masoretic manuscripts)
v., vv.	verse, verses

Ancient Bible Versions

Aq	Greek (hexaplaric) version of Aquila
B19a	Leningrad Codex, a medieval Hebrew (Masoretic) manuscript and basis for the standard printed edition of the Hebrew Bible, *Biblia Hebraica Stuttgartensia*
IH	Jerome's *iuxta Hebraeos* translation (i.e., his translation of the Hebrew Bible)
LXX	Septuagint (the Seventy)
MT	Masoretic Text
OL	Old Latin translation, based on the Septuagint
Pesh	Syriac Peshitta
Sym	Greek (hexaplaric) version of Symmachus
Targ	Aramaic Targum
Th	Greek (hexaplaric) version of Theodotion
Vg	Vulgate

Modern Bible Versions

RSV   Revised Standard Version

Lexicons and Other Linguistic Aids

BDB   Brown, Francis, S. R. Driver, and Charles A. Briggs. *A Hebrew and English Lexicon of the Old Testament*. Oxford: Oxford University Press, 1906. Reprinted with revisions, 1951.

FC   Fathers of the Church: A New Translation. Washington, DC: Catholic University of America Press, 1947–.

Field   Field, Frederick. *Origenis Hexaplorum Quae Supersunt; sive Veterum Interpretium Graecorum in Totum Vetus Testamentum Fragmenta*. 2 vols. Oxford: Clarendon, 1875.

Jastrow   Jastrow, Marcus. *A Dictionary of the Targumim, the Talmud Babli and Yerushalmi, and the Midrashic Literature*. New York: Pardes Publishing, 1950.

KB   Koehler, Ludwig, and Walter Baumgartner, et al. *The Hebrew and Aramaic Lexicon of the Old Testament*. 5 vols. Leiden: Brill, 1994-2000.

Kennicott   Kennicott, Benjamin. *Vetus Testamentum Hebraicum cum variis lectionibus*. Oxford: Clarendon, 1776-1780.

Lambdin   Lambdin, T. *Introduction to Biblical Hebrew*. Upper Saddle River, NJ: Prentice Hall, 1971.

Lampe   Lampe, G. W. H. *A Patristic Greek Lexicon*. Oxford: Clarendon Press, 1961.

LCL   Loeb Classical Library

LS   Lewis, Charlton T., and Charles Short. *A Latin Dictionary*. Oxford: Oxford University Press, 1879.

LSJ   Liddell, Henry George, and Robert Scott. Revised and Augmented by Sir Henry Stuart Jones. *A Greek-English Lexicon, with a Revised Supplement*. Oxford: Oxford University Press, 1996.

OLD   Glare, P. G. W. *Oxford Latin Dictionary*. Oxford: Oxford University Press, 1996.

OS   De Lagarde, Paul. *Onomastica sacra*. Göttingen: Vandenhoeck and Ruprecht, 1887.

Sok   Sokoloff, Michael. *A Syriac Lexicon*. Winona Lake, IN: Eisenbrauns; Piscataway, NJ: Gorgias Press, 2009.

Sok, *DJPA*   Sokoloff, Michael. *A Dictionary of Jewish Palestinian Aramaic*. 2d ed. Ramat-Gan, Israel: Bar Ilan University Press; Baltimore: Johns Hopkins University Press, 2002.

Soph   Sophocles, E. A. *Greek Lexicon of the Roman and Byzantine Periods*. 2 vols. New York: Charles Scribner's Sons, 1900.

Sout   Souter, Alexander. *A Glossary of Later Latin*. Oxford: Oxford University Press, 1949.

Series

CC   Corpus Christianorum

CSEL   Corpus Scriptorum Ecclesiasticorum Latinorum

FC	Fathers of the Church: A New Translation. Washington, DC: Catholic University of America Press, 1947–.
LCL	Loeb Classical Library
NPNF	Nicene and Post-Nicene Fathers, series 2
SC	Sources Chrétiennes

Classical and Other Early Sources

Aelian
Nat. An.   *De Natura Animalium (The Nature of Animals)*

Alexander of Aphrodisias
Fat.   *De Fato*

Aristotle
An. Pr.   *Analytica Priora (Prior Analytics)*
Hist. An.   *Historia Animalium (History of Animals)*

Aulus Gellius
Noct. Att.   *Noctes Atticae (Attic Nights)*

Cicero
Brut.   *Brutus*
De Or.   *De Oratore*
Div.   *De Divinatione*
Fin.   *De Finibus*
Inv.   *De Inventione Rhetorica*
Nat. D.   *De Natura Decorum*
Off.   *De Officiis*
Or. Brut.   *Orator ad M. Brutum*
Top.   *Topica*
Tusc.   *Tusculanae Disputationes*

Dionysius of Halicarnassus
Dem.   *De Demosthene*

Euripides
Herc. Fur.   *Hercules Furens (The Madness of Hercules)*

Hesiod
Op.   *Opera et Dies (Works and Days)*
Theog.   *Theogonia (Theogony)*

Homer
Od.   *Odyssea (Odyssey)*

Horace
Carm.   *Carmina (Odes)*

| *Ep.* | *Epistulae (Epistles)* |

Josephus
| *Ant.* | *Antiquities of the Jews (Antiquitates Judaicae)* |
| *J.W.* | *Jewish Wars (Bellum Judicarum)* |

Ovid
| *Am.* | *Amores* |
| *Metam.* | *Metamorphoses* |

Persius
| *Sat.* | *Satirae* |

Philo
Agr.	*De Agricultum (On Agriculture)*
Congr.	*De Congressu Eruditionus Gratia*
Fug.	*De Fugit et Inventione (On Flight and Finding)*
Leg.	*Legum Allegoriae (Allegorical Interpretation)*
Mos.	*De Vita Mosis (On the Life of Moses)*
Plant.	*De Plantione (On Planting)*
Q.G.	*Quaestiones et Solutiones in Genesin (Questions and Answers on Genesis)*
Somn.	*De Somniis (On Dreams)*

Plato
Leg.	*Leges (Laws)*
Prot.	*Protagoras*
Resp.	*Respublica*

Pliny
| *Nat.* | *Naturalis Historia (Natural History)* |

Plutarch
Comm. Not.	*De Communibus Notitiis contra Stoicos*
Mor.	*Moralia*
Stoic. Rep.	*De Stoicarum Repugnantiis*

Symmachus
| *Ep.* | *Epistulae (Letters)* |

Terence
| *Ad.* | *Adelphi* |

Virgil
Aen.	*Aeneid*
Ecl.	*Eclogae*
Georg.	*Georgica*

Early Christian Sources

Ambrose

Exp. Luc.	*Expositio Evangelii Secundum Lucam*
Fid.	*De Fide*
Tob.	*De Tobia*

Athanasius

Ep.	*Epistulae*

Augustine

Doctr. Chr.	*De Doctrina Christiana* (*Christian Instruction*)
Enarrat. Ps.	*Enarrationes in Psalmos* (*Enarrations on the Psalms*)
Ep.	*Epistulae*
Mor. Eccl.	*De Moribus Ecclesiae Catholicae* (*The Way of Life in the Catholic Church*)
Nat. Grat.	*De Natura et Gratia* (*Nature and Grace*)
Tract. Ev. Jo.	*In Evangelium Johannis Tractatus* (*Tractates on the Gospel of John*)
Trin.	*De Trinitate* (*The Trinity*)

Diodore of Tarsus

Comm. Ps. 118

Eusebius of Caesarea

Comm. Isa.	*Commentariorum in Isaiam* (*Commentary on Isaiah*)
Hist. Eccl.	*Historia Ecclesiastica* (*Ecclesiastical History*)
Onom.	*Onomasticon*

Hilary

Tract. Ps.	*Tractatus super Psalmos* (*Tractates on the Psalms*)

Irenaeus

Epid.	*Epideixis tou Apostolikou Kerygmatos* (*Demonstration of the Apostolic Preaching*)
Haer.	*Adversus Haereses* (*Against Heresies*)

Jerome

Chron.	*Chronicon Eusebii a Graeco Latine Redditum et Continuatum*
Comm. Am.	*Commentariorum in Amos*
Comm. Eccl.	*Commentariorum in Ecclesiasten*
Comm. Eph.	*Commentariorum in Epistulam ad Ephesios*
Comm. Ezech.	*Commentariorum in Ezechielem*
Comm. Gal.	*Commentariorum in Epistulam ad Galatos*
Comm. Habac.	*Commentariorum in Habacuc*
Comm. Hos.	*Commentariorum in Osee* = *Commentary on Hosea*
Comm. Isa.	*Commentariorum in Isaiam*
Comm. Jer.	*Commentariorum in Jeremiam*
Comm. Joel	*Commentariorum in Joelem*

Comm. Jon.	*Commentariorum in Jonam*
Comm. Mal.	*Commentariorum in Malachiam*
Comm. Matt.	*Commentariorum in Matthaeum*
Comm. Nahum	*Commentariorum in Nahum*
Comm. Obad.	*Commentariorum in Obadiam*
Comm. Ps.	*Commentarioli in Psalmos*
Comm. Tit.	*Commentariorum in Epistulam ad Titum*
Comm. Zach.	*Commentariorum in Zachariam*
Comm. Zeph.	*Commentariorum in Zephaniam*
Ep.	*Epistulae*
Expl. Dan.	*Explanatio in Danielem*
Lucif.	*Altercatio Luciferiani et orthodoxi seu dialogues contra Luciferianos*
Jo. Hier.	*Adversus Joannem Hierosalymitanum Liber (Against John of Jerusalem)*
Jov.	*Adversus Jovinianum Libri II (Against Jovinian)*
Nom. Hebr.	*De Nominibus Hebraicis (Liber Nominum) (Book of Hebrew Names)*
Pelag.	*Adversos Pelagianos Dialogi III (Against the Pelagians)*
QHG	*Quaestionum Hebraicarum liber in Genesim*
Ruf.	*Adversus Rufinum Libri III (Apology Against Rufinus)*
Tract. Ps.	*Tractatus in Psalmos*
Vigil.	*Adversus Vigilantium*
Vir. Ill.	*De Viris Illustribus (On Illustrious Men)*
Vit. Paul.	*Vita S. Paulii Primi Eremitae (Life of Paul the First Hermit)*
Let. Aris.	*Letter of Aristeas*

Origen
Cels.	*Contra Celsum (Against Celsus)*
Comm. Matt.	*Commentarium in Evangelium Matthaei*
Ep. Afr.	*Epistula ad Africanum*
Fr. Jer.	*Fragmenta in Jeremiam*
Hom. Exod.	*Homiliae in Exodum*
Hom. Jer.	*Homiliae in Jeremiam*
Philoc.	*Philocalia*
Princ.	*De Principiis (On First Principles)*
Rhet. Her.	*Rhetorica ad Herennium*

Rufinus
Apol. Hier.	*Apologia Adversus Hieronymum*
Orig. Princ.	*Orig. Princ. Origenis Libri Peri archon seu De Principiis Libri IV*

Sozomen
Hist. Eccl.	*Historia Ecclesiastica*

Tertullian
Adv. Jud.	*Adversus Judaeos (Against the Jews)*

Theodore of Mopsuestia
Comm. Joel   *Commentariorum in Joelem*

Theodoret
Comm. Jer.   *Commentariorum in Jeremiam*

Medieval and Renaissance Sources
Erasmus
Adagia

Thomas Aquinas
STh   *Summa Theologica*

TRANSLATOR'S INTRODUCTION

Since the thirteenth century, Jerome of Stridon has been officially regarded as one of the four doctors of the Latin church (*Doctores Ecclesiae*), along with Ambrose, Augustine and Gregory the Great. Jerome's chief legacy lies in his work as a biblical translator and commentator. In the Roman Catholic Church, Jerome is honored on his feast day, June 30, as the "greatest teacher of the church in expounding the Sacred Scriptures" (*Doctor in exponendis Sacris Scripturis Maximus*).[1] Insight into the meaning of the biblical text is one thing that we should expect to find as we read Jerome's *Commentary on Jeremiah*.

Yet, Jerome offers more than just insight into the historical meaning of Scripture. Jerome was a significant figure in the development and spread of Christian asceticism in the fourth and early fifth centuries, and his comments on the biblical text often reflect his striking views on the ideals of strict Christian discipline. As a native Latin speaker who moved east and mastered Greek, Jerome was one of the last Christian thinkers truly able to converse with Christian theological writings in both the East and the West. Jerome received the best classical (i.e., "pagan") education available in his day, and he made constructive use of non-Christian learning in his biblical exegesis, laying the groundwork for much biblical scholarship to follow. Jerome was also unique among preserved Christian writers in his extensive knowledge of Hebrew and his awareness of Jewish traditions. Jerome's contact with Hebraic sources makes his Old Testament exegesis especially valuable today.

Jerome was an intense personality. He spent much of his life in conflict with those around him, although he also enjoyed some close personal friendships. He was highly learned and somewhat elitist in his views about language and interpretation, and his ideal standards for Christian living were more rigorous than most other Christians would tolerate. He could be vain, petty in conflict and overly harsh in his criticisms. Furthermore, unlike some other Christian writers of his era, he was not adept at covering over his flaws; rather, he tended to wear them on his sleeve. For all of these reasons, he can be difficult for the modern reader to relate to; indeed, most Christians in his own day had a hard time relating to him. But his personal flaws do not detract from the wealth of learning and insight contained in his scriptural exegesis, especially as he compiled and set forth in an orderly fashion the insights drawn from Christians (Greek and Latin), Jews

---

[1]For example, the encyclical *Divino Afflante Spiritu*, given by Pope Pius XII in order to promote biblical studies, was delivered on June 30, 1943, in recognition of Jerome's contribution to Christian biblical scholarship.

and the classical tradition. Over time, Jerome's reputation in the church was established through recognition of his remarkable gifts as a translator, exegete and advocate for Christian asceticism. Throughout the Middle Ages and into the Renaissance, Jerome was a model for Christians who wanted to learn from Jews, read classical authors and practice Christian self-discipline. It is as a biblical commentator that we will see him at work in this volume, but the reader will clearly see that Jerome brings to the task of exegesis his whole vision for the Christian life.

Jerome's Life and Works

Jerome was born in approximately A.D. 347 and spent his early life in Stridon, a small town near the border between the Roman provinces of Dalmatia and Pannonia (perhaps in modern Croatia or Slovenia).[2] He received his primary education in his hometown under the supervision of his Christian parents, who were wealthy enough to employ teachers for Jerome and his brother. A classical education was necessary for success in administration or law within the Roman Empire, so at the age of eleven or twelve Jerome was sent to Rome in order to study literature and rhetoric with the best teachers. Among Jerome's teachers was the well-known literary scholar Aelius Donatus, who was the author of important commentaries on classical authors and of a Latin grammatical textbook used for centuries afterwards. Following his training in grammar and literature, Jerome also studied rhetoric, and he probably had some exposure to philosophical writers as part of his formal education. Jerome's parents were obviously intent on preparing their son for life as a Christian and as a Roman aristocrat. As he later recollects, "From my cradle, I have been nourished on Catholic milk" (*Ep.* 82.2), and, "Almost from the cradle, my life has been spent in the company of grammarians, rhetoricians and philosophers" (*Pref. IH Job*).

In the late 360s, when his education in Rome was completed, Jerome traveled to the city of Trier in Gaul. This was the residence of the emperor Valentinian, and therefore a logical place for the young Jerome to start his career in civil service. Yet, soon after his arrival, Jerome decided to give up his plans for a secular career and pursue instead a life devoted to the service of God. This may have been the result of his reading Athanasius's *Life of Antony*, the story of the first monk, who renounced the world and adopted an ascetic life in the desert of Egypt. Jerome began at this time to acquire the writings of Christian authors, and he departed Trier in order to go to Aquileia, where he joined a fellowship of young ascetics, consisting of both women and men, whose company included his friend Rufinus, Chromatius (who later became bishop of Aquileia) and Evagrius (later bishop of Antioch).

---

[2]Jerome *Vir. Ill.* 135. I am essentially following the chronology worked out by Ferdinand Cavallera, *Saint Jérôme: Sa vie et son oeuvre*, 2 vols. (Louvain: Spicilegium Sacrum Lovaniense Bureaux, 1922), 2:3-12. In support of this chronology, Jerome says in his *Comm. Hab.* 3:14-16 that he was a boy in the school of *grammatice* (see below) when the emperor Julian died in 362. See Michael Graves, *Jerome's Hebrew Philology* (Leiden: Brill, 2007), 13.

In around 372, the fellowship in Aquileia broke up, and Jerome went east toward Antioch. At first he stayed with Evagrius, who had already departed Aquileia for his home city. Then, perhaps in 375, Jerome went into the desert of Chalcis in Syria in order to try a monastic life based on withdrawal from society; but Jerome never took to this lifestyle, as his letters from this period demonstrate, and within a year or two he returned to the household of Evagrius. This is where Jerome remained until 380, when he journeyed to Constantinople to attend the church council of 381. During his time in Antioch, Jerome significantly improved his command of Greek, which he had learned in only a rudimentary way as a student in Rome. In addition, in the desert Jerome picked up some of the basics of the local Semitic language, which he called Syriac, and he began his study of Hebrew under the tutelage of a Jewish convert to Christianity. Jerome also heard lectures in Antioch by Apollinaris of Laodicea, whom he later claimed proudly as a teacher in scriptural interpretation, even though he rejected Apollinaris's teaching on the person of Christ.[3] To this period belong Jerome's earliest literary productions, including many letters, a lost allegorical commentary on Obadiah and his *Life of Paul the First Hermit*, a fascinating tale about the supposed monastic predecessor of Antony. Jerome was already showing himself to be both a man of letters and a devoted (even extreme) Christian.

Although his time in Constantinople was brief, Jerome had significant experiences there. Chief among these were his interactions with Gregory of Nazianzus, from whom he deepened his understanding of Greek theology and developed his early admiration for Origen. In Constantinople, Jerome continued his literary output with an exegetical letter on the sixth chapter of Isaiah, a Latin translation and update of Eusebius of Caesarea's *Chronicon* (a chronicle of the world from Abraham to Constantine) and translations into Latin of Origen's homilies on Isaiah, Jeremiah and Ezekiel. In 382, Jerome headed for Rome together with bishops Epiphanius of Salamis and Paulinus of Antioch in order to attend an ecclesiastical assembly. Jerome returned to Rome with knowledge of Greek language and theology, Eastern monastic experience and biblical learning, including some Hebrew, that was quite rare for any Latin Christian of his time.

In Rome, Jerome came quickly into favor with Bishop Damasus. Jerome functioned as a secretary for Damasus, composing official correspondences for the East and West. Jerome also served Damasus as an advisor in biblical learning; thus, at the Roman bishop's urging, Jerome translated Origen's homilies on the Song of Songs and undertook to revise the then-current Latin versions of the Psalms and the Gospels according to the best available Greek texts. The letters that Jerome wrote during his stay in Rome show him to be growing ever more competent and enthusiastic in his Hebrew studies, as he

---

[3]Jerome *Ep.* 84.3: "At Antioch I frequently heard the teaching of Apollinaris of Laodicea and attended his lectures; and yet, although he instructed me in the Holy Scriptures, I never accepted his contentious conclusion as to their meaning." Cf. Jerome *Vir. Ill.* 104; *Chron.* 365; *Ep.* 70.3; *Comm. Dan.* prol. Apollinaris was an admirer of Athanasius and defender of the Nicene confession, but he held that the divine Logos within Jesus took the place of a human soul, and for this he received serious censure.

read Hebrew with Jews and compared the Hebrew text with the traditional Greek Old Testament (the Septuagint [LXX]) and the Greek version of Aquila (see below). Jerome showed the same enthusiasm for his rigorous ascetic ideals, promoting poverty, fasting, self-denial, and above all, virginity. From this period comes Jerome's treatise *Against Helvidius*, defending the perpetual virginity of Mary. The most ardent followers of Jerome's program of biblical learning and asceticism were well-born women in Rome, many of whom looked to Jerome for guidance in Christian discipleship. Prominent among these women were Marcella, a leader among ascetic women in Rome and Jerome's best Hebrew student, and the wealthy widow Paula, who, together with her daughter Eustochium, shared Jerome's devotion to serious Scripture study and Christian self-discipline.

Unfortunately for Jerome, not everyone in Rome appreciated his ideals for the Christian life. Jerome came under criticism for revising the Latin Gospels and changing some of the traditional wording, even though he was basing himself on the original Greek. This would not be the first time that Jerome was maligned for his pioneering biblical scholarship. More significantly, however, many in Rome began to feel that Jerome's program of ascetic denial was too harsh. For example, a young woman named Blesilla, a follower of Jerome's teaching, died from complications related to excessive fasting, and Jerome was widely blamed. It was also regarded as a point of suspicion that Jerome spent so much time in the company of women. When Damasus died in 384 and Jerome no longer enjoyed the patronage of the Roman bishop, formal charges were brought against him, and he was forced to leave the city in 385. Jerome decided to return to the East, this time accompanied by his closest friend, Paula.

Jerome and Paula, together with Paula's daughter Eustochium and a company of servants, journeyed to Palestine and immediately made a trip to Egypt. While in Egypt, they listened to the teaching of Didymus the Blind in Alexandria and visited the monks in the desert. Then, in 386 the group returned to Bethlehem, where Paula, who was quite well-off, provided the resources to establish a pair of monasteries, one for men supervised by Jerome and the other for women overseen by Paula. These monasteries were centers for the poor and for pilgrims from the West, where aid was given to those in need and where Jerome, for his part, was afforded the time he needed to write.

Jerome lived in Bethlehem for the rest of his life, and his arrival in 386 marked the beginning of a very productive time for him as an author. Jerome composed several reference works that served to demonstrate to readers the value of Hebrew learning, such as his *Book of Hebrew Names*, *Book of Hebrew Place Names* and *Hebrew Questions on Genesis*. Jerome wrote exegetical works on the Psalms and Ecclesiastes, both of which reflected his ever-increasing command of Hebrew and Jewish traditions, and he produced commentaries on Galatians, Ephesians, Titus and Philemon. The monastic life continued to hold Jerome's attention, as he wrote two more "lives" of idealized ascetic characters, *The Life of Hilarion* and *The Life of Malchus the Captive Monk*. Jerome likewise continued his work as a translator, rendering into Latin Origen's homilies on Luke, Didymus's treatise *On the Holy Spirit* and several books of the Old Testament (e.g., Proverbs, Chronicles and Job) in accordance with Origen's version of the LXX (see below). Throughout his early years in Bethlehem and for the rest of his life, Jerome stayed in constant contact with his friends in Rome through letters. Most of his works were written with this audience in mind. For Jerome, publication meant sending his compositions back to Rome where his friends, such as Marcella and Pammachius, would pay for copies to be made and circulated among those interested in Jerome's learned and ascetically oriented writings.

A new phase of Jerome's life began in 391 with the start of his translation of the Old Testament from Hebrew into Latin.[4] Jerome referred to this translation as his version of the Old Testament *iuxta Hebraeos* ("according to the Hebrews"); it was not called the Vulgate ("common" edition) until centuries later. Partly because of the newness of the work he was doing on the biblical text, and partly because of his reliance on Jewish sources, Jerome was sharply criticized for making this translation, as for example by Augustine, who only later in life came to recognize the value of Jerome's version.[5] Jerome completed his translation *iuxta Hebraeos* (his IH edition) in 405, and with each book that he translated he included a preface in which he explained his work and defended himself against his detractors. Controversy likewise surrounded Jerome during these years because of his ascetical views. In 393, Jerome wrote two books *Against Jovinianus*, in refutation of a certain Jovinianus, who argued that fasting is no better than eating with gratitude to God, and virginity is no better than faithful Christian marriage. Even though Jovinianus's views had already been condemned in Rome by the time Jerome composed his refutation, the forcefulness with which Jerome extolled virginity and disparaged wedlock offended many Christians in Rome, to the extent that Jerome's friends tried to remove the work from circulation in order to save further damage to his reputation. The IH translation project and *Against Jovinianus* represent well Jerome's dual concerns for high-level biblical scholarship and high-intensity Christian self-discipline. Jerome's writings in these areas gave rise to sharp disagreements, but his reputation continued to grow. One can see Jerome's estimation of his own importance as a literary figure in his book published

---

[4] Jerome comments on his translation of the Old Testament based on the original Hebrew: "Therefore, with full knowledge and recognition (of the difficulties and potential criticisms), I send forth my hand into the flame" (*Pref. IH Isa.*).

[5] Augustine first criticizes Jerome for his Hebrew translation project in *Ep.* 28 (written in 394 or 395), in which he wonders how Jerome could possibly improve on the LXX. Augustine spells out his belief in the authority of the LXX in *Doctr. Chr.* 2.15 (written in 396). Later, in *Ep.* 71 (written in 403), Augustine expresses concern that Jerome's Hebrew-based translation could cause a rift between East and West, and he raises the problem of how Jerome's work could be checked for accuracy, since no other Christian knows Hebrew. Augustine also tells the story of a bishop in the town of Oea who introduced Jerome's translation of Jonah into his congregation and almost lost control of his church because of the strife that resulted. Jerome answers Augustine point by point in his *Ep.* 112 (written in 404), defending his translation of the plant in Jon 4:6 as "ivy" rather than the traditional LXX and Old Latin translation, "gourd." Augustine shows only slight concessions to Jerome's position in his *Ep.* 82 (written in 405). Yet, in *City of God* 18.42-44 (written sometime after 420), Augustine allows for both the LXX and the Hebrew text to be inspired, and he refers to Jerome as "a most learned man, skilled in all three languages" (i.e., Hebrew, Greek and Latin). Moreover, in *Doctr. Chr.* 4.7.15 (composed in the late 420s), Augustine chooses to quote Amos in Jerome's IH version rather than the LXX.

around 392, *On Illustrious Men*. In this work, Jerome surveyed the great (mostly) Christian writers in history, beginning with Peter and ending with himself, allotting to himself the longest entry for any living writer.

Yet, the greatest and most painful controversy in Jerome's life began later in 393, when Epiphanius, bishop of Salamis, came to Palestine in order to secure signatures on a document condemning Origen for some of his speculative theological ideas that had come to be regarded as heretical (see below). To state the matter briefly: in spite of his former praise of Origen (e.g., "the greatest teacher of the churches after the apostles," *Nom. Hebr.*, pref.) and his earlier enthusiasm for translating Origen's exegetical writings, Jerome agreed to sign the condemnation; but Rufinus, Jerome's boyhood friend who also translated Origen's works and who now lived in Jerusalem, refused to condemn Origen. This caused a bitter and public feud between Jerome and Rufinus, which involved not only the Eastern bishops Epiphanius (against Origen) and John of Jerusalem (in favor of Origen) but also significant members of the church in Rome and their networks in the Latin-speaking world (e.g., Augustine was aware of the conflict and deeply saddened by it [*Ep.* 73.6]). After a brief reconciliation in 397, arguments and allegations erupted again in 398, culminating in 401 in Rufinus's *Apology Against Jerome* and Jerome's *Apology Against Rufinus* (401-402), in which both men attacked each other, and Jerome was particularly virulent in assailing his opponent's integrity and orthodoxy. This dispute showed Jerome at his worst: too ready to strike back with venom when he felt that he had been slighted, and unmeasured in his attack, so as to escalate minor grievances into major conflicts. Jerome became more and more outspoken against Origen's doctrinal errors from this time forward, even though he continued to consult Origen's exegetical works and profit from them. Furthermore, Jerome continued to attack Rufinus for following the heresies of Origen, even after Rufinus's death.

Still, this period was not entirely lacking in scriptural study for Jerome. During the brief reconciliation with Rufinus in 397-398, Jerome completed a commentary on Matthew, and during the middle of the 390s he began his series of commentaries on the minor prophets. Near the end of this phase of his life, however, he faced what was probably his greatest personal loss. In 404, approximately one year before the completion of his IH translation, Paula, his closest friend and partner in the cause of Christian monasticism in the Holy Land, died. Jerome's *Epistle* 108, a long letter written in recollection and praise of Paula, reveals the depth of his admiration for her and was instrumental in Paula eventually receiving the status of sainthood.

Jerome's last years kept him busy with controversy and scholarship. Unresolved issues related to the conflict over Origen still demanded Jerome's attention in 406 and 407. For example, an old adversary named Vigilantius, who had earlier accused Jerome of sharing in Origen's errors, came again into Jerome's view, and in 406 Jerome composed his *Against Vigilantius*, in which Jerome combined harsh personal invective with refutations of Vigilantius, who apparently criticized certain practices related to the homage paid to relics, night vigils at martyrs' basilicas and the sending of alms to Jerusalem. Jerome maintained his commitment to the monastic life, translating into Latin some monastic rules associated with the Egyptian Pachomius (ca. 292-346) and later taking into his monastery many people from the West who fled to the Holy Land after the sack of Rome in 410. As a result of the sack of Rome, Pelagius and his followers spread out to North Africa and beyond, and eventually their teachings came to Palestine. Jerome took up the task of correcting them in a relatively measured work, the *Dialogue Against the Pelagians*, written in 415. In the following year, Jerome's monastery was attacked and burned by people identified by Jerome as followers of Pelagius. This hardship of Jerome's old age may have slowed his work to some extent, but it did not deter him from continuing to write. Jerome's later commentaries, such as the *Commentary on Jeremiah*, strongly reflect the background of the Pelagian debate, while still keeping in view the errors of Rufinus and Origen. The final fifteen years of Jerome's life saw him at the height of his powers as a biblical scholar. Jerome completed his commentary on the minor prophets in 401, wrote an abbreviated commentary on Daniel in 407 and then followed up with commentaries on Isaiah (408-410), Ezekiel (410-414) and Jeremiah. Jerome began his commentary on Jeremiah in 414 and reached the end of chapter 32 by the time of his death in 419.

The Commentary on Jeremiah

Jerome was in his mid-sixties when he began to write his *Commentary on Jeremiah* in 414. He had been studying Hebrew seriously for more than thirty years, and he had already translated the book of Jeremiah from Hebrew into his native Latin, with the help of Jewish teachers and previous Greek translations. As shown by the detailed linguistic discussions in the commentary and the numerous citations and allusions to biblical and non-biblical texts, Jerome was still mentally sharp and full of energy, in spite of his often-poor health. Jerome composed this work "through the hand of secretaries" (bk. 1, prol.), that is, by dictating to a scribe who did the writing (bk. 2, prol.). As can be seen in his comments on Jeremiah 22:10-12 and Jeremiah 22:18-19, where he corrects at verses 18-19 the interpretation he gave at verses 10-12, Jerome did not go back and revise himself but marched along through the book passage by passage, taking each text as it came and doing his best to tie each passage into the flow of thought based on what came before.

Jerome dedicated his *Commentary on Jeremiah* to Eusebius of Cremona, a priest and long-time friend, to whom Jerome had dedicated his *Commentary on Matthew* in 398. This Eusebius had been instrumental in the conflict between Jerome and Rufinus over the purported heresies of Origen. In 398, Rufinus completed a translation of Origen's *On First Principles* designed to put Origen's teaching in a positive light. Eusebius of Cremona obtained a copy of this translation, falsified it (according to Rufinus *Apol. Hier.* 1.19-20) and gave it to Jerome's friends in Rome, so that they could ask Jerome to make a new translation that would expose Origen's errors (*Ep.* 83). By dedicating this commentary to Eusebius of Cremona, Jerome signaled his intention to continue to refute the heresies of Origen and to criticize Rufinus, who had died in 410.

Jerome does indeed continue to heap abuse on Rufinus, whom he scornfully refers to as Grunnius, that is, "Grunter," which alludes to the grunting sound made by a pig.[6] Jerome based this name for Rufinus on M. Grunnius Corocotta, the title character in a popular piece of satire from Jerome's day called "The Last Testament of a Little Pig."[7] In the *Commentary on Jeremiah*, Jerome criticizes Rufinus for promoting the errors of Origen (e.g., Jer 28:12-14; 29:14-20) and for paving the way for the errors of Pelagius (bks. 1-4, prols.; Jer 22:24-27). It is unfortunate that Jerome felt the need to keep assailing Rufinus even after the latter's death. Just after Rufinus passed away, Jerome wrote about him in the preface to his *Commentary on Ezekiel*: "The scorpion lies buried under the soil of Sicily among the vanquished giants Enceladus and Porphyrion; the many-headed hydra has at last ceased to hiss against me" (bk. 1, prol.).[8] The *Commentary on Jeremiah* shows that even eight years later Jerome had not forgotten the grudge that he held against his boyhood friend who had become a bitter enemy.

By the time of the *Commentary on Jeremiah*, Jerome seems to have regarded Origen as the paradigmatic heretic, and he suggests often that Origen was the founder of Pelagianism (e.g., bk. 4, prol.). Beyond this, at a few points in the commentary Jerome mentions and refutes specific interpretations of Origen, touching on aspects of Origen's thought that were considered problematic by many in Jerome's day (e.g., Jer 24:1-14; 25:15-17; 27:2-4; 27:9-11). In *Epistle* 61.2, Jerome mentions four key points that he found objectionable in the teachings of Origen: Origen's conception of the resurrected body did not show enough continuity with our present bodies; Origen taught that souls "fell" into bodies as a result of sin; Origen suggested that the devil might repent and be saved; and Origen identified the seraphim in Isaiah 6 as the Son and the Holy Spirit, thus making them less than divine.[9] It is unclear to what extent Jerome is fairly representing the views of Origen, since there is much at stake for Jerome to make Origen out to be a heretic.[10] Examples of Jerome's criticisms of Origen in the *Commentary on Jeremiah* include Origen's reading of the cup of divine wrath (Jer 25:15-17) as restorative rather than punitive, and Origen's interpretation of Jeremiah's charge to Judah that they should accept the

---

[6]See *Ep.* 119.11; *Comm. Ezech.* 33:23-33; *Ep.* 125.18; *Comm. Isa.*, bk. 12, prol.; *Comm. Jer.*, bk. 1, prol.; bk. 4, prol.; *Comm. Jer.* 22:24-27; 28:12-14; 29:14-20.

[7]See *Comm. Isa.*, bk. 12, prol.; *Ruf.* 1.17. Cf. D. S. Wiesen, *St. Jerome as a Satirist* (Ithaca, NY: Cornell University Press, 1964), 229.

[8]On the hydra, see bk. 3, prol. Regarding Enceladus and Porphyrion, see Horace *Carm.* 3.4.53-64; Virgil *Aen.* 3.570-587.

[9]On this last question, see Jerome *Ep.* 18 dealing with Is 6.

[10]For different approaches to Origen's orthodoxy, see Joseph W. Trigg, *Origen: The Bible and Philosophy in the Third-Century Church* (Atlanta: John Knox, 1983); Henri Crouzel, *Origen*, trans. A. S. Worrall (Edinburgh: T&T Clark, 1989). See also the excellent new work by Ronald E. Heine, *Origen: Scholarship in the Service of the Church* (Oxford: Oxford University Press, 2010).

yoke of Babylon (Jer 27:2-4; 27:9-11) as a charge to souls that they should willingly accept bodies. When Jerome alludes to Origen, it is always in order to criticize him, but he still makes constructive but unacknowledged use of Origen's homilies on Jeremiah (e.g., Jer 29:21-23).

Still, the most prevalent theological adversary in the *Commentary on Jeremiah* is Pelagius. This makes sense in light of Jerome's context: he wrote the *Dialogue Against the Pelagians* in 415, when he was just getting under way with this commentary, and his monastery in Bethlehem was attacked and burned in 416 by men thought by Jerome to be associated with Pelagianism. Jerome traces Pelagianism back to Origen and Rufinus, and he references his former refutations of Jovinianus when condemning Pelagius for his openness to remarriage after the death of a spouse (bk. 1, prol.; Jer 16:1-4). If there is a consistent theological thread that runs throughout Jerome's *Commentary on Jeremiah*, it is his opposition to Pelagianism.[11]

The essential claim that Jerome ascribes to the Pelagians and attempts to refute is that Christians can achieve perfection in this life. Jerome accuses them of arrogance, of making themselves out to be equal with God and of following the teachings of Stoic and Pythagorean philosophy rather than Scripture. Jerome asserts that we cannot be perfectly free from sin in this life and that we should not boast in the power of our own will, as the Pelagians do, but in the love and justice of God.[12] Jerome is certainly capable of finding in the biblical text genuine connections with his anti-Pelagian theological agenda; for example, the statement of Jeremiah 8:6 that "no one speaks what is right; no man repents of his wickedness," taps into the larger theme in Jeremiah of the apparent inability of the people of Israel to follow God, which leads to their exile in Babylon and their eventual restoration through God's initiative (cf. Jer 31:31-33). The prophet Jeremiah's observation that no one says or does what is right—not even among the people of God—is theologically relevant to the question of Pelagianism, that is, the ability of the human will to respond rightly to God.

However, there are times when Jerome's arguments against the Pelagians seem arbitrary. Thus, at Jeremiah 25:3, Jerome observes that the prophet repeats God's commands over and over, thus showing (against the Pelagians) that God's commands once given are not enough (i.e., we also need the special inner work of God's grace). Yet, based on Jerome's *Dialogue Against the Pelagians* (e.g., *Pelag.* 1.10; 1.14), one could see Pelagius responding that, if obedience comes from God's working and not from the human will, what is the point of continuing to repeat these commands to the people? Do not these repeated appeals demonstrate that it is possible for the people to obey? In the end, Jerome

---

[11]See Philip Rousseau, "Jerome on Jeremiah: Exegesis and Recovery," in *Jerome of Stridon: His Life, Writings and Legacy,* ed. A. Cain and J. Lössl (Farnham and Burlington: Ashgate, 2009), 73-83.

[12]Important passages where Jerome address Pelagianism include Jer 2:6; 3:11; bk. 2, prol.; Jer 5:26-27a; 8:6; 9:23-24; 10:11; 10:23; 11:3b-4; 17:1; bk. 4, prol.; Jer 25:3; 26:4-6; 30:10-11.

has done the meaningful work of putting the book of Jeremiah into conversation with the issues raised by Pelagianism; it can be left up to Jerome's readers to decide where he is most or least successful.

Jerome and the Ancient Versions of the Bible

One of the most prominent features of Jerome's Old Testament commentaries is their extensive interaction with different versions of the Bible. Jerome grew up reading Latin translations of the Bible that were based on the LXX, the traditional Greek version used by most Christians.[13] This Septuagint-based Latin Bible known to Jerome may conveniently be called the Old Latin translation (OL), but in reality it was not a single translation but a conglomeration of translations done over many years. Jerome generally referred to it as the "common edition" (*editio vulgata*). By Jerome's day, the careful reader could observe many differences between one copy of the Latin Bible and another, and this sense of confusion only increased if one could consult the available Greek editions.

The problem was twofold. First, there had been no single authoritative Latin version, and many people tried their hand at translating this or that portion of Scripture from Greek into Latin; as Augustine said, "In the early days of the faith, whoever chanced upon a Greek codex, and thought himself to have even a little skill in both Greek and Latin, ventured to make his own translation" (*Doctr. Chr.* 2.11.16). Second, there was no single authoritative version of the Greek LXX. This collection of Greek translations of the Hebrew Scriptures was produced by Jews between the third and first centuries B.C.E., and it was largely adopted by early Christians as their Old Testament, serving as the primary scriptural foundation for the New Testament and early Christian worship and literature. Yet, partly due to a sense of inaccuracy vis-à-vis the current Hebrew text, and perhaps partly due to Christian appropriation, certain Jews in the second century C.E. produced new versions of the Hebrew Scriptures into Greek. Aquila, a convert to Judaism from Pontus in Asia Minor, produced a literalistic version of the Hebrew Bible; Symmachus, a Jew (or perhaps Jewish Christian), made a more idiomatic translation; and a third edition, not far different from the LXX, was ascribed to a certain Theodotion, who apparently lived in the second century but primarily revised an earlier translation, since some readings cited as Theodotion already appear in the New Testament.[14]

These translations, in use among Jews by the early third century C.E., came to the awareness of Origen, who used them to create a multi-column Old Testament known as

---

[13]The term "Septuagint" in its strictest sense applied only to the original translation of the Pentateuch into Greek, but it later came to be applied to the entire Greek Old Testament. For an introduction to the LXX and the whole topic of the Greek Bible in antiquity, see Natalio Fernandez Marcos, *The Septuagint in Context: Introduction to the Greek Versions of the Bible*, trans. W. G. E. Watson (Leiden: Brill, 2001). Early Christians, such as Jerome, believed that the traditional Greek Old Testament had been translated by seventy (or seventy-two) men, and so they refer to the Seventy (Roman numeral LXX), meaning "the seventy translators" (e.g., bk. 1, prol.). In modern usage, we usually refer to this version as the Septuagint.

[14]On these figures, see Marcos, *Septuagint in Context*, 109-54.

the Hexapla.[15] This massive piece of scholarship consisted of six versions of the Old Testament presented in parallel columns for easy comparison: the first column gave the original Hebrew in Hebrew letters, the second gave the Hebrew words transliterated into Greek letters, the third column gave the literalistic version of Aquila, the fourth gave the more idiomatic rendering of Symmachus, the fifth gave Origen's own version of the LXX, and the sixth column gave Theodotion. In Origen's fifth column, he identified units of text that were present in the Hebrew but lacking in the LXX, and he added them into his copy of the LXX, borrowed from one of the other Greek versions (usually Theodotion), and he marked this with an asterisk. Furthermore, wherever a detail was present in the LXX but missing in the Hebrew, Origen would indicate this with an obelus. Origen's aims in this process were partly apologetic (to help Christians know better how to argue from Scripture with Jews), partly textual (to help find the right reading of the LXX) and partly interpretive (to help Christians discover the full range of possible meanings of biblical words).[16] But Origen's work had a profound impact on the history of the LXX beyond what he imagined or intended.

Many people copied Origen's fifth column without his critical signs (asterisks and obeli), thereby introducing words and phrases taken from the hexaplaric versions (Aquila, Symmachus and Theodotion) into common use in their churches.[17] By the time of Jerome, many churches in Palestine used copies of Origen's LXX (i.e., the fifth column of the Hexapla without the critical signs), not necessarily knowing the critical work that stood behind it. Moreover, in Egypt most churches read an edition of the LXX produced by a certain Hesychius, and from Constantinople to Antioch Christians used an edition of the LXX produced by Lucian the Martyr. Jerome saw the whole world in conflict over this "threefold variety" (*trifaria varietas*).[18] Confronted with this great diversity of editions of the LXX, the alternative Jewish translations of Aquila, Symmachus and Theodotion, and the variety of readings floating around in copies of the Latin Bible, Jerome realized that the only way to solve the problem of the Old Testament text was to learn Hebrew and get back to the "Hebrew truth" (*hebraica veritas*).

The Hebrew text is the primary focus of Jerome's attention in his commentaries on the prophets, but he makes constant use of other versions. His commentaries are broken up into sections that treat individual segments of the biblical text. For each segment of text (the lemma; plural is lemmata), Jerome starts out by giving his own translation into Latin based on the Hebrew. Jerome often follows this with a second translation of the whole

---

[15]See Marcos, *Septuagint in Context*, 204-22. The standard edition of the Hexapla is Frederick Field, *Origenis Hexaplorum Quae Supersunt; sive Veterum Interpretium Graecorum in Totum Vetus Testamentum Fragmenta*, 2 vols. (Oxford: Clarendon, 1875).

[16]See Timothy Michael Law, "Origen's Parallel Bible: Textual Criticism, Apologetics or Exegesis?" *Journal of Theological Studies* 59 (2008): 1-21.

[17]This had important apologetic value for Jerome, since it showed that translators after the time of the original LXX were already being read in churches with approval; e.g., see *Chron.*, pref.; *Pref. IH Isa.*; *Pref. IH Job.*

[18]See the preface to Jerome's IH translation of the biblical book of Chronicles.

lemma, this time based on the LXX. It is Jerome's normal practice in most of his prophets commentaries to give the second translation according to the LXX in full, but in the *Commentary on Jeremiah* it is quite common for Jerome to give the biblical lemma only once—based on the Hebrew—and then to give alternative translations for specific words or phrases where the LXX differs in a significant way.[19] It should be assumed in the commentary that the main translation of the biblical lemma is Jerome's rendering based on the Hebrew, which usually matches his IH translation. If Jerome gives the LXX in full, he will introduce it with the letters LXX. When Jerome gives alternatives (e.g., at Jer 2:11, "Has a nation changed gods"—or "their gods"), it can be assumed that the alternative translation (in this case, "their gods" instead of "gods") is the LXX, unless otherwise indicated in a footnote. The Hebrew text is generally the center of attention for Jerome's literal exposition of the text, and the LXX is often used as part of Jerome's spiritual interpretation (see below).

Besides discussing the LXX in comparison with the Hebrew, Jerome also cites the Jewish translations known from Origen's Hexapla, Aquila, Symmachus and Theodotion. Since Jerome did not have printed dictionaries or grammars that he could consult, and he did not always have a Jewish teacher available to ask, he used these translations as dictionaries and as linguistic commentaries on the Hebrew text. Jerome particularly appreciated Aquila for his literal adherence to the Hebrew, Symmachus for his clarity in rendering the sense of the passage and Theodotion for being closest of the three to the LXX.[20] Jerome uses these hexaplaric versions in his exegesis, but he does not slavishly follow any of them, and sometimes he disagrees with all of them (e.g., Jer 7:17-19; 23:18; 32:35a). In a few instances, Jerome makes reference to a second edition of Aquila or a second edition of Symmachus. These are probably not second complete editions of these translations but alternative translations made selectively in the margins of Jerome's copies of Aquila and Symmachus.[21] Jerome uses all of these translations as scholarly commentaries, but he evaluates and employs them based on his own understanding of the Hebrew text.

The paragraphs above describe the ancient versions of the Bible that Jerome refers to explicitly in his commentaries. In addition to these, there are a few other ancient biblical texts that I will reference in my notes throughout the commentary. As will be discussed below, Jerome relied on the help of Jewish teachers to help him read and understand the Hebrew text. We obviously do not have transcripts of the conversations between Jerome and these teachers—how fascinating it would be if we did! But we can

---

[19]This feature of the *Commentary on Jeremiah* is due partly to the sheer size of the work and partly to the radical differences between the Hebrew and Greek texts of Jeremiah, which make it difficult at times to match up the two texts in clear correspondence.

[20]E.g., see Jerome *Chron.*, pref.; *Pref. IH Job.*

[21]See Graves, *Jerome's Hebrew Philology*, 94; Marcos, *Septuagint in Context*, 119-20; and Field, *Origenis Hexaplorum Quae Supersunt*, 1:xxv, xxxvi-xxxvii. In the footnote to Jer 23:15, I also refer to a reading of "the Hebrew." Various Christian commentators from the fourth and fifth centuries mention readings of "the Hebrew," but it is not clear in most cases whether they are referring to a person or a text; see Marcos, *Septuagint in Context*, 161-63.

perhaps catch a glimpse into the information given to Jerome by these Jewish teachers by looking at ancient translations of the Bible into Aramaic. The most important of these translations is the Aramaic Targum to Jeremiah (Targ). Although no Aramaic translation of Jeremiah existed until after Jerome's time, the later Targum to Jeremiah preserves earlier traditions on how Jews interpreted the Hebrew text at the basic linguistic level. When Jerome agrees in a distinctive way with the Targum, he may well be reflecting an ancient Jewish reading tradition, which he learned directly from a Jewish teacher.

The second Aramaic translation that we will reference is the Syriac Peshitta (Pesh). Syriac is a dialect of Aramaic used in Jerome's day (and our own) by Christians living in Mesopotamia and further east. Although there is no evidence that Jerome ever consulted a written Syriac version of the book of Jeremiah, the Peshitta may have been based on a Jewish version, or as a Semitic Christian text it might reflect influence from Jewish traditions. Thus, in a more indirect way, the Peshitta might give us a window into what Jerome heard about the Hebrew text from his Jewish teachers. A related text that we will mention is the Syro-Hexapla. This was a translation of Origen's version of the LXX (the fifth column of the Hexapla) into Syriac made by Paul, bishop of Tella, in the early seventh century. The Syro-Hexapla is important because it sometimes preserves the critical signs that Origen used in his fifth column, and so it is an important source for understanding Jerome's use of the hexaplaric versions (Aquila, Symmachus and Theodotion).

Regarding Jerome and his ancient versions of the Bible, we may conclude by making a brief comment about his Hebrew text. Never in the *Commentary on Jeremiah* does Jerome indicate that he is aware of textual diversity in the Hebrew. His Hebrew text generally agrees with what we know later as the Masoretic Text (i.e., the medieval Jewish text that serves as the basis of modern English translations), except that Jerome's Hebrew Bible does not include any written indications of vowels or accents, as do the later Masoretic manuscripts. Where we have evidence in Jerome, in places where the Masoretic tradition distinguishes between what is written (Ketiv) and what is read (Qere), Jerome agrees once with the Ketiv (Jer 6:6b-7a) and three times with the Qere (Jer 8:7; 19:1-3a; 31:38-40).[22]

Influences on Jerome's Exegesis

Jerome was quite proud of the fact that he was not self-taught.[23] According to Jerome, the key to acquiring knowledge is to sit under great teachers, and this he attempted to do throughout his entire life. He was indeed a lifelong learner. As mentioned above, Jerome studied as a teenager in Rome with the greatest literary scholar of his day, Aelius Dona-

---

[22]On the Ketiv/Qere readings in the Hebrew Bible, see Michael Graves, "The Origins of Ketiv-Qere Readings," *Textual Criticism* 8 (2003); <http://purl.org/TC>.

[23]See Jerome *Ep.* 84.3; 50.1-2; *Ruf.* 1.20; *Pref. LXX Par.*

tus, whom Jerome affectionately referred to as "my teacher."[24] In *Epistle* 84.3, Jerome reflects on his various teachers: "As a youth, I was carried along by a strong love of learning, and I did not, according to the presumption of certain people, teach myself. At Antioch I frequently heard the teaching of Apollinaris of Laodicea. . . . Yet, I went on to Alexandria to hear the teaching of Didymus. . . . And again, in Jerusalem and in Bethlehem, at great price and effort I had Bar Hanina as my teacher at night."[25] These comments may be taken as representative of the influences on Jerome's exegetical method: classical, Antiochene, Alexandrian and Jewish. Each of these traditions had a significant influence on how Jerome interpreted Scripture.

Jerome and Classical Learning

As a young child, Jerome learned the basics of reading and writing from the schoolmasters employed by his parents in his hometown of Stridon. Jerome was sent to Rome for further education at around twelve years old, and his first course of study was *grammatice*, literary studies. In Jerome's world, *grammatice* did not refer merely to the study of grammar in our sense of the word, but to the mastery of language through the interpretation and appreciation of great literature.[26] His studies in *grammatice* prepared Jerome to receive instruction in rhetoric, which started in his late teens. While rhetoric focused on expression, it also included continued exposure to the literature of great speakers of the past. Thus, by the time Jerome was in his early twenties and ready to begin his career, he had been thoroughly grounded in the thought patterns and texts of classical antiquity.

At some point after Jerome gave up his ambitions for a secular career and devoted himself to the service of the church, he came to experience an inner conflict between his love of classical literature and his love for Christ. When he first seriously encountered the language of Scripture, he found it repellent in comparison with the language of classical authors such as Quintilian, Cicero and Pliny, and it took some effort on his part, including learning Hebrew, to overcome this initial aversion.[27] During his stay in Rome, when he was vigorously promoting Christian asceticism and was immersed in scriptural study, Jerome wrote a lengthy letter to Paula's daughter Eustochium, instructing her on how to devote her life properly to Christian virginity. In this letter, Jerome reports a dream that he had while in the Syrian desert, in which a heavenly Judge summoned him before the judgment seat and condemned him by saying, "You are a follower of Cicero, and not of Christ" (*Ep.* 22.30). According to Jerome, he vowed to stop reading secular literature and to devote himself exclusively to the books of God. In a symbolic way, this vow definitely captured the tone of the rest of his life. He did indeed commit himself

---

[24]Jerome *Chron.* 354; *Ruf.* 1.16; *Comm. Eccl.* 1:9.

[25]On Bar Hanina, see below on Jerome's Hebrew teachers.

[26]On Jerome and *grammatice*, see Graves, *Jerome's Hebrew Philology*, 13-75.

[27]On Jerome's initial negative reaction to Scripture and his development of an appreciation for Scripture as literature, see Michael Graves, "The Literary Quality of Scripture as Seen by the Early Church," *Tyndale Bulletin* 61 (2010): 169-72.

until the day of his death to expounding sacred Scripture.

At the same time, Jerome's renunciation of secular literature did not hold up at the literal level. It is true that Jerome claimed that his constant references to classical authors were due to his remarkable memory, which always retained the impress left on him by the classics (*Ruf.* 1.30). But it has been shown that Jerome knows classical sources later in life that he never used earlier, such as Pliny the Younger and Cicero's philosophical works, suggesting that he read these works in his later years.[28] Moreover, as Rufinus pointed out, Jerome taught classical authors to children while living in Bethlehem (*Apol. Hier.* 2.11). In reality, instead of viewing Jerome's dream as a failed commitment not to read the classics, it is better to see Jerome's sentiments as expressed in *Epistle* 22 as a reflection of his desire to devote all of his being, including his strong knowledge of classical literature, to Christ and the interpretation of Scripture.

The influence of Jerome's classical education is most obvious when he quotes directly from a pagan author. His favorite authority to cite is Virgil, whom he quotes nine times.[29] An example may be taken from Jerome's comments on Jeremiah 4:12b: "And now I—but I speak my judgments on them!" Jerome identifies this as the literary figure *aposiōpēsis*, which he illustrates by citing Virgil's *Aeneid* 1.135, the same passage used by Quintilian to illustrate this figure in *The Orator's Education* 9.2.54.[30] Besides named authors, Jerome also sometimes quotes a "saying of the philosophers" (e.g., Jer 5:26-27a) or an "old saying" taken from a pagan author (e.g., Jer 1:11-12). When the ultimate source of the quotation is Greek, Jerome is most often dependent on Latin authors for his information, but there are times when Jerome may have read the Greek pagan author.[31]

Yet, a more substantive influence on Jerome's biblical scholarship can be seen in his systematic application of the principles of *grammatice* to his literal exposition of Scripture. The four parts of *grammatice*, as given by the first-century B.C.E. Latin scholar Varro, were *lectio* (reading aloud), *enarratio* (explanation), *emendatio* (textual criticism) and *iudicium* (literary judgment).[32]

The first element of interpretation, *lectio*, consisted in reading the text out loud correctly. Because most texts in Jerome's time lacked punctuation, even the act of reading a text out loud constituted a significant level of interpretation. Through oral expression, one could indicate the proper division of words and clauses and show by voice inflection

---

[28]See H. Hagendahl, *Latin Fathers and the Classics: A Study of the Apologists, Jerome and Other Christian Writers* (Göteborg: Almqvist and Wiksell, 1958), 309-28.

[29]See Jer 4:12b; 6:4b-5; 6:20; 10:3b-5; 11:5a (twice); 13:25b-27a; 18:14 (twice). Jerome also relies on Virgil for his mythological references (e.g., bk. 3, prol.).

[30]Direct parallels can also be found between Jerome's explanations of biblical language and the definitions given by his teacher Donatus in his grammatical manuals; see Graves, *Jerome's Hebrew Philology*, 14-15.

[31]See William C. McDermott, "Saint Jerome and Pagan Greek Literature," *Vigilae Christianae* 36 (1982): 372-82.

[32]Varro's description of *grammatice* was based on the Greek model of *grammatikē*, the four parts of which were *anagnōstikon* (reading aloud), *exēgētikon* (explanation), *diorthōtikon* (textual criticism) and *kritikon* (literary judgment), as seen in the scholia to the *Technical Grammar* written by Dionysius Thrax (c. 170-c. 90 B.C.E.). See Graves, *Jerome's Hebrew Philology*, 17-20.

who was the speaker in a dialogue and whether a sentence should be read as a statement or a question. In the *Commentary on Jeremiah*, Jerome talks about the pronunciation of Hebrew consonants (e.g., Jer 19:1-3a) and the vocalization of words (e.g., Jer 9:22); the division of clauses (e.g., Jer 12:11b-12); the interrogative tone of a sentence (e.g., Jer 8:12a); and the identity of the speaker, that is, whose *persona* (e.g., the Lord, Jeremiah, the city of Jerusalem, the people) is speaking the words in the text.[33]

Jerome's greatest emphasis as a commentator lay in the area of *enarratio*: the exposition of the text, the explanation of difficulties, linguistic analysis and the discussion of background information. Roman grammarians such as Donatus explained difficult words (*glossemata*), resolving ambiguities and sometimes appealing to Greek (or even Punic or the like) in order to expound the meaning. Jerome devotes considerable attention to biblical *glossemata*, resolving ambiguities by going back to the Hebrew (e.g., Jer 2:1-2a) and even bringing in additional languages (such as Syriac, at Jer 6:6b-7a). Jerome explains features of the grammar (e.g., Jer 2:12-13) and syntax (e.g., Jer 31:37) of the text, using standard classical categories. Jerome follows the grammatical model by identifying various tropes and figures in Jeremiah, such as *hyperbolē* (e.g., Jer 4:23-26), *metaphora* (e.g., Jer 6:2-4a) and *synekdochē* (e.g., Jer 15:10a). Throughout the commentary Jerome offers paraphrases of the biblical text, often introducing his paraphrase with the phrase *sensus est* ("The sense is," which is the standard grammarian terminology). Many times, Jerome paraphrases both the Hebrew text and the LXX in order to show how they differ in general sense. Through his use of paraphrase in particular, Jerome's appropriation of *enarratio* went beyond the atomistic approach that sometimes characterized ancient commentary.[34]

One final element of *enarratio* that deserves special attention is Jerome's exposition of *historia*, or narrative background material. In the classical sense, *historia* would include any background material relevant to the interpretation of a discourse or poem, including even mythological narratives to which allusions were made in the text. For Jerome, most of the *historia* necessary for the interpretation of the prophets is to be found in the Bible itself (e.g., the book of Kings), which he took to be historical in the modern sense. Jerome often associates *historia* with the Hebrew text, as at Jeremiah 22:18-19, where he interprets the text by bringing in what "the Hebrew *historia*" narrates, and then proceeds to explain the historical background of the text through the biblical books of Kings and

---

[33]Jerome uses the rhetorical term *persona* to indicate who is the speaker in the text; see Jer 2:2b; 2:14-15; 8:18; 11:18-20; 14:17; 15:10b; 15:11; 15:17-18; 17:11; 25:38; 26:1-3.

[34]Over the span of his career, Jerome tended to move away from the fragmented exegesis of the grammarians and toward more holistic readings, as shown by his practice of taking larger blocks of text to discuss as a whole (e.g., see Jerome's comments at Jer 17:21-27). Cf. Jerome *Comm. Matt.* 25:13: "I always admonish prudent readers that they should not acquiesce to superstitious interpretations and things said in a cut-up way according to the whim of those who make up such things; rather, one should consider what came before, what comes in the middle, and what comes after, and one should connect together everything that is written." See Pierre Jay, *L'exégèse de saint Jérôme d'après son "Commentaire sur Isaïe"* (Paris: Études Augustiniennes, 1985), 76-87.

Chronicles. Jerome's frequent appeal to the *historia* of the text demonstrates that he values the historical context of Jeremiah.

The third stage, *emendatio*, encompassed more than just textual criticism in the modern sense—it extended to the correction of both manuscript errors and faults of language. Jerome never presumes to correct the style or usage of the Hebrew Bible, but he does reflect the practice of *emendatio* in his remarkably advanced views on textual criticism.[35] In this area, Jerome broke new ground in the study of the Bible by combining the insights derived from classical *emendatio* with his return to the "Hebrew truth." Jerome understood the critic's job to be to restore the original form of the text by correcting errors in transmission, which could arise through scribal carelessness or when scribes (wrongly) thought they were fixing a mistake.[36] Jerome recognized the potential text-critical value of ancient translations of the New Testament,[37] and he was generally aware of the value of good manuscripts;[38] but for the Old Testament, the single standard for any reading was the Hebrew text that Jerome consulted, the originality of which he virtually never questioned.[39]

Jerome gives considerable attention in the *Commentary on Jeremiah* to identifying places where the Hebrew contains something lacking in the LXX, or, less often, where the Hebrew lacks something present in the LXX.[40] Jerome also treats differences between the LXX or other Greek versions and the Hebrew where the key to resolving the conflict is a presumed misreading of the Hebrew text on the part of the Greek translators. Especially interesting examples include errors due to the misreading of similar Hebrew letters (e.g., Jer 15:12; 31:2) and an error due to the LXX's alleged misunderstanding of the sense (Jer 22:29-30), where Jerome solves a theological conundrum through his textual criticism. A final feature of Jerome's *emendatio* on the book of Jeremiah is his occasional references to the critical signs used in Origen's Hexapla (see above). On three occasions, Jerome explains that material found in the Hebrew but absent from the LXX was supplied by Origen in the Hexapla, borrowed from the version of Theodotion and marked with an asterisk (Jer 2:1-2a; 29:14-20; 30:10-11).

Iudicium, the final stage of *grammatice*, involved giving an overall assessment of the aesthetic quality and stylistic features of a work. The grammarian would make observations about what a given author was best at expressing, the most outstanding features of his style and the general spirit embodied in his work. Other aspects of this artistic criti-

---

[35]See K. K. Hulley, "Principles of Textual Criticism Known to St. Jerome," *Harvard Studies in Classical Philology* 55 (1944): 87-109.

[36]See Jerome *Ep.* 27.1; 71.5; 106.30; *Pref. Gospel*. At Jer 22:29-30, Jerome gives the categories of textual deviation as "what has been changed, what has been added and what has been subtracted."

[37]See especially the *Pref. Gospel*.

[38]E.g., see Jerome *QHG* 23.2; *Comm. Hos.* 1.10; *Comm. Isa.* 58:11; *Tract. Ps.* 77:2.

[39]Cf. Graves, *Jerome's Hebrew Philology*, 54.

[40]When Jerome does discuss material present in the LXX but absent from the Hebrew, it is often to show that the LXX is wrong (e.g., Jer 10:20; 31:10-14).

cism included the comparison of one author with another and the assessment of how the author in question fit into the literary canon. As part of *iudicium*, grammarians rendered judgments on the authenticity of works ascribed to particular authors. Such a decision could be made for a given work by carefully comparing its stylistic qualities with the usual style of the author, making the question of authenticity a natural outgrowth of the task of *iudicium*.

Because Jerome's focus as a commentator was on the theological and moral message of Scripture, he does not give much attention to *iudicium*. Jerome only rarely comments on the aesthetic dimension of Jeremiah (e.g., at Jer 6:2-4a; 22:18-19); this is perhaps because he considered Jeremiah to be a rustic fellow from a small village.[41] But in one component of *iudicium*, the question of authenticity, Jerome was thoroughly invested. Jerome's grammatical training in this area is evident in *On Illustrious Men*, in which he indicates that the book of Hebrews is not considered to be one of Paul's letters "because of its dissonance with his style and expression" (*Vir. Ill.* 5.10; cf. 15.2); he says that 2 Peter is considered by many not to belong to Peter "because of its disagreement in style with the previous letter" (that is, 1 Peter; *Vir. Ill.* 1.3); and regarding the writer Modestus, he says, "Other works circulate under his name, but they are repudiated by scholars as pseudepigraphic" (*Vir. Ill.* 32.2). In this last comment, he uses the same word ("pseudepigraphic") in rejecting these works falsely ascribed to Modestus as he does when rejecting the so-called Epistle of Jeremiah in the prologue to book 1 of the *Commentary on Jeremiah*. Jerome rejected the letter of Jeremiah and the book of Baruch because, although they may be in the LXX, they are not in the Hebrew. For Jerome the Christian grammarian, the "Hebrew truth" served as the ultimate standard for authenticity.

Jerome and Jewish Learning

Jerome began his study of Hebrew under the instruction of a Jewish convert to Christianity during his stay in the Syrian desert between 375 and 377.[42] In *Commentary on Jeremiah* 25:26c, Jerome describes how the rudiments of the Hebrew alphabet were taught by reciting the letters forwards, backwards and then "transposed," and his description matches what we know from rabbinic sources. Jerome refers frequently to his first Hebrew teacher, with whom he apparently read quite a lot.[43] Jerome references several other Hebrew teachers, most of whom were Jews whose assistance Jerome needed for specific projects, such as the Jewish scholars who helped him translate Chronicles, Job and the Aramaic Tobit (*Pref. LXX Par.*; *Pref. IH Job*; *Pref. Tobit*). Jerome's best-known Hebrew teacher was a certain Bar Hanina, who apparently taught Jerome at night; Jerome likened

---

[41]See bk. 6, prol.

[42]*Ep.* 125.12. Jerome says that he took up Hebrew in order to help strengthen his mind in combat against sinful thoughts; other factors that probably led Jerome to study Hebrew include his natural curiosity and his sense of the significance Hebrew would have for interpreting and appreciating the Old Testament.

[43]E.g., Jerome *Comm. Eccl.* 1:14; 3:9-11; 4:13-16; *Comm. Isa.* 22:17; *Comm. Am.* 3:11; *Comm. Obad.* 20-21; *Ep.* 18A.10.

this to the nighttime visit of Nicodemus in John 3 (*Ep.* 84.3; *Ruf.* 1.13). In *Epistle* 36.1, written during his stay in Rome, Jerome mentions a Jew who brought him numerous volumes (mostly biblical texts?) that needed immediate attention so that they could be returned to the synagogue as soon as possible.[44] Jerome could not have attained competence in reading Hebrew without the help of these Jewish teachers, and it is worth reflecting on their impact on his biblical interpretation.

In Jerome's day there were no written Hebrew grammars or dictionaries. Moreover, since Hebrew was not a broadly spoken language but was used only within pockets of Judaism for specific purposes, it was impossible for Jerome to develop his skills by living in a Hebrew-speaking environment, as he did with Greek.[45] Jerome was able to acquire reading and perhaps hearing proficiency in Hebrew by learning from Jewish teachers and by consulting the "Jewish" hexaplaric versions, Aquila, Symmachus and Theodotion. No Christians in the mainstream church made use of Hebrew or copied Hebrew manuscripts. The only copies of the Hebrew Bible available to Jerome were preserved by Jews. Jewish sources were necessary to understand the basic meanings of Hebrew words and the grammar of Hebrew. It is not surprising, therefore, that Jerome sometimes included Jewish interpretations of the Hebrew text as part of his return to the "Hebrew truth." Of course, Jerome used his own wits to sort out which linguistic reading to favor among those presented to him by Jewish teachers or the hexaplaric versions, and he could choose to adopt or reject Jewish traditions relating to the broader interpretation of the text. But Jerome did indeed absorb a great deal of Jewish linguistic exegesis and a considerable amount of broader Jewish exegesis into his commentaries.[46]

Although Jewish exegesis in Jerome's day could be highly creative and was not overly literal by today's standards, Jerome's Jewish contemporaries read the Hebrew Bible in such a way that "Israel" referred to the national people (and not a spiritual group), Nebuchadnezzar was a Babylonian king (and not the devil), and so forth, so that it corresponded to the literal (*ad litteram*) or historical (*iuxta historiam*) sense of the text as described by Christians. For Jerome, most Hebrew and Jewish exegetical material belonged to the exposition of the text at the literal level; the only major exceptions were Hebrew proper name etymologies, which belonged to the spiritual exposition (see below). Generally, Jerome appropriated what he learned from Jews through the grid of his training in formal literary interpretation (*grammatice*); for example, Hebrew language data could be used to solve grammatical difficulties or describe literary figures; also, Jewish traditions about biblical times and the lives of biblical characters were interpreted by Jerome as information useful for explaining the *historia* of the text (e.g., Jer 7:30-31).[47] The value

---

[44]See Graves, *Jerome's Hebrew Philology*, 92.

[45]See ibid., 76-85.

[46]Rufinus sharply criticized Jerome for his reliance on Jewish learning (*Apol. Hier.* 2.32-37).

[47]Cf. Adam Kamesar, "The Evaluation of the Narrative Aggada in Greek and Latin Patristic Literature," *Journal of Theological Studies* 45 (1994): 39, 65-68. An interesting illustration of Jerome's way of dealing with this material can be seen in his *Comm.*

placed by Jerome on the literal sense of the Hebrew sometimes led him to correct the well-intentioned but uninformed spiritual readings of his fellow Christians.[48] At the same time, Jerome could also use the Hebrew to discover a Christian theological meaning that was absent from the LXX (e.g., Jer 23:36b-40; cf. *Comm. Isa.* 2:22).

As a final note on the influence of Jewish learning on Jerome, it is necessary to say something about Jerome's sources for his Jewish traditions. In a few places, Jerome reports an exegetical tradition as if he received it directly from a Jew, when in fact it appears that he borrowed it from Origen or Eusebius of Caesarea.[49] Yet, such examples of simple borrowing are rare. In general, Jerome offers much more by way of Jewish traditions than any of his Christian predecessors, and he adds new Jewish material to the traditions that he appropriates from others.[50] At the same time, even if we acknowledge that Jerome learned Jewish traditions firsthand from Jews, there are still some complexities involved in assessing what Jerome reports about "the Jews" or "the Hebrews."[51]

First, when Jerome reports a supposed Jewish custom or tradition and supports his statement with a reference to the Bible, it is always possible that he is deriving this information from Scripture and not from the actual practice of contemporary Jews.[52] Second, because Jerome associated Jewish exegesis with the literal sense, in some cases Jerome may identify his literal exposition as what "the Jews" say, not because he received an explanation of the given passage from a Jew but because it is the literal explanation and therefore constitutes what the Jews might be expected to say.[53] Third, Jerome often mentions the "Jews" in the same breath as "our Judaizers," namely, Christians whose views Jerome regards as excessively "Jewish"; in these cases, the primary target is not Jews but Jerome's Christian interlocutors.[54] Fourth, Jerome occasionally describes an interpretation as what "the Jews/Hebrews think," but the Jewish sources preserved from late antiquity give a different interpretation altogether (e.g., Jer 15:17-18; 22:10-12). This does not

---

Mal., in which Jerome reports a Jewish tradition saying that "Malachi" ("my messenger") is actually Ezra, and for the rest of the commentary he supplies background information from the book of Ezra in order to explain the individual prophecies of Malachi.

[48] See Jer 17:9-10; 13:18-19; 23:18. Cf. *Comm. Am.* 4:12-13; *Comm. Isa.* 63:1 ("many, led astray by pious error, think . . .").

[49] E.g., see Jerome *Comm. Isa.* 22:2; 22:15-25; Eusebius of Caesarea *Comm. Isa.* 22:15-19; 36:11.

[50] See Hillel Newman, "How Should We Measure Jerome's Hebrew Competence?" in *Jerome of Stridon: His Life, Writings and Legacy*, ed. A. Cain and J. Lössl (Farnham and Burlington: Ashgate, 2009), 134; Graves, *Jerome's Hebrew Philology*, 2-7.

[51] Following an earlier trend in Origen, Jerome shows some tendency to refer to "the Jews" in polemical contexts and to refer to "the Hebrews" when reporting Jewish traditions useful for interpreting the Bible. But this distinction is not maintained consistently in the *Commentary on Jeremiah*.

[52] This may perhaps be an issue with the custom described at Jer 16:5-8. One should be especially cautious about any descriptions of contemporary Jews that are reminiscent of Gospel portrayals of the Pharisees.

[53] This might be the case at Jer 14:8b-9a. Cf. Jerome *Comm. Zeph.* 2:12-15, where Jerome describes the historical sense (*iuxta historiam*) and wraps up his discussion by saying, "these things are said in the Jewish manner" (*haec Judaice dicta sint*), that is, as we would expect the Jews to expound the passage.

[54] See Jer 11:18-20; 13:17c; 17:21-27; 19:10-11a; bk. 6, prol.; Jer 31:23-24; 31:27-30; 38-40; and the notes to these passages. Many of these contested interpretations deal with the future earthly thousand-year reign of Christ—an idea that Jerome soundly rejected. Although Jerome may be correct that Jews share with these Judaizing Christians belief in a future earthly messianic kingdom, the details of the views that Jerome describes probably belong to the Christian millenarians, not the Jews.

necessarily mean that Jerome's Jewish tradition is inauthentic. For most exegetical questions (certainly in the book of Jeremiah), there was no single authoritative interpretation that represented what all Jews thought. Even rabbinic texts, which represent a select group among Jews in Jerome's day, can give multiple different interpretations of the same passage. Thus, when Jerome's tradition contradicts what is found in a rabbinic text, it may be that Jerome's Jewish informant gave a different answer from what we find in rabbinic texts. Any given statement of Jerome on what "the Hebrews say" should be taken as no more than the explanation given to Jerome by a single Jewish scholar.

Jerome's *Commentary on Jeremiah* contains numerous Jewish traditions for which parallels can be found in rabbinic sources.[55] A striking example is Jerome's report about the seven types of gold in his comments at Jeremiah 10:6-10. Another fascinating case is at Jeremiah 31:15, where Jerome gives a Jewish tradition that does not aid his own interpretive agenda but was so interesting to Jerome that he decided to give it anyway. Jerome made much constructive use of this material in his *Commentary on Jeremiah*; but he also expresses negative views about Jews at various points. We will need to address this below in "Understanding Jerome for Today."

Jerome and the Christian Spiritual Sense

Jerome's aim was not only to explain the literal (*ad litteram*) and historical (*iuxta historiam*) sense of the biblical text but also to expound the abiding meaning of the text as seen through the lens of Christ. Jerome typically gives a twofold interpretation of each passage, one historical and the other spiritual.[56] Jerome associated the literal sense with the "Hebrew truth" and with Jewish learning.[57] Jerome did not have a negative view of the historical sense but saw it as an important part of the meaning of Scripture, which nevertheless needed to be combined with the spiritual sense.[58] Jerome saw his task as "to mix together our tropology with the *historia* of the Hebrews" (*Comm. Zech.*, prol.); and elsewhere he says, "I formerly resolved to deliver to Latin ears the secrets of Hebraic learning and the hidden knowledge of the teachers of the synagogue, insofar as it touches on the sacred Scriptures; for this reason, I must outline the *historia* in the passages which are most obscure. Likewise, I must set forth that which I have received from the authors of the church" (*Comm. Zech.* 6:9-15; cf. *Comm. Jer.*, bk. 3, prol.). We have already seen how

---

[55]*Talmud Yerushalmi* and some of the earlier midrash collections (e.g., *Genesis Rabbah, Leviticus Rabbah*) are roughly contemporary with Jerome, but even later documents can contain older traditions that ultimately go back to the fourth or fifth century (cf. Jer 20:14-18). For descriptions of the various rabbinic texts referenced in the footnotes of this commentary, see H. L. Strack and G. Stemberger, *Introduction to the Talmud and Midrash*, ed. and trans. M. Bockmuehl (Minneapolis: Fortress, 1996).

[56]Cf. Jerome *Comm. Isa.* 45:8: "the interpretation of this passage is twofold."

[57]E.g., Jerome *Comm. Isa.* 23:18: "Thus far the visions of Isaiah . . . we have treated with a 'historical' interpretation, keeping close to the tracks of only the Hebrew truth."

[58]Jerome's comments at Jer 13:16-17 illustrate how he accepts the historical sense but believes that it is unacceptable to neglect the higher sense; in this passage, Jerome criticizes the Jews and "our Judaizers" for following only the simple *historia* that kills (alluding to 2 Cor 3:6).

the classical system of *grammatice* and Jewish learning provided tools for Jerome to use in explaining the historical sense. Now, we may consider how Jerome incorporated traditions that he received "from the authors of the church" in order to perceive the Christian spiritual meaning of the book of Jeremiah.

For Jerome, all Old Testament texts can have some application to Christ and the church. On a few occasions, Jerome thinks that the text speaks of Christ in a directly prophetic way (*iuxta prophetiam*), so that no higher meaning is necessary.[59] In other cases, Jerome grounds his spiritual meaning in the historical sense by pointing out some way in which the wording of the text was not properly realized in the historical fulfillment, so that a further fulfillment in Christ is necessary. The text is seen to be fulfilled "in part" in Old Testament history, but "more fully" in Christ (e.g., Jer 7:27-28; 16:14-15; 31:10-14). This is similar to Antiochene exegesis of the prophets and can be traced back to Jerome's reading of Antiochene commentaries and perhaps to the influence of Apollinaris of Laodicea.[60] Most often, however, the christological meaning is explained as the second component of Jerome's double exposition (historical, then spiritual), where Jerome sees an analogy between the historical meaning and the spiritual. Thus, regarding the "scorching wind" that comes against Jerusalem (Jer 4:11-12a), Jerome says, "According to *historia* you should understand the 'scorching wind' as Nebuchadnezzar, who consumed the entire world. But according to tropology, the 'scorching wind' is the adversarial power [the devil], who comes from the desert and the wilderness, where there is no shelter of God, and tries to destroy God's church." This kind of exegesis operates from the belief that God works according to certain patterns and that the manner of God's dealing with biblical Israel naturally offers paradigms for how God acted through Christ and deals with the church. The historical meaning is valid and useful for Jerome, but it is expected that a Christian expositor should unfold these paradigms and explain how the text relates to Christ and the church. As Jerome says, "Whatever was said at that time to the Israelite people now is referred to the church, so that 'holy prophets' become 'apostles and apostolic men,' and 'lying and frantic prophets' become 'all the heretics'" (*Comm. Ezek.* 13:1-3a; cf. *Comm. Jer.* 30:18-22). This represents the Alexandrians' influence on Jerome's exegesis.

Jerome uses several traditional Christian terms to identify the spiritual meaning of the text. In general, these terms are used without any distinction between them. They may be regarded as synonyms. A common term in Jerome is "tropology" (Gk *tropikōs*; Lat *tropologia*), which in the field of rhetoric referred to the figurative sense of a word as opposed to its literal or proper sense, but in Christian exegesis after Origen became a technical term for the spiritual sense.[61] Another regular term in Jerome is the word *anagogy* (Gk

---

[59]"Where the prophecy is perfectly clear, and the true sequence of the *historia* is explained through the translation, the interpretation of the tropology is superfluous" (*Comm. Zech.* 11:4-5).

[60]Cf. Theodore of Mopsuestia *Comm. Joel* 2:28-32 (LXX) and Diodore of Tarsus in the prologue to his *Comm. Ps. 118*. Jerome does not call this manner of prefiguring Jesus *theoria*, as the Antiochenes do, but the idea is essentially the same.

[61]In the Latin Middle Ages, "tropology" came to be used for a spiritual interpretation that focused on a moral application of the text.

anagōgē, "elevation"), which also goes back to Origen as used in this sense. Other terms, such as *intellegentia spiritalis* ("spiritual understanding"), *sacramenta* ("mysteries") and the Greek *allēgoria* appear in Jerome's exegesis. Jerome usually offers only a twofold exposition, but occasionally, influenced by Origen, Jerome operates with a threefold system of scriptural senses.[62]

One final element of Jerome's spiritual exegesis that requires explanation is his exposition of etymologies of proper names. It was a common belief among learned readers in the Greek tradition that the etymologies of proper names conveyed essential information about the things named. This thinking stemmed from theories of Plato and the Stoics regarding the connection between words and things.[63] By the time of the New Testament, pagan Greek scholars regularly practiced symbolic exegesis of proper name etymologies when reading Homer.[64] In due time, Hellenized Jews, such as Philo, applied this practice to the Bible.[65] From there, it became part of the tradition of Christian spiritual exegesis.[66]

In the early centuries of the Christian era, various name lists (*Onomastica*) circulated in Greek, which listed proper names in the Bible together with their supposed etymological meanings. Jerome's *Book of Hebrew Names* was a translation and mild revision of an earlier Greek list that Jerome ascribed to Philo (on the authority of Origen) but which may have gone back earlier than Philo.[67] Such name lists represented one of the only avenues prior to Jerome through which information about the Hebrew language made its way into the Christian world. Although Jerome generally broke new ground in the realm of Christian Hebrew scholarship, he did inherit a long tradition going back to Philo and Origen of using Hebrew etymologies as part of allegorical exegesis. Whereas the rest of Jerome's Hebrew philology focused on the literal sense, Jerome continued to employ the traditional Hebrew etymologies in the traditional way, that is, allegorically.

Jerome's dependence on earlier Greek sources, both commentators (such as Origen) and name lists, can be seen in the footnotes of the commentary, where I identify parallels

---

[62]On Jerome and the spiritual sense, see P. Jay, "Jerome," in *Handbook of Patristic Exegesis,* ed. C. Kannengiesser, 2 vols. (Leiden: Brill, 2004), 2:1105-9; idem, "Saint Jérôme et le triple sens de l'Écriture," *Revue des études augustiniennes* 26 (1980): 214-27; J. Gribomont, "La terminologie exégétique de S. Jérôme," in *La terminologia esegetica nell'antichità,* ed. C. Curti, J. Gribomont et al. (Bari: Edipuglia, 1987), 123-34; A. Penna, *Principe e carattere dell'esegesi di S. Girolamo* (Rome: Pontifical Biblical Institute, 1950), 93-167.

[63]See Robert Lamberton, *Homer the Theologian* (Berkeley: University of California Press, 1986), 44-54; A. A. Long, *Hellenistic Philosophy,* 2d ed. (Berkeley: University of California Press, 1986), 131-39.

[64]A brief and readable account of this topic is given by R. M. Grant, *The Letter and the Spirit* (London: SPCK, 1957), 3-30.

[65]See Lester Grabbe, *Etymology in Early Jewish Interpretation: The Hebrew Names in Philo* (Atlanta: Scholars Press, 1988), 49-87.

[66]See Nicholas De Lange, *Origen and the Jews* (Cambridge: Cambridge University Press, 1976), 117-19.

[67]In the prologue to his *Book of Hebrew Names,* Jerome reports that Origen ascribed this list to Philo. Eusebius of Caesarea *Hist. Eccl.* 2.18.7 also says that Philo was credited with a book on the interpretation of Hebrew names. Yet, it is doubtful that Philo knew Hebrew well enough to produce such a list; see David Winston, "Philo and Rabbinic Literature," in *The Cambridge Companion to Philo,* ed. Adam Kamesar (Cambridge: Cambridge University Press, 2009), 235. This ancient Greek list explaining the meanings of Hebrew names may have been a source used by Philo in the production of his own etymological allegories.

between Jerome's etymologies and those of Philo, Origen and the *Onomastica*.[68] Jerome learned Hebrew from Greek translations (Aquila, Symmachus and Theodotion) and from Jews with whom he probably spoke Greek,[69] and he similarly regarded Greek *Onomastica* and Origen as legitimate sources of Hebrew information, even though they sometimes reflect errors that one would not expect to find in Jerome. Occasionally, Jerome corrected these errors (e.g., "Sesach" at Jer 25:26c), but often he did not (e.g., "Mahseiah" at Jer 32:12). In general, Jerome's aim in giving these etymologies was not to explain the literal sense of the text according to the Hebrew but to give a traditional Christian interpretation. Thus, understandably, he usually gave a traditional etymology already known to earlier Greek sources.

Understanding Jerome for Today

Jerome wrote his *Commentary on Jeremiah* for Christians who were serious about the study of Scripture and devoted to proper Christian thinking and living. Christians today who share these commitments will find much that is immediately meaningful for them in Jerome's comments. At the same time, Jerome lived in a cultural context very different from the western world in the twenty-first century. Moreover, his comments obviously cannot reflect the advances in scholarship that have come about subsequent to his time. I would therefore like to make a few suggestions on how best to profit from reading Jerome's *Commentary on Jeremiah* today. I obviously cannot address every concern, but by touching on some significant issues, I hope to encourage faithful and thoughtful reflection on the whole task of reading this ancient commentary.

First, Jerome's perspectives on whomever he regards as the "other" are generally uncharitable and reflect the narrow mindset of the Greco-Roman world. Jerome criticizes theological adversaries harshly and without much sense for the possibility of middle ground, even when his own views, when expressed in calmer moments, are moderate. His depictions of the beliefs of others, such as Pelagians or Origenists, must be interpreted not as straight fact but through the lens of Jerome's rhetoric. Furthermore, Jerome inhabits an intellectual world that does not ascribe to women the same dignity as men, in spite of his friendships with extremely capable women, such as Paula and Marcella. Thus, we should not be surprised to find Jerome mocking Pelagius as a "crazy old woman" (Jer 17:1) in the tradition of Roman satire,[70] or frequently drawing the connection between contemporary heresies and "weak women."[71] Moreover, many of Jerome's statements about

---

[68]The ancient name lists are cited according to the edition published by Paul de Lagarde, *Onomastica sacra* (Göttingen: Vandenhoeck and Ruprecht, 1887). This work is a collection of Greek lists of biblical proper name etymologies and Jerome's *Book of Hebrew Names* and *Book of Hebrew Place Names*. De Lagarde's *Onomastica sacra* is abbreviated OS and is followed by the marginal page number and the relevant line number(s).

[69]Graves, *Jerome's Hebrew Philology*, 84-85.

[70]See Wiesen, *St. Jerome as a Satirist*, 113-65, on the anti-woman heritage that Jerome received from the Roman satire tradition.

[71]Jer 3:12-13; 23:28-29 (cf. Jer 29:21-23). See also Jerome *Ep.* 53.7; 130.17; 133.4; *Vigil.* 3; *Comm. Isa.* 57:6. Jerome is following 2 Tim 3:6-7.

Jews reflect the Christian-Jewish polemics of the fourth and fifth centuries[72] and should be regarded as unacceptable. Jerome believes that "the rejection of the Jews is the occasion of our salvation" (Jer 30:23-24; cf. Jer 10:12-16; 15:9), and he comments with approval on the calamities that befell Jews (e.g., Jer 2:14a; 18:17; 19:10-11a).[73] Such ideas are not commensurate with Christian faith and should not be promoted or accepted by Christians.

While it can and should be difficult for us to read such views expressed by a major Christian figure of the past, it is also important to remember Jerome's social location and the limits that we all face as people living in a given time and place. The negative attitudes that Jerome sometimes expressed about women are balanced by the respect and esteem that he showed to his women friends, such as Marcella, whom Jerome approvingly says taught men, including priests, in Rome (*Ep.* 127.7). Likewise, Jerome's whole argument on behalf of the "Hebrew truth" presumed that the Jews continued to possess essential truth for understanding the Scriptures, and Jerome's personal contacts with Jewish teachers must have resulted in some genuine friendships, despite Jerome's acquiescence in his writings to standard anti-Jewish polemics. Thus, even though Jerome did not transcend the limitations of his age in these areas, his experiences and his reflective nature allowed him to take some steps in the right direction.

As for the substance of Jerome's commentary, I will make a few observations on how best to profit both from Jerome's literal exposition and from his spiritual exposition.

Regarding Jerome's exegesis at the literal/historical level, it may be acknowledged that his *Commentary on Jeremiah* reveals certain deficiencies when compared with modern commentaries of comparable scholarship. Jerome believes that his Hebrew text always represents the original text of Jeremiah vis-à-vis the LXX, whereas modern scholars generally conclude that the LXX more often reflects an earlier Hebrew text.[74] Also, there are times when Jerome would have benefited from today's knowledge of ancient Near Eastern Semitic languages; for example, at Jeremiah 7:18, it would have helped Jerome to know that there is an Akkadian word, *kamānu* ("cake"), that is related to the Hebrew word *kwnym*. Most important, Jerome does not give as much attention as do the best modern commentaries to broad themes that extend throughout the entire book. All of these criticisms are valid from this perspective.

At the same time, Jerome's literal exegesis is certainly more than just a relic from the distant past. Jerome constantly shows how one passage connects with another, how the flow of thought unfolds within a passage and how the historical context of Jeremiah illuminates the individual prophecies. Jerome's extensive use of paraphrase makes him a

---

[72]On this context, see Robert Wilken, *John Chrysostom and the Jews* (Berkeley: University of California Press, 1983).

[73]Jerome even invokes New Testament charges made against Jews for the death of Jesus in his anti-Jewish polemics (e.g., Jer 17:1; 17:21-17). We have been able here to give only a selection, not an exhaustive list, of unacceptable passages.

[74]For a brief and clear discussion of the Hebrew and Greek texts of Jeremiah, see Louis Stulman, *Jeremiah*, Abingdon Old Testament Commentaries (Nashville: Abingdon, 2005), 7-9. For a more technical treatment and bibliography, see Emanuel Tov, *Textual Criticism of the Hebrew Bible*, 2d rev. ed. (Minneapolis: Fortress, 2001), 319-27.

helpful guide for grasping the sense of a passage, and he can be quite adept at summing up the key idea. Thus, at Jeremiah 1:7-8 (v. 8: "Be not afraid of them, for I am with you to deliver you, says the Lord"), Jerome astutely observes, "The Lord rescues the prophet not in the sense that he will avoid persecutions and difficulties—since we read that he suffered many things—but such that, while enduring all these things, he will overcome them and not yield to the difficulties."

Moreover, Jerome's treatments of individual words remain valuable for serious students of Scripture. Many of Jerome's comments on the meaning of Hebrew terms are well in line with modern scholarship (e.g., Jer 3:2a; 7:17-19; 13:18-19; 19:1-3a). In other cases, Jerome's analysis is suggestive for possible solutions, or else he transmits information that could be useful for clarifying the text.[75] Jerome reports numerous readings from the Greek translations of Aquila, Symmachus and Theodotion, whose renderings show how the Hebrew word in question was understood in the second century C.E. or earlier. Furthermore, Jerome's distinctive views about Hebrew words represent Jewish traditions from the late fourth or early fifth century C.E.[76] The interpretations given by Jerome and the hexaplaric versions are centuries older than the medieval traditions (vocalization, accents, etc.) of the Masoretic Text. Although one should not read the Hebrew Bible strictly through the lens of Jerome and the ancient versions (and the evidence transmitted is not always uniform), it is difficult to justify placing great confidence in the medieval Masoretic tradition while ignoring the earlier evidence of late antiquity. I hope that modern scholars will make more use of Jerome's commentaries and the hexaplaric versions in their study of the Hebrew Bible.[77]

Regarding Jerome's spiritual interpretation, one can likewise identify both limitations and possibilities for insight. As for limitations, even setting aside the element of anachronism involved with all readings that seek contemporary meaningfulness, Jerome's dichotomy between the historical and the spiritual senses was sometimes so drastic that a clear connection between the two is not obvious. This lack of natural flow from one sense to the other is most evident when Jerome capitalizes on textual obscurity or proper name etymologies for his spiritual interpretation. Conversely, Jerome is most successful as a Christian spiritual interpreter when he takes his lead from the literal interpretation and follows it through into the Christian fulfillment of the original motif. Much of the Old Testament communicates through cultural symbols and archetypes (e.g., land flowing

---

[75]In order to help readers see how Jerome's Hebrew comments correspond to modern scholarship, whenever Jerome discusses a Hebrew word, I always give in a footnote the meaning of the word as given by the most up-to-date Hebrew-English lexicon, *The Hebrew and Aramaic Lexicon of the Old Testament*, ed. L. Koehler and W. Baumgartner et al., 5 vols. (Leiden: Brill, 1994-2000).

[76]See Jerome's comments on *mgwr* at Jer 20:3. Although my emphasis here is naturally on Jerome, I also want to stress the importance of classical rabbinic sources and medieval Jewish commentators, such as Rashi, Kimchi and Ibn Ezra, for interpreting the Hebrew Bible.

[77]Although the most recent edition of the Hexapla is from the nineteenth century (see n. 15), exciting work is presently under way to create an up-to-date edition of the Hexapla. See <www.hexapla.org>.

with milk and honey), and Jerome often succeeds in showing how the pattern is summed up in Jesus. In his *Commentary on Nahum* 2:1-2, Jerome expresses his struggle to hold the two senses of Scripture together: "It is essential that I steer the course of my discussion between *historia* and allegory, as if I were threatened with shipwreck and steering carefully between rocks and crags."[78]

As an example of Jerome's spiritual exegesis, we may consider his comments on Jeremiah 1:10: "See, I have set you this day over nations and over kingdoms, to pluck up and to break down, to destroy and to overthrow, to build and to plant." Jerome begins with a textual detail, noting that the verb "to overthrow" is absent from the LXX. After this, Jerome describes the key point of the passage that sets the stage for the rest of the book: "that the two favorable actions come after the four harsh ones." Indeed, Jeremiah's prophetic career will involve announcing harsh judgments, which must, as the prophet asserts, precede restoration. As Jerome explains, "good things cannot be built until the bad things are destroyed, and the best cannot be planted until the worst is wiped out." Jerome then connects this principle from Jeremiah to the teachings of Jesus, reminding us that the plant not planted by God must be uprooted (Mt 15:13) and that the structure not built on the rock will fall (Mt 7:25-27). In other words, if the foundation is bad, what is above it will not stand. Next, Jerome applies this to his day by equating the weak structure with perverse doctrine that is not built on Jesus. Humility is the product of doctrine that is truly built on Jesus, and so perverse doctrine is that which is built on prideful human wisdom; it is this pride that must be eliminated before what is humble can be built in its place. The church is built on this foundation of humility, as Paul says, "You are God's building, God's field" (1 Cor 3:9), because humility is the way of Christ, who first defeated the prideful power of the devil (allusion is made to the temptation of Jesus) and afterwards was exalted.[79] Finally, at the end of his discussion, Jerome affirms that the text does apply to Jeremiah, based on what we read about Jeremiah in the rest of the book. Thus, Jerome describes the sense of the passage for the book of Jeremiah, lays out the basic principle and then applies it, through the lens of the New Testament, to his own Christian readers and to Christ. He explains the spiritual meaning, but he also maintains the *historia*.

Although most Christians today do not talk about multiple senses, or about tropology, Jerome's spiritual readings can be understood and appreciated today as the perceptions of literary motifs or cultural archetypes. Our vocabulary may be different, but the basic concepts are quite similar. For example, in Jeremiah's day, the people refused to acknowledge their sinfulness, as Jeremiah expresses in Jeremiah 2:23a: "How can you say, 'I am not defiled, I have not gone after the Baals'?" Jerome applies this text through tropology

---

[78]Jerome goes on to quote Virgil *Aen.* 3.420-421: "Scylla lurks on the right side; implacable Charybdis guards the left."

[79]Jerome grounds the idea of Christ's exaltation in an etymological interpretation of the name Jeremiah. The etymology itself is superfluous to his interpretation.

to people of his day who refuse to acknowledge their vices. Jerome probably has in mind the Pelagians. It is the same motif. Similarly, in Jeremiah's day, greedy people turned the temple into a den of robbers (Jer 7:11), and Jerome compares this with the church (= the temple) being led astray by greed, as when Christians prefer the wealth of kings to a wretched-looking coat. This was an important theme for Jerome the ascetic. As another example, Jerome says that the "land flowing with milk and honey" (as promised in Israel's covenant with God) was originally a hyperbolic expression for a land that abounded in material things, but for Christians it represents the church, which abounds in good teaching about Christ (Jer 11:5a). This is a traditional Christian appropriation of the concept of place as it relates to God's blessings (see Heb 4; 11:10). Today's Christian readers and preachers can discover much profit in Jerome's spiritual interpretations. Despite differences in categories and terms, the same Christian faith continues to speak throughout the centuries.

Text and Translation

The edition used as the basis of this translation is that prepared by Siegfried Reiter, *Sancti Eusebii Hieronymi in Hieremiam Prophetam Libri Sex* (Leipzig: Freytag, 1913), which is volume 59 in the series Corpus Scriptorum Ecclesiaticorum Latinorum (CSEL). In the few places where I have deviated from Reiter's reading, I have indicated this in the footnotes. Reference is also made to the older edition of the *Commentary on Jeremiah* edited by Dominic Vallarsi, *Sancti Eusebii Hieronymi Stridonensis Presbyteri Operum. Tomus Tertius* (Verona, 1735).

In keeping with the goals of the series, I have attempted to make the commentary as readable as possible within the confines of the commentary genre in general and the technical nature of some of Jerome's comments.

When discussing a Hebrew word, Jerome often gives his own transliteration of the word into Latin. In the translation of Jerome's comments I have left these transliterations exactly as Jerome gave them, so that today's English readers can see how Jerome heard these Hebrew words and represented them in Latin. In addition, I always provide a footnote that gives a standardized transliteration of the Hebrew word according to the medieval Masoretic tradition. For example, at Jer 1:11-12 Jerome discusses a word play between two similar sounding Hebrew words. The text of the commentary gives these words as *saced* and *soced*, which is precisely how Jerome transliterated them into Latin. In the footnote below, however, I give the transliterations as *šāqēd* and *šōqēd*, which follows modern conventions for transliterating Hebrew into English according to the Masoretic pronunciation.

The biblical texts cited in the lemmata and quoted by Jerome in his comments are translated with reference to modern English translations, so as to be recognizable to English readers, but they do not match any English translation of the Old Testament. In each case, I have tried to capture the essential elements of Jerome's understanding of the text that he is translating (as shown by his Latin), whether it is the Hebrew text, the LXX or one of the hexaplaric versions (Aquila, Symmachus or Theodotion). It should be noted that, although Jerome almost always follows his own translation of Jeremiah "according to the Hebrews" in giving the lemmata in the commentary, he often quotes the Old Latin edition (based on the LXX) when quoting a passage from elsewhere in the Bible. This is especially noticeable in his quotations of the Psalms. This probably reflects the fact that he is quoting these "remote" verses from memory, which also explains why these quotations are not always exact.

EUSEBIUS HIERONYMUS (JEROME)
Commentary on the Prophet Jeremiah
In Six Books

Prologue

After explanations of the twelve prophets, Isaiah, Daniel and Ezekiel, I am at last setting my hand to Jeremiah, dedicating a brief commentary on this book to you, brother Eusebius,[1] so that you may join this evangelical man[2] to the Evangelist Matthew, whom I discussed in a concise way many years ago at your urging. And since the book of Jeremiah is very long, and in most passages the *historia* is described clearly, I will offer this one word of warning to your good judgment: that you should not seek from this commentary extensive explanations, especially concerning those issues that have already been discussed in the other prophetic books or whose interpretations are obvious in and of themselves. I will endeavor to write, through the hand of secretaries, in such a way that nothing is lacking with respect to the ideas, even if much is lacking with respect to the words. I will prepare for you the warp, weft and heddle; it is up to you to make the beautiful garment. As a result, you will be able not only to hear us but also to teach others.

The book of Baruch, which is included in the popular edition of the Seventy but is not found in the Hebrew, and the pseudepigraphic letter of Jeremiah,[3] I have judged to be totally unworthy of treatment. But out of the Hebrew founts I have endeavored to straighten out the order of Jeremiah, which had been confused by scribes, and to complete what was lacking in the book, so that you may have the new out of the old, and the true prophet in place of the false and corrupted one. You should pay little attention to the rabid frenzy of our detractors, who criticize not only our words but even the syllables of our words, because they wrongly suppose that they know something themselves if they disparage the works of others.

For example, an unlearned detractor recently burst forth who thought my commentary on Paul's epistle to the Ephesians was reprehensible.[4] Yet, while snoring in extreme dementia, he failed to recognize the laws of commentary writing, according to which one reports many opinions from various authors— sometimes leaving out their names and sometimes mentioning them—so that it is left up to the judgment of the reader to decide which

---

Prologue   [1]Eusebius of Cremona, a presbyter, was a long-time friend of Jerome and one of Jerome's supporters in the controversy surrounding the translation of Origen's *On First Principles*. Jerome had earlier dedicated to Eusebius his *Comm. Matt.*, which was written in 398.   [2]Jeremiah.   [3]Baruch and the Epistle of Jeremiah are ancient Jewish works preserved as part of the Greek Old Testament. A copy of the Epistle of Jeremiah was found among the Qumran scrolls, and both Baruch and the Epistle of Jeremiah were included in Athanasius's list of canonical scriptures (*Ep.* 39.3-4). Because they were not extant in Hebrew or part of the Hebrew canon as Jerome knew it, he did not regard them as worthy of treatment. The Epistle of Jeremiah was not written by Jeremiah, so Jerome was justified in using the Greek term *pseudepigraphon* ("falsely written") to describe it. Jerome lists the books of the Old Testament according to the Hebrew canon in the preface to his IH translation of Samuel and Kings (the Helmeted Preface). See Patrick W. Skehan, "St. Jerome and the Canon of the Holy Scriptures," in *A Monument to St. Jerome*, ed. F. X. Murphy (New York: Sheed & Ward, 1952), 259-87.   [4]This is Pelagius, whom Jerome accused of following the heresies of Origen and Rufinus (see bks. 3 and 4, prol.). In answer to Jerome's charge that Pelagius was reviving the errors of Origen (through Rufinus), Pelagius apparently took up Rufinus's observation that Jerome had depended heavily on Origen in his *Comm. Eph.* (see Rufinus *Orig. Princ.* pref. 2; Jerome *Ruf.* 1.8). See R. F. Evans, *Pelagius: Inquiries and Reappraisals* (New York: Seabury Press, 1968), 19-21; R. E. Heine, *The Commentaries of Origen and Jerome on St. Paul's Epistle to the Ephesians* (Oxford: Oxford University Press, 2002), 5-7.

interpretation ought to be chosen as best.[5] He failed to grasp this even though I said in the preface to the first book of the same work that I would be explaining either my own ideas or those of others, and that the comments were going to come both from old writers and from us. Not seeing this, his precursor Grunnius formerly tried with great effort to slander us, but I answered him in two books.[6]

The other charges which that fellow[7] puts forth as his own—the same old charges with now a different accuser—have already been cleared, so that I may omit reference to my volumes against Jovinianus, in which he is shown to be grieved that virginity is preferable to marriage, that marriage is preferable to bigamy and that bigamy is preferable to polygamy.[8] Nor does that complete dolt, weighed down with Scottish porridge, remember that we said in that very work, "I do not condemn second marriages, or even third marriages, or—if it could happen—eighth marriages. I will say more than that: I would even receive a fornicator who was penitent. Whatever is equally lawful ought to be weighed on an equal scale."[9] Let him read the apology of the same work,[10] which Rome received with gladness many years ago against his teacher. Then, let him take note that he is blaspheming with the voices of others and that he is so unskilled that not even his slanders are his own; instead, he uses against us the rabid frenzy of enemies long ago buried. But now we must enter on the work set out for us.

Book One

1:1-3: *The words of Jeremiah, the son of Hilkiah, of the priests who were in Anathoth*

in the land of Benjamin, to whom the word of the Lord came in the days of Josiah the son of Amon, king of Judah, in the thirteenth year of his reign. It came also in the days of Jehoiakim the son of Josiah, king of Judah, and until the end of the eleventh year of Zedekiah, the son of Josiah, king of Judah, until the deportation of Jerusalem in the fifth month.

Many prophets, such as Isaiah, Hosea and Joel, lived before the captivity of the ten tribes of Israel or the two tribes of Judah and Benjamin; others lived after the captivity, such as Daniel, Haggai and Zechariah; but Jeremiah and Ezekiel composed their prophecies when the captivity was imminent, the one being in Judah, the other in Babylon. Although Jeremiah was at this point only a boy, he began to prophesy in the thirteenth year of Josiah the son of Amon king of Judah, and he prophesied during his reign for nineteen years. Afterwards he prophesied under his son Jehoiakim for eleven years, and then under Zedekiah, who was the last king of Judah, for eleven years, all the way to the fifth month when Jerusalem was taken captive by the Babylonians. Of course, three months each are being reckoned in the above-mentioned years for Jehoahaz and Jehoiachin, the first of whom was led away to Egypt, and the second together with his mother was led to Babylon. Thus, from the beginning of his prophetic career to the captivity of Jerusalem, in the course of which he himself was also taken captive, he prophesied for forty years. In addition, he prophesied one year beyond this time when he was led away to Egypt, where he prophesied in Tahpanhes, as is related in this very book.[1]

---

[5]On the laws or conventions of commentary writing, see Jerome *Ruf.* 1.16; 3.11; *Comm. Jer.* 25:26c; *Comm. Isa.* bk. 11, prol.; *Ep.* 20.2; 61.1. [6]The two books of Jerome *Ruf.* On the name Grunnius ("Grunter") for Rufinus, see the Introduction. [7]Pelagius. [8]Pelagius is now said to be the heir of Jovinianus, who challenged Jerome's extreme views on the superiority of virginity over marriage. By bigamy, Jerome is referring to remarriages after being widowed, a practice that Pelagius did not view so negatively (e.g., *Libellus Fidei* 10). Jovinianus accused Jerome of disparaging marriage, and Pelagius took up the charge as well, but Jerome claims to have already answered this charge in *Jov.* [9]Jerome *Jov.* 1.15. [10]See Jerome *Ep.* 48, which is an apology for *Jov.* **Book One** [1]Jer 43.

In place of "the words of Jeremiah," the Seventy put "the word of God that came to Jeremiah," which means that the words of Jeremiah are the word of the Lord. Moreover, he was from the line of priests who inhabit the area north of Jerusalem at the third milestone,[2] in the village of Anathoth. The great clemency of the Lord is astonishing: with the captivity already near and the Babylonian army besieging Jerusalem, he nevertheless provokes the people to repentance, preferring to save the converted rather than to destroy wrongdoers. In place of "deportation," which all the others translated with one voice, the LXX put "captivity."[3] After the beginning of Jeremiah's prophesying, in the thirty-fifth year of his prophetic career, Ezekiel began to prophesy to those who had been taken captive with him.

1:4-5: *Now the word of the Lord came to me saying, "Before I formed you in the womb I knew you, and before you were born I consecrated you; I appointed you a prophet to the nations."*

This is not (as heresy supposes) because Jeremiah existed before his conception, but because the Lord, to whom things not yet made are already made, foreknew that he was going to exist, as the apostle says: "he who calls things that are not as though they were."[4] That he was sanctified in the womb we can also understand according to this statement of the apostle: "He who set me apart from the womb of my mother and called me through his grace was pleased to reveal his son to me, in order that I might preach him among the Gentiles."[5] John the Baptist was also sanctified in the womb. He received the Holy Spirit, stirred in the womb and spoke through the mouth of his mother.[6]

Furthermore, when he says, "I appointed you a prophet to the nations," he wishes this to be understood: later on in this very prophet, we are going to read that he prophesied not only to Jerusalem but also to many of the surrounding nations. Certain people understand this passage to be about the Savior, who was in the strictest sense a prophet to the nations and who called all nations through the apostles. For that one, before being formed in the virgin's womb and coming forth from his mother's body, was truly sanctified in the womb and known to the Father—indeed, he was always in the Father, and the Father was always in him.[7]

1:6: *Then I said, "Ah Lord God! Behold, I do not know how to speak, for I am a lad."* LXX: *Then I said, "O Lord God, I do not know how to speak, for I am a youth."*[8]

He pleads against his office, which in view of his age he cannot fulfill, showing the same modesty as Moses, who said that he was slight and meager of voice.[9] But Moses was summoned, as it were, at a great and robust age, whereas Jeremiah is given the grace of boyhood, which is adorned with modesty and reserve.

1:7-8: *But the Lord said to me, "Do not say, 'I am only a lad'; for to all to whom I send you, you shall go, and whatever I command you, you shall speak. Be not afraid of them, for I am with you to deliver you, says the Lord."*

---

[2]Three Roman miles from Jerusalem. One Roman mile (one thousand paces) is roughly equivalent to 1500 m (OLD 1109). That Anathoth was three milestones from Jerusalem was also noted in Eusebius *Onom.* 27. See Jer 11:21-23. [3]Jerome agrees with Aq, Sym and Th ("all the others") in translating the word as "deportation" (*transmigratio*), which attempts to capture the sense of the Hebrew *glh* ("to go into exile"). The Greek term for "captivity" (*aichmalōsia*) is a common equivalent for *glh* in the LXX. [4]Rom 4:17. [5]Gal 1:15-16. [6]Lk 1:41-42. [7]Jn 10:38; 14:10-11. [8]The term that Jerome uses for "boy" (*puer*) refers to any nonadult male, strictly speaking up to the seventeenth year. The LXX's term for "youth" (*neōteros*) usually refers to those in the prime of life (e.g., between twenty and forty). The Hebrew *n'r* can refer to a boy or to a young man in the prime of life. [9]Ex 4:10; 6:12.

He says, "You should not consider your age, for (as you learn from another prophet) understanding is gray hair for men,[10] and it is only by your willingness that you will go forward. You will have me as a companion, and with my help you will fulfill all things. 'Open your mouth wide, and I will fill it.'[11] Nor should you consider the great number of those to whom and against whom you will be speaking, but instead consider me, who 'am with you to deliver you, says the Lord.'" Yet, the Lord rescues the prophet not in the sense that he will avoid persecutions and difficulties—since we read that he suffered many things—but such that, while enduring all these things, he will overcome them and not yield to the difficulties.

1:9: *Then the Lord put forth his hand and touched my mouth; and the Lord said to me, "Behold, I have put my words in your mouth."*

It should be observed that here the hand of God is sent to touch the mouth of the prophet, to whom it is said, "Behold, I have put my words in your mouth," whereas in Isaiah it is written: "Then flew one of the seraphim to me, having in his hand a burning coal that he had taken with tongs from the altar. And he touched my mouth and said, 'Behold, this has touched your lips; your guilt is taken away, and your sin forgiven.'"[12] In Isaiah, since the prophet is of a sound and complete age, and since he confesses candidly that he has unclean lips and dwells in the midst of a people of unclean lips, one of the seraphim is sent to touch his mouth—not with his hand but with tongs and a burning coal—to take away his guilt and forgive his sin. Here, however, it is the hand of God that is sent—the hand through which he administers all things and which elsewhere is called an "arm"[13]—not to

take away sins, of which he had committed few on account of his youth, but to grant the gift of speaking. Moreover, Ezekiel swallowed a scroll that was written on both within and without, thus containing both the divine mysteries and the simple *historia*. As for Jeremiah, his mouth is touched and the words of the Lord are granted to him, so that he may receive the confidence to preach. And beautifully according to the letter a "hand" is sent, so that the prophet, seeing the likeness of a human hand, will not recoil from the touch of the hand.

1:10: *"See, I have set you this day over nations and over kingdoms, to pluck up and to break down, to destroy and to overthrow, to build and to plant."*

That which we have added from the Hebrew, "to overthrow" or "to throw down," is not found in the LXX. And one ought to consider carefully that the two favorable actions come after the four harsh ones. For good things cannot be built until the bad things are destroyed, and the best cannot be planted until the worst is wiped out. For "every plant that my heavenly Father has not planted will be rooted up,"[14] and any structure that does not have its foundation built on the rock, but instead was built on sand, will be overthrown by the word of God and will fall down.[15] This structure, namely, every sacrilege and perverse doctrine, which Jesus will consume with the breath of his mouth and will destroy by the appearance of his coming, will be put to ruin forever.[16] Furthermore, whatever is exalted against the knowledge of God,[17] where people are trusting in their own wisdom (which is foolishness with God),[18] he will destroy and throw down, so that what is humble may be built in its place, and so that things suited to ecclesiastical truth may be built and planted

---

[10]Wis 4:9; that is, if you have understanding, then you have the equivalence of old age. [11]Ps 81:10. [12]Is 6:6-7. [13]E.g., Jer 27:5; 32:17. [14]Mt 15:13. [15]Mt 7:25-27. [16]2 Thess 2:8. [17]2 Cor 10:5. [18]1 Cor 3:19.

on the site of the haughty things that were destroyed and plucked up. In this way the saying of the apostle may be fulfilled: "You are God's building, God's field."[19]

Many interpret this passage as relating to the person of Christ. For "Jeremiah" is translated "the exalted one of the Lord,"[20] who destroyed the kingdoms of the devil that were shown on the top of the mountain[21] and who did away with the adversarial powers, canceling the bond of errors on the cross.[22] Beyond the truth of the *historia*, the psalm speaks about these powers in a tropological[23] way: "Why do the nations conspire, and the peoples plot in vain? The kings of the earth set themselves, and the rulers take counsel together."[24] In place of those plucked up, destroyed, ruined and brought down lower, the church of God is built and planted. There is no doubt, however, that this text applies to the person of Jeremiah, since we read in the following chapters that he receives in his hand a cup filled with wine and is commanded to make all the surrounding nations drink from it.[25]

1:11-12: *And the word of the Lord came to me, saying, "Jeremiah, what do you see?" And I said, "I see a 'watching rod.'"* *Then the Lord said to me, "You have seen well, for I am watching over my word to perform it."*

In place of "watching rod," the LXX translated "nut-tree staff." We must therefore elaborate on the matter, so that the Latin reader may understand the Hebrew etymology. In Hebrew the word *nut-tree* is *saced*, whereas the Hebrew word for "a watch" or "watchful" or "to watch" is *soced*; thus, in a later passage this same word is used for a "watching panther." Because of the similarity between these two words, the prophet takes the word that means "nut-tree" and plays on the word *watching*.[26] A similar example can be found in the book of Daniel, following Theodotion's version, where from the *schinos* and *prinos* trees, that is, from the "mastic tree" and the "oak," "cutting" and "sawing" are decreed for the adulterous elders.[27] Likewise at the beginning of the book of Genesis, it says that "Woman," which in Hebrew is *issa*, was taken out of "Man," *is*; thus "Wo-man"—"because she was taken out of Man."[28] For "nut-tree staff," Aquila and Symmachus gave "watching rod" as a translation. Theodotion, on the other hand, put "almond-tree rod."

With this rod God is watching and examining the sins of the people, so that he may strike and apprehend those at fault. Similarly, the apostle writes to sinners: "What do you wish? Shall I come to you with a rod, or with love in a spirit of gentleness?"[29] This is also the same rod or staff of which David speaks: "Thy rod and thy staff, they comfort me."[30] And it is beautiful how it says "they comfort me," since

---

[19]1 Cor 3:9. [20]This etymology of Jeremiah (*yrmyhw*), based on the Hebrew verb *rwm* ("to be exalted") and *yhw* ("the Lord"), was available in the onomastica (OS 192.91) and Origen (*Fr. Jer.* 60). See also Jerome *Nom. Hebr.* (OS 62.6); cf. Jer 23:9b; 32:6-7. [21]Mt 4:8. [22]Col 2:14-15. [23]Jerome uses the Greek term *tropikōs*, which in the field of rhetoric referred to the figurative sense of a word as opposed to its literal or proper sense, but in Christian exegesis after Origen it became a technical term for the spiritual sense of the text. [24]Ps 2:1-2. [25]Jer 25:15. [26]Jerome is pointing out the word play present in the Hebrew text between the words for "nut-tree" (Jer 1:11; Heb *šāqēd*) and "watching" (Jer 1:12; Heb *šōqēd*). The "later passage" to which Jerome refers is Jer 5:6, where reference is made to a "watching (Heb *šōqēd*) panther." [27]Jerome is referring to the Greek play on words found in the story of Susanna (Sus 54-55, 58-59). Jerome says that he is following Th, which differs considerably from the version of Susanna transmitted as the LXX. Julius Africanus, in his *Epistle to Origen*, had taken the Greek word play as evidence that Susanna was composed in Greek and therefore not authentic to the Old Testament. Origen acknowledged the possibility that Susanna might have been written in Greek, but he also suggested that this may have been an original Hebrew word play translated into Greek; in any case, Origen defended Susanna as Christian Scripture on the basis of church usage (*Epistle to Africanus* 4-6, 12). In his *Expl. Dan.* 13:54-59, Jerome essentially sides with Africanus, arguing that one must prove the Hebrew origin of the word play in order to defend Susanna's scriptural status. Yet, Jerome is still willing to use this Greek word play as an illustration of the kind of literary device found here (Jer 1:11-12). [28]Gen 2:23. The Hebrew words for "man" (*'yš*) and "woman" (*'šh*) resemble each other. [29]1 Cor 4:21. [30]Ps 23:4.

the Lord strikes only so that he may afterwards heal.

Moreover, just as a nut or an almond has a hard, bitter shell, but when the rough and hard outside is removed the sweetest fruit can be found, so also with the labor of continence: it seems bitter at present, but it brings forth the sweetest fruits. From this principle also comes this old saying: "The roots of education are bitter, but the fruits are sweet."[31]

Some people understand the "watching" (or "nut-tree") rod to be the Lord, about whom Isaiah speaks: "There shall come forth a rod from the stump of Jesse."[32] Some also say that the rod of Aaron, which was thought to have died, blossomed in the resurrection of the Lord.[33]

1:13-14: *The word of the Lord came to me a second time, saying, "What do you see?" And I said, "I see a boiling pot, facing away from the north." Then the Lord said to me, "Out of the north evil shall be opened out"—or "shall blaze forth"[34]—"on all the inhabitants of the land."*

Torments are assigned to sinners in specific degrees, so that gradually they may come to salvation. Those who do not wish to be healed by the rod when it strikes are sent to the boiling bronze pot that is heated facing away from the north. Ezekiel explains more fully that this pot signifies the king of Babylon and the city of Jerusalem.[35] And beautifully it concludes: "Out of the north evil shall blaze forth on all the inhabitants of the land." This applies either to the land of Judah, or, undoubtedly, to the whole earth, as is written in the Apocalypse: "Woe on all the inhabitants of the earth."[36] For the saints are not inhabitants of the earth but are foreigners

and sojourners, as one of them says: "For I am a foreigner on the earth, and a sojourner like all my fathers";[37] and as another says, "Few and evil have been my days, in which I have been a sojourner on the earth."[38] In the same way, Peter also wrote his catholic epistle to the foreigners and sojourners in Pontus, Galatia and Cappadocia.[39]

And Solomon says according to the mystical understanding, "The north wind, although called by a favorable name, is harsh,"[40] for those, that is, who have become stiff from its cold and have extinguished the heat of faith.

1:15-16: *"For lo, I am calling all the tribes of the kingdoms of the north, says the Lord; and they shall come and every one shall set his throne at the entrance of the gates of Jerusalem, against all its walls round about, and against all the cities of Judah. And I will utter my judgments against them, for all their wickedness in forsaking me; they have burned incense to other gods and worshiped the works of their own hands."*

No one can doubt that many nations and the kings from these various nations were subjected to the king of Babylon, and that when Jerusalem had been besieged they put their thrones and tents round about the city, and especially at the exits of the gates, lest any of them who had been shut in should be able to break out. And not only Jerusalem but also all the cities of Judah were surrounded by a similar blockade. "And when," he says, "the city has been captured, I will tell them that my judgments were correct and that each of them received what they deserved, not for any other faults to which the human condition is subject, but chiefly for idolatry, through which they deserted me and worshiped the works of their hands."

---

[31]This saying is found in many ancient sources and was ascribed to various notable figures, including Isocrates (Libanius *Chriae* 3) and Aristotle (Diogenes Laertius 5.18) in Greek, and Cato (Diomedes *Ars Grammatica* 1. *De Decl. Chriarum*) in Latin. [32]Is 11:1. [33]Num 17:1-11. [34]Jerome matches Aq and Sym (Heb *pth*, "to open"). [35]Ezek 24:1-5. [36]Rev 8:13. In Greek as in Hebrew, the word that means "land" can also mean "earth." [37]Ps 39:12. [38]Gen 47:9. [39]1 Pet 1:1. [40]Prov 27:16 (LXX).

Certain people understand this passage in a positive sense: those who through their sufferings had been boiled in the bronze pot and purged[41] now become leaders in Jerusalem. And after the Lord shows this compassion on them he rebukes them, because they had previously abandoned God and worshiped images. But this is an impetuous and perverse interpretation. Let not the unlearned commentator practice this trickery.

1:17a: *"But you, gird up your loins; arise, and say to them everything that I command you."*

Job was commanded to gird up his loins, as were the apostles,[42] so that, with their loins girded up (loins that Elijah and John the Baptist mortified with leather girdles),[43] they might be able to hold their lamps in their hands, that is, the lamps of evangelical preaching.[44] Therefore, whoever is going to speak the words of God should gird up his loins, knowing that all the strength of the devil is in the loins, and that justly it says in the Psalms: "My loins are filled with disgrace."[45] But since he has girded up his loins, he will hear that which is written: "Awake, O sleeper, and arise, and Christ shall give you light."[46] Thus, always watchful and arising from sleep he will speak just as God commanded him.

1:17b: *"Do not be dismayed by them; for I will make you to be not dismayed before them."*

Or, as the Seventy and the other translators say, "lest I dismay you before them." This is the sense according to our translation: "You should not be dismayed by them; for with me as your helper, you will not be able to fear them." According to the Seventy, "You should not be dismayed by them; have confidence in my command! For if you will not offer what you have and so cease from being dismayed, then I will forsake you and hand you over to dismay. And to whatever extent I appear to be making you dismayed, to that extent I am leaving you to your own fear." The passage also shows that the truth is bitter and that one should not fear the multitude of people who will not endure the chastisement of a rebuke but instead will plot treacheries against the one by whom they were rebuked. And that which follows according to the Seventy, "For I am with you, to deliver you, says the Lord," is not found in the Hebrew. But the sense is: "I will rescue you, not in such a way that nothing will be plotted against you, but so that you will not be lacking, even while enduring treacheries."

1:18-19: *"For I have given you today[47] to be a fortified city, an iron pillar and a bronze wall, against the whole land, against the kings of Judah, its princes, its priests and the people of the land. They will fight against you; but they shall not prevail against you, for I am with you, says the Lord, to deliver you."*

The divine word explains why the prophet need not be afraid. He says, "I have given (or assigned) you today"—that is, in the present life, which is why it says "today"—"as a fortified city," not as a single house, or a tower or any other fortification, but as a whole city, which set on a hill cannot be hid,[48] and concerning which it is written, "Glorious things are spoken of you, O city of God,"[49] and "I am a strong city, a city under siege."[50] And he says "an iron pillar," about which the apostle writes, "the pillar and bulwark of the truth."[51] Furthermore, Peter and John, who were

---

[41]Jer 1:13-14. [42]Job 38:3; 40:7; Lk 12:35. [43]1 Kings 1:8; Mt 3:4. [44]Lk 12:35. [45]Ps 38:7 (LXX [37:8]). [46]Eph 5:14. [47]Or, "Behold, I have assigned you on this day." The renderings "given" and "today" are attempts by Jerome to follow the Hebrew (*ntn* and *hywm*) more closely. At the same time, Jerome avoids the traditional "behold" (Heb *hinnēh*; LXX: *idou*) in an attempt to capture the sense of the Hebrew (cf. Lambdin 169). [48]Mt 5:14. [49]Ps 87:3. [50]Is 27:3 (LXX). [51]1 Tim 3:15.

considered pillars of the church, gave the right hand of fellowship to Paul and Barnabas.[52] And this is not even sufficient, but he says "a bronze wall," which is neither damaged by rust nor ruined by the pounding of rain, but instead becomes stronger with age. Such you will be against the kings, the princes and the people of not just any old place, but of the earth.[53] They have a taste for earthly things but do not understand the heavenly;[54] they bear the image of dust, and not of heaven.[55] "These," he says, "will fight against you; but they shall not prevail against you." Why, I ask? What cause of fortitude is so great that neither kings nor princes nor priests nor people can prevail against one man? He goes on to say, "For I am with you, says the Lord, to deliver you." Whenever the kings of Judah (which is translated "confession"),[56] its princes, priests and people—that is, the bishops, presbyters, deacons and the vile and ignoble mob—seek to rise up against a holy man, he may have firmness of faith and may cease from being afraid, because he shall overcome by the Lord's help.

2:1-2a: *The word of the Lord came to me, saying, "Go and proclaim in the ears of Jerusalem . . ."*

This is not found in the LXX but was added under asterisk from the edition of Theodotion.[57] But in place of the Hebrew word *carath*,[58] which we interpreted as "proclaim" or "preach," Theodotion translated "read." For this word, in view of its ambiguity, can signify "reading," "proclaiming" or "preaching." Finally, we can understand the "ears of Jerusalem" to be the ears of its inhabitants.

2:2b: *"Thus says the Lord, I remember your youth when I was compassionate with you, and my love for you at your betrothal, when you followed me in the wilderness, in a land not sown."* LXX: *"Thus says the Lord, I remember the devotion of your youth and your love in maturity."*[59]

This is discussed more fully in Ezekiel, when the Lord joins himself in matrimony with Jerusalem, and under Jerusalem's *persona* of a wife he unites with her in embraces.[60] Likewise, in order to show the intensity of his affection, he calls her girl, maiden, and betrothed; after all, to whatever extent we have not yet obtained something, to that extent we strive to obtain it. "And when," he says, "you followed me in the wilderness, as betrothal and legal wedding gifts I bestowed on you the ornament and necklace of words."[61] And all of this is ascribed not to her merit but to his compassion, after which his love follows. What we translated as "in the wilderness, in a land not sown" is not found in the LXX.

2:3: *"Israel was holy to the Lord, the first fruits of his harvest. All who ate of it became guilty; evil came on them, says the Lord."*

When it says that Israel was the first fruits of the Lord, it shows that the people have been gathered from among the nations since the

---

[52]Gal 2:9. [53]See n. 45. [54]Phil 3:19. [55]1 Cor 15:49. [56]The etymology for Judah (*yhwdh*) from *ydh* (Hiphil; "to confess") was traditional; see Gen 29:35 (LXX); OS 169.82; Philo *Plant.* 134; *Leg.* 1.80; 3.146; Origen *Fr. Jer.* 11. Cf. Jer 32:42-44. [57]The fifth column of Origen's Hexapla contained an edition of the Greek Old Testament that, using the LXX as its base, added words that were found in the Hebrew but not in the LXX (marked with an asterisk) and used an obelus to identify words that were present in the LXX but lacking in the Hebrew. Jerome is referring to Origen's edition, saying that the material found in the Hebrew but lacking in the LXX was supplied by Origen from Th. [58]Heb *qārā'tā* (Qal, perfect, second person masculine singular), from *qr'* ("call, shout, summon, proclaim, read" [KB 1128-30]). Because Jeremiah read at least some of his prophecies from a scroll (e.g., Jer 36), Th's interpretation is not unreasonable. Cf. Jer 3:12; 19:1-3a. [59]The LXX's "maturity" (or "completion") arose because the Hebrew word for "betrothal" (*klwlh*) is similar to the word for "completion" (*klyl*). In some manuscripts of the LXX, the following phrase is present at the end of the verse: "in that you followed the Holy One of Israel, says the Lord." [60]Ezek 16:8-14. [61]Ezek 16:11.

beginning, as it is written in another passage: "Remember your congregation, which you have gotten of old."[62] Moreover, the first fruits are to be given to the priests,[63] not to their enemies. And what follows, "All who ate of it became guilty; evil came on them, says the Lord," has this sense: just as those who eat of the first fruits who are not from the priestly line are answerable for their crime, so also those who defile Israel will be subjected to evils, as the saint says in the twenty-sixth psalm: "When hurtful people drew near against me in order to devour my flesh, my persecutors and my enemies themselves became weak and fell."[64] And they will not be exempt from punishment simply because they are following a command from God,[65] but evil will come on them: "For it is necessary that temptations come, but woe to the man by whom the temptation comes!"[66]

2:4-5: Hear the word of the Lord, O house of Jacob, and all the families of the house of Israel. Thus says the Lord: "What wrong did your fathers find in me that they went far from me, and went after worthlessness, and became worthless?"

Another prophet also relates this idea: "O my people, what have I done to you? In what have I wearied you? Answer me! For I brought you up from the land of Egypt and redeemed you from the house of bondage."[67] The names of both Jacob[68] and Israel are used with reference not only to the twelve tribes but also to all the people, since it was Jacob himself who came to be known as Israel.[69] He reckons the offense as deriving from the parents, not because the sins

of the parents are imputed to the children,[70] but because the children are being similar to their parents and because they will be punished both for their own wickedness and for the wickedness of their parents. We often read that God has compassion on children on account of their holy parents.[71] Yet, the ancestors of this sinful people have forsaken God—and not just for a moment, but for a long time. In place of God they have followed worthlessness, namely, idols, which are of no benefit to those who worship them and which have been made in the likeness of their worshipers, as it is written: "Those who make them are like them; so are all who trust in them."[72]

2:6: "They did not say, 'Where is the Lord who brought us up from the land of Egypt, who led us through the wilderness, through a land uninhabitable and impassable, through a land of thirst and the image of death, through a land where man does not walk, and no one dwells?'"

Instead of "man" the LXX translated "son of man," and in place of "image of death," Theodotion has "shadow of death."[73] Since the *historia* is clear, this should be contemplated according to anagogy:[74] As long as we are in this age and are being led out of Egypt, we are brought up by degrees. We first pass through the places of "wilderness" and the "uninhabitable" land, which a holy person ought not to inhabit; then it says the "impassable" land, so that it shows the difficulty of the journey; "through a land of thirst," where we always desire more and are never content with our

---

[62]Ps 74:2. [63]Lev 23:10; Num 18:12-13. [64]Ps 27:2 (LXX [26:2]). [65]Even though Babylon was called by God to afflict Israel, it will still be punished, because it has consumed the "first fruits" of the Lord (i.e., Israel; cf. Jer 25:26; 50:1–51:64). [66]Mt 18:7. [67]Mic 6:3-4. [68]"Jacob" is lacking in the manuscripts but must be added in accordance with the sense. [69]Gen 32:28. [70]Ex 20:5. [71]E.g., Ex 32:13; 1 Kings 11:12-13, 34; 15:4-5; 2 Kings 8:19; 2 Chron 21:7. [72]Ps 115:8. [73]Lit.: " 'shadow of death' was added (i.e., in the Hexapla) from Theodotion." Heb *ṣlmwt* ("gloom," KB 1029). Aq, Sym, Th, Targ and Pesh: "shadow of death" (*ṣēl*, "shadow," and *māwet*, "death"). Jerome: "image of death" (*selem*, "image," and *māwet*, "death"). [74]Following Origen and other Greek fathers, Jerome uses the Greek term *anagōgē* ("elevation") to refer to the higher or spiritual sense.

present station; "and the image (or 'shadow') of death," for we always stand in danger, and everywhere the devil sets his traps; "through a land where man does not walk"—the person, that is, who has obtained perfected stature, since we all will rise up "to mature manhood, to the measure of the stature of the fullness of Christ."[75] Of course, Christ, who is the man of God and the Son of man, never inhabited these places but always hastened on to greater things. From this it is obvious that one does not reach perfection while on the road, but at the end of the road and in the mansion prepared in heaven for the saints,[76] about which it is said, "you who stand in the house of the Lord, in the courts of the house of our God!"[77] In vain, therefore, heresy—a new one that has come from an old—supposes that perfect victory happens here,[78] when in reality the future holds struggle, combat and an uncertain end.

2:7: "And I brought you into the land of Carmel to enjoy its fruits and its good things. But when you came in you defiled my land and made my heritage an abomination."

"To compensate for the toil of your difficult journey, I gave to you an abundance of all things"—for this is what "Carmel" signifies. In Hebrew it is *Chermel*, and in our language it gives the meaning "recognition of circumcision."[79] And so, just as that people polluted and defiled the land with their idolatry, a land that was holy and fertile with all things, so also with us, when we receive the knowledge of the true circumcision and consume its fruit, if negligence then creeps in, we defile the land of God and make his inheritance an abomination.

2:8: "The priests did not say, 'Where is the Lord?' Those who handle the law did not know me; the shepherds transgressed against me; the prophets prophesied by Baal and went after idols."

After such great benefits, they turned their privileges of honor into something contemptible, in that the priests did not seek the Lord; the doctors of the law, who should have been teaching others, did not know him; the shepherds became transgressors through negligence; and the prophets, who were preaching among the people, did not speak by God but by an idol and venerated things that they themselves had made. These words should be used against the leaders of our order, who devour the people of God like a loaf of bread and by their evil works fail to call on the Lord.

2:9: "Therefore, I still contend with you, says the Lord, and with your children I will dispute."

Lest it appear that the Lord is merely assaulting them by force, he contends with them by reason, as if with an equal, in accordance with what David sings and the apostle appropriates: "That you may be justified in your words and prevail when you are judged."[80] He says "still" in order to testify that he has often done this already. And when he adds "with your children," it shows that there is obstinacy in the children of these evil people similar to that of their parents. In a hidden way, however, it signifies that their children, at the coming of the Lord, did follow in their ancient denial of God.

---

[75]Eph 4:13. [76]Jn 14:2. [77]Ps 135:2. [78]Pelagianism, derived from Origenism. [79]The LXX had "into Carmel," but Jerome, agreeing with Aq, Sym and Th, renders MT precisely, "into the land of Carmel." In addition to being the name of a place, the word *Carmel* (*hcrml*, lit., "the Carmel") in Hebrew can also refer to an orchard or fruit garden (KB 499), and so the "abundance" to which Jerome refers. The meaning "recognition of circumcision" is based on a creative etymology (from *nkr* [Hiphil], "to recognize," and *mûl*, "to circumcise") that was already traditional in Greek sources by Jerome's time; see OS 171.30; 193.26; 203.5. [80]Ps 51:4; Rom. 3:4. Jerome follows the wording of Romans.

2:10-11: *"For cross to the islands of Chettim and see, or send to Kedar and examine with care; see if there has been such a thing. Has a nation changed gods"—or "their gods"—"even though they are no gods? But my people have changed their glory for an idol"—or "for that which does not profit."*

He makes a comparison about something incomparable and draws a parallel between the true God and false ones. "Go," he says, "to the islands of Cyprus," which are either the islands of Italy or the islands of the western regions, since there is near to the land of Judah an island Cyprus, on which there is a city called Chettim.[81] This is where Zeno, the founder of the Stoics, came from. Kedar, by contrast, is the wilderness region of the Ishmaelites, whom they now call the Saracens.[82] An oracle is delivered against Kedar near the end of this very prophet,[83] and David mentions it when he says, "I have lived among the inhabitants of Kedar; my soul has wandered much."[84]

The sense of the passage is this: "Go out to the west or send to the wilderness, and see if any nation has done what you have done. None of these nations have rejected their own gods, nor have they traded in their gods of wood and stone for gods of gold; rather, they followed an ancient error and held to what their elders had accepted. And they did this, even though their gods are not gods, but only the images of men made by hand. But my people have exchanged the truth for a lie and have preferred an idol to me, although the idol will not be of any profit to them in their time of need." We may also direct this passage against those who, with greater zeal, follow vice rather than virtue. The apostle warns these people, saying, "I am speaking in human terms, because of your

natural limitations. For just as you once yielded your members to impurity and to greater and greater iniquity, so now yield your members to righteousness for sanctification."[85]

2:12-13: *"Be appalled, O heavens, at this; be utterly desolate, O its gates,[86] says the Lord, for my people have committed two evils: they have forsaken me, the fountain of living waters, and hewed out cisterns for themselves, broken cisterns, that can hold no water."* LXX: *"Heaven was appalled at this and shuddered exceedingly beyond measure, says the Lord,"* and the rest as above.

Heaven, to whom it was said, "Hear, O heaven, and I will speak,"[87] and "Hear, O heaven, and give ear, O earth,"[88] seeing the commands of God trampled on, shuddered and could not hide its astonishment. For all creation groans and grieves over the sins of human beings.[89] Moreover, the people of God have committed two wrongs: first, they forsook God, the fountain of life, who gave to them a command, saying, "I am the Lord your God, who brought you out of the land of Egypt";[90] second, the issue written about in the same passage, "You shall have no other gods before me."[91] But in place of God they followed demons, which are called "broken cisterns," because they are not capable of containing the commandments of God. And one should take note of this: although God is an eternal fountain possessing living water, the land was nevertheless filled with cisterns and reservoirs drawn from torrential streams or some other turbid and rainy waters.

And he mentions the gates of the heavens, which are written about in the twenty-third psalm: "Lift up your heads, O gates! And the king of glory will come in."[92] Instead of this,

---

[81]Heb *ktyym*, identified by Jerome as Cyprus. Cf. Jos. *Ant.* 1.128; Eusebius *Onom.* 174. Jerome adds (in the *Liber Locorum*): "Even today the Cypriots call the city Chettim." [82]Jos. *Ant.* 1.220; Eusebius *Onom.* 118. On the Saracens, cf. Ammianus Marcellinus 14.4.1. [83]Jer 49:28-32. [84]Ps 120:5-6 (LXX [119:5-6]). [85]Rom 6:19. [86]RSV has "be shocked" instead of Jerome's "O its gates." Jerome, like Aq and Sym, derives the word from *ša'ar* ("gate"), whereas the RSV, following MT and the LXX, reads *š'r* ("to shudder"). [87]Deut 32:1. [88]Is 1:2. [89]Rom 8:22. [90]Ex 20:2. [91]Ex 20:3. [92]Ps 24:7 (Ps 23:7 LXX).

the LXX translated "Lift up your gates, O rulers." I have discussed this more fully in its place.[93] And let no one be disturbed that Aquila and Symmachus translated "heavens," whereas the LXX and Theodotion translated "heaven." For the Hebrew word *samaim* is of common number, so that both "heavens" and "heaven" reflect the same word, just like "Thebes," "Athens" and "Salona."[94]

2:14a: *"Is Israel a slave? Is he a homeborn servant?"*

I believe that it is based on this verse that the Jews, carried away with pride, said to the Savior, "We are descendants of Abraham and have never been in bondage to anyone. How is it that you say, 'You will be made free'?"[95] They did not know that everyone who sins is a slave to sin[96] and that each individual person is a slave to whatever has control over him or her. Therefore, even though they were born from Abraham the friend of God,[97] because of their own sin they have been made like the sons of Ham, to whom it was said, "Cursed be Canaan; a slave shall he be to his brothers."[98]

2:14b-15: *"Why then has he become a prey? The lions have roared against him, and he has raised a cry. They have made his land a waste; his cities are in ruins, without inhabitant."*

The divine word asks the question, so that it can itself provide the answer. By lions he means the leaders of Babylon, who have made the land a waste and destroyed its cities with fire. Or else, according to anagogy[99] we may understand the lions as the adversarial powers or the leaders of the heretics, who desolate the land of the church and ravage all its cities

with heretical fire and with that burning about which it is written: "They are all adulterers, like an oven is their heart."[100] For these people have truly raised a cry, and in this very prophet under the *persona* of a partridge they called out and gathered what they had not hatched, getting rich but not by right.[101] Therefore, their cities have been wasted and destroyed, since they did not have God as an inhabitant, as Scripture says: "without inhabitant."

2:16-17: *"Moreover, the men of Memphis and Tahpanhes have defiled you up to the crown of your head. Have you not brought this on yourself by forsaking the Lord your God, when he led you in the way?"*

What we have rendered as "when he led you in the way" is not found in the LXX. He names the two greatest cities of Egypt, Memphis and Tahpanhes, and he says that their men have defiled Israel up to the crown of the head. This should be taken in the same sense as what Isaiah said: "From the sole of the foot even to the head, there is no soundness in it."[102] So great was the libido of the Egyptians, who were exceedingly fleshly, that none could resist its "members."[103] On the contrary, they defiled everyone. And all of this befell Israel precisely because they forsook the Lord their God at that very time when they especially should have been following their leader.

2:18: *"And now what do you gain by going to Egypt, to drink the waters of the Sior? Or what do you gain by going to Assyria, to drink the waters of the river?"*

For *Sior* we gave the translation "turbid," which is what the Hebrew word means, in place of

---

[93]See Jerome *Comm. Ps.* 23 (CC 72:200).　[94]Heb *šāmayim*, which occurs only in the plural (dual) form. Jerome illustrates this grammatical point with three Latin words that occur only in the plural.　[95]Jn 8:33.　[96]Jn 8:34.　[97]Jas 2:23.　[98]Gen 9:25.　[99]Following Origen and other Greek fathers, Jerome uses the Greek term *anagōgē* ("elevation") to refer to the higher or spiritual sense.　[100]Hos 7:4, 6.　[101]Jer 17:11.　[102]Is 1:6.　[103]The Latin *membrum* ("limb") could refer to the genital member.

which the common edition has *Geon*.[104] Since he had earlier talked about the men of Memphis and Tahpanhes who had defiled Israel up to the crown of the head, he now more clearly mentions Egypt itself. And it is obvious that the Nile does have turbid waters, and that the river of the Assyrians is the Euphrates, since Scripture says that the land of the promise is from the river of Egypt to the great river, the Euphrates.[105] And all who forsake Christ, the fountain of life, and dig for themselves cisterns of heresy, which are not able to hold the waters of true teaching, will by necessity be subject to lions that reduce their land to waste and destroy all the churches. These people will be polluted up to the crown of their head, and they will drink from turbid waters. They will also drink from the streams of the Assyrian river and of the north, from where evil things burst forth against the land.

2:19: "Your wickedness will chasten you"—or "Your rebellion will instruct you"[106]—"and your apostasy will reprove you. Know and see that it is evil and bitter for you to forsake the Lord your God; the fear of me is not in you, says the Lord GOD of hosts."

Let us take note: once "wickedness" (or "rebellion") has glutted the rebel so much that, as with the quails, he has reached the point of nausea,[107] then the rebellion can instruct him—if he will repent. He is commanded to look at what he has forsaken and what he has followed, and how he has spurned the good, sweet fruit and chosen the bitter. All of this happened because he forsook the Lord his God and because the fear of the Lord was not in him. For "the fear of the Lord is the beginning of knowledge."[108] It is because he lacks the fear of the Lord that he is handed over to evil and bitterness.

2:20: "For long ago you broke my"—or "your"—"yoke and burst my"—or "your"—"bonds;[109] and you said, 'I will not serve.' For on every high hill and under every green tree you bowed down as a harlot"—or "there you were spread out in fornication."[110]

He speaks to Israel as to a harlot, because Israel broke the marital covenant and said, "I will not serve," that is, "I will not serve the Lord"—or "my husband." Instead, she bowed down to idolatry "on every high hill and under every green tree," since the places dedicated to idols are always pleasant and high up. It is also possible for this passage to be directed at the one who, having started off as a Christian with some learning in sacred literature, prostrates himself to demons through his desire for secular literature, which is signified by the "high places," and through his delight in pleasantness of expression, which is pointed to by the "green tree." Under the pretext of "learning" and the "loftiness of knowledge" these demons pollute the souls of believers and cause them to spread their feet to all who pass by.[111]

---

[104]The OL (the "common edition"), following the LXX, took the Hebrew word *šiḥôr* to be the name of a river in Egypt, identifying it as the Gihon (Gen 2:13; modern scholars suggest *šiḥôr*, the "pond of Horus" [KB 1477]). Jerome had translated it as "turbid" in IH (cf. *šḥr* I, KB 1465), but he puts the Hebrew word itself (*Sior*) here in the lemma of the commentary because he can explain what it means. [105]Gen 15:18. [106]Jerome matches Aq, Sym and Th (Heb *r'h*, "evil, wickedness"). [107]Num 11:19, 31-35. [108]Prov 1:7. [109]The first two verbs could be read either as second person (as if Aramaic) or first person (MT). Jerome's IH edition and the LXX take them as second person, whereas Aq, Th and Targ read first person. Jerome, however, gives the first person as the first option for the pronouns that follow (= IH). This could very well reflect the Hebrew text that he is using. The LXX has second person pronouns (= MT). [110]As usual, the second option reflects the LXX, except that the transmitted LXX reads: "there I will be spread out in my fornication." The spreading of the heels betokens the spreading of the legs, which represents a posture designed to invite "fornication," either literal or metaphorical (i.e., idolatry). [111]Jerome was a lover of secular literature and well-turned phrases, and his comments here are written out of his own struggle with this issue. In *Ep.* 22.30, Jerome reports a dream in which he is rebuked for preferring Cicero to Christ, and he vows never again to read secular literature. Yet, the imprint of secular literature never departed from Jerome's mind, and Jerome seems to have returned to reading secular authors later in life; see the Introduction.

2:21: "Yet I planted you a choice vine, wholly of pure seed. How then have you turned degenerate and become an alien vine?" LXX: **"Yet I planted you as a fruit-bearing vine, wholly pure. How then have you turned into bitterness and become an alien vine?"**

In place of a "choice" or "fruit-bearing" vine, the Hebrew has *sorec*, which is also used in the Song of Isaiah.[112] It is the best kind of vine, and the Lord says that he had planted Israel from a shoot of this vine. But now he marvels at how a choice vine of pure seed could have turned into bitterness, and so become an alien vine. Indeed no one is safe, if what the Lord has planted—a pure seed and a *sorec* vine—is altered so much by its own vice that it withdraws from the Lord through bitterness and is made an alien vine. And the mercy of the Creator can be seen clearly in this: that the one who said in the Gospel "I am the true vine"[113] granted to his disciples and to those who believe in him that they may be a "choice" or "true" vine, if they determine to remain in him who was planted.

2:22: "Though you wash yourself with lye and use much of the borith plant, the stain of your guilt is still before me, says the Lord God."

In place of "*borith* plant,"[114] which we rendered as it is written in the Hebrew, the LXX translated "grass," so as to indicate a cleaning plant that, according to the custom of the Palestinian province, springs up in green and moist places and has the same power for washing filth as natron. Yet our natron or "plant of cleansing" is repentance; and the ecclesiastical word, which chastises and rebukes the wrongdoer, is similar to stinging natron. The one

who has been stained by only a light spot of sin is cleansed by light admonitions, whereas the graver sins that lead to death cannot be washed cleaned by natron or the *borith* plant but require graver torments. For "what sort of work each one has done the fire will test," and "with fire it will be revealed."[115] And beautifully the prophet adds, "the stain of your guilt is still before me," because "even if you appear clean to other people, you are still not clean to me, since I know the conscience of every person." Thus it is said in another passage: "No man living is righteous before you."[116]

2:23a: "How can you say, 'I am not defiled, I have not gone after the Baals'? Look at your way in the valley!"

The word *valley* or *vale*, which in Hebrew is *ge*, was rendered by the LXX as *polyandrion*, which in our language can be translated as "tomb of many."[117] "In vain," he says, "you refuse to acknowledge your evil deeds, and you claim to be clean, even though you are polluted with the filth of idolatry, and shamelessly you deny that you have worshiped the idols of the Baals. Look at the valley of the sons of Hinnom,[118] which is watered by the springs of Siloam, and there you will see the shrine of Baal, whom you have venerated, even as you were forsaking God." And that which is added next, (**2:23b**) **"know what you have done,"** opens the shut eyes of the denier, so that he will see what he is ashamed to look at.

According to tropology,[119] let us reprove the shameless deeds of those who refuse to acknowledge their vices. For people of this sort walk not on the straight and narrow path that leads to life but on the wide and spacious path that leads to death, through which many

---

[112]Is 5:2. The precise meaning of the Hebrew *śrq* is not clear. KB 1362 defines the word as "a valued, bright-red species of grape." Jerome's "choice" agrees with Targ (Jer 2:21) and with Sym (Is 5:2). [113]Jn 15:1. [114]For *bōrît*, KB 159 gives "alkaline salt, extracted from soap-plants." [115]1 Cor 3:13. [116]Ps 143:2. [117]Heb *gay'* ("valley"; Gk *polyandreion* ["common burial-place," LSJ 1436]). [118]Jer 32:35. [119]The Latin word *tropologia* is taken from a Greek rhetorical term that refers to the figurative sense of a word as opposed to its literal or proper sense. In Christian exegesis after Origen it became a technical term for the spiritual sense of the text.

enter.[120] It is for this reason, by signification, that the place is named *polyandrion*, the "tomb of many." Or, alternatively, according to *historia* the name "tomb of many" was given because many people were killed and destroyed by the evil of idolatry.[121]

2:23c-24: *"A restive runner interlacing her tracks, a wild ass used to the wilderness, in her heat sniffing the wind! Who can restrain her lust? None who seek her need weary themselves; in her month they will find her."* LXX: *"In the evening her voice has cried out. She has extended her ways over the waters of the desert. She was carried along by the desires of her soul; she was handed over to them. Who can turn her back? None who seek her need weary themselves; in her humiliation they will find her."*

In this passage, the edition of the Seventy differs significantly from the Hebrew truth. Yet, each has its own sense. Since earlier she said, "I am not defiled,"[122] he now describes her fornication as one might speak to a woman who has acted shamefully. "Just as," he says, "a restive beast"—which we have rendered with the more general term "runner," and which Aquila, Symmachus and Theodotion translated more accurately as "restive dromedary"[123]—"interlaces her tracks and quickly comes to her fodder, and just as a wild ass in the desert lustfully takes in the wind of her breath or the spirit of her lover"—for among the Hebrews both "wind" and "spirit" are signified by the same term, *ruha*[124]—"so also Israel (or Jerusalem) was carried by her unrestrained passion to the desire of her lust, and she burned with a complete love for idols. There was none who could, through their warnings, turn her away

from this passion. This was not due to any lack of ability on the part of the prophets but to the perverse wickedness of her desire."

"None," he says, "who seek her need weary themselves; in her month and in her uncleanness they will find her." In place of "month," Aquila translated *neomēnia*, that is, Kalends.[125] Symmachus translated the word as "month," and the LXX and Theodotion put "humiliation."[126] According to the LXX the sense is this: Jerusalem the harlot, like that woman described in Proverbs,[127] was crying out with her voice in the evening and was enticing her lovers into desire, uncovering the ways of her shamefulness and spreading her feet to all who pass by. Hers was a place of charm with flowing waters, and it was all the more delightful since all around was desert solitude, so that no one could see her committing fornication. The LXX says, "By the desires of her soul *epneumatophoreito*,"[128] all of which could mean "by a perverse spirit she was led," or perhaps "she drew in the refreshment of her love," or else, "she sang her songs of shamefulness." It goes on to say that "she was handed over to them," that is, to her vices and to her desire. No one was able to turn her back. All who wished to come into her would find her in the humiliation of her shamefulness, and there was no way to satisfy her love of pleasure.

2:25: *"Keep your feet from going unshod and your throat from thirst. But you said, 'I am hopeless; I cannot do it! For I have loved strangers, and after them I will go.'"* LXX: *"Turn away your feet from the rough way and your throat from thirst. She said, 'I will act vigorously, since I have delighted in strangers and after them I will go.'"*

---

[120]Mt 7:13-14. [121]Jer 32:35. [122]Jer 2:23a. [123]The term "dromedary," which refers to a kind of camel, is derived from a Greek word that means "running." Jerome agrees with the identification given by the hexaplaric versions, but he gives a more general term, "runner," as the translation in the lemma. [124]Heb *rûaḥ*. Cf. Jer 10:12-16; 10:14; Jerome *Comm. Hos.* 4:17-19. [125]The first day of a new month, sometimes used simply as a term for "month." [126]MT reads *hōdeš* ("month"). [127]Prov 7:6-27. [128]Jerome gives the Greek verb that matches "she was carried along" in the LXX lemma above. The word is unusual, perhaps coined by the LXX, and seems to mean "to be borne as by the wind" (LSJ). Jerome gives several paraphrases of the whole clause in an attempt to capture the overall sense.

At the Passover the people are commanded to have shoes on their feet.[129] And the apostle preaches that those who are equipped with the gospel should have their feet shod,[130] so that, while they are walking through the wilderness of this age, they do not leave themselves vulnerable to venomous creatures that should be trampled on and crushed by the evangelical foot. We keep our throat from thirst when we take up the precepts of the Savior, who said, "If anyone thirst, let him come to me and drink."[131] She, despairing of better things, confesses that she will not do what the Lord has commanded; and she provides her reason, saying, "I have loved strangers and will follow them." She thinks that by this impudent confession she can set aside the charges against her.

Furthermore, according to the Seventy, the "way" of sinning is a rough one, which can be turned into a level "way" by the Lord. And whoever follows heretics, let him be disgraced by the statement of these verses: "I am hopeless," or "I will hold to my intention vigorously," and "I am comfortable in my error." In fact, it is obvious that the one who follows teaching that is strange and alien to ecclesiastical doctrine will love "strangers" and will follow their tracks, whether they are demons or the leaders of heretics, who are strangers to God.

2:26: "As a thief is shamed when caught, so the house of Israel shall be shamed: they, their kings, their princes, their priests and their prophets."

However much the face of a thief may be bold and insolent, he will still be ashamed when he is caught in the act of stealing. Therefore Israel, when it (**2:27a**) *"says to a tree, 'You are my father,' and to a stone, 'You gave me birth'"*—thus calling things that they them-selves have made their parents—will be shamed when it is caught in its idolatry. And lest we think that he is saying this about the people, he says, "their kings, their princes, their priests and their prophets." Let us make use of this testimony whenever our "princes" and those who think of themselves as leaders in the church are caught in foul sins.

2:27b: "For they have turned their back to me, and not their face."

Those who reject the words of God turn their backs against him and not their face. For when a teacher gives a command, it is an indication of obedience to listen while facing the teacher with head bowed. But when a person turns his back, it is a sign of contempt, as it is written in another passage: "And they turned to me a stubborn shoulder."[132] "They despise my precepts so much," says God, "that they do not even wish to hear them. Instead, they show the haughtiness of their spirit through the posture of their body."

2:27c: "But in the time of their trouble they say, 'Arise and save us!' "

Those who did not acknowledge God in good times will acknowledge him in times of suffering.

2:28a: "But where are your gods that you made for yourself? Let them arise, if they can save you, in your time of trouble."

It is a shameless demand that they should seek help in a time of distress and necessity from one whom they despised in times of peace. This should be read with a tone of rebuking: "Let your gods, whom you made for yourselves, save you! Although God is the creator of humanity, people have attempted to make

---

[129]Ex 12:11. [130]Eph 6:15. [131]Jn 7:37. [132]Zech 7:11.

'god,' and so necessity will show you how little can be done by these 'gods' that you formerly worshiped without worry."

2:28b: *"For as many as your cities are your gods, O Judah."*

Each of the individual cities was worshiping false gods, in some cases the same as each other, and in other cases various and diverse. Thus, not even in impiety did they reflect a consensus, but superstition fighting against itself resulted in a diversified error. And what follows, "And according to the number of streets in Jerusalem they sacrificed to Baal," was added by the Seventy.

2:29: *"Why do you complain against me? You have all rebelled against me, says the Lord."*

Human perversity is prone to making excuses for itself. The people wish it to appear as if they are suffering unjustly, when in fact they are suffering what they deserve. Furthermore, they ascribe to God's justice the failure that belongs to them. Thus it says, "In vain do you offer these excuses and complain that the judge is unfair, because it is from your own impiety that you are suffering." And what follows, "And all of you acted unjustly against me," and so on, was added by the Seventy.

2:30a: *"In vain have I smitten your children, they took no correction."*

In place of the last phrase the Seventy put "you took no correction." The sense in the Hebrew is: "They themselves who were smitten refused to take correction"; whereas in the LXX the sense is: "I struck your children in order that you might learn a lesson from their deaths. And lest you should think that I am unwilling

to punish the sinners themselves, learn from the blows that I inflicted on your children that I am eager to treat you with an even harsher medicine."

2:30b: *"Your own sword devoured your prophets."*

"It was not my prophets but your prophets that were devoured; and not by my sword but by your own sword—raised by your own sins." Furthermore, the Seventy do not have "your" but simply translated "The sword devoured your prophets," thus referring either to the enemies' sword or to God's sword, with which the people's sins are pierced through.

2:31a: *"Like a ravaging lion is your generation."*[133] LXX: *"Like a ravaging lion, and you were not afraid."*

He says, "The sword that devoured your prophets"—this no doubt refers to the soothsayers of Baal and other idols—"has ravaged all things like a lion. And still your whole generation, which should have reformed after the slaying of a select few, has persisted in evil." But according to the Seventy this is the sense: "The sword of the Lord"—which means the sword of the enemies—"has torn apart and devoured your false prophets like a lion that voraciously consumes its captured prey. Nevertheless, you could not be converted to better things even by the punishment inflicted on your prophets."

2:31b: *"See the word of the Lord. Have I been a wilderness to Israel, or a land of late blooming? Why then do my people say, 'We have departed, and we will not come back to you'?"* LXX: *"Hear the word of the Lord. Thus says the Lord: Have I been a wilderness to Israel,*

---

[133]Jerome takes the phrase "like a ravaging lion" (from the end of Jer 2:30 in modern Bibles) as the beginning of a new sentence together with the first words of Jer 2:31.

or a land full of thorns?[134] *Why has my people said, 'We will not submit to you and we will not come to you'?"*

Moses saw the voice of God,[135] and the apostle John says that he saw and touched the word of God.[136] He is perplexed at how the people of Israel regarded God as a wilderness, while they followed idols as one follows the great crowd of cities. It is a land of late blooming, since it does not receive the rains of doctrine or the discipline of the gospel; and it is full of thorns, because it has not been cultivated. In addition, the people at that time were especially accursed of God in that they departed from the Lord and did not want to be turned back to their God. It is a great offense not to wish to appease the one whom you have offended.

2:32: *"Can a virgin forget her ornaments, or a bride her breast sashes? Yet my people have forgotten me days without number."*

Through these things we learn that Christ is the bridegroom of the virgin church, which has neither spot nor wrinkle.[137] Moreover, if he is the bridegroom, then those words that were spoken by John the Baptist are about him: "He who has the bride is the bridegroom."[138] Therefore, she who departs from the Lord ruins her "ornaments," and she loses her understanding of doctrine, which is signified by the "breast." Thus also John the Evangelist reclined close to the breast of Jesus,[139] and the breastpiece of the sacrifice—among other things—was separated out by the priests.[140] The more times we forget God, the greater the punishment will be for our sin, since we were not able to master the sin for so long a period of time.

2:33-34: *"Why do you endeavor to present your way as good, in order to seek love? And what is more, you have taught others your evils and your ways. Also on your wings"—or "hands"[141]—"is found the life blood of the guiltless poor; I did not find them breaking in, but in all these things"—or "under every oak tree."[142]*

"In vain," he says, "you desire to defend yourself by skill of words and to present your deeds as good, so as to appear worthy of love. And what is more, you have even taught others your ways and have become an example to all of evil deeds. And indeed on your wings"—or "hands"—"is found the blood of the innocent, whom you have sacrificed to idols, or whose lives you have destroyed just as if you had sacrificed them." We have added from the Hebrew the word *poor*, which is not found in the LXX.[143] "And moreover," he says, "I have not found that these poor, innocent people were killed while breaking in"—it was common for a thief to be killed during his crime[144]—"but rather they were killed in all these circumstances that I have mentioned above"—or "under every oak tree." In Hebrew the word in question is *ella*,[145] which can signify "these things," so that the sense is "in all of these things that I mentioned," or else it can signify "oak tree," so that the sense is: "under the oak and terebinth trees under whose shade and foliage you enjoyed the evils of idolatry."

2:35-36a: *"You say, 'I am without sin and innocent; surely your anger has turned from me.' Behold, I will bring you to judgment for saying, 'I have not sinned.' How lightly you gad about"—or "because you have had so much*

---

[134]Jerome's copy of the LXX read "full of thorns," but the preserved copies of the LXX have "dry, barren." Jerome's translation "late blooming" agrees with Aq. [135]Ex 20:18 (in Hebrew); cf. Ex 33:17-23. [136]1 Jn 1:1. [137]Eph 5:27. [138]Jn 3:29. [139]Jn 13:23. [140]Ex 29:26-27; Lev 7:30-34; Num 6:20; 18:18. [141]Jerome matches Aq and Sym. [142]Jerome reads these words with Jer 2:34; the RSV connects them to Jer 2:35. [143]This word was supplied in the Hexapla. [144]Ex 22:2-3. [145]The two words are spelled with the same consonants in Hebrew but are vocalized slightly differently: *'ēlleh* means "these (things)" (= MT), and *'ēlāh* means "oak tree" (= LXX).

contempt"—"repeating your ways a second time!"

These words should be used against those who are unwilling to acknowledge their sins but instead claim in times of affliction and anguish that they are suffering unjustly. And in doing this, they provoke God's anger even more, since it is a second and greater sin for them to refuse to mourn for what they have done, and instead to make vain excuses for their sins. "I will bring you to judgment," he says, "for saying, 'I have not sinned,'" as if somehow it is even worse than their previous sin to have one thing in their conscience and saying something else with their words. Let the new heresy be instructed by the old: the anger of God is even greater when the offender is unwilling to confess his sin humbly but instead claims that he is righteous.

2:36b-37: *"You shall be put to shame by Egypt as you were put to shame by Assyria. From it too you will come away with your hands on your head, for the Lord has demolished your confidence"*—or *"hope"*—*"and you will not prosper by it."*

In order to deflect the onslaught of the Egyptians, they fled to the Assyrians, whose assistance was of no use; for we read that the Assyrians were defeated by the Egyptians.[146] On the other hand, so that they might escape the anger of Assyria, they relied on the help of the Egyptians, whom the *historia* narrates were overcome by the Assyrians.[147] Therefore they are rebuked, because they lost their faith in God and relied on human aid, which is always so broken and toppled that nothing useful can be found in it. Thus it says, "From it too you will come away," that is, "from Egypt you will

come away," in the same manner that you went away from the Assyrians, with your hands on your head, and you will mourn the fact that you expected aid to come from the Egyptians. Let us remember the *historia*, when Tamar was ravished and violated by Amnon, her exceedingly wicked brother. She put her hands on her head, which she had sprinkled with ashes, and in this way she returned to her house.[148]

3:1a: *"It is commonly stated:"*—for which the LXX simply translated *"it is said"*[149] *"If a man divorces his wife and she goes from him and becomes another man's wife, will he return to her? Would not that woman"*—or *"that land"*[150]—*"be greatly polluted? You have played the harlot with many lovers"*—or *"shepherds"*!

The Hebrew word *rehim*, which is written with four letters, *res, ain, ioth* and *mem*, can signify both "lovers" and "shepherds." If we read it as *rehim*, it means "lovers," but if we read it as *rohim*, it means "shepherds."[151]

3:1b: *" 'Nevertheless, return to me!' says the Lord—or 'and you returned to me!' says the Lord."*

In the Hebrew, even after her fornication God is willing to receive the penitent and admonishes her to return to him; but in the Seventy, he does not summon her to repentance but condemns the harlot's impudence, because she dared after her adultery to return to her husband. And with the statement, "Would not that woman be greatly polluted?" where in the Hebrew we read "land" instead of "woman," he is leaving behind the analogy and speaking more plainly about the land of Israel, which is being compared with an adulterous woman.

---

[146]2 Chron 28:21; 2 Chron 12:1-12. Cf. Josephus *Ant.* 10.14-23. [147]2 Kings 17:1-6; 18:21. [148]2 Sam 13:14, 19. [149]MT has *lě'mōr*, which is usually translated "saying." Its meaning here is not clear. "It is commonly stated" is Jerome's attempt to capture the sense. Jerome also reports the simpler translation found in his copy of the LXX (our evidence for the LXX lacks the word). [150]The first option is Jerome's IH version and matches the LXX as preserved. The second option represents Jerome's copy of the LXX (= MT; reflected in Syro-Hexapla). [151]See Jer 6:2-4a.

Let us make use of this testimony against those who, abandoning the faith of the Lord and becoming entangled in the errors of heretics, after many fornications and deceiving many souls pretend that they are returning to the pristine truth, not so that they may remove the poison from their breast but so that they may introduce it to others.

3:2a: *"Lift up your eyes to the bare heights, and see! Where have you not been lain with? By the waysides you have sat awaiting lovers like a brigand in the wilderness"—or "like a crow in the wilderness."*[152]

In place of "brigand" and "crow" in the Hebrew is written *arabe*, which can signify Arabs, a race given to brigandage even to this day. They make incursions into the borders of Palestine and lie in wait on the roads for those going down from Jerusalem to Jericho, a fact which the Lord also calls to mind in the Gospel.[153] "So lift up your eyes, O Jerusalem! Look all around, and see! Where have you not been lain with in fornication? For just as brigands customarily lie in wait to ambush travelers in deserted places in the evening, so also you, like the adulterous woman in Proverbs,[154] sit waiting on the road in the evening in order to destroy the souls of adulterers when they have intercourse with you. In this way the whole land is polluted with your adultery." And more significantly, according to anagogy[155] it admonishes those who promise to forsake their heretical errors that they must lift up their eyes to the bare heights. For unless they are able to see straight, they will not be able to condemn their former wickedness.

3:2b-3a: *"You have polluted"—or "destroyed"*[156]*—"the land with your vile harlotry. Therefore the showers have been withheld, and the spring rain has not come"—or "you have had many shepherds in your stumbling."*

The land has been "destroyed" or "polluted" through the destruction brought about by those who perished because of the "harlotry" of idol worship. As a result, the blessing that was on all things has been removed, leaving them to suffer a drought of the word of God.[157] Or else, they had shepherds who caused them to stumble against God: those who ought to have been teachers, keeping others from error, emerged rather as authors of impiety.

3:3b: *"Yet you have a harlot's brow; you refuse to be ashamed."* LXX: *"Yet you have a harlot's face; you have acted shamefully toward all."*

Since above she said, "I have not sinned"[158]— and she sinned all the more by denying her evil deeds—he now charges her, as an insolent woman of extreme impudence, that she is not merely exhibiting her insolent expression before one or two individuals but is in fact being shameless before everyone. We should make use of this word against the public assembly of heretics, who glory in their own errors.

3:4-5a: *"So then, from now on call me, 'My Father—you are the guide of my virginity.' Will you be angry forever, will you be indignant to the end?"*

Let the heretics be ashamed, they who are

---

[152]Heb *'rby*, which, depending on the vocalization, could be taken as related to "Arab" (Jerome and Targ) or could be a form of the word *crow* (*'ōrēb*, LXX). Sym translated the word as "inn, lodging" (perhaps *'ărābāh* III, KB 880), and Aq transliterated it.   [153]Jerome is thinking of the parable of the Good Samaritan (Lk 10:30), although the Gospel text says nothing about Arabs. For the perceived connection between Arabs and brigandage, see Diodorus Siculus 2.48; *b. Sukkah* 52b.   [154]Prov 7:9-12.   [155]Following Origen and other Greek fathers, Jerome uses the Greek term *anagōgē* ("elevation") to refer to the higher or spiritual sense.   [156]The preserved LXX matches Jerome; the alternative rendering ("destroyed") could have been in Jerome's copy of the LXX.   [157]Amos 8:11.   [158]Jer 2:35.

unwilling to be converted to better things or to return to the Father, their Creator; and let them hear: "From now on call to me, 'My Father—you are the guide of my virginity.'" He himself has pledged your soul in marriage with his embraces, and he teaches the soul how it should pray and repent. As great as the mercy of the one who shows the way of wholeness after there has been fornication, so great is the wretchedness of the harlot who does not wish to receive healing after she has been wounded.

3:5b: "Behold, you have spoken, and you have done evil, and you have been capable."

Instead of offering words of repentance, you have blasphemed with words of pride. You have fulfilled your evil intentions and have shown your fortitude against men, that you are capable of doing all that you have talked about with words.

3:6-10: The Lord said to me in the days of King Josiah: "Have you seen what she did, that faithless one, Israel, how she went up on every high hill and under every green tree, and there played the harlot? And even though she had done all this, I said, 'Return to me!' but she did not return, and her false sister Judah saw it. She saw that for all the adulteries of that faithless one, Israel, I had sent her away with a decree of divorce; yet her false sister Judah did not fear, but she too went and played the harlot. Because harlotry was so light to her, she polluted the land, committing adultery with stone and tree. Yet for all this her false sister Judah did not return to me with her whole heart, but in pretense, says the Lord."

The torments of some are the remedies of others; when a murderer is punished he receives the just return for what he has done, but others are deterred from evil. But when the ten tribes that are called Israel were captured by the Assyrians and taken to Media, the two tribes, Judah and Benjamin, who should have feared similar punishments for themselves and turned with their whole mind to God, instead surpassed the evils of the ten tribes and followed after idols to such an extent that they set up in the temple a statue of the god Baal, which in Ezekiel is called an image set up to provoke the zeal and jealousy of the Lord.[159] It speaks here under the metaphor of two sisters, since they were born from the one stock of Abraham, Isaac and Jacob; it calls the first one "faithless," and the second it calls "false." For the first was thoroughly faithless to God, immediately setting up golden calves to be worshiped at Dan and Bethel,[160] whereas the second, who possessed the temple and the religion of the true God, departed from the Lord little by little in imitation of her sister, and so is called "false."

According to anagogy,[161] it is a prophecy about heretics: deceived by heretical subtlety, they think that they are pursuing the knowledge of the Name, but in fact they are going up on the hill of pride and displaying their fornication under every green and pleasing tree, having been seduced by the pleasures of the flesh. Yet, although these heretics are delivered to Satan for the destruction of the flesh,[162] it often happens that the members of house of "Judah" (that is, of "confession"[163] and of the true faith) are not deterred by their example, but they commit sins much greater than the heretics. In this way, they pollute the land of the church because harlotry is a trivial thing to them, and they commit adultery with stone and tree, that is, following those teachings that are contrary to God. But if an ecclesiastical person wishes to correct the one

---

[159]Ezek 8:3. [160]1 Kings 12:28-29. [161]Following Origen and other Greek fathers, Jerome uses the Greek term *anagōgē* ("elevation") to refer to the higher or spiritual sense. [162]1 Cor 5:5. [163]Cf. Jer 1:18-19.

who is erring, cut off the putrid flesh and restore to repentance those who have followed falsehood—and still the heretics follow their ancient error under the pretense of ecclesiastical truth—then it can be said concerning them: "Yet for all this her false sister Judah did not return to me with her whole heart, but in pretense."

But this prophecy was given during the times of the just king Josiah, under whom Jeremiah began to prophesy.[164]

3:11: And the Lord said to me, "Faithless Israel has shown herself just in comparison with false Judah."

"Israel," he says, "is more just—when compared with Judah—because Israel perished first and without warning, whereas Judah could have corrected itself by seeing Israel's sufferings." Let the new heresy give heed to the old, because Israel is said to be "just" in comparison with one who is worse. This comparison is hardly surprising concerning sisters from the same nation, since even Sodom is called "just" in comparison with Jerusalem, as the Lord says through Ezekiel: "Sodom is more just than you."[165] Likewise, the tax collector was justified in comparison with the Pharisee.[166]

3:12-13: "Go, and proclaim"—or "read"—"these words toward the north, and say, 'Return, faithless Israel, says the Lord. I will not turn aside my face from you,'—or 'I will not set my face against you'[167]—'for I am holy,'—or 'merciful'[168]—'says the Lord. I will not be angry forever. Only acknowledge your guilt, that you rebelled'—or 'behaved impiously'—'against the Lord your God and scattered'—or 'poured out'—your favors among

strangers under every green tree, and that you have not obeyed my voice, says the Lord.'"

The Hebrew word *carath* may be understood as "to call," "to proclaim" or "to read"; this is why Aquila and Symmachus translated it "proclaim," while the LXX and Theodotion put "read."[169] The message is directed toward the north against Babylon and the Assyrians. It addresses both the ten and the two tribes[170] and announces their return. "I will not," he says, "turn aside my face from you," or else, "I will not set my face against you," so that "I will not receive you with the severity of a judge but with a look of compassion." "For I am holy and compassionate, so I will no longer remember your iniquities or call to mind the fact that you departed from the Lord, took delight in idols instead of the Lord and committed adultery under every shady and green tree."

This is something that is suitable to say to heretics or to those in the church who are negligent, who are daily being provoked to repentance by ecclesiastical people and to whom one can apply the words "you have not obeyed my voice." Every heretic lives in the "north" and has lost the warmth of faith. He cannot hear what the apostle says, "be aglow with the Spirit,"[171] and because he has given himself over to pleasures, he departs from the Lord and scatters his favors among strange doctrines, pursuing gratification. For no heresy is founded except on the palate and the belly, so as to seduce "weak women who are burdened with sins."[172] These heretics "will listen to anybody and can never arrive at a knowledge of the truth."[173] Concerning them it is rightly said, "they who eat up my people as they eat bread,"[174] or as Christ said about them, they "devour widows' houses."[175] "And

[164]Jer 1:2; 3:6. [165]Ezek 16:46-52. [166]Lk 18:9-14. [167]Jerome does not match Aq, Sym or Targ; "hurl (Heb *npl*, Hiphil) my face against (*b*) you." [168]Jerome agrees with Aq and Sym; Heb *hsyd*, "faithful, godly" (KB 337). [169]Cf. Jer 2:1-2a; 19:1-3a. [170]The ten northern tribes (Israel) and the two southern tribes, Judah and Benjamin (Judah). [171]Rom 12:11. [172]2 Tim 3:6. [173]2 Tim 3:7. [174]Ps 14:4.

when I have compassion on you," he says, "you should not think that you are just, but rather you should always remember your guilt, acknowledge that you have committed fornication against the Lord and bow down your proud neck." In this way, the one who offended God through arrogance may appease him through humility. By contrast, that which we said above, "I will not set my face against you," matches this prophetic statement: "Hide your face from my sins, and blot out all my iniquities."[176]

3:14-16: *"Return, O faithless"—or "wandering and leaving"—"children, says the Lord, for I am your husband"—or "I will rule over you"—"and I will take you, one from a city and two from a family, and I will bring you to Zion. And I will give you shepherds after my own heart, who will feed you with knowledge and understanding. And when you have multiplied and increased in the land, in those days, says the Lord, they shall no more say, 'The ark of the pact'—or 'testament'[177]—'of the Lord.' It shall not come to mind or be remembered or missed; it shall not be made again."*

The Jews think that this was fulfilled after the return from Babylon under Cyrus the king of Persia, and under Zerubbabel the son of Shealtiel, even though not all of the people returned at that time. They think that the return from Babylon is indicated by the phrase "I will take you, one from a city and two from a family." But it is better to understand this passage as being fulfilled in the coming of Christ, when the remnant was saved, as the apostle explains: "If the Lord of hosts had not left us children, we would have fared like Sodom and been made like Gomorrah."[178]

Then, they are brought to Zion, about which it is written, "Glorious things are spoken of you, O city of God."[179] And they are given shepherds after God's own heart, namely, apostles and apostolic men, who fed the multitude of the faithful not with Jewish ceremonies but with the knowledge and understanding of Christ, and through the preaching of the gospel they have children[180] throughout the whole world. They will not trust in the ark of the Lord, which was the container of the law of Moses; instead, they themselves will be the temple of God.[181] And they will not, according the errors of the Nazareans,[182] enslave themselves to sacrifices that have been abolished but will practice spiritual worship. But others think that this passage will be fulfilled at the end of time, when all Israel will be saved by means of the full number of the Gentiles coming in.[183]

3:17: *"At that time Jerusalem will be called the throne of the Lord, and all nations shall gather to it, to the presence of the Lord in Jerusalem, and they shall no more stubbornly follow their own evil heart."*

The Lord, to whom the people previously said, "You who are enthroned above the cherubim, shine forth,"[184] will surely not at that time sit above the ark of the testament and the cherubim; rather, all who believe with a perfect mind will be the throne of God. Or even better, one should understand this as the whole church, when all the nations are gathered to the presence of the Lord in Jerusalem (where there is a "vision of peace"[185]) and shall no more stubbornly follow their own evil heart. Thus, they will fulfill what was lacking and stop following their own errors, and they

---

[175]Mk 12:40; Lk 20:47; Mt 23:14. [176]Ps 51:9. [177]Cf. Jer 31:31-34. [178]Rom 9:27-29; cf. Is 1:9; 10:22. [179]Ps 87:3. [180]Rom 9:29. [181]1 Cor 3:16; 2 Cor 6:16; Eph 2:21. [182]The Nazareans were a group of Jewish Christians living in the city of Beroea in Syria, whom Jerome met during his stay in the Syrian desert. According to Jerome, the Nazareans preserved the original Hebrew version of the Gospel of Matthew (*Vir. Ill.* 3). [183]Rom 11:25-26. [184]Ps 80:1. [185]This is the traditional etymological interpretation of Jerusalem; see Philo *Somn.* 2.250; OS 169.66, 174.91, 203.99; Origen *Hom. Jer.* 9.2. Cf. Ezek 13:16.

will say with the prophet, "My soul clings to you; your right hand upholds me."[186]

3:18: *"In those days the house of Judah will join the house of Israel, and together they shall come from the land of the north to the land that I gave your fathers for a heritage."*

Strictly speaking this was fulfilled in the coming of Christ, when some from all the twelve tribes believed in the gospel,[187] forsaking the land of the harsh, cold north—that is, leaving the power of the devil—and receiving the land of the promise, which had been pledged to their fathers, to Abraham, Isaac and Jacob. I published a short book recently on the land of the promise.[188]

3:19: *" 'I thought how I would set you in my sons, and give you a pleasant land, a heritage most beautiful of a host of nations. And I thought you would call me, my Father, and would not turn from following me.' "*

In place of "a heritage most beautiful of a host of nations," which the LXX translated "a chosen heritage of God Almighty of the nations," Theodotion gave a more meaningful translation, "an illustrious heritage of fortitude that is strongest of the nations," signifying Christ, who is the commander and Lord of all nations that believe in his name and his suffering. Christ said to Israel, "You would call me 'my Father,' " and "He who believes in me, believes in the Father."[189] And Christ promised, "I will set you in my sons," that is, "among the number of my sons," namely, "among the people of the nations who have believed in me and to whom I have given a pleasant land." For

"to all who received him, he gave power to become children of God."[190]

3:20: *" 'Surely, as a faithless wife despises her lover, so have you despised me, O house of Israel, says the Lord.' "*

This is the voice of Christ to the people of the Jews, to whom he had said, "I would set you in my sons and give you a pleasant land, and you would call me, 'my Father,' and not turn from following me."[191] He says, "Just as a faithless wife despises her lover" (and not her husband), if she has had intercourse with her lover and she perceives that he will be subject to her sexual desire (so that in him the law of nature has been inverted, according to which law she had previously been subjected to the man; as the Lord says, "Her desire will be for you"),[192] so also the house of Israel, that is, the people of the Jews, have despised the Lord their Savior to their own ruin.

3:21-22a: *"A voice on the highways"*—or *"lips"*[193]—*"is heard, the weeping and pleading of Israel's sons because they have perverted their way, they have forgotten the Lord their God. 'Come back, O returning sons, and I will heal your faithlessness'—or 'grief'—in place of which Symmachus translated 'backsliding.' "*[194]

God gladly receives penitents. He hastens to meet the son who was overcome by poverty and filth, and he immediately clothes him with his former garments and restores honor to him who returns, provided that he returns with weeping and pleading,[195] since he had perverted his way with vice and forgotten the Lord his God and

---

[186]Ps 63:8. [187]Jas 1:1. [188]Cf. Jerome *Ep.* 129. [189]Jn 12:44; 14:8-14. [190]Jn 1:12. [191]Jer 3:19. [192]Jerome is attempting to cite the pronouncement made by the Lord to the woman in Gen 3:16, "your desire shall be for your husband," but he is quoting it as if it were spoken to the man about the woman. His precise wording, which reflects the LXX (*apostrophē = conversio,* perhaps "turning to," and so "desire"), may be influenced by Song 7:10. [193]Jerome's translation presumes *šĕpî* ("bare heights"), whereas the LXX derives the word from *śāpāh* ("lip"). Aq has "level (places)," and Sym has "even (places)." Jerome is perhaps closer to Targ (*ngdyn*, "paths, passes" [Jastrow 872]). [194]Heb *mšwbh* ("falling away, apostasy," KB 643). [195]Lk 15:20, 22-23.

Father. It is to such a person that the prophetic word now speaks: "Come back, O returning sons!—and I call you 'sons' precisely because you have acknowledged your sins and are returning to your parent." "And when," he says, "you have returned to the Lord, he will heal all your 'grief' or 'faithlessness,'" by which you departed from God; or else, he will heal your "backsliding." For, although we return to the Lord by our own will, we could not be saved unless he drew us and by his aid strengthened our desire.[196] Let us understand this passage with reference to the people of the Jews who are returning to the Lord, and with reference to heretics who have forsaken the Lord.

3:22b-23: *"Behold, we come to you; for you are the Lord our God. Truly the hills are a delusion, and the multitude"—or "strength"[197]—"of the mountains. Truly in the Lord our God is the salvation of Israel."*

Let him say this who is penitent and who is leaving behind all haughtiness and the "multitude" or "height" of the mountains and hills through which he was exalting himself against God. And, prostrating himself, let him say in humility, "Truly in the Lord our God is the salvation of Israel."

3:24: *"But from our youth confusion has devoured all for which our fathers labored, their flocks and their herds, their sons and their daughters."*

All the efforts of the heretics (about whom it is written, "those who search into obscurity have failed"[198]) have been crushed by confusion from the youth of those whom they deceived, namely, their sons and daughters, who either progressed in their heresy or were simply capti-vated by luxury. For this reason they say:

3:25: *"Let us lie down in our shame, and let our dishonor cover us; for we have sinned against the Lord our God, we and our fathers, from our youth even to this day; and we have not obeyed the voice of the Lord our God."*

Let this be said by Israel when it has not obeyed its Lord; that is, let it be said by every heretic when he repents. Yet, it is also a part of salvation to confess and acknowledge one's sins.[199] It says, "Recite your iniquities first, so that you may be justified."[200] For truly Israel rejected Christ its Lord and God, and they sinned against him not only when he appeared in the flesh but also after his coming, so that they say, "We and our fathers, from our youth even to this day, have not obeyed the voice of our God, who said to our fathers, 'If you believed Moses, you would believe me, for he wrote of me.'"[201]

4:1a: *"If you return to me, O Israel, says the Lord, you will be converted."*

Instead of this, the Seventy translated: "If Israel returns to me, says the Lord, he shall return." The sense is this: "If Israel will return to me, then he will return from captivity," or else, "Since Israel has offered to me what he has, he shall be restored," since "to him who has will more be given, but for him who has not, even what he has will be taken away."[202] Furthermore, according to the Hebrew, this is the sense: "If you return to me, O Israel, and at the same time you long for salvation and acknowledge that you have sinned and not obeyed my voice, then you will be fully con-verted. Believe in the one whom you denied, and your conversion will be complete."

---

[196]Jn 6:44.   [197]Jerome matches Aq and Sym; Heb *hmwn* ("turmoil," "multitude," "army," "wealth," KB 250).   [198]Ps 64:6 (LXX [63:7]).
[199]Not only must one lie down in shame, as this verse describes, but also one must actively confess sin.   [200]Is 43:26 (LXX).   [201]Jn 5:46.
[202]Mt 13:12; 25:29; Mk 4:25; Lk 8:18; 19:26.

4:1b: *"If you remove your abominations from my presence and do not waver."*

When we waver and say, "as for me, my feet had almost wavered,"[203] we do not suffer this because of the helplessness of our nature but because we have set up our abominations and idols against the Lord.

4:2: *"And if you swear: 'the Lord lives in truth, in justice and in uprightness,' then nations shall bless him, and him shall they praise."*

How is it that the Gospel prohibits us from swearing?[204] Here, the word *swear* is used as part of a confession and for the purpose of condemning the idols by which Israel had been swearing; now the abominations are being removed and Israel is swearing by the Lord. As for the phrase "the Lord lives," it is an oath taken in the Old Testament for the purpose of condemning things that are dead, by which all idol worshipers swear. In addition, it should be carefully noted that this oath holds these three as companions: truth, justice and uprightness. If these things are lacking, there will be not an oath, but perjury. He says, "And when Israel has done this and there is an apostolic teacher of the Gentiles,[205] then all the nations shall 'bless him' or 'be blessed in him,' and 'him shall they praise,' because salvation has come out of Israel."

4:3-4: *"For thus says the Lord to the men of Judah and Jerusalem: 'Break up your fallow ground, and sow not among thorns. Circumcise yourselves to the Lord, remove the foreskin of your hearts, O men of Judah and inhabitants of Jerusalem, lest my wrath go forth like fire and burn with none to quench it, because*

of the evil of your thoughts"—or *"deeds."*

In place of what we translated as "Circumcise yourselves to the Lord, remove the foreskin of your hearts," Symmachus put "Purify yourselves to the Lord, remove the evil of your hearts," understanding "circumcision" as "cleansing" and "foreskins" as "vice." This admonition is given to the men of Judah and Jerusalem—who adhere to the true faith and inhabit the church—that they should not sow among the thorns, which (as the evangelical word indicates) choke the sowing of God,[206] but rather they should work the fallow ground, digging up the thorn bushes and removing the brambles, so that the pure soil may take in the pure seed. Or, as it says in another passage: "Do not throw your pearls before swine, and do not give dogs what is holy."[207] For how is it possible for one whose spirit is filled with the cares of the world to hear the word of God, to take in the seed and to produce fruit?[208] As for what follows, "Circumcise yourselves to the Lord, remove the foreskin of your hearts," this is said to none other than the men of Judah and the inhabitants of Jerusalem, so that they will forsake the letter that kills and follow the Spirit that gives life.[209] "For if you will not do this," he says, "then my wrath will go forth like fire, and it will burn with none to quench it." This is the reason why he warns us and announces his judgment ahead of time: so that he might not be compelled to do to us what we wanted to have happen to the Ninevites, to whom the message was preached that they could turn away the coming wrath of God by repentance.[210] Yet, all these punishments will happen to us on account of our evil "thoughts" or "deeds." Where are those who say that they have not sinned in

[203]Ps 73:2.   [204]Mt 5:33-37.   [205]1 Tim 2:7.   [206]Mt 13:7; Mk 4:7.   [207]Mt 7:6.   [208]Mt 7:22; Mk 4:18-19.   [209]2 Cor 3:6.   [210]According to Jerome (*Comm. Jon.* 3:4b), Jonah's proclamation, "Yet forty days, and Nineveh shall be overthrown," constituted a demand for repentance.

their thoughts, seeing that all vices, according to Gospel truth, come out of the heart?[211]

4:5: *"Declare in Judah, and proclaim in Jerusalem, and say, 'Blow the trumpet through the land'; cry aloud and say, 'Assemble, and let us go into the fortified cities.'"*

Let this be heard by Judah and Jerusalem, in which there is "confession of faith" and where the "peace" of Christ dwells,[212] to whom it was said through Isaiah: "Get you up to a high mountain, O Zion, herald of good tidings; lift up your voice, O Jerusalem, herald of good tidings!"[213] He cries aloud, and thus he commands, "Let us go into the fortified cities!" The wars of the heretics rise up;[214] let the fortifications of Christ hold us fast. (**4:6**) Raise the standard of the cross atop the "tower"[215] and on the loftiness of the church. "Flee for safety," you who fear, "stay not," but hasten to the aid of Christ. "For I bring evil," he says, "from the north, and great destruction." "Indeed, I bring Nebuchadnezzar, who is permitted by me to exist in this world so that your bravery and victory may be confirmed."

4:7: *"A lion has gone up from his thicket, a destroyer of nations has set out; he has gone forth from his place to make your land a waste; your cities will be ruins without inhabitant."*

This is, as we say, the true Nebuchadnezzar, about whom Peter also speaks: "Your adversary the devil prowls around like a roaring lion."[216] He has gone up, if you will, from the abyss in which he is to be bound[217] and has petitioned not to be sent back, and so he has set out as a destroyer or devastator of nations. It is written about him, "He will rule over all his enemies,"[218] and he boasts in the presence of the

Lord: "I have been going to and fro on the earth, and walking up and down on it."[219] For who is there that is untouched by the devil's poisons except the one who alone is able to say, "The ruler of this world is coming. He has no power over me"?[220]

This "ruler of the world" is constantly making all the land of the church a waste, so that some who have come out from the church make war against the church; about them John the Evangelist says, "They went out from us, but they were not of us; for if they had been of us, they would have continued with us."[221] The cities of the land of Judea are ruined, but the assemblies of the heretics flourish. And if anyone is a patron of the authors of perverse doctrines, then it can be said of this person, "A lion has gone up from his thicket, a destroyer of nations has set out," and so forth.

4:8: *"For this gird yourselves with sackcloth, lament and wail; for the fierce anger of the Lord has not turned back from us"*—or, as the LXX translated, ***"from you."***

There is no other way that we can avoid the lion, the savage beast, except by repenting and converting to the Lord, not only in mind but also in deed. For as long as the lion is ravaging the church and the land of Judah and devastating Jerusalem, the anger of God is evident.

4:9: *"In that day, says the Lord, the heart of the king and the heart of the officials shall fail; the priests shall be benumbed and the prophets astounded."*

When the plunderer is ravaging the church of the Lord and the anger of the Lord against us persists, all aid is useless. "The heart of the king shall fail," although the king's heart

---

[211]Mt 15:19. [212]On Judah, see Jer 1:18-19; 3:6-10; on Jerusalem, see Jer 3:17. [213]Is 40:9. [214]Ps 2:2. [215]"Zion" is understood to mean "tower." Cf. Jer 6:2-4a. [216]1 Pet 5:8. [217]Rev 11:7; 17:8; 20:1-3. [218]Ps 10:5 (LXX [9:26]). [219]Job 2:2. [220]Jn 14:30. [221]Jn 2:19.

should be in the hand of God.[222] And "the heart of the officials shall fail," although they are thought to be wise; for God has made foolish the wisdom of the world, since through this wisdom they did not know God.[223] The priests also, who ought to teach the law of the Lord and defend the people under them from the fury of the lion, are struck with a certain numbness and "shall go insane"—for thus the Seventy translated, interpreting "numbness" as a loss of mind. And "the prophets shall be astounded"—or, as Aquila translated the Hebrew word *iethmau*,[224] "shall be demented." For who would not go crazy, who would not lose heart, once he has seen that his own officials, kings, priests and prophets are under the power of the lion?

4:10: *Then I said, "Ah, Lord God,"*—in place of which the LXX translated ***"O Lord God"*** — ***"surely you have utterly deceived this people and Jerusalem, saying, 'It shall be well with you'; whereas the sword has reached their very soul."***

Since above he said, "At that time Jerusalem will be called the throne of the Lord, and all nations shall gather to it, to the presence of the Lord in Jerusalem,"[225] and now he says, "The heart of the king and the heart of the officials shall fail; the priests shall be benumbed and the prophets astounded,"[226] the prophet is confused, and he thinks that God has spoken falsely to him. The prophet does not understand that the first statement is a promise for the far distant future, whereas the second statement is for the near future. This agrees with what the apostle says: "Has God rejected his people? By no means!"[227] And "the sword has reached their very soul"

when nothing pertaining to life is left remaining in the soul. At the same time, it also shows this: unless the sword goes first in order to cut away and purge the vices of the soul, peace and promise will not follow.

4:11-12a: *At that time it will be said to this people and to Jerusalem, "A scorching wind"—or "wind of error"*[228]***—"from the highways in the desert toward the daughter of my people, not to winnow or cleanse, a spirit too full for this comes for me."***

When the sword has reached to the very soul and the threshing floor has been spent, then a scorching wind will come from the desert. This scorching wind will not cleanse and winnow or carry away the chaff so that the grain may be stored in barns. Instead, a "full spirit" comes, not for the people but "for me," "so that my wheat may be scattered."[229] Among the Hebrews, the same word *ruha*[230] stands both for "wind" and "spirit," and we should understand either "wind" or "spirit" based on the nature of the passages involved.

Others explain this passage in the following way: After the threshing floor has been cleansed, the remnant will be saved, so that it is written, "a spirit of fullness will come to me,"[231] and as the Evangelist says, "from his fullness have we all received,"[232] and we will receive the grace of the Holy Spirit.

Moreover, according to *historia* you should understand the "scorching wind" as Nebuchadnezzar, who consumed the entire world. But according to tropology,[233] the "scorching wind" is the adversarial power [the devil], who comes from the desert and the wilderness, where

---

[222]Prov 21:1. [223]1 Cor 1:20-21. [224]Heb *yitmāhû*, from *tmh* ("be astonished, amazed, horrified," KB 1744). [225]Jer 3:17. [226]Jer 4:9. [227]Rom 11:1. [228]Jerome agrees with Sym. [229]In other words, the "full spirit" from God will come not to do what the people want (cf. Lk 12:18) but to do God's task, to bring judgment against his people (the "wheat") and scatter them among the nations. [230]Heb *rûah*. [231]Jer 4:12 (LXX). [232]Jn 1:16. [233]The Latin word *tropologia* is taken from a Greek rhetorical term that refers to the figurative sense of a word as opposed to its literal or proper sense. In Christian exegesis after Origen it became a technical term for the spiritual sense of the text.

there is no shelter of God, and tries to destroy God's church.

4:12b: *"And now I—but I speak my judgments on them!"*

This is an example of *aposiōpēsis*, as in Virgil: "Whom I—! But better it is to calm the troubled waves."[234] He is about to speak something favorable, but he stops himself and then adds more harsh things to the harsh judgments already stated. For God speaks these judgments on his people so that they will know that it is just that they suffer what they are suffering.

4:13: *"Behold, he comes up like clouds, his chariots like the whirlwind; his horses are swifter than eagles—woe to us, for we are ruined!"*

Perceiving the events that are soon to take place, he describes the Babylonian army: the rumbling of their chariot wheels is compared with a violent storm, and the swiftness of their horses is associated with the eagle. Despite the fact that the prophet says this and as it were points out the coming enemies with his finger, the people still groan and fail to heed what is to come, paying attention only to what has already happened, saying, "Woe to us, for we are ruined."

One should apply this same message to the church, because daily the army of the true Nebuchadnezzar assails us, and the chariots of Pharaoh and all his cavalry of eagles mount their attack.[235] If an ecclesiastical person were to understand this, trusting in that saying,

"When you will return and groan, then you will be saved,"[236] then he would say, "Woe to us, for we are ruined!"

4:14: *"O Jerusalem, wash your heart from wickedness, that you may be saved. How long shall your evil thoughts lodge within you?"*

To the people who say, "Woe to us, for we are ruined," the prophet—or rather, God through the prophet—responds, "O Jerusalem, wash your heart from wickedness," using that water about which Isaiah also spoke: "Wash yourselves; make yourselves clean,"[237] namely, the water of saving baptism, the water of repentance. Moreover, he says this to the chief city of the Jews, so that through the city the people may be understood: "How long will you be subject to evil thoughts, which come out of your heart?"[238] In the sacred Scriptures, we must understand that "heart" is used for the soul and the mind.

4:15: *"For a voice of one announcing from Dan and making known an idol"—or "affliction"[239]—"from Mount Ephraim."*

The divine word is speaking now according to the location in the land of Judea. For the tribe of Dan, which is near to Mount Lebanon and the city known today as Paneas,[240] is in the north, from where Nebuchadnezzar is going to come. And he describes as coming from Mount Ephraim an "idol" (or "Bel"), or else "affliction" (or "iniquity"), since after the tribe of Dan comes the land of Ephraim, as one comes to Jerusalem. "Dan" is interpreted as "judgment,"[241] and "Ephraim" is interpreted as

---

[234]*Aposiōpēsis* is a figure of thought whereby someone begins to say something but cuts himself or herself off before finishing. Jerome illustrates this figure with a quotation from *Aen.* 1.135 (LCL), the same passage used to illustrate *aposiōpēsis* in Quintilian 9.2.54. [235]As he does with Nebuchadnezzar, Jerome uses Pharaoh here as a symbol for the devil. The "cavalry of eagles" may express the swiftness of this "army"; it may also be in view that the image of an eagle was the standard for a Roman legion, so that the word *eagle* could stand for a legion. [236]Is 30:15 (LXX). [237]Is 1:16. [238]Mt 15:19. [239]Heb *'wn* ("disaster," "sin/injustice," "deception," "false, idolatrous cult," KB 22). [240]Caesarea Philippi. [241]This etymology for Dan (Heb *dyn*, "to plead a cause, execute judgment") was widely known in Greek sources; see OS 172.5, 177.81, 190.17, 202.65; Philo *Leg.* 2.96; *Agr.* 95; *Somn.* 2.35.

"richness."[242] Therefore, the "judgment" of the Lord will come with all "richness" of torment on the land that offends the Lord.

4:16-17: *"Say to the nations: Behold, it is heard in Jerusalem, 'Besiegers come from a distant land; they shout against the cities of Judah. Like keepers of a field are they against her round about, because she has rebelled against me,' says the Lord."*

He desires for all of the surrounding nations to know the decree of God and to know that, once Jerusalem has been scourged, all of them will receive discipline. "It is reported widely in Jerusalem," he says, "that enemies are coming from a distant land and that there is arising against the city the din of a shouting army, which will so thoroughly barricade the city with fortifications and trap the citizens inside, that you would think them not so much military enemies as keepers of a field or vineyard. But this state of affairs has not come about because of the strength of the enemy but because of the guilt of Jerusalem, since she has rebelled against me." For if the adversarial powers do not have authority over swine,[243] how much less do they have authority over people, especially people who once belonged to the city of God!

4:18: *"Your ways and your doings have brought this on you. This is your doom, and it is bitter; it has reached your very heart."*

He makes an *apostrophe*[244] toward the city of Jerusalem: that her ways and thoughts—since she sinned both in deed and in word—have caused all of these things that have happened to take place; and that her doom, which is

bitter through her own doing, has reached her very heart and penetrated to the inner parts of her soul. Therefore, whatever happens to us happens to us because of our own vice. We turn a sweet God into bitterness, and we drive him, against his will, to treat us harshly.

4:19-20: *"My belly, my belly! I writhe in pain! The feelings of my heart are in disorder; I cannot keep silent; for I hear the sound of the trumpet, the alarm for war. Disaster follows hard on disaster, the whole land is laid waste. Suddenly my tents are destroyed, my curtains in a moment."*

Where we, following Symmachus, have put "are in disorder," and in Hebrew it is written *homae*, the LXX and Theodotion translated *maimassei*.[245] Even now I do not know what this word means. But Aquila used the word *ochlazei*, which itself also has the sense "to be in a tumult." I know that there is great contention about this word among many; let what I have said about it suffice. The voice of the prophet is introduced, and through the prophet the voice of God, who says that he writhes in pain over the contrition of his people, and that, like a human being, his insides are torn apart, just as the Savior grieved over the death of Lazarus[246] and bewailed Jerusalem,[247] lest silence conceal his grief. All the trumpet ringing and the din of war throw his feelings into disorder, while calamity is piled on top of calamity, and the whole land of the two tribes is laid waste. "Before I had a chance to think," he says, "what had been my tents and curtains were destroyed by raging Babylon, and what was my sanctuary was made into plunder for the enemy." Moreover, God says this same thing when he sees

---

[242]This is a traditional Greek interpretation of Ephraim; see OS 164.67; Origen *Fr. Jer.* 56. Cf. Jer 31:3-6; Jer 31:15 on Ephrathah. [243]Mt 8:31-32; Mk 5:12-13; Lk 8:32-33. [244]*Apostrophe* is a rhetorical figure whereby the speaker turns from his current listeners and addresses some other person or persons, as when the speaker turns from the judge and directly addresses his opponent (see Quintilian 9.2.38-39; 9.3.24). [245]Heb *hmh* ("be tumultuous," "roar," "groan," KB 250). Jerome gives the reading for the LXX and Th in Greek; *maimassei* means "to quiver." [246]Jn 11:33-35. [247]Lk 19:41-42.

the disorder and discord of sedition in the church, when the partridge cries out in his assemblies[248] and when the peace of God is turned into war. And so it goes on to say:

4:21: *"How long must I watch people fleeing,*[249] *and hear the sound of the trumpet?"*

"They are either fleeing from the king of Babylon, or they are fleeing from me and pulling away from being subject to me."

4:22: *"For my people are foolish, they do not know me; they are stupid children, they have no understanding. They are skilled in doing evil, but they do not know how to do good."*

The cause of the contrition, of the devastation, of the fleeing and of the trumpet sound is that the people have become foolish, not by nature but by the exertion of their will. This foolishness is shown by the fact that they do not know God. Instead of wise children they have become foolish children who lack understanding. For what could be more foolish than Israel, when the ox knows its owner and the donkey its master's crib,[250] but Israel does not know the Lord? What could be more foolish, when Israel despises the Lord when he is present with them even though they were always longing to see him? And regarding the next phrase, "They are skilled in doing evil, but they do not know how to do good": "skilled" here should be understood in a bad sense, as when "the children of this world are more shrewd . . . than the children of light," and the dishonest steward is reported to have done certain things shrewdly;[251] or when the serpent in paradise is said to be "more subtle" than any other wild creature.[252] True wisdom, therefore, is wisdom that is joined with the

fear of the Lord. Generally speaking, where there is treachery and deception, one should not use the word *wisdom* but "craftiness" or "cunning." In place of what we said, "For my people are foolish, they do not know me," the LXX translated, "For the leaders of my people do not know me," so that the guilt of the teachers is greater than the guilt of the people when the people lack the knowledge of God.

4:23-26: *"I looked on the earth, and lo, it was waste and void; and to the heavens, and they had no light. I looked on the mountains, and lo, they were quaking, and all the hills moved to and fro. I looked, and lo, there was no man, and all the birds of the air had fled. I looked, and lo, Carmel was a desert, and all its cities were laid in ruins before the Lord, before his fierce anger."*

The prophet perceives by the Spirit what is going to take place, so that the people will be terrified when they hear of it; and once they have repented, they will avoid suffering what they dread. The land is void because the inhabitants have been wiped out. The heavens do not have light because the people cannot see, due to the magnitude of their terror. Even the mountains and hills are not safe places to hide; through *hyperbolē*[253] they are seen as quaking and moving to and fro. He looked here and there and glanced all around, and not even a bird could be found; for both the lifeless elements and the irrational animals sense the anger of God and become terribly afraid. The whole world now shows this to be true. Even the winged creatures, which generally accompany human habitation, will depart and perish after the multitude of people have been cut off. Likewise Carmel, which is close to the Great Sea,[254] although planted with olives and thick

---

[248]Jer 17:11. [249]MT vocalizes the word *ns* as *nēs* ("standard" or "banner"), whereas Jerome, like LXX and Pesh, interprets the word as a participle from *nws* ("to flee"). [250]Is 1:3. [251]Lk 16:8. [252]Gen 3:1. [253]The Greek rhetorical term *hyperbolē* refers to an expression that exaggerates the truth, either to magnify or denigrate something (see Cicero *Top.* 45; *Rhet. Her.* 4.44). [254]The Mediterranean.

with orchards and vineyards, will come to such a state of desolation that it will be as barren as a desert. All the cities will also be deserted. And the cause of this calamity is that the anger of the Lord has been roused by the sin of the wayward people.

Whatever we have said according to *historia* concerning Jerusalem and Judea, let us refer it to the church of God, since the church has offended God. Either because of sins or because of the ravaging of persecution, where formerly there was a choir of virtues and rejoicing, there now is a multitude of sins and sorrows.

4:27-28: *For thus says the Lord, "The whole land shall be a desolation; yet I will not make a full end. The earth will mourn and the heavens above will lament because of that which I have spoken. I have purposed and I have not relented, nor have I turned back from it."*

The compassion of God is intermingled with his wrath: the whole land is desolated, but a full end is not to be made, so that some might comprehend his mercy. Heaven above will appear gloomy and the earth itself will mourn, because the Lord's judgment continues on to the very end, and he has not relented concerning the things that he has purposed and spoken. The "relenting"[255] of God is spoken of whenever a sentence of judgment predicted by God is lifted and his fierce anger does not continue on to the very end. Thus, God threatened judgment through Jonah, but the multitude of tears and groans from the people overcame the impending sword.[256]

4:29: *"At the noise of horseman and shooter of arrows"*—or *"stretcher of the bow"*[257]—*"every city"*—or *"region"*—*"takes flight; they enter*

thickets; they climb among rocks"—and that which follows, *"and they enter 'groves' or 'caves,'"* was added by the LXX; *"all the cities are forsaken, and no man dwells in them."*

The divine word describes the raging Babylonian army, and how all the people forsake the city because they are terrified of this army, and each person goes into the thickets; and still they are not able to deflect the wrath of the Lord. And, as we said above,[258] whatever is understood by *historia* against Jerusalem should be referred to the church, since the church has offended God and has been handed over to "enemies," either in times of persecution or else to "vices" and "sins."

4:30a: *"And you, O desolate one, what are you doing?"*

In place of "desolate," which in Hebrew is *sadud*,[259] and which Aquila alone translated as "desolate," the others[260] translated "miserable" and "pitiable," because of the unchastity that has offended the merciful God. And so it continues:

4:30b: *"When you dress in scarlet and deck yourself with ornaments of gold and enlarge your eyes with paint, you beautify yourself in vain. Your lovers despise you; they seek your life."*

Through the metaphor of an adulterous woman he says, "Once you have offended God and abandoned your creator as if he were your husband, it is vain for you to search for ornaments. Your demon lovers despise you; they do not really seek the filth of your debauchery but the ruin of your life." This same idea should be understood spiritually

---

[255]The Hebrew word *nhm* can refer to repentance (thus Jerome's *paenitentia*). This is the same Hebrew word used at Gen 6:6; 1 Sam 15:11; Jon 3:10. [256]Jon 3:10. [257]The Hebrew idiom is "shooter of the bow" (rendered literally by Aq and Sym). Jerome turns this into "shooter of arrows," whereas the LXX rendered it as "stretcher of the bow." [258]Jer 4:23-26. [259]Heb *šādûd*. [260]Sym, Th.

against those who have ruined marital affection and the chastity of pure faith. He says, "If you dress in scarlet" (you have accepted faith in the blood of Christ), "if you deck yourself with ornaments of gold" (you have contemplated the spiritual sense and understanding) "and if you enlarge your eyes with paint" (you have a zeal for mysteries and for knowing the secrets of God), then "you beautify yourself in vain." For you had also prepared these things for your lovers, and your narrow bed is not able to hold both them and God. And so God will not accept your ornaments, since previously you satisfied your lovers with them.

4:31: *"For I heard a cry as of a woman in travail, anguish"—or "groaning"[261]—"as of one bringing forth her first child, the cry of the daughter of Zion gasping for breath, stretching out her hands, 'Woe is me, for I am fainting before those who have been killed!' "[262]*

Using the likeness of a woman bringing forth her first child, that is, who is bearing her first offspring,[263] he describes the city of Jerusalem wailing and crying out. For just as a woman in labor who has not yet experienced the pain of childbirth passes out (she suffers anguish, can scarcely breathe and collapses with her hands spread out), so also the daughter of Zion, when she has seen her children killed, bursts out with these words: "Woe is me, for I am fainting before those who have been killed!" Two images are brought in for comparison in this one passage: the image of the woman giving birth and the image of the woman grieving. Thus, whatever a woman suffers in childbirth or in the death of her children, Jerusalem suffers in the death of its people.

5:1-2: *"Run to and fro through the streets of Jerusalem, look and take note! Search her squares to see if you can find a man, one who does justice and seeks faith; that I may pardon her. Though they say, 'As the Lord lives,' yet they swear falsely."*

So great is God's love of justice that he does not promise to spare the city if ten righteous men can be found in it, as he did when Abraham was asking and God was responding,[264] but even if one person who does justice and seeks "faith"—or as Symmachus translated, "truth"[265]—is found in Jerusalem (which is about to be destroyed), then God will have compassion on the city. And since there could be found among the people some who pretended to worship God and who swore by the Lord, he anticipates this (because God does not delight in empty words but in the truth of faith) and says, "I pay no regard to those who swear by me but swear falsely; but I do regard those whose heart and lips are in agreement."[266]

5:3: *"O Lord, do not your eyes look for faith? You have smitten them, but they felt no anguish; you have consumed them, but they refused to take correction. They have made their faces harder than rock; they have refused to repent."*

After the previous words of the Lord, through which he ordered the prophet to "run to and fro through the streets of Jerusalem,"[267] the prophet now speaks to the Lord: "O Lord, do not thy eyes look for 'faith' "—which in Hebrew is *emuna*[268]—not the works of the Jews, in which they exult according to the ceremonies of the Law, but the faith of Chris-

---

[261]Jerome agrees with Sym and one edition of Aq (= MT). [262]Jerome and the LXX read this last word as a passive participle, whereas MT vocalizes it as active. [263]There is only one word in Hebrew (and Latin) that represents "one bringing forth her first child." Jerome is making clear the meaning of the word for his Latin readers ("that is . . ."). [264]Gen 18:32. [265]Cf. Jer 5:3. [266]Is 29:13; Mt 15:8; Mk 7:6. [267]Jer 5:1. [268]Heb *'mwnh* ("faithfulness, honesty," KB 62-63). This word is translated "faith" by the LXX at Jer 5:1 and Jer 5:3 (so also Aq, preserved only at Jer 5:3) but is rendered as "truth" by Sym in both passages.

tians, through which we have been saved by grace.[269] Moreover, from this passage we learn that punishments are inflicted so that vices may be corrected; and so it says, "You have smitten them, but they felt no anguish; you have consumed them, but they refused to take correction." For through all these torments and scourges Jerusalem is to be restored. Yet, in spite of all this, they do not even feel shame for their sins but instead have made their faces hard like a rock and refuse to be converted to better things.

5:4-5a: "Then I said, 'These are only the poor, they have no sense,'—or 'they are not capable'[270]—'for they do not know the way of the Lord, the law of their God. I will go to the great, and will speak to them; for they know the way of the Lord, the law of their God.' "

When he speaks here of the poor and the great, he is not comparing poverty with wealth but the people with the leaders. This is the sense: "As I saw the stubbornness of the faithless people and how they hardened their faces and refused to take correction, I had this thought: 'Perhaps the ignoble masses are not able to understand the doctrine of God; and so their condition is excusable, since due to ignorance they are not capable of knowing God's commands. Therefore, I will go to the priests and to those who preside over the people, and I will speak to them. For they understand the will of the Lord and know his commands.' " Furthermore, he says this as an expression of uncertainty, as in the Gospel: "I will send my son; perhaps they will respect him."[271] Thus, through the open-endedness of the statement and the sense of doubt in the words, the freedom of the human will is shown.

5:5b-6: "But they all alike had broken the yoke, they had burst the bonds. Therefore a lion from the forest shall slay them, a wolf at evening[272] shall destroy them. A leopard is watching against their cities, everyone who goes out of them shall be torn in pieces; because their transgressions are many, their apostasies are great."

"But I concluded," he says, "that the teachers were worse than the students, and that however much greater was the authority of the wealthy, so much greater was the excess of their sins." For they broke the yoke of the Law, as the apostle says: "Now therefore why do you make trial of God by putting a yoke on the neck of the disciples which neither our fathers nor we have been able to bear? But we believe that we shall be saved through the grace of the Lord Jesus, just as they will."[273] Indeed, they broke the bonds of God's laws, and not simply the bonds of the Pharisees' laws. Concerning the Pharisees, it says in the second psalm: "Let us burst their bonds asunder and cast their cords from us."[274]

Therefore, because they did those things, "a lion from the forest," namely, the Babylonian kingdom, "shall slay them." The phrase "a wolf at evening shall destroy them" signifies the Medes and the Persians, which Daniel portrays in his vision as a "bear," in whose mouth were three rows.[275] The phrase "a leopard is watching against their cities" prefigures the onslaught of Alexander and the quick advance from the west to India. He calls him a "leopard" because of his inconstancy, and since he contended against the Medes and the Persians after having subjected many nations to himself. And of this leopard it says, "And the beast had four heads, and dominion was given to it."[276] But since he is not prophesying about the

---

[269]Eph 2:8. [270]Jerome agrees with Aq and Th. Heb y'l (Niphal; "to turn out to be a fool," KB 381). [271]Lk 20:13. [272]MT 'rbwt, vocalized as from 'ārābāh ("desert"), thus, "wolf of the desert." Jerome, Aq, Targ and Pesh derive the word from 'ereb ("evening"; cf. Hab 1:8; Zeph 3:3). [273]Acts 15:10-11. [274]Ps 2:3. [275]Dan 7:5. [276]Dan 7:6.

future but is narrating the *historia* of the past or of things that are now about to take place, he passes over the Roman Empire in silence, although the Roman Empire may be spoken of by the phrase "everyone who goes out of them shall be torn in pieces."[277] And he provides the reason why all these things were allowed: "because their transgressions are many." And they continued in their transgressions, so that it says "their apostasies are great."

What we said at the beginning, that the Hebrew word *sacad* means "watching," is demonstrated in the present passage.[278] For where we have said "a leopard is watching," in the Hebrew it is written *nemer sacad*.[279] According to tropology,[280] the prophet refers to those who think themselves to be great in church, since they break their yoke and burst their bonds, and for that reason they are handed over into disgraceful passion, so that they do things that are inappropriate.

5:7-9: *"How can I pardon you? Your children have forsaken me and have sworn by those who are no gods. When I fed them to the full, they committed adultery and trooped to the houses of harlots. In my view, they became like horses, paramours to women,*[281] *and stallions, each neighing for his neighbor's wife. Shall I not visit them for these things? says the Lord; and shall not my soul avenge itself on a nation such as this?"*

This is a catalogue of the sins of Jerusalem, where God says that he does not know any way

that he can have compassion on them. "Your children," he says, "have forsaken me"—not "my children" but "your children," since they "have sworn by those who are no gods." "When I fed them to the full, they committed adultery"—this should be heard by those who, having received wealth from the Lord, brood over it and are slaves to luxury. "They became like horses, paramours to women." In place of "stallions," the Hebrew has *mosechim*,[282] which all translated with one voice as *helkontes*,[283] that is, "dragging ones," so as to highlight the great size of their genitalia, as in Ezekiel: "whose 'members' were like those of donkeys."[284] And this is what is written in another passage: "they are like the senseless beasts,"[285] and they have indeed become like them. Likewise, he shows the great madness of their desire by calling it not a "craving" for pleasure but a *chremetismos*,[286] that is, a "neighing," which serves as a metaphor for the desire of a raving horse.

"And since you have done these things," he says, "are you not deserving of 'visitation'?" It should be noted that the word for "visiting" is used for punishments and penalties, as it is written: "Then I will visit their transgression with the rod."[287] "And shall not my soul avenge itself on a nation such as this?" After they have been condemned for sins, they are not called the "people" of God but a "nation"—a nation from which the soul of God has departed, as it is written: "Your new moons, your sabbaths and your appointed feasts my soul hates."[288] And that which is said in the Old Testament

---

[277]In other words, Jeremiah is primarily prophesying about events that are in the past (Babylon, Medes and Persians, Alexander), with a little bit of contemporary history and soon-to-be-fulfilled prophecy woven in (Roman Empire). Cf. Jer 25:26c. [278]Cf. Jer 1:11-12. [279]Heb *nāmēr šōqēd*. [280]The Latin word *tropologia* is taken from a Greek rhetorical term that refers to the figurative sense of a word as opposed to its literal or proper sense. In Christian exegesis after Origen it became a technical term for the spiritual sense of the text. [281]In Jer 5:8, the words "in my view" and "to women" do not directly translate anything in the Hebrew and were not used by Jerome in his IH translation. Jerome probably adds them into the lemma here in order to clarify the metaphor. [282]Heb *mškym*. According to KB 1488, this word is a Hiphil participle from *škh* (or *'šk*), meaning "possessing testicles" (cf. *'ešek*, "testicle"). Jerome derives the word from *mšk* ("to pull, drag"), but he also sees in the word a reference to genitalia. [283]The "all" refers to Aq, Sym and Th. [284]Ezek 23:20. [285]Ps 49:12, 20. [286]Jerome gives the Greek noun related to the verb used by the LXX. [287]Ps 89:32. Both at Jer 5:9 and at Ps 89:32, the word in question is the Hebrew word *pqd*, which has a wide range of meanings, including "to visit" and "to punish." Cf. Jer 32:3b-5; Jerome *Comm. Isa.* 24:21-23; *Comm. Ezech.* 9:1; *Comm. Am.* 3:1. [288]Is 1:14.

for effect is said in the New Testament in view of the reality, as when Jesus says, "I have the power to lay down my soul, and I have the power to take it up again."[289]

5:10-11: *"Go up through her walls"—or "ramparts"*[290]*—"and destroy, but make not a full end; strip away her branches"—or "supports"—"for they are not the Lord's. For the house of Israel and the house of Judah have been utterly faithless to me, says the Lord."*

He commands the nations, about whom it was said above, "a lion from the forest shall slay them, a wolf shall destroy them, and a leopard watches against their cities,"[291] that they should go up through the "walls" or "ramparts" of Jerusalem and destroy it but not make a full end, so that a remnant may be saved who will proclaim the glory of God among the nations. Thus he mixes severity with clemency. And with the next phrase, "strip away her branches (or "supports")," he orders that her sources of aid be removed. God destroyed this aid because of their sin, that is, because the house of Israel and the house of Judah (which signifies the ten tribes and the two) had been faithless to the Lord. Let the church take heed of this: that the "walls" and "ramparts" of those who have no hope in the Lord and are faithless to him will soon be broken down; nevertheless, a full end will not be made—on account of the clemency of the Judge, not on account of the merits of the wrongdoers.

5:12-13: *"They have denied the Lord and said, 'He is not the one'—or 'these things are not so';*[292] *'no evil will come on us, nor shall we see sword or famine. The prophets will become wind; the response'—or 'word'*[293] *—'is not in them.' Thus shall it be done to them."*

"They have denied the Lord," or "they have lied to the Lord,"[294] and have said, "He is not the one by whose judgment all these things were done; rather, all these things happened by chance, and what the prophets threatened will not come about. We will not see the sword or endure the famine of a siege. Whatever the prophets spoke, they spoke as wind, and all their useless utterances have come and gone. They have had no 'response,' that is, 'oracle'— or else the 'word' of God was not in them." Because they denied the Lord in this way, they will indeed suffer all the things that the following discourse describes.[295] Let the church take heed of this when it is negligent and rejects the providence of God: that the church will indeed suffer the sword and famine, unless it will believe that the things spoken about will come to pass.

5:14: *"Therefore thus says the Lord, the God of hosts: 'Because you have spoken this word, behold, I am making my words in your mouth a fire, and this people wood, and the fire shall devour them.' "*

You have said, "The prophets will become wind, and what they threaten will not come about."[296] "Therefore, O prophet, I am making my words in your mouth to have the power of fire, and this people shall turn into wood, so that the faithless will be burned up by your prophetic word." Accordingly, God is said to be a "devouring fire,"[297] so that, if anyone builds on the foundation of Christ with hay, wood or straw, it will be consumed within us.[298]

5:15-18: *"Behold, I am bringing on you a nation from afar, O house of Israel, says the Lord. It is a sturdy nation, it is an ancient nation, a nation whose language you do not*

---

[289]Jn 10:18.   [290]Jerome matches Aq. The Hebrew is obscure (cf. KB 1653).   [291]See Jer. 5:6.   [292]MT, like Jerome, Aq and Sym, has the singular pronoun.   [293]Heb *dibbēr* (noun). Jerome renders this unusual form as "response." The LXX translates "word," assuming the common vocalization of these consonants, *dābār*.   [294]"They have lied to the Lord" (LXX).   [295]Jer 5:15-17.   [296]Jer 5:13.   [297]Deut 4:24; Heb 12:29.   [298]1 Cor 3:12-15.

know, nor can you understand what they say. Their quiver is like an open tomb, they are all mighty men. They shall eat up your harvest and your food; they shall eat up your sons and your daughters; they shall eat up your flocks and your herds; they shall eat up your vines and your fig trees; your fortified cities in which you trust they shall destroy with the sword. But even in those days, says the Lord, I will not make a full end of you."

"Not, as you falsely believe, are the prophets speaking as wind,[299] nor will these things come about only in the distant future. On the contrary, right now I am already bringing on you the nation of the Babylonians, which will come from afar. "It is a sturdy nation," which in Hebrew is written *ethan*.[300] "It is an ancient nation," over which Nimrod the giant formerly held rule.[301] It is "a nation whose language you do not know," and as it is written in the Hebrew, "nor can you understand what they say."[302] For it is a comfort in the face of disaster if you have enemies whom you are able to petition and who can understand your entreaties. And that which follows, "their quiver is like an open tomb," which is not found in the edition of the LXX, refers to the Babylonian soldiers. There is no doubt that the kingdoms of Assyria, Babylon, Medea and Persia had very skilled archers.

It goes on to describe the devastation of the land of Judah, the killing of many people, the driving away of cattle, the demolition of cities and walls, and the fact that everything will be swallowed up by the enemy's sword. Nevertheless, in spite of all these calamities, he will not break them down all the way to the point of extermination. Instead, he will save a remnant: either those who were led to Babylon and were later allowed to go back to cultivate the fields of the land of Judah, or else those who, after the flames of persecution, maintained their faith in the Lord either by flight or by confession.

5:19: *"And when your people say, 'Why has the Lord our God done all these things to us?' you shall say to them, 'As you have forsaken me and served a foreign god'—or 'foreign gods'[303]—'in your land, so you shall serve strangers in a land that is not yours.' "*

It is tremendous folly on their part not to know why they are suffering these things, since they have sinned so much; and the response to their question is brief: "Just as you served a foreign god" (that is, Baal) or "foreign gods" (namely, the gods of all the nations around the land of Judah), "so you shall serve strange gods in a land that is not your own," no doubt Babylonian gods in the land of Chaldea. "For if you delight in foreign religion, why is it necessary for you to engage in this error from far away? Go live among the people—or rather, go be slaves to the people—whose gods you honor!"

This can also be said with regard to heretics, about whom it is written: "They went out from us, but they were not of us; for if they had been of us, they would have continued with us."[304] For a long time the heretics worshiped the idols of their lies under God's name, but the Lord drives them out of the church, so that they may honor outside the church what they previously worshiped within it, so as to separate the chaff from the wheat.[305]

BOOK TWO

This second book on Jeremiah, O brother Eusebius, we are dictating with hurried voice,

---

[299]Jer 5:12-13. [300]Heb *'ētān* ("constant, continual," KB 44-45). Jerome's interpretation matches Aq. [301]Gen 10:8-10. [302]This last phrase is not represented in the LXX. [303]Lit., "gods of foreignness," thus the LXX's plural "foreign gods" (cf. Targ: "idols of the nations"). Because the plural form *'ĕlōhîm* is also used to refer to God, Jerome renders the word as singular. [304]1 Jn 2:19. [305]Mt 3:12; Lk 3:17.

turning aside our ears for a while lest we hear the judgment of blood and bemoan the souls of those who have been slain.[1] In spite of their reputation for virtue, they fall into arrogance daily and regard themselves as on a par with God,[2] so that equality with God, which the impious heresy of the Arians denied to the Son, they ascribe to all people, setting their mouths to the heavens[3] and leaving nothing more for the saints' future state of blessedness.[4] We have responded to their raving, as we have been able,[5] and if the Lord grants us life we will respond more fully.[6] But now the path once begun must be pursued—namely, the path of dictating this commentary! We should avoid increasing the length of the work beyond proper measure, but we should also avoid cutting short our explanations with excessive brevity. The one burdens the minds of readers, but the other fails to satisfy the needs of the studious.

5:20-21: *"Declare this in the house of Jacob, proclaim it in Judah: 'Hear this, O foolish and senseless people, who have eyes but see not, who have ears but hear not.'"*

In many ways he draws sinners back to salvation. He calls them a "foolish" people since they have abandoned the author of wisdom, and he likens them to idols, about which it is written, "They have eyes but do not see. They have ears but do not hear. Those who make them are like them; so are all who trust in them."[7] Strictly speaking, he says this to "Judah" and the "house of Jacob," since Israel had already gone into exile among the Assyrians many years before. He also makes the general point that, even apart from the commandments, we should be able to understand what is right by our natural senses.

5:22-24: *"Do you not fear me? says the Lord. Are you not grieved"—or "afraid"—"before me?*[8] *I placed the sand as the bound for the sea, an eternal command that cannot pass away; though the waves toss, they cannot prevail"— or "though the sea is stirred up, it will not prevail"; "though they swell"—or "resound"— "they cannot pass over it. But this people has a stubborn and rebellious heart; they have turned aside and gone away. They do not say in their hearts, 'Let us fear the Lord our God, who gives the rain in its season, the autumn rain and the spring rain, and keeps for us the fullness of the yearly harvest.'"*

He recounts the benefits they received in order to rebuke them for being ungrateful. He says, "Do you not fear me, considering that I have shown you such great things? I, who keep in check so powerful an element, the great mass of rushing water that is bounded by the shore at my command (as it is written: "he set a command that cannot pass away"[9])—I do not expect love as from those who have been perfected, but simply fear as from those who are just beginning. Even things that do not have the sense of hearing[10] listen to me and respond, but my people (that is, formerly mine) have become fools by their own vice. They not only belittle but even exasperate their otherwise pleasant God."

"They have turned aside from me," he says, "and turned their backs to me, and they have gone away with hurried steps; nor has their silent conscience caused them to return to me, so that they might say in their hearts, 'Let us fear him who gives the rain, the autumn rain and the spring rain, and who provides for us through all these good things the fullness of the yearly harvest.'" In place of "fullness," the first edition of Aquila and Symmachus

---

Book Two   [1]Rufinus had recently (410) died.   [2]Is 14:14.   [3]Ps 73:9.   [4]This is Jerome's characterization of the teaching of Pelagius, whom he associates with Origen and Rufinus.   [5]Jerome *Ep.* 133.   [6]Jerome *Pelag.*   [7]Ps 115:5-8.   [8]Heb *hyl* ("writhe, tremble," KB 310). [9]Ps 148:6.   [10]The sea and the waves, which heed God's commands.

translated "weeks," for in Hebrew the word is written *sabaoth*, which, due to its ambiguity, can mean either "sevens" or "fullness."[11]

5:25: *"Your iniquities have turned these away, and your sins have kept good from you."*

Therefore, if the sea ever crosses its bounds or the rains are withheld, it is not that the hand of the Lord is shortened,[12] so that he cannot perform these tasks. On the contrary, it is our sins that have diverted these benefits away from us, so that they are transferred to those who have not sinned. He says, "They have hindered the good that was already set to come to them," as it is written according to the literal sense: "I will also command the clouds that they rain no rain on it."[13] We may also understand the autumn rain and the spring rain as the law and the gospel, and even the various callings from the first hour to the eleventh in which the workers of the vineyard are promised the same reward of eternal life.[14]

5:26-27a: *"For impious men are found among my people; they lurk like fowlers. They set traps and snares so as to catch men. Like a trap filled with birds, thus their houses are filled with treachery."*

The reasons are given as to why the autumn and spring rains were withheld and all good things did not come: it is because there were found among God's people "impious" people. He did not say "unjust" or "sinful," as the new heresy wishes, but "impious."[15] Impiety openly denies God, whereas the one who has committed injustice or sin, if he will confess his error, easily moves God to pity.

That which we said, "they lurk like fowlers," is not found in the LXX. Aquila and Symmachus translated the word *lurk* as *iasir*, thus "*iasir* like a fowler's net,"[16] since even those among them who seem good and upright set traps like a fowler, as they hunt each other to death and fill their houses with the losses and expenses of others, thereby fulfilling this saying of the philosophers: "Every rich man is either unjust or is the heir of an unjust person."[17] Would that these things were being done only by those who are clearly seen to be on the outside (whom the Lord judges) and not by those within our own assemblies. Avarice, the root of all evils, has such a hold on us that we do not consider the mouths of those who come to us, but the hands![18]

5:27b-29: *"Therefore they have become great and rich, they have grown fat and sleek. They have transgressed my words most wickedly; they do not judge rightly. The cause"*—or *"justice"*[19]—*"of the fatherless they have not established; and they do not judge in favor of the justice of the needy"*—or *"the widow."*[20] *"Shall I not visit them for these things? says*

---

[11]Heb *šbʿwt* or *śbʿwt* (the written distinction between *š* and *ś* did not exist in Jerome's day, although Jerome is aware of the difference in pronunciation between these two "letters"; see Jerome *QHG* 26:32-33). The word could be read as from *šābûʿa* ("period of seven") or from *śābʿâ* ("satiety, abundance"). See Jer 15:9. [12]Is 50:2; 59:1. [13]Is 5:6. Jerome specifies the literal sense for this quote because the higher sense of this passage does not relate to literal rain on a vineyard but to the nations of Israel and Judah (see Is 5:7). [14]Mt 20:1-16. [15]The Hebrew word *ršʿ* ("wicked") usually has the sense of being guilty before God (see KB 1295), thus Jerome's *impietas*. The "new heresy" of which Jerome speaks is Pelagianism, which teaches (according to Jerome) that one can fully master sin. But Jerome wishes to argue that our greatest danger is not sin, which can be absolved through confession, but impiety, that is, the pride of Pelagianism that amounts to denial of God. Pelagians set traps for people by parading their supposed virtues and leading Christians astray. [16]The Hebrew text of this verse is extremely difficult. Aq and Sym transliterated the Hebrew word *yšwr* as *iasir*. Jerome seems to think that they meant to connect this word with the Hebrew *yāšār* ("upright") to emphasize that even those who appear upright are really laying traps for others. [17]Plato *Leg.* 5.12.743; Jerome *Ep.* 120.1; *Tract. Ps.* 1; Erasmus *Adagia* 1.9.47. [18]When looking at those coming into the church, we pay attention more to their wealth (their hands) than to their confession of the faith (their mouth). Cf. 1 Tim 6:10. [19]Jerome translates the Hebrew word *dyn* as "cause" ("of the fatherless") in order to distinguish it from *mšpṭ* "justice" ("of the needy"). The LXX had translated both of these Hebrew words with the same Greek word. [20]Jerome agrees with Aq and Sym (= MT).

the Lord, and shall not my soul avenge itself on a nation such as this?"

If I were to point out each individual instance where something was left out of the edition of the Seventy, it would take a long time. "They set traps for others," he says, "and rejoice at the want of others; therefore they have become great and rich." It is because they have done the above-mentioned things that "they have grown fat and sleek," in accordance with what is written: "He became fat and sleek; the beloved one kicked."[21] "And they have transgressed my words," since, cognizant of their wealth, they spoke to themselves this saying from the Gospel: "Soul, you have ample good laid up for many years; take your ease, eat, drink, be merry."[22] Moreover, they have transgressed in their wickedness, and despising all people they do not set the justice of God before their eyes. They spurn the fatherless and the "needy," in place of which the Seventy said "widows," which is not what it says in the Hebrew. Strictly speaking, *hebionim*[23] means "needy," not "widows." And that which follows, "Shall I not visit them for these things? says the Lord, and shall not my soul avenge itself on a nation such as this?" I have already discussed above.[24]

5:30-31: *"An appalling and horrible thing has happened in the land: the prophets prophesy falsely,"—or "unjustly"[25]—"and the priests applaud with their hands; my people love to have it so, but what will you do at the end"[26]— or "after these things?"*

Earlier he said, "I will go to the great and will speak to them; perhaps they know the way of the Lord. But they all alike had broken the yoke, they had burst the bonds."[27] Now he explains who the "great" are—namely, the prophets and the priests, the first of whom predict the future, and the second determine what should be done according to the Law. "Look!" he says, "while the prophets prophesy falsely, the priests applaud with their hands!" And in order to show that the people who are being led astray by such things are not without guilt, it is written: "my people love to have it so"—or rather, "they were formerly 'my people,' but because they loved to have such things be so, they ceased to be mine." What, then, will they do when the end time of judgment or the inevitable captivity comes? It is for this reason that an appalling and terrible thing is happening: because neither among the leaders nor among the people was there found even one person who thinks rightly.

6:1: *"Strengthen yourselves, O sons of Benjamin, from the midst of Jerusalem! Blow the trumpet in Tekoa, and raise a signal"—or "standard"[28]—"on Beth-haccherem; for evil is seen"—or "peers out"—"from the north, and great destruction."*

That Jerusalem is located in the tribe of Benjamin no one is unaware.[29] As for Tekoa, we see with our own eyes today that Tekoa is a little village situated on the mountain and separated from Jerusalem by twelve thousand paces. In this area there is another village, which in the Syrian and Hebrew language is called Bethacarma, which is also positioned on the mountain. What he is saying, therefore, is this: "Because any time now Nebuchadnezzar is going to come from the north and captivity is near at hand, O inhabitants of Jerusalem, take up arms, blow the trumpet in Tekoa and raise a standard on Beth-haccherem, so that you may be able to offer resistance against the enemies!" "Benjamin" is interpreted "son of the

---

[21]"Kicked in rebellion." See Deut 32:15 (LXX). [22]Lk 12:19. [23]Heb *'ebyônim*. [24]See Jer 5:7-9. [25]Jerome matches Sym (MT: *bšqr*, "in falsehood"). [26]Cf. the IH edition: "What will happen at its end?" [27]Jer 5:5. [28]In this case, the first option ("signal") is the LXX (= Aq), the second ("standard") is the IH edition (cf. Sym). [29]Eusebius *Onom.* 106; cf. Josh 18:16.

right hand";[30] "Tekoa" is "trumpet";[31] and "Beth-haccherem" is "house of the vineyard."[32] We refer all these things to the church, so that, if the church were to do wrong and be attacked with persecution, it ought to prepare itself to offer resistance.

6:2-4a: "I have likened[33] the daughter of Zion to a comely and delicately bred woman. Shepherds with their flocks shall come to[34] her; they have pitched"—or "they shall pitch"[35]—"their tents around her, each one will graze the flock that is under his hand. Consecrate"—or "prepare"[36]—"war against her; up, and let us attack at noon!"

What is described here is the beauty of Jerusalem, which is the same thing as Zion: the first term refers to the whole city, while the second refers to the fortress of the city, since "Zion" may be interpreted as "fortress," that is, "watchtower."[37]

Zion is compared with a comely woman, and just as lovers are said to come to the woman, so also shepherds are said to come to the city. Very elegantly the Hebrew word, which is written with the four letters *res, ain, iod* and *mem*, can be read *reim*, in which case it means "lovers," or *roim*, in which case it means "shepherds."[38] Thus, either "lovers" of the comely maiden may be understood, in accordance with the metaphor, or else "shepherds" may be understood, in keeping with the destruction of the city. Whereas the one group rushes to defile the harlot, the other rushes to

blockade and overthrow the city.

We ought to understand the shepherds and their flocks as the leaders of the Chaldeans and their armies. "They pitch their tents around her" in blockade of the city, and "each one will graze the flock that is under his hand"—namely, his troops and divisions. They say to their flocks, "Consecrate war against Jerusalem!" for it is a command of the Lord. "Up, and let us attack at noon!"—let us fight, not at night and in concealment but in full light; for no one can resist us.

6:4b-5: "Woe to us, for the day declines, for the shadows of evening lengthen"—or "fail!" "Up, let us attack by night, and destroy her houses"—or "foundations!"[39]

The Chaldeans say, "Up, and let us attack at noon, and let us fight in bright light!" Now Jerusalem responds, "Woe to us, for the shadows of evening lengthen!" as in this quote from Virgil:

Even now the housetops yonder are smoking

and longer shadows fall from the mountain heights.[40]

And this is the sense: "If we are suffering these things in the day, what will we suffer at night?"

And again, those who above said, "Consecrate war against Jerusalem, rise up!" now summon themselves to fight, saying, "Up, let us attack by night," so that our opponents will not know the time of our victory, but they will

---

[30]On this etymology for Benjamin (*bn ymyn*) in the Greek tradition, see OS 178.84; 201.52; Origen *Hom. Jer.* 19.13; *Fr. Jer.* 11. See also Jer 17:21-27; 20:1-2; 31:15; 32:8a; 32:42-44. [31]The Hebrew verb *tq'* can mean "to blow the trumpet" (KB 1785). [32]*bêt* ("house of") *hakkerem* ("the vineyard"). [33]Jerome reads this verb as if from *dmh* I (Piel; "to liken" [see KB 225]). [34]The Hebrew preposition *'el* can mean "against," but in Jerome's view the phrase fits the metaphor of the lovers coming to the woman, Zion. This idiom ("to come to") can have sexual overtones; see Gen 16:2; 30:3; 38:8; Deut 22:13; 2 Sam 16:21. [35]Jerome's "have pitched" reflects that the Hebrew verb has shifted to the perfect inflection. [36]Heb *qdš* (Piel; "to consecrate to God," "to sanctify" [KB 1073-74]). [37]On "Zion" in the Greek tradition, see OS 174.90; 198.63; Origen *Fr. Jer.* 32; cf. Lampe 1240. One possible etymology for "Zion" (*sywn*) among modern scholars is "castle" or "citadel" (KB 1022). Cf. Jer 4:6; 31:3-6, 21. [38]The consonants here can be pronounced as if from *rēa'* ("friend" or "neighbor," or "lover"; see Jer 3:1, 20; Hos 3:1; Song 5:16); or they can be pronounced as if from *rō'eh* ("shepherd," the final *h* being absent from the plural). Jerome takes this to be an intentional and even artistic Hebrew word play. [39]Jerome seems to match Aq and Sym, *bareis* (*baris*, "large house, tower" [LSJ 307]). [40]Virgil *Ecl.* 1.82-83 (LCL).

know its strength; "and let us destroy her palaces," which in vain are surrounded by sturdy walls.

6:6a: *"For thus says the Lord of hosts: 'Hew down her timber'—or 'trees';*[41] *'pour out'—or 'bring together'*[42]*—'a mound around Jerusalem.'"*

They say, "We are safe from being conquered immediately, because of this command of the Lord given to the Chaldeans: 'Cut down trees and bring together a mound around Jerusalem, to be used for future fortifications!'" This shows even before it happens that the besiegers are not going to capture the city immediately but will capture it only after a long siege, as we read about later.[43]

6:6b-7a: *"This is the city of visitation"—or "of falsehood";*[44] *"there is nothing but slander"—or "oppression"*[45]*—"within her. As a cistern"—or "pool"*[46]*—"keeps its water cold, so she keeps her wickedness cold."*

The Lord commands that trees be cut down and that mounds be poured out all around, because the time has come for Jerusalem to receive punishment for her sins, the greatest of which is *sykophantia*, since she oppressed the innocent through "slander." Just as a "cistern" or "pool" keeps its water cold, so also the wickedness that is in Jerusalem destroys all warmth of life. And this should be noted: that

people are called to be "aglow with the Spirit,"[47] whereas evil things are said to be cold. Thus, it is written that in the last days, when wickedness is multiplied, "most men's love will grow cold."[48] I think the same thing is also meant by this passage: "Lest I become like those who go down to the cistern."[49] Moreover, the Latin reader should understand this; let it suffice for me to say it once: the word *lacus* according to the Greeks does not mean "pool" but "cistern," which in the Syriac and Hebrew language is *gubba*. Yet, in the present passage the word is *bor*, which all the Greek translators rendered unanimously as *lakkos*.[50]

6:7b-8: *"Violence and destruction are heard within her; sickness and wounds are ever before me. Receive discipline, O Jerusalem, lest I be alienated from you; lest I make you a desolation, an uninhabited land."* LXX: *"Impiety and misery will be heard within her, before her always. With pain and with the lash you will be disciplined, O Jerusalem, lest I be alienated from you, lest I make you a desolate land in which no one dwells."*

Through these words we learn that the Lord chastises every son whom he receives.[51] The very reason why Jerusalem is disciplined with torments and wounds is so that she may be set right, and so that God may not be alienated from her and she be reduced to a wasteland. Therefore, if we ever encounter severe difficulties, let us call to mind for our own comfort

---

[41]The Hebrew word is grammatically singular. [42]Jerome uses *effundite* ("pour out"; *fundite* in the IH edition) in order to represent the Hebrew word *špk*, normally "to pour" or "to shed" but also "to heap up" (KB 1630). The transmitted LXX also translates the word as "to pour," and hexaplaric evidence is lacking for this word. The second option, "bring together" (*conportate*), could be the reading of Jerome's copy of the LXX, or it could be Jerome's attempt (following Aq or Sym?) at a more contextually appropriate translation. [43]Jer 32:2, 24; 37:5; 39:1-2; 52:4-5. [44]Heb *hpqd*. See Jer 5:7-9 on the meaning of "visitation." [45]Jerome agrees with Aq, who translated the Hebrew *'šq* ("oppression, extortion," KB 897) with the Greek word *sykophantia* ("slander"). [46]The Hebrew has *bwr* and the LXX has *lakkos*, both of which mean "cistern" according to Jerome. The OL had translated the Greek *lakkos* into Latin as *lacus* ("pool"), which can refer generally to any kind of hollow of water, such as a pond, a cistern or even a basin. In his comments, Jerome uses his linguistic knowledge in order to clarify the proper meaning of the LXX's *lakkos*. [47]Rom 12:11. [48]Mt 24:12. [49]Ps 28:1. The Hebrew *bwr*, translated by Jerome as "cistern" at Jer 6:7, is also used at Ps 28:1, where most translations render it as "the pit." [50]When Jerome gives the Hebrew as *bwr*, he is in agreement with the Ketiv against the Qere (see the Introduction). Technically speaking, *gubba* is a Syriac word (cf. *Vit. Paul.* 6), but it may also have been in use among Hebrew speakers in Jerome's day. [51]Heb 12:6.

this verse: "With pain and with the lash you will be disciplined, O Jerusalem."

6:9: *"Thus says the Lord of hosts: 'They shall glean thoroughly as a vine the remnant of Israel; like a grape gatherer pass your hand again to your basket.' "* LXX: *"For thus says the Lord of hosts:*[52] *'Glean! Glean as a vine the remnant of Israel! Return like a grape gatherer to his basket.' "*

Some take these words in a good sense, others in a bad. In a good sense: "Even though Jerusalem will be laid waste, a remnant will be saved." In a bad sense: "Let not even one cluster or a small grape be left on the vine, but let everything be gathered in. And whatever you find you should throw into a basket like a grape gatherer, so that you lead away captives to Babylon just like a gatherer takes grapes to the winepress."

6:10: *"To whom shall I speak and give warning, that they may hear? Behold, their"*—or *"your"*—*"ears are uncircumcised and cannot listen."*[53]

They cannot hear because they are unwilling to "circumcise" their ears. The fact that this is impossible for them does not void the punishment, since the impossibility derives from their own contempt and infidelity. Therefore, anyone who does not accept the words of God and who does not understand his precepts is said to have "uncircumcised ears." It should be noted that there are three kinds of circumcision in the Scriptures: of the foreskin, of the heart[54] and of the ears. Similarly the Lord says, "He who has ears to hear, let him hear."[55] The reason why we do not accept the word of God is because we are not willing to do so. As a consequence, the word of God becomes a reproach for us. That which was given for our salvation is turned into punishment because of our vice.

6:11a: *"Therefore I am full of the wrath of the Lord; I am weary of holding it in."* LXX: *"I fulfilled my wrath; yet I held back, and I did not utterly destroy them."*

According to the Hebrew, this is said out of the *persona* of the prophet: that he foresees the coming anger of God, that he is filled with the Lord's furious wrath and that he can no longer bear up under it; what is more, he dare not intercede on behalf of the people's sins. But according to the LXX there is a new sense, so that the Lord himself is speaking: "I fulfilled my wrath" by striking this sinful people; and yet he restrained his fury and did not pour it forth fully, so that a remnant would be saved. But it seems to me that this sense contradicts itself. For if he "fulfilled" his wrath, how could it have been "held back," so that it was not fulfilled?

6:11b-12a: *"Pour"*—or *"he poured"*[56]—*"it out on the children in the street and on the gatherings of young men; both husband and wife shall be taken, the old folk and the very aged. Their houses shall be turned over to others, their fields and wives together."*

Perhaps the prophet, in the Spirit, is commanding the Babylonians who are to come that they should pour out the wrath of the Lord on the children, and that those of innocent age likewise should not be spared; or, more likely, he is narrating what has already happened to the "gatherings of young men" who set out to fight the Babylonian army. "Both the husband and wife shall be

---

[52]Jerome's copy of the LXX contained the phrase "of hosts," which is found in only a select number of Greek witnesses preserved for the LXX. [53]Jerome's "their ears" agrees with MT and most ancient versions, whereas Jerome's copy of the LXX read "your ears," as is preserved in a few witnesses to the LXX. [54]Deut 10:16; 30:6; Jer 4:4; 9:26. [55]E.g., Mt 11:15; Mk 4:9; Lk 8:8. [56]Jerome's "pour" (imperative) matches MT. Jerome's copy of the LXX read, "He poured" (most LXX witnesses: "I will pour").

taken"—those with the dearest names for each other will experience captivity together. "The old folk and the very aged" shows that the most advanced age is not "old" but "very aged."[57] In our language, we call these people "elderly" or "decrepit." It goes on: "Their houses shall be turned over to others"—because of the evil of captivity; "their fields and wives together"—both their spouses and their possessions are turned over to the enemies. Whatever we understand according to the letter as it relates to Jerusalem, we refer according to the spiritual understanding to the church, if the church has offended God.

6:12b-14: *"For I will stretch out my hand against the inhabitants of the land, says the Lord. For from the least to the greatest of them, every one is greedy for unjust gain; and from prophet to priest, every one deals falsely. They have healed the wound of my people with dishonor, saying, 'Peace, peace,' when there is no peace."*

What is written in the Hebrew as "I will stretch out my hand against sinners" or "against the inhabitants of the land" in the LXX is always written as "I will raise my hand."[58] Both of these actions are characteristic of one who is about to strike, according to what is written: "and the hand of the Lord is stretched out"—or "lifted up"—"still."[59] Moreover, the "inhabitants of the land" are always associated with vice, as it says frequently in the Apocalypse: "Woe to the inhabitants of the land!"[60]

"From the least to the greatest of them, every one is greedy for unjust gain"—this follows the apostolic saying: "Greed is the root of all evils."[61] "And from prophet to priest, every one deals falsely"—the one by prophesying falsehood, the other by interpreting the

law of God perversely (for a prophet says in another place, "seek the Law from the priests"[62]). "And after they did all this," he says, "they announced to my people all kinds of favorable things, as if they desired to heal the wounds and shame of my daughter. They said, 'Peace, peace,' when there was no peace at all."

This should properly be understood with respect to priests and teachers who promise favorable things to the rich and to those whom they see to be stationed in the highest positions of honor. These priests and teachers preach the clemency of God instead of preparing the rich and the highly stationed for punishment and wrath.

6:15a: *"Were they ashamed when they committed abomination? No, they were not at all ashamed; they did not know how to blush."*

This should be read curtly according to the Hebrew. "After they had done all these things," he says, "were they at all ashamed? Did they blush at their evil deeds? No, they just intensified their scorning and did not know how to blush." Either the expression "did not know how" is used here for "did not want"; or else scorning and vice were so deeply rooted within this evil people that they could not even understand how to blush.

6:15b: *"Therefore they shall fall among those who fall; at the time that I punish them, they shall be overthrown, says the Lord."*

He says, "Because they did not know how to blush, and they lacked not only the deed of repentance but also the awareness and knowledge of how to repent, those among them who formerly stood will fall. They shall be overthrown on account of their own vices, and

---

[57]The Hebrew idiom is "full of days" (thus Jerome's *plenus dierum*). [58]Although the expression "to raise up the hand" does occur in the LXX, it is not used in Jer 6:12 and is not the most common way to express this idiom in the LXX. Jerome's statement that this idiom is "always" expressed this way in the LXX is incorrect. [59]Is 5:25. [60]Rev 8:13. [61]1 Tim 6:10. [62]Hag 2:11.

when the time comes for their punishment and penalty they will be gathered together with those who are falling." Indeed, not only is it important to be on guard against sin, but also it is great impiety to refuse to understand sin or to make no distinction between good works and evil works.

6:16-19a: *"Thus says the Lord: 'Stand by the roads, and look, and ask for the ancient paths, where the good way is; and walk in it, and find refreshment'— or 'purification'*[63]*—'for your souls.' But they said, 'We will not walk'—or 'go'—'in it.' I set watchmen over you, saying, 'Give heed to the sound of the trumpet!' But they said, 'We will not give heed.' Therefore hear, O nations,"—or "the nations heard"—"and know, O congregation,"—or "and you who shepherd the flocks"* (or according to Symmachus: *"know the testimony that is against them"*)[64]*—"what will happen to them. Hear, O earth!"*

There is a Gospel parable that, if understood, supplies the right understanding of this passage. In this parable, a good merchant sells all of his pearls so that he can use the money to buy one pearl of great value.[65] This means that through the patriarchs and prophets we come to him who said, "I am the way."[66] Therefore, one should "stand" on the prophets and diligently contemplate and "ask for the ancient (or eternal) paths," which are well worn with the tracks of many saints (the Greek word for "paths," *triboi*, expresses this better).[67] This path is the "good way" in the Gospel, and we should walk in it.[68] The good way, once it has been found, supplies "refreshment" or "purification" to the souls of those who believe.

But some respond in the negative: "We will not walk in the way of the gospel." The

prophet says this specifically with respect to the Jews. Immediately he continues: "I set watchmen over you." There is no doubt but that this indicates the chorus of apostles, as in Ezekiel: "Son of man, I have made you a watchman for the house of Israel."[69] "And I commanded that you give heed to the 'sound of the trumpet,'" that is, the 'commands of the gospel' or the 'teaching of the apostles,'" according to Isaiah: "Get you up to a high mountain, you who preach the gospel to Zion; lift up your voice like a trumpet, you who announce the gospel to Jerusalem."[70] Those who say, "We will not give heed," are the ones who were invited but refuse to come to the feast.[71] For this reason it is said, "Hear, O nations!" This is what the apostles did: "It was necessary that the word of God should be spoken first to you. Since you thrust it from you and judge yourselves unworthy of eternal life, behold, we turn to the nations."[72]

"And know, O congregation"—this is not the Jewish congregation but the congregation of all nations; or it is "you who shepherd the flocks"—the bishops, presbyters and the whole ecclesiastical order; or else, "know the testimony that is against them," for "the testimony of the Lord is sure, making wise the simple."[73] To these the Lord says, "Fear not, simple flock,"[74] and, "Behold, I and my children whom God has given to me."[75]

"Know, therefore, what will happen to the people who do not believe." As for what is added, "Hear, O earth!"—the whole earth is summoned to hear, as we read at the beginning of Isaiah: "Hear, O heavens, and give ear, O earth."[76] The whole earth is summoned to hear what God is going to do to the people of the Jews.

---

[63]Jerome agrees with Aq; Heb *mrgw'* ("resting place," KB 631). [64]Jerome: "Hear, O nations, and know, O congregation." LXX: "The nations heard, and you who shepherd the flocks" (a better rendering of the LXX would be "and they who shepherd their flocks"). According to our evidence, the rendering "know the testimony that is against them" is that of Aq, not Sym. [65]Mt 13:45-46. [66]Jn 14:6. [67]The Greek *tribos* can be used in a metaphorical sense, referring to the "path of life." [68]Mt 7:14. [69]Ezek 3:17. [70]Is 40:9. Jerome's recollection of this verse fails him in a few details, including the fact that the key phrase, "like a trumpet," is not there. [71]Mt 22:3; Lk 14:16-20. [72]Acts 13:46. [73]Ps 19:7. [74]Lk 12:32. [75]Is 8:18. [76]Is 1:2.

6:19b: *"I am bringing evil on this people, the fruit of their thoughts,"—or "apostasy"*[77]— *"because they have not given heed to my words; and as for my law, they have rejected it."*

He calls "evil" the punishments and penalties that he is bringing, not on the nations who are called to the truth of the gospel but on this people who said, "We will not give heed."[78] The people will receive the "fruit" of their "thoughts" or "apostasies," as blessed David says: "You shall eat the fruit of the labor of your hands."[79] And the reason for all of this is clear: they did not heed the words of the Lord, and they rejected his law.

6:20: *"To what purpose does frankincense come to me from Sheba, or sweet cane from a distant land? Your burnt offerings are not acceptable, nor your sacrifices pleasing to me."*

That frankincense comes from Sheba no one doubts; thus the Virgilian phrase "And its hundred altars steam with Sabaean incense."[80] Moreover, "sweet cane," which in Hebrew is *cane*,[81] and which the LXX and Theodotion translated as "cinnamon," is shown by the prophetic word to come from a faraway land, which we understand to be India, from where many perfumes come through the Red Sea. This particular kind of spice physicians call *quill-cassia*.[82] And this is the sense: "It is in vain that you offer to me your sweet-smelling spices and your burnt offerings, even though you have performed acts of anointing that were commanded in the law;[83] for you have not done my will in the law." This is what was said above: "They have not given heed to my words; and as for my law, they have rejected it."[84] This may rightly be applied to those who offer sacrifices from what has been taken

by violence and from the plundering of the destitute[85] and then suppose that by this mercy taken from iniquity they are ransoming their sins.[86] Scripture says, "The ransom of a man's soul is his wealth"[87]—yet, not wealth derived from iniquity but wealth gathered by hard work and righteousness.

6:21: *"Therefore thus says the Lord: 'Behold, I will lay before this people devastations, and they shall be devastated by them,'—or 'weakness, and they shall become weak by them'*[88]— *'fathers and sons together, neighbor and friend shall perish.'"*

We see that everything the Lord threatened against this people has been fulfilled. For daily they are devastated by their blasphemies; there is nothing of strength in them, but every one among them is weak. Sons follow the blasphemies of their fathers, and every day they receive this curse: "His blood be on us and on our children!"[89] And not only they but also their "neighbors and friends"—all who follow the law and the prophets according to the letter that kills and not according to the Spirit that gives life—all of them perish equally, because all have sinned equally.[90]

6:22-23: *"Thus says the Lord: 'Behold, a people is coming from the north country, a great nation is stirring from the farthest parts of the earth. They lay hold on bow and shield,'—or 'spear'*[91]—*'they are cruel'—or 'impudent'—'and have no mercy, the sound of them is like the roaring sea; they ride on horses, set in array as a man for battle, against you, O daughter of Zion!'"*

Strictly speaking, this prophecy relates to the Babylonians, who are going to come against

---

[77]Heb *mhsbh* ("thought"; Jerome = Aq). The LXX's "apostasy" reflects the Hebrew *mšwbh*. [78]Jer 6:17. [79]Ps 128:2. [80]Virgil *Aen.* 1.416-417. [81]Heb *qāneh*. [82]Jerome gives the Greek name *kassia syringos*. See Galen 14.73 (ed. C. G. Kühn); cf. Dioscurides *Of Medicinal Materials* 1.13. [83]Ex 25:6; 30:25; 35:8. [84]Jer 6:19. [85]Mal 1:13. [86]Dan 4:27. [87]Prov 13:8. [88]Heb *mkšlym* ("stumbling blocks"), *wkšlw bām* ("they shall stumble on them"). [89]Mt 27:25. [90]2 Cor 3:6. [91]Heb *kydwn* ("scimitar," KB 472).

the people of Jerusalem. The whole array of their weapons and the charge of the attackers is described so that the people of Jerusalem, struck with terror at the sound of all this, might repent and plead for God's mercy. Finally, he gives them an opportunity to ask when he says "against you, O daughter of Zion!" We can make use of this testimony in a time of persecution, when all the madness of the devil is stirred up against us without mercy. Like the most violent waves of the sea they crush those who resist.

6:24: *"We have heard the report of it, our hands fall helpless; anguish has taken hold of us, pain as of a woman in travail."*

The prophet (or rather, the Lord through the prophet) threatened the people that the Babylonians would come; and now the people respond that even before the Babylonians come, they are overwhelmed with fear, they cannot lift their hands, and anguish has seized them like the pain of a woman in travail. They assert that nothing they have experienced is more severe than this pain.

6:25: *"Do not go into the field or walk on the road, for the enemy has a sword, terror is on every side."*

The Gospel teaches that one should not go out into the field or come down from the house-top[92] but should instead heed this: "Escape to the mountain,"[93] to where we are told to hasten and go up in Isaiah and in Micah.[94] According to the letter, the people are commanded not to

go outside or beyond the city walls but to protect themselves with strong fortifications.

6:26: *"O daughter of my people, gird on sackcloth, and roll in ashes; mourn as for an only-begotten"*—or *"beloved"*[95]—*"son, most bitter"*—or *"pitiable"*[96]—*"lamentation; for suddenly the destroyer"*—or *"misery"*—*"will come on us."*—or *"on you."*

Since earlier he said, "Do not go forth into the field or walk on the road, for the enemy has a sword, terror is on every side,"[97] thereby forbidding them to flee, he now teaches them what they should do: namely, be converted to repentance, which is the firmest and most secure armor. Where we said "mourn as for an only-begotten son," in place of "only-begotten" in the Hebrew it is written *iaid*, which means "only" rather than "only-begotten."[98] If "beloved" or "lovable" had been meant, as the LXX translated, then *ididia* would have been written, which is the name that God gave to Solomon.[99] Nothing is more painful than to lose a "lone" or "only" son. And for what we translated "suddenly the destroyer (or "misery") will come on us," the LXX put "on you," although God said, with much more compassion, that whatever is going to come on his people he regards as also coming on himself.[100] The "destroyer" signifies properly either Nebuchadnezzar or the devil.

6:27-30: *"I have made you a strong tester among my people, that you may know and test their ways. All the leaders are crooked,"*—or *"disobedient"*[101]—*"going about deceptively"*—

---

[92]Mt 24:17-18. [93]Gen 19:17. [94]Is 2:3; Mic 4:2. [95]Jerome matches Aq and Sym. [96]Jerome matches Aq and Sym. [97]Jer 6:25. [98]Even though Jerome had used *unigenitus* ("only-begotten") for the Hebrew word *yāḥîd* in his IH edition and in the lemma of the commentary, he now clarifies that *yāḥîd* does not technically express the idea of being only-*begotten* but means "only" or "alone" (*solitarius*). [99]The Hebrew name Jedidiah (see 2 Sam 12:25) is made up of two elements: the divine name at the end (*yh*) and the word *beloved* (*yādîd*) at the beginning. Jerome is telling the reader what the Hebrew text would have needed to be for the translation of the LXX to be correct. It seems that he also wishes for the reader to see how similar the Hebrew words are (*yāḥîd* and *yādîd*), so as to explain the error. [100]The presentation of God in the Hebrew text ("on us") is more compassionate than that of the LXX ("on you"), since according to the Hebrew God includes himself as one of the recipients of the destruction. [101]Jerome agrees with Aq; Heb *sôrĕrîm*. According to KB 770, this verb is from *srr* and means "to be stubborn." Aq and Jerome are deriving it from *swr* ("to turn aside," KB 748).

47

or "perversely"; "they are bronze and iron, all of them act corruptly. The bellows"—which the Greeks more vividly call physētēra[102]*— "blow fiercely, the lead is consumed by the fire; in vain the metal caster"—or "silversmith"*[103]*— "melts down the metal, for the wicked are not removed. Refuse silver they are called, for the Lord has rejected them."*

The prophet is given to the unbelieving people as a "strong" tester, which in Hebrew is *mabsar*, which means either "fortified" according to Aquila or "enclosed" or "encompassed" according to Symmachus and the LXX.[104] Thus, the prophet as a "strong" tester is like a strongly protected city, such that he need not fear the wicked plots of the people. "Once you have tested them," he says, "and you have come to know the ways of my delinquent people, then you will understand that silver mixed with copper can in no way be purified." For just as lead is mixed together with impure and polluted metals in order to separate out foreign substances, and if by chance the metals are not purged, then all the lead is consumed and reduced to nothing, so also all the eloquence of doctrine and the prophetic word perish in those who despise to hear them. We may say that they are also like deaf snakes that shut their ears so that they cannot hear the sound of the charmers. For "in vain the metal caster (or 'silversmith') melts down the metal, for the wicked are not removed." Thus, they are not called 'silver' but "refuse silver," "for the Lord has rejected

them." Moreover, the leaders are deviating from the Lord, or "disobedient," going about "deceptively" or "perversely."

7:1-2: *"The word that came to Jeremiah from the Lord: 'Stand in the gate of the Lord's house, and proclaim'—or 'read'*[105]*—'there this word, and say, Hear the word of the Lord, all you men of Judah who enter these gates to worship the Lord.' "*

This passage is not in the edition of the LXX but was added out of the Hebrew from Theodotion. The prophet is commanded to stand in the Lord's gate, through which the multitude of people enter in order to pray to the Lord, so that they may be able on this occasion to hear what the Lord commands. Through this we understand the hardness of the Jewish people. They had prophets who were like liars and madmen, yet they listened to the words of the Lord not because they were the Lord's words but only because they were forced to do so on this occasion where everyone was assembled at this place.

7:3: *"Thus says the Lord of hosts, the God of Israel, make good"—or "amend"*[106]*—"your ways and your pursuits,"—or "your inventions"*[107]*—"and I will dwell with you in this place"—or "I will make you dwell in this place."*[108]

A merciful physician desires to heal the wounded with every kind of remedy possible.

---

[102]The Greek word for "bellows" is etymologically connected to the word "to blow." [103]Jerome matches Aq and Sym. [104]Heb *mbṣr* ("fortified city," KB 542-43, but some doubt is expressed as to the sense at Jer 6:27). Jerome's copy of the LXX contained the word *enclosed*, as is found in many LXX witnesses, although the grammatical form in Greek agrees not with "tester" but with "people" (or "peoples"), that is, "enclosed people/s." Other LXX witnesses have "tested peoples." The evidence for Aq is diverse: Jerome says that Aq translated "fortified," but one MS indicates that Aq and Th put "strong." Yet, Jerome differs from all the Greek versions in construing "strong" or "fortified" with "tester" and not with "people." The Hebrew word order is: "A tester-I have made you-among my people-strong." In Hebrew, "strong" could be taken either with "people" or with "tester." [105]The alterative rendering ("read") is Th. Cf. Jer 2:1-2a; 3:12; 19:1-3a. [106]Heb *yṭb*, "to be good," in the Hiphil (thus, "make good"); cf. Aq and Sym. [107]Heb *m'll* ("deeds," KB 614). The LXX and Jerome in the IH edition translated this word as "pursuits." The rendering "doings" is Jerome's updated translation (Aq and Sym are lacking). Cf. the IH edition at Ezek 14:23; 24:14; 26:19; Hos 7:2; 12:3; Zech 1:6. [108]Jerome presumes the Qal of *škn*, "I will dwell with you" (= Aq), whereas the LXX (= MT) presumes the Piel, "I will make you dwell."

But when he says "make good (or "amend") your ways," he shows that their ways are perverse and that there is nothing good in them. And since it is natural for each person to love his native soil and to regard nothing as dearer than his native land, he sets forth the rewards for obedience: "I will dwell with you," he says, "so that I may keep you safe from occupation." Or, according to Symmachus, who says, "I will confirm you in this place," he is saying, "I will establish you with a secure dwelling."

7:4-7: "Do not trust in these deceptive words: 'This is the temple of the Lord, the temple of the Lord, the temple of the Lord.' For if you amend well"—or "if you amend"[109]—"your ways and your pursuits, if you truly execute justice, one with another, if you do not cheat"—or "oppress"—"the alien, the fatherless or the widow, or shed innocent blood in this place, and if you do not go after other gods to your own hurt, then I will dwell with you"—or "make you dwell"[110]—"in this place, in the land that I gave of old to your fathers forever."

That which the LXX added at the beginning of this passage, deceptive words "that will not profit you in any way," is not found in the Hebrew. This warning was given to the Jewish people at that time, and it is given today to us in the church who appear to be firmly established, that we should not put our trust in the splendor of our buildings, and in our paneled ceilings overlaid with gold and in our walls adorned with mosaics of marble, and say, "This is the temple of the Lord, the temple of the Lord, the temple of the Lord." For the "temple of the Lord" is that place in which true faith dwells, where there is holy conversation and a chorus of all the virtues.

Then he adds, "If you correct your ways, if your thoughts are not diverted toward error but you follow justice and refrain from doing evil, if you do not shed innocent blood, the blood of the simple and those made to stumble,[111] and if you do not go after other gods, adoring perverse dogmas that you have projected from your heart to your own hurt, then I will dwell with you in this place, which you call the temple of God, and in the land that I gave to your ancestors, who are the apostles and apostolic men (or "then I will make you dwell with a secure standing"[112]), from beginning to end."

This may also apply to virgins who boast of their purity and display their chastity with an impudent expression on their faces, even though their consciences reflect a different state of affairs. They do not know this apostolic definition of virginity: "to be holy in body and spirit."[113] For what does it profit to have a pure body if the mind is depraved and the other virtues that the prophetic word describes are lacking?

7:8-10: "Behold, you trust in words of deception"—or "deceptive words"[114]—"to no avail. Will you steal, murder, commit adultery, swear falsely, burn incense to Baal and go after other gods that you have not known, and then come and stand before me in this house, which is called by my name, and say, 'We are delivered because we have done all these abominations?' —or 'We have refrained from doing all these abominations!' "[115]

This list of sins shows that it is useless for them to put their trust in the temple. For what does it profit them to go boldly to the threshold of the house of God and stand with their

---

[109]Jerome's "well" is an attempt to translate the Hebrew cognate infinitive absolute form modifying the main verb. The alternative leaves this form untranslated. [110]See n. 108. [111]Mt 18:6. [112]This paraphrase is a blending of the LXX and Sym; see Jer 7:3. [113]1 Cor 7:34. [114]Jerome's rendering is more literalistic. [115]Jerome matches Aq and Sym (= MT).

heads held high, when not only their hearts but also their hands are stained with robbery, murder, adultery, perjury, sacrilege and the worship of gods that they have not known? This happens spiritually in the church whenever people reflect on their present good fortune and fail to reckon with their sins, supposing that these sins have escaped God's notice because punishment did not come right away. Moreover, they burst forth in such great madness that they think themselves "delivered" simply because after their evil deeds they also withdrew from worshiping the Lord.

7:11: "Has this house,"—or "my house,"[116]— "which is called by my name, become a den of robbers in your eyes? Behold, I myself have seen it, says the Lord."

Part of this passage is taken up in the Gospel: "It is written, 'My house shall be called a house of prayer,' but you make it a den of robbers,"[117] or, as it is written in another Gospel, "a house of trade."[118] The church of God is turned into a den of robbers when robbery, murder, adultery, perjury, sacrilege, the invention of heresy, and all such evils are going on within it, when its leaders are inflamed with the fire of greed and when the wealth of kings takes the place of a wretched (but in truth not wretched) cloak. Thus he adds, "Behold, I myself have seen it, says the Lord." "My eyes have seen what you think in secret; the darkness of your treasure houses has not escaped my notice." He who, though he was rich, yet for our sakes became poor,[119] is ashamed of our riches and says, "Woe to you that are rich, for you have received your consolation."[120]

7:12: "Go now to my place that was in Shiloh, where I made my name dwell at first, and see

what I did to it for the wickedness of my people Israel."

He draws from the past in order to teach in the present. To those who say, "This is the temple of the Lord, the temple of the Lord, the temple of the Lord," and who delight in the splendor of this costly edifice, he recounts the *historia* of Shiloh, where the tabernacle of God first resided.[121] It is also written about this in the psalm: "He forsook his dwelling at Shiloh."[122] Just as that place was reduced to ruin and ashes, so also the temple will come to ruin, since it is the abode of similar sins. Therefore, just as Shiloh was an example for the temple, so also the temple should be an example for us, when we come to the time of this testimony: "When the Son of man comes, will he find faith on earth?"[123]

7:13-15: "And now, because you have done all these things, says the Lord, and when I spoke to you, rising early and speaking, you did not listen, and when I called you, you did not answer, therefore I will do to the house that is called by my name, and in which you trust, and to the place that I gave to you and to your fathers, as I did to Shiloh. And I will cast you out of my sight, as I cast out all your kinsmen, all the offspring of Ephraim."

That which we translated "rising early and speaking" is not present in the LXX. God rises early, not because he has any need of the dawn but because the spirit of humankind is better able to hear and do what is said after the quiet of night, when the strength of the body has been restored and the spirit, more lively, is not occupied with pleasures and with the desire for food. Thus, we also read in the psalm: "In the morning you hear my voice, in the morning I prepare a sacrifice for you, and

---

[116]Jerome agrees with Aq, Sym and Th (= MT). [117]Mt 21:13; Mk 11:17; Lk 19:46. [118]Jn 2:16. [119]2 Cor 8:9. [120]Lk 6:24. [121]Josh 18:1; 1 Sam 4:3. [122]Ps 78:60. [123]Lk 18:8.

watch";[124] and in Isaiah: "My soul rises up to thee in the early morning (or "at dawn"), O God, for your judgments are a light on the earth."[125] So also the apostle Paul calls the brothers "sons of light" and "not of night or of darkness"; they are not like "those who sleep," who do not understand the commands of God.[126] Therefore, because God rose in the early morning and summoned them to be free from the darkness, he threatens that he is going to bring judgments on the temple in Jerusalem similar to those he brought on Shiloh, where the tabernacle was first located,[127] so that similar sins might be cut down by similar judgments. And just as God cast out the offspring of Ephraim, that is, the ten tribes, which are called Israel but which had leaders from the tribe of Ephraim on account of Jeroboam the son of Nebat[128] (this nation is also called Joseph), so also he vows that he is going to cast out Jerusalem and the tribe of Judah (along with Benjamin). He cast out the ten tribes; he will cast out the two. And whatever was said to that people, let us understand it as applying to us if we do similar things.

7:16: *"As for you, do not pray for this people, and do not lift up for them praise or prayer,"*— or *"do not ask that they be shown mercy"*[129]— *"and do not get in my way, for I do not hear you."*

Lest it appear that the prophet is asking God not to bring about what he has been threatening, God commands the prophet not to pray for the people, who are sinners and offer no

repentance. And when he says "do not get in my way," it shows that the prayers of the saints are able to check the anger of God. Thus, the Lord says to Moses, "Let me alone, that I may consume this people; but of you I will make a great nation";[130] and in the psalm it is written, "Then Phinehas stood up and interposed, and the plague was stayed. And that has been reckoned to him as righteousness."[131] Aaron also took his censer with fire and stood among the people who were about to be consumed, and the anger of God was stayed.[132] And so that we do not think that God is cruel for not allowing him even to ask, he explains the reason why he will not listen, saying:

7:17-19: *"Do you not see what they are doing in the cities of Judah and in the streets of Jerusalem? The children gather wood, the fathers kindle fire, and the women knead dough, to make cakes"—or "chavonas"*[133]— *"for the queen"—or "host"*[134]—*"of heaven; and they pour out drink offerings to other gods, to provoke me to anger. Is it I whom they provoke? says the Lord. Is it not themselves, to their own confusion?"*

He says, "Do you want to know, O prophet, why I said to you, 'Do not pray for this people'? It is because they have done the following: both inside and outside, in the streets and on the byways, the children collect wood, the fathers kindle fire, and the women knead dough with flour, in order to make *chavonim*," which we translated as "cakes," or else as "preparations,"[135] "so as to indicate every kind of sacrifice to the queen of heaven." We should

---

[124]See Ps 5:3. [125]Cf. Is 26:9. Jerome's memory fails him at several points in citing this verse. For "in the early morning," Jerome had given a more accurate rendering of the Hebrew in his IH edition (*in nocte*), but here he translates the phrase *de nocte* (literally, "from the night," an idiom for early morning), under the influence of the present context. [126]Cf. 1 Thess 5:5-8. [127]See n. 121. [128]Cf. 1 Kings 11:26. [129]Jerome is in basic agreement with Aq and MT. Jerome's rendering of the LXX represents a text found in some MS witnesses and Tertullian. Other copies of the LXX read, "Do not resolve to petition about them." [130]Ex 32:10. [131]Ps 106:30-31. [132]Num 16:46-48. [133]Heb *kwnym* (from *kawwān*, "sacrificial cake" [KB 466]). The LXX, Aq, Sym and Th merely transliterated the word. [134]Jerome's reading ("queen," as in MT) matches all of the hexaplaric versions. For the LXX's "host," cf. Jer 8:2. [135]The translation "preparations" comes from connecting the word *kwnym* to the verbal root *kwn*, which in the Hiphil means "to prepare."

interpret the "queen of heaven" to be the moon; but if it is the "host of heaven," then all of the stars are meant.

And after this it says, "they pour out drink offerings to other gods"—not that they really are gods, but under the names of gods the people are burning incense to demons—and by doing this, they "provoke me to anger." "These wretched people do not understand that their obstinacy does not harm me, as I am in no way altered by anger, but rather it is they who are harmed, to their own confusion and eternal disgrace." Therefore, whatever we do, we do not harm God, who cannot be harmed. Instead, we make preparations for our own destruction, storing up wrath for the day of wrath.[136] He mentions the various household members, the "children," the "fathers" and the "mothers" (or "wives"), in order to show that there was no age group that was dissenting from this impiety.

7:20: "Therefore thus says the Lord God: Behold, my anger and my wrath are kindled"—or "will fall in drops"[137]—"on this place, on man and beast, on the trees of the field and the fruit of the ground; it will burn and not be quenched."

Since above he said, "Is it I whom they provoke?"[138] how can he now say, "Behold, my anger and my wrath will fall in drops on this place"? This is the sense: "I, by my nature, do not become angry; but they have acted in such a way as would provoke me to anger, so I appear to them to have changed my nature. Therefore, they perceive me as being angry because they have done all they could to make me so." And beautifully it does not say "my anger will be poured out on this place," but rather, "my anger will fall in drops," thus

indicating moderation in punishment. And if there is so much severity in a drop of God's wrath, what would happen if a whole rain shower were poured out? But the idea of "kindling" can be understood thus: that which he refused to do for a long time he is now compelled to do because of the multitude of their sins. And since God has become angry, both human beings and human affairs will experience a similar annihilation. "It will burn"—no doubt the anger of the Lord—"and not be quenched," since the people are not doing the things through which it could be quenched.

7:21-23: Thus says the Lord of hosts, the God of Israel: "Add your burnt offerings to your sacrifices, and eat the flesh. For in the day that I brought them out of the land of Egypt, I did not speak to your fathers or command them concerning burnt offerings and sacrifices. But this command I gave them, 'Obey my voice, and I will be your God, and you shall be my people; and walk in all the way that I command you, that it may be well with you.'"

Having condemned their temple, he consequently condemns their sacrifices and charges them obliquely that they offered sacrifices not out of reverence for him but out of a desire for sumptuous feasts. Regarding the statement, "I did not speak to your fathers or command them, in the day that I brought them out of the land of Egypt, concerning burnt offerings and sacrifices," he clearly means that at first he gave them the Decalogue on stone tablets written with the finger of God,[139] but after the offense of idolatry in the passage about the calf,[140] he ordered that sacrifices be made to him rather than to demons, setting aside the true religion of the commandments of God

---

[136]Rom 2:5. [137]Jerome's rendering is "are kindled," whereas "will fall in drops" represents Aq and Sym. The LXX translated "are poured out." The verb that Jerome uses, *conflare*, can be used for "melting down" or "smelting"; on this meaning for the Hebrew word *ntk*, see KB 732-33 and Middle Hebrew. [138]Jer 7:19. [139]Ex 31:18; Deut 9:10. [140]Ex 32.

and granting by concession the blood of sacrificial victims and the need for animal flesh.

7:24-25a: *"But they did not obey or incline their ear, but walked in their own choices"—or "desires"*[141]*—"and the stubbornness of their evil hearts, and went backward and not forward, from the day that your fathers came out of the land of Egypt to this day."*

Although God said, "Obey my voice, and I will be your God,"[142] "they did not obey or incline their ear" but instead did the desires of their hearts, acting contrary to the opinion of the apostle who forgot what was behind and strained forward to what was ahead,[143] so that they longed for what was behind and despised what was to come. And when he says "from the day that your fathers came out of the land of Egypt to this day," he says that they spent all the time in between offending God. This is why the grace of the gospel was necessary. For the gospel saved them not by their own merit but by the mercy of the Lord.

7:25b-26: *"I have sent to you my servants the prophets by day, rising at dawn and sending them; yet they did not listen to me or incline their ear but stiffened their neck. They did worse than their fathers."*

Just, therefore, is the anger of God, which was kindled against (or will fall like drops on) these people who are contemptuous, have stiff necks and refuse to listen to the word of God. We have explained above the manner in which God sends prophets both in the day and in the early morning (or at dawn).[144]

7:27-28: *"So you shall speak all these words to them, but they will not listen to you. You shall call to them, but they will not answer you. And you shall say to them, 'This is the nation that did not obey the voice of the Lord their God and did not accept discipline; faith has perished; it is cut off from their lips.'"*

"Lest you doubt," he says, "that they have stiffened their neck and done worse than their fathers,[145] I will give an opportunity for repentance. But I am not saying 'they will not listen' in order to bring about that outcome. Rather, since this is what is going to happen, I predict it. But at any rate, speak my words to them even though 'they will not listen to you; you shall call to them, but they will not answer you.' For their pride is so great that, although you call them to listen, none of them will deem it worthwhile to answer. And so you will say to them: 'This is the nation that did not obey the voice of the Lord their God and did not accept discipline.'" Beautifully, as I already said before,[146] he calls them not a "people" but a "nation."

Although this happened in part during the prophet's time, happening first as a shadow and an image,[147] it was fulfilled more fully in Christ, when they were not willing to accept discipline and despised the voice of their Lord. Thus elegantly he adds "faith has perished"—which properly speaking is the faith of Christians; "it is cut off from their lips"—namely, every confession of the Son of God and of the faith.

7:29: *"Cut off your hair and cast it away; raise a lamentation on the height,"—or "on your lips"*[148]*—"for the Lord has rejected and forsaken the generation of his wrath."*

We read that Job, when he heard of the death of his sons and daughters, shaved his head.[149] Among the ancients it was a custom that all

---

[141]Heb *mô'ēṣâ* ("plan," KB 558). [142]Jer 7:23. [143]Phil 3:13. [144]See Jer 7:13-15. [145]Jer 7:26. [146]See Jer 5:7-9. [147]Heb 10:1. [148]Heb *š/śpym*. Jerome's translation, "on the height" (= MT, cf. Sym), presumes *śĕpî* ("bare height"), whereas the LXX's "on your lips" presumes *śāpâ* ("lip"). [149]Job 1:20.

who were grieving would shave their hair. Nowadays, on the contrary, it is conventional for those who mourn to let their hair down. In the prophets, all lamentation and wailing is taken up for this reason: "because the Lord has rejected and forsaken the generation of his wrath." No doubt this indicates the people of the Jews. And properly speaking this should be referred to the time of Christ, when faith perished and was cut off from the lips of people who blasphemed the Lord.[150]

7:30-31: *"For the sons of Judah have done evil in my sight, says the Lord; they have set their abominations in the house that is called by my name, to defile it. And they have built the high places"—or "altar"*[151]*—"of Topheth, which is in the valley of the son of Hinnom, to burn their sons and their daughters in the fire, which I did not command, nor did it come in to my mind."*

That the sons of Judah set up a statue of Baal in the temple of God we learn from the beginning of Ezekiel.[152] The "high places" (which in Hebrew is *bamath*[153]) or "altar" of Topheth, which is in the valley of the sons of Hinnom, represents the place that is watered by the springs of Siloam and is pleasant and wooded, and today offers the delights of gardens. This error of paganism also infested all the provinces, where they offered sacrificial victims at the heads of springs and in pleasant groves; every religious observance of depraved superstition was observed.

Topheth in the Hebrew language is interpreted "width,"[154] and it is said that this is the place written about in the book of Joshua the son of Nun,[155] a place in the valley of the sons of Ennom, which in Hebrew is *gehennom*.[156] Ge, in fact, means *pharanga*,[157] that is, "valley." *Hennom* is either the name of a man or else means "grace."[158] And based on this passage the Hebrews report that the place was called *gehenna* because all the Jewish people who offended God perished there in that very spot where they consecrated their own sons to idols through fire or offered them up as burnt offerings,[159] actions that they were neither commanded to do nor ordered to perform by any sanction of law. But if Jephthah offered up his virgin daughter to God, it was not the sacrifice itself that pleased God, but the spirit of the one who made the offering.[160] For if a hound or a donkey or any unclean animal had met the father first when he returned from slaying the enemy, he was not supposed to offer it up.

7:32-33: *"Therefore, behold, the days are coming, says the Lord, when it will no more be called Topheth or the valley of the son of Hinnom but the valley of slaughter: for they will bury in Topheth, because there is no room elsewhere. And the dead bodies of this people will be food for the birds of the air and for the beasts of the earth; and none will drive them away."*

This refers to a time of siege that they endured from the ninth year of the reign of Zedekiah up to the eleventh year.[161] This valley will no longer be called *gehennom* (that is, the "valley of *hennom*" or "of the sons of Ennom") but "the

---

[150]Jer 7:28. [151]Jerome agrees with Sym. [152]Ezek 8. [153]Heb *bāmôt*. [154]On the location of Topheth, see Eusebius *Onom.* 102. The meaning "width" is based on an etymological connection with the Middle Hebrew (and Aramaic) root *pth* ("to be open/wide"). [155]Josh 15:8; 18:16. [156]Heb *gê' hinnōm* ("the valley of Hinnom"). [157]The Greek word for "valley," which the LXX used to translate *gê'*. See also Jer 2:23a. [158]The Hebrew word related to "grace" is *hinnām*, not *hinnōm*. Jerome may have misread the first letter, or he may be passing on an already established creative etymology. For a creative reading of *hinnōm* as *hinnām*, see *b. Erubin* 19a on Gehenna: "a valley that is as deep as the valley of Hinnom (*hinnōm*) and into which all go down for gratuitous (*hinnām*) acts." [159]In addition to *b. Erubin* 19a (n. 158), see also *Lamentations Rabbah* 1.9.36, where it is said that Topheth (*tōpet*) received its name because of the "seduction" (*topteh*, from *pth*) to idolatry that took place there. See 2 Kings 17:17. [160]Judg 11:29-40. [161]2 Kings 25:1-2.

valley of slaughter," because so many people will be killed there. The slaughter will be so great that in the place of their previous religious observances there will be innumerable tombs. And those whom they will not be able to bury will be torn by birds and eaten by beasts, and there will be none to drive them away, because everyone will fear a similar end and thus fail in their obligation to bury the dead.

We are rushing past the things that are clear so that we may spend more time on whatever passages might be obscure. For the vast size of the book itself can be an aversion to the reader; how much the more so if our discussion of the book is too long!

7:34: "And I will make to cease from the cities of Judah and from the streets of Jerusalem the voice of mirth and the voice of gladness, the voice of the bridegroom and the voice of the bride; for the land shall become a waste."

Just as the place of idolatry would become a tomb, so that on the very spot where they offended God their unburied corpses would lie exposed, so also from the (now ruined) city of Jerusalem and from the other cities under its jurisdiction all gladness will be taken away, and all things will be filled with sadness, groaning and desolation.

8:1-3: "At that time, says the Lord, the bones of the kings of Judah, the bones of its princes, the bones of the priests, the bones of the prophets and the bones of the inhabitants of Jerusalem shall be brought out of their tombs; and they shall be spread before the sun and the moon and all the host of heaven, which they have loved and served, which they have gone

after and which they have sought and worshiped; and they shall not be gathered or buried; they shall be as dung on the surface of the ground. Death shall be preferred to life by all the remnant that remains of this evil family in all the places where I have driven them, says the Lord of hosts."

We have seen all the things that the prophetic word describes happen in our own time, not only to Jerusalem, which suffered under the Babylonians and Romans, but also to the whole world, to the point where tears have run dry and all places are filled with the bones of the dead.

It was customary for them, following an ancient practice, to hide gold and certain ornaments in the tombs of both men and women, and greedy people would break these tombs open and dig them up, exposing the remains to the sky and light. First, the bones of the kings and officials were dug up, and then the bones of the priests and prophets and finally the bones of everyone in Jerusalem, so that all of their bones were taken out of their burial mounds and exposed to the sun and moon, in view of all the stars. Thus, after they abandoned God they were left exposed before those very things that they served, and in this way they decayed and decomposed into a heap of dung and ashes. So if anyone was able to flee from the multitude and escape to some other place, he would still prefer death to life, reckoning destruction to be the best relief for his unhappy soul.

8:4: "You shall say to them, Thus says the Lord: When men fall, do they not rise again? He who turns away, does he not return"—or "does he not turn away?"[162]

---

[162]The Hebrew verb *šwb*, which is used twice at the end of Jer 8:4, can refer to both "turning away" (i.e., apostasy) and "returning" (i.e., repentance). The first alternative ("does he not return?") is Jerome's IH translation. In all likelihood, therefore, the second alternative ("does he not turn away?") represents Jerome's copy of the LXX, since this reading is found in a few LXX MSS, whereas most LXX witnesses have "does he not return."

After these great disasters he now calls those who remain to repent; or else, before the disasters that he threatens take place he urges them toward conversion, providing an opportunity for repentance. That which is written according to the Hebrew, "He who turns away, does he not turn away?" signifies this: if one who has turned away from God wishes to change for the better, that person is able to change the wrath of God into something more favorable, withstand the coming disaster and through prayer avoid destruction.[163]

8:5: "Why then has this people in Jerusalem turned away in obstinate backsliding? They hold fast to deceit, they refuse to return."

"The more I called them to repentance," he says, "the more they withdrew from me, not simply in their fondness for going astray but in their zeal for committing transgressions." For they vigorously "hold fast to deceit"—to idols or to any depravities contrary to truth and justice. And "they refuse to return." He does not say "they are unable"; rather, they pursue injustice with full zeal.

8:6: "I have given heed and listened, but no one speaks what is right; no man repents of his wickedness, saying, 'What have I done?' Every one turns to his own course, like a horse plunging headlong into battle."

Although they were called to repentance, they gave no thought to listening. Not only did they offend the Lord and speak blasphemy, but also, like horses rushing into battle at blazing speed, they failed to ponder their sin and say, "What have I done?"

We understand these things to have been said either concerning the whole human race, since it is prone to error, or concerning the time of the Savior, since "all have turned aside, together they have gone wrong; no one does good, not even one."[164] Therefore he himself cries out, "Save me, Lord, for there is no longer any that is godly."[165] But if this is how things are, then where are those who say that by our will we can be made free from all sin?[166] "No one," he says, "speaks what is right," since we will render account on the day of judgment even for a careless word.[167]

8:7: "Even the kite in the heavens knows her times; and the turtledove, swallow and stork keep the time of their coming; but my people know not the ordinance of the Lord."

In place of "kite," which is what Symmachus translated, the LXX and Theodotion put the Hebrew word itself, *asida*,[168] whereas Aquila translated "heron." Again, in place of "swallow," Symmachus translated "cicada," which in Hebrew is *sis*.[169] Furthermore, in place of what we put as "stork," both Aquila and Symmachus translated *agur*,[170] as it is written in the Hebrew, for which the LXX translated "field sparrows." But the sense is one and the same, which is also written in the beginning of Isaiah: "The ox knows its owner, and the donkey its master's crib; but Israel does not know, my people does not understand."[171] Even little birds understand their times, and they know when they ought to shun the coldness of winter by hastening to warm places and when they should return again to their normal regions at the beginning of spring. We should understand the word

---

[163]Since the same verb is used twice in the Hebrew, Jerome uses the same Latin verb twice in his rendering "according to the Hebrew." It is interesting that what Jerome identifies as the Hebrew reading matches his rendering of the LXX but disagrees with his IH translation. Perhaps in the IH translation he followed the sense of the passage, but here he takes note that it is the same Hebrew form that is repeated, and so he tries to interpret both verbs with the same basic sense of "turning away," although in his paraphrase Jerome takes the first "turning away" as intransitive (= Qal) and the second as transitive (= Hiphil). [164]Rom 3:12; Ps 14:3. [165]Ps 12:1. [166]This is directed against the followers of Pelagius. [167]Mt 12:36. [168]Heb *hăsîdâ*. [169]Heb *sîs* (= Qere). [170]Heb *'āgûr*. [171]Is 1:3.

heavens here to refer simply to the air that is above.

8:8: *"How can you say, 'We are wise, and the law of the Lord is with us'? But behold, the false pen of the scribes has made it into a lie."*

He says this to the scribes and Pharisees, who boast of their knowledge of the law and write iniquity whenever they write. And he says:

8:9a: *"The wise men shall be put to shame, they shall be dismayed and taken"*

. . . not because those who do such things really are wise; but he calls them "wise" so that they may be condemned by their own judgment, and, conversely, so that foolishness may overcome their "wisdom," as Paul says: "You who teach others, will you not teach yourself?"[172] And since

8:9b: *"They have rejected the word of the Lord,"* therefore, ***"No wisdom is in them."***

And so it is in vain that those who ruin doctrine by their works boast about their knowledge of the law.

8:10-11: *"Therefore I will give their women"* —or ***"wives"***[173]—***"to others and their fields to conquerors, because from the least to the greatest every one is greedy for unjust gain; from prophet to priest every one deals falsely"*** —or ***"does injustice."***[174] ***"They have healed the wound of my people lightly, saying 'Peace, peace,' when there is no peace."***

They have received the just recompense for their deeds, because those who rejected the word of the Lord have been abandoned by him.

"Their wives," he says, "and their possessions I will hand over to their enemies. And lest it be thought that my sentence is cruel, let the hearer understand the causes: 'from the least to the greatest every one is greedy for unjust gain'—for greed is the root of all evils.[175] 'From prophet to priest'—those who ought to restrain others from sinning are the first to join in sin. And they all 'do injustice'—as they pillage the possessions of others—or, surely, they 'deal falsely'—such that no truth is in their mouth."[176]

And after doing these things, they—as if they were good doctors—wanted to heal with words the wounds of those very people who had been struck by the blows of all their shameful deeds! We witness this daily among our own people, too, as the apostle says: "You who preach against stealing, do you steal? And so on."[177] There are some who, when they see the wealthy and sinners among us, desire to heal the contrition of the daughter of God's people, that is, the church. But this leads to the disgrace of those who are deceived and the disgrace of those who are deceiving others. They say to those who are covered with every evil deed, "Peace, peace," when there is no peace and the war of sins is near on them.

8:12a: *"Were they ashamed when they committed abomination? No, they were not at all ashamed; they did not know how to blush."*

This should be read as a question,[178] so that the sense is: "Did they blush at their crimes? Did they recognize the abominations that they committed? No, but they broke out in such great madness that they desired neither to emend their wickedness out of shame nor to confess their evils in hope of mercy."

---

[172]Rom 2:21. [173]The same Hebrew (and Greek) word is used both for "women" in general and for "wives." [174]The end of Jer 8:10 is lacking in the LXX. Jerome's "deals falsely" is a closer equivalent to the Hebrew *šeqer* than "does injustice," which is Th (preserved under asterisk). [175]1 Tim 6:10. [176]Mic 6:12; Zeph 3:13. [177]Rom 2:21-23. [178]Jerome uses the Greek term *erōtēmatikōs* ("as a question"). Nothing in the Hebrew explicitly marks this as a question, which is why Jerome must explain it.

8:12b: *"Therefore they shall fall among the fallen; when I punish them, they shall be overthrown, says the Lord."*

This is the reward for those who did not know how to blush: those whose rank was higher than the people share in the people's downfall. *"From the least to the greatest every one is greedy for unjust gain; from prophet to priest every one deals falsely."*[179] And the time "when I punish them" is the approaching captivity.

8:13: *"When I gather them, says the Lord, there are no grapes on the vine or figs on the fig tree; even the leaves are withered, and what I gave them has passed away from them."*

That there is a time coming when the wrongdoers will be overthrown he teaches clearly by saying "when I gather them"—no doubt in Jerusalem, to be besieged by the Babylonians and undergo the hardship of famine. He says, "And when time goes by, and autumn succeeds summer, and in winter the leaves fall from the trees, then you will see all of these things (i.e., the vine, the fig tree, etc.) from afar, but you will not receive any food from them. For 'there are no grapes on the vine' for you who will not enjoy what the vines produce, nor are there 'figs on the fig tree' for a besieged people who see the fruit of their own trees snatched away by the enemy." "The leaves fall," he says, "when summer and autumn are spent. For they saw what I gave them pass away, and with even greater anguish they lost their great abundance, which they were not permitted even to touch."

8:14-15: *"Why do we sit still? Gather together, let us go into the fortified city"*—or *"cities"*[180]—*"and be silent"*—or *"be cast out"*[181]—*"there; for the Lord our God has cast us away*[182] *and has given us poisoned water to drink, because we have sinned against the Lord. We looked for peace, but no good came; for a time of healing, but behold, terror."*

The voice of the people is introduced as responding, both confessing their sins and exhorting one another to gather into the fortified cities—or into one city, Jerusalem. For the rest of the cities had already been captured. "And let us be silent," he says, "for the Lord has made us silent"—since we do not have confidence in prayer; or else, "let us be cast away (or "cast out") there" like dung. God himself has given us poisoned water to drink because we have changed this sweet God into bitterness. And the reason why we should drink such waters is clear: "we have sinned against the Lord" and "we looked for peace"—we who had done no good works and yet still thought that a time of healing was near to us, even though all things were filled with fear and terror.

The changing around of the speakers, especially in the prophets, makes it difficult to understand the meaning.[183] But things that appear to be obscure become clear if they are explained in their own times, places and circumstances.

8:16: *"The snorting of their horses is heard from Dan; at the sound of the neighing of their fighters"*—or *"cavalry"*[184]—*"the whole land*

---

[179]Jer 8:10. [180]The first option is indeed Jerome's IH translation, but the Hebrew text as we have it matches the LXX ("cities"). Jerome's copy of the Hebrew apparently had the singular ("city"), as can be seen from his comments here and at Jer 8:16. [181]Heb *niddēmâ*. Jerome agrees with Aq, Sym, Pesh and Targ in interpreting the word as "to be silent" (*dmm* I, KB 226). For the LXX's "to cast out," see *dmm* III, KB 226. [182]Heb *hădimmānû*. Jerome gives only the LXX here ("cast us away"), but in his IH edition and in his comments below he translates "made us silent" (see n. 181), agreeing with Aq, Sym and the Pesh. [183]Jerome is commenting on how the people, speaking in the first person plural, are introduced in vv. 14-15 without warning. Jerome often comments on the changing around of the speakers (*personarum mutatio*) in the prophets and the psalms (e.g., Jer 31:25-26; *Expl. Dan.* 11:1; *Tract. Ps.* 80:8). [184]Heb *'abbîr* ("strong, powerful," KB 6). Cf. Aq and Sym: "powerful ones."

quakes. They came and devoured"—or *"will come and devour"*[185]—*"the land and all that fills it, the city and those who dwell in it."*

The people did not therefore say, as the LXX translated, "Let us go into the fortified cities," but rather, "into the fortified city," referring to Jerusalem.[186] For just now it says "the city and those who dwell in it."

Nebuchadnezzar is described as coming with his army from Dan through Phoenicia, where the Jordan River rises. The LXX describes these things as future, but the Hebrew, in accordance with the truth of the matter, recounts them as already having taken place.

**8:17(-18): *"For behold, I am sending among you"* "serpents, adders"—or "evil (serpents)"*—or, as the LXX translated, *"deadly (serpents)"*[187]—*"which cannot be charmed, and they shall bite you," says the Lord, "incurably with the grief of your weakened heart."*[188]

Whoever these are who come from Dan, whose snorting was heard and who reduced the whole land to desolation, the prophetic word now describes this same group under a different figure, calling them "serpents"—"evil," or "deadly," or, as Aquila translated, "adders," which in Hebrew are called *sapphonim*.[189] For this word Aquila's second edition put "watchmen," and I do not understand what it was intending, except perhaps that it was misled by the similarity between the words.[190]

He says "which cannot be charmed"—for in vain they pour out prayers to God against the ancient serpent,[191] the twisting serpent,[192] since they despised God's precepts. Let us use

this passage against those who, despising the sayings of the Savior, are handed over to adversarial powers.

**8:18: *"My grief is beyond grief, in me my heart is mourning."*

Instead of this, as we said above, the LXX joined these words to the previous sentence, thus rendering: " 'And they shall bite you,' says the Lord, 'incurably with the grief of your weakened heart.' " In Hebrew, however, it is not so much "grief," which in Greek is said *odynē*, as *meidiama*, which we can translate as the "opening" of the mouth when it is contracted with grief, having the likeness of a smile.[193] Moreover, these things should be read expressively,[194] out of the *persona* of God, who mourns the overthrow of Jerusalem and cannot bear her miseries.

**8:19a: *"Hark, the voice crying of the daughter of my people from a far-off land."*

He describes the weeping and crying of the city of Jerusalem after the enemies have entered into the city.

**8:19b: *"Is the Lord not in Zion? Is her king not in her?"*

Either the Lord himself is the king, or else the Lord is the Father and the king is the Son, according to what is written under the name of Solomon: "Give the king thy justice, O God, and thy righteousness to the royal Son!"[195] The reason is clear why the sound of crying is heard in Jerusalem and the cry comes from a far-off

---

[185]Jerome's past tense rendering matches the vocalization of MT. [186]Jer 8:14-15. [187]Jerome's "adders" (*regulos*) agrees with Aq (*basiliskous*). The rendering "evil" is Sym. [188]These last words reflect Jerome's understanding of the LXX (v. 18). According to Jerome, these words represent a separate thought unit, and so he discusses them below on their own. [189]Heb *ṣpʿnym* ("poisonous snake, viper," KB 1050). [190]In Hebrew, "watchmen" would be *ṣpym*. [191]Rev 12:9; 20:2. [192]Is 27:1. [193]The Greek word *meidiama* may be Aq's rendering. Properly speaking, *meidiama* means "smile." Since Jerome thinks that the Hebrew word in question means "grief," he may be trying to reconcile his own understanding of the Hebrew with the meaning given by Aq. [194]Jerome uses the Greek term *emphatikōs*. [195]Ps 72:1.

land; it is because the Lord is not in her, and her king has withdrawn from her.

8:19c: *"Why have they provoked me to anger with their graven images and with their foreign idols?"*

"The Lord has withdrawn from them," he says, "because they provoked me to anger by worshiping idols, even though I was their Lord and king."

8:20: *"The harvest is past, the summer is ended, and we are not saved."*

Yet, the people who have been shut in by the long siege say that the seasons have changed, the cycle of the year has come around and all of their hope has failed and passed away.

8:21: *"For the wound of the daughter of my people is my heart wounded, I mourn, and dismay has taken hold of me."*

God responds that he appears to be distressed because of the distress of Jerusalem. Using a human analogy, he is consumed with dismay.

8:22: *"Is there no balm in Gilead? Is there no physician there? Why then has the scar of the daughter of my people not been healed?"*

Not only in the present passage but also in many other testimonies of Scripture[196] we find the "balm of Gilead" put for "repentance" and for "medicine." Now we find God wondering at why the wounds of Jerusalem have in no way been cured and why her scars have not yet brought healing to the skin—the reason being that there are no prophets and priests, by whose medicine the people ought to be cured.

9:1: *"O that my head were waters, and my eyes a fountain of tears, that I might weep day and night for the slain of the daughter of my people!"*

"Even if I were wholly transformed into weeping," he says, "and there were not merely drops of tears but the abundance of a river, still I would not be able to weep properly for the slain of the daughter of my people. For their evils are so great that they overwhelm all grief by their magnitude." This can be understood as spoken both out of the *persona* of the prophet and out of the *persona* of the Lord.

9:2a: *"O that I had in the desert a wayfarers' lodging place! I would leave my people and go away from them!"* LXX: *"Who would give to me in the desert a remote stopping place, that I might forsake my people and go away from them!"*[197]

He says, "It is better to live in a remote desert than to remain in the midst of such great human crimes." Thus also the Savior said in the Gospel: "How long am I to be with you?"[198] And in another passage it is written: "In that time, he who understands will sit and keep silent, for it is an evil time."[199]

9:2b-3: *"For they are all adulterers, a company of treacherous men. They bend their tongue like a bow of falsehood and not of truth; they have grown strong in the land, for they proceed from evil to evil, and they do not know me, says the Lord."*

Sinners pass from evil to evil when they exchange one idol for another idol and transition from sin to sin, or else when they pass from the evil of siege to captivity. Concerning the saints, in fact, it says, "They go from

---

[196]Jer 46:11; 51:8. [197]Jerome's "lodging place" matches Aq. Jerome interprets the second clause of the LXX as a purpose clause, even though it is not specifically marked as such in the Greek. [198]Mt 17:17; Mk 9:19; Lk 9:41. [199]Amos 5:13; Mic 2:3; Lam 3:28.

strength to strength,"[200] but concerning sinners it says, "They proceed from evil to evil." And the cause of all these miseries is that "they do not know" the Lord and are a "company of treacherous men," who arm their tongues "like a bow" bent in blasphemy. "They have grown strong in the land," so that they deserve to hear, "Dust you are and to dust you will go."[201]

9:4-6: *"Let every one beware of his neighbor and put no trust in any brother; for every brother is a supplanter, and every neighbor goes about like a slanderer. Every one mocks his brother, and no one speaks the truth; their tongue has learned to speak lies"—or "they have taught their tongue to speak lies";[202] "they labor so that they may do iniquity"—or "they do iniquity and do not cease, so as to repent." "Your habitation is in the midst of deceit in deceit; they refuse to know me, says the Lord."—or "Usury on usury and deceit on deceit; they did not wish to know me."*

This passage should be used in a time of persecution and distress, when faith is either rare or nonexistent, when neither brother nor neighbor can be trusted, when a person's enemies are those of his own household,[203] when, in accordance with the Gospel, father delivers up son and son delivers up father[204] and when two are divided against three and three against two.[205] And by adding "they have taught their tongue to speak lies" or "their tongue has learned to speak lies," he shows that their habit of lying has become a lying nature and that they are working diligently to do iniquity. And as for what follows, "Your habitation is in the midst of deceit in deceit," strictly speaking this word is directed toward

the prophet, since he dwells in the midst of lying people, or, as the LXX translated, "Usury on usury and deceit on deceit," because every day they increase their wicked deeds. They will not repent of their past behavior, but they make up for crimes omitted with new crimes! They act with complete eagerness as they do all of these things, so that they do not know the Lord, who commanded that these things should not be done.

9:7: *Therefore thus says the Lord of hosts: "Behold, I will burn them"—or "I will examine them by fire"[206]—"and test them, for what else can I do, because of my people"—or "because of the evil of my people?"*

Whenever we are subject to trials, receive evil from God and are tested by persecutions, it is so that whatever impure materials are in us may be purified by the fires of tribulation and misery. For we are silver examined by the fire of the Lord, refined on the ground, purified seven times.[207]

9:8-9: *"Their tongue is a wounding arrow; it speaks deceitfully; with his mouth each speaks peaceably to his neighbor, but in his heart he plans an ambush for him. Shall I not visit them for these things? says the Lord; and shall not my soul avenge itself on a nation such as this?"*

Every heretic who wounds the hearts of those who listen and do not know what is written, "Keep your heart with all vigilance,"[208] possesses a wounding arrow and speaks deceitfully. With his mouth he promises peace to his neighbor, but secretly he prepares an ambush. In the following lines where he says, "Shall I

---

[200]Ps 84:7. [201]Eccl 3:20; Gen 3:19. The Latin word (*terra*) that Jerome uses for "dust" (or "ground, soil") is the same word translated "land" in Jer 9:3. [202]The first option represents the LXX (presuming the Qal of *lmd*); and the second option is Jerome's rendering (presuming the Piel of *lmd*), agreeing with Aq, Th and MT. [203]Mic 7:6b; Mt 10:36. [204]Mt 10:21. [205]Lk 12:52-53. [206]Heb *srp* ("smelt, refine," KB 1057). The first option ("burn") is Jerome's IH edition and matches the LXX as preserved. No hexaplaric readings are available; the basis for the alternative ("examine by fire") is not known. [207]Ps 12:6. [208]Prov 4:23.

not visit them for these things? says the Lord; and shall not my soul avenge itself on a nation such as this?" the prophet makes use of repetition in order to emphasize, since he has enumerated each one of their evil deeds, that he is acting justly in what he is doing to them.

9:10: *"I will take up"—or "Take up"[209]—"weeping and wailing for the mountains and a lamentation for the beautiful places"—or "paths"[210]—"of the wilderness, because they have been burned"—or "they failed"[211]—"so that no man"—or "no person"[212]—"passes through, and they do not hear the sound of one possessing"—or "the sound of substance"; "both the birds of the air and the beasts have fled and are gone."*

As Babylon is approaching and ravaging the whole land, he prophesies the desolation of the region. There is wailing on the mountains and weeping in the desert (or on the paths of the wilderness), all has failed and been burned, there is no one to walk through the land since all have been killed, and nothing remains that can breathe and live. In place of "one possessing," the LXX translated "substance," which in Hebrew is *macne*.[213] But "substance" here is not understood as *ousia*, that is, "essence," but as "wealth" or "riches."[214] And when he adds "both the birds of the air and the beasts have departed and gone," he shows, as I have often said, that the whole world senses the anger of God. Not only the birds of the air but also the

fish of the sea withdraw.

According to tropology,[215] weeping goes up over the mountains and lamentation over the beautiful places of the wilderness when the leaders of the church sin, when nothing of the substance of God is found in the church and when there is not heard in it the voice of the Lord who possesses the church through holy and apostolic men. Both the "birds of the air" and the "beasts"—namely, those who are able to ascend to the sublime and those who are irrational and simple—have gone from the assembly of God.

9:11: *"I will make Jerusalem a heap of sand"—or "deportation"[216]—"and a lair of dragons;[217] and I will make the cities of Judah a desolation, without inhabitant."*

Since all the ecclesiastical men and teachers have gone away, Jerusalem is given over to deportation (or is made a heap of sand), so that the heretical word prevails within her and she is made a lair of dragons. Her cities are reduced to desolation, and there is not found in her the habitation of the divine word or him who says, "I will live and walk among them, and I will be their God."[218]

9:12-14: *Who is the man so wise that he can understand this? To whom has the mouth of the Lord spoken, that he may declare it? Why is the land ruined and laid waste like a wilderness, so that no one passes through? And*

---

[209]Jerome matches Aq and Sym (= MT). [210]Heb *n'wt*. Jerome's "beautiful places" (= Aq) presumes the Hebrew *nā'weh* (KB 657). Many modern versions read as if from *nāwâ* ("grazing place," KB 678). The rendering "paths" is the LXX. [211]Jerome matches MT. [212]The Hebrew has *'iš* ("man"), which Jerome renders literally as *vir*. The LXX uses *anthrōpos*, which is the more general word for "person" (Lat *homo*). [213]Heb *mqnh*. Jerome takes the word as a participle from *qnh* ("to acquire"), and he translates it with the Latin word *possideo*, which means "to possess, acquire," and can also mean "to occupy, abide in." The LXX understood the Hebrew word to be *miqneh* ("property" or "cattle"). [214]Jerome, probably following the OL, uses the word *substantia* to translate the LXX's *hyparxis* ("property"). But since *substantia* can also stand for the Greek *ousia*, Jerome must clarify that the underlying Greek of the LXX is not "essence" (a philosophical term) but "property." [215]The Latin word *tropologia* is taken from a Greek rhetorical term that refers to the figurative sense of a word as opposed to its literal or proper sense. In Christian exegesis after Origen it became a technical term for the spiritual sense of the text. [216]Jerome agrees with Aq; cf. Heb *gal* ("heap," KB 190). The LXX understood the Hebrew as from *glh*, "to go into exile," and thus "deportation." [217]Heb *tnym*. Jerome and the LXX both translate "dragons" (from Heb *tannin*, KB 1764). Many modern translations have "jackals" (from Heb *tan*, KB 1759). [218]2 Cor 6:16; Lev 26:12.

the Lord says, "Because they have forsaken my law, which I set before them, and have not obeyed my voice or walked in accord with it but have turned aside after the depravity of their own hearts and have gone after the Baalim, as their fathers taught them."

The prophet asks if it is possible to find in Jerusalem any wise person to whom the word of God has come, who could announce the will of the Lord and explain why Judah has been reduced to such desolation that no one remains to pass through it, since everyone has been killed. Then he introduces the Lord as responding and explaining the reasons: they forsook his law that he had given to them, they did not obey his voice, and they did not do the things he commanded, but instead they turned aside after the depravity of their own hearts. Therefore we should trust not in our own hearts but in the Lord, for "deceitful is the human heart,"[219] and "out of the heart come evil thoughts."[220] "And they have gone after the Baalim," he says, "as their fathers taught them." (Baal is an idol of the Sidonians. Baal is singular in number, whereas Baalim is plural in number.) Thus, one should not follow the error of parents and elders, but we should follow the authority of the Scriptures and the command of God who instructs us.

9:15-16: *"Therefore thus says the Lord of hosts, the God of Israel: Behold, I will feed this people with wormwood"—or "troubles"[221]— "and give them poisonous water to drink. I will scatter them among the nations whom neither they nor their fathers have known; and I will send the sword after them, until I have consumed them."*

This prophecy can relate to a near time when they were captured by the Babylonians, and it can relate properly to this time, since they have been scattered among nations whom neither they nor their ancestors had known and they have been divided among the nations and fed wormwood—or necessities and troubles. And they received poisonous water to drink, which either signifies the magnitude of their calamities and the eternal yoke of their captivity, or else it indicates that they are going to receive the antichrist instead of Christ because of their ignorance of the law of God. Moreover, the sword is sent after them so that they are consumed to the point of ruin; or else the sword divides them and does not permit them to have unity in evil, so that they perish precisely because they are evil.

9:17-19a: *Thus says the Lord of hosts: "Consider"—or "Understand"[222]—"and call for the mourning women to come; send for the skillful women to hurry"—or "to speak";[223] "let them make haste and raise a wailing over us"—or "over you"—"that our"—or "your"— "eyes may run down with tears, and our"—or "your"—"eyelids gush with water. For a sound of wailing is heard from Zion"—or "in Zion."*

On account of the coming overthrow and captivity of Jerusalem he commands them to summon the mourning women, who customarily provoke the people to tears by wailing with a doleful voice and by beating their shoulders with their hands. This custom persists up to today in Judea, such that women with disheveled hair and naked breasts stir up all to weeping by their measured voices. Moreover, God (or the prophet) unites himself with them by adopting the manner of one sharing in their

---

[219]Jer 17:9. [220]Mt 15:9. [221]Heb *la'ănâ* ("wormwood; metaph. meaning bitterness," KB 533). The hexaplaric versions all translate "bitterness." The LXX has *anagkē* ("necessity, trouble"). [222]Jerome's copy of the LXX contained "Understand" (also Aq and Th), as is found in some MSS. Other LXX MSS omit the word. Sym has a Greek word that essentially means "consider." [223]The Hebrew is "to come," just as earlier in the verse. Jerome's "hurry" may reflect a desire to introduce variety.

suffering, so that whatever the people experience he says that he experiences and feels. As for what he adds, "For a sound of wailing is heard from Zion," it follows immediately afterwards what that sound is:

9:19b: "How have we been ruined and utterly shamed? It is because we have left the land, because they have cast down"—or "we have thrown aside"—"our dwellings."

This is the sound of those wailing over Zion: "How have we been ruined and utterly shamed?" Immediately they themselves answer and explain the reason for their devastation, saying, "It is because we have left the land" by our vice and sin, and "they have cast down our dwellings," which they possessed previously but neglected. Let them say this also to those who formerly trusted in the mob and now are "persecuted"; indeed, they have been ruined and shamed precisely because they left the land of the Lord and abandoned his dwellings.

9:20-21: "Hear, O women, the word of the Lord, and let your ear receive the word of his mouth; teach to your daughters a lament, and each to her neighbor a dirge. For death has come up into our windows, it has entered our palaces, cutting off the children from the streets and the young men from the squares."

In the above section he said "call for the mourning women to come; send for the skillful women to hurry."[224] Now he speaks to these women (as if they were present) in condemnation of the priests, teachers and all the men. Since the men have stopped paying heed to right teaching, he wishes for these women to

hear the word of the Lord and receive the words of his mouth and to teach their daughters and neighbors a lament and the reason for their tears: "For death has come up into our windows, it has entered our palaces." Yet, this can also be understood spiritually, in that the death that comes from sin enters the body through all the senses, so as to bring ruin to the soul. At the same time, this can be understood in connection with the onslaught of the Babylonians: the strength and speed of their attack is so great that they are not waiting to unlock the doors but are going up through the windows and the roofs in order to destroy the palaces of Jerusalem. Moreover, the children who are out in the streets leaving Jerusalem will perish; likewise the young men will perish, to whom John also wrote,[225] who are not going through the straight and narrow path that leads to life but are walking through the squares, about which it is written, "How wide and easy is the way that leads to death."[226]

9:22: Speak, "Thus says the Lord: 'The carrion of man'—or 'dead bodies of men'[227]—'shall fall like dung on the land'—or 'field'—'like sheaves after the reaper, and none shall gather them.'"

Regarding the Hebrew word that is written with three letters, *daleth, beth* and *res*—for it does not have the vowels within it—in view of the surrounding context and the decision of the reader if it is read as *dabar*, then it means "word"; if it is read *deber*, it means "death"; and if it is read *dabber*, it means "Speak!"[228] Out of all this, the Septuagint and Theodotion joined this word to the previous passage, so that they said "cutting off the children from the streets and the young men from the squares by death."[229]

---

[224]Jer 9:17. [225]1 Jn 2:13. [226]Mt 7:13-14. [227]The Hebrew words are grammatically singular as in Jerome's version. [228]The Hebrew consonants can be read as the noun *dābār* ("word," KB 211), the noun *deber* ("bubonic plague," KB 212) or as the Piel imperative *dabbēr* ("speak!" KB 210). [229]Jer 9:21. What Jerome reports here for the LXX is attested for Th and was apparently found in the hexaplaric edition of the LXX under asterisk. Most LXX MSS lack "by death" and the following phrase, "Thus says the Lord."

But Aquila and Symmachus translated the word as *laleson*, "Speak!" so that God commands the prophet to say the things that follow: "Thus says the Lord, etc." This is the sense: When death has come up through our windows and has entered the palaces of Jerusalem, and when children and young men have perished from the streets and squares, then their "carrion"—or the "dead bodies" of the deceased—will be like the stubble that is left after the reapers, which remains ungathered because it is useless. Through these things he wishes to show that the carnage to come will be so great that there will be no one to bury those who have fallen.

9:23-24: *Thus says the Lord: "Let not the wise man glory in his wisdom, let not the mighty man glory in his might, let not the rich man glory in his riches; but let him who glories glory in this, that he understands"—or "comprehends"—"and knows me, that I am the Lord who practices steadfast love, justice and righteousness in the earth; for in these things I delight,"—or "in these things is my will"— "says the Lord."*

All human pride is taken away as wisdom, strength and wealth are reckoned as nothing, and the sole basis of glorying is said to be this: that one understands and comprehends that he is Lord, who practices steadfast love, justice and righteousness in the earth; that all things are governed by the providence and justice of God; and that things that seem to us not to have any reason are filled with justice and reason.[230] For in these things alone does God delight, and in these is his will. Where, then, are those who say that a person is guided by his own choosing and has been given the power of free choice, so that

the steadfast love and justice of God are abolished? Thus the apostle, taking up this testimony, sets an example: "Let him who glories glory in the Lord."[231]

9:25-26: *"Behold, the days are coming, says the Lord, when I will punish all those who are circumcised—Egypt, Judah, Edom, the sons of Ammon, Moab, and all who dwell in the desert that cut the corners of their hair; for all these nations are uncircumcised, and all the house of Israel is uncircumcised in heart."*

Out of all nations there is a certain group, especially those bordering Judea and Palestine, among whom the people practice circumcision even up to today. The primary nations in this group are the Egyptians, the Idumeans, the Ammonites, the Moabites and all the territory of the Saracens, who live in the desert and about whom it is said, "all who dwell in the desert that cut the corners of their hair." Therefore Judah, who was included among the nations mentioned above, should boast, not in the fact that it lacks a foreskin but in the fact that it is circumcised in conformity with the law of God, since these other nations that have not kept the commands of the law and are ignorant of the God of Israel also have this practice. Circumcision, which was given as a sign, is of no benefit unless the precepts of the Lord are fulfilled. So also the hair, which signifies the nation, is of no benefit without the strength of bodies and the bravery of fighters. And that which follows, "for all these nations are uncircumcised, and all the house of Israel is uncircumcised in heart," has this sense: Except for the Egyptians, Idumeans, Ammonites, Moabites and the Ishmaelites who dwell in the desert (most of whom are circumcised), all other nations in the world are

---

[230]Wis 14:3. Cf. Origen *Princ.* 4.1.7; *Philoc.* 2.4-5. On the Stoic background of this line of reasoning, see A. A. Long and D. N. Sedley, *The Hellenistic Philosophers*, 2 vols. (Cambridge: Cambridge University Press, 1987), 1:54 O, Q, R, T; Plutarch *Comm. Not.* 1065.a-c. [231]1 Cor 1:31; 2 Cor 10:17.

uncircumcised in the flesh. Yet, while all these nations are uncircumcised in the flesh, the whole house of Israel is uncircumcised in the heart, not the flesh; but this uncircumcision leads to death. For the flesh is one thing, the spirit is another.

10:1-3a: *Hear the word that the Lord speaks to you, O house of Israel. Thus says the Lord: "Learn not the way of the nations, nor be dismayed at the signs of the heavens because the nations are dismayed at them, for the customs of the people are false."*

Strictly speaking, he says this against those who worship celestial bodies and things that have been set as signs for years, times, calculations and days, and who suppose that the human race is governed by these celestial bodies and that earthly affairs are ordered according to celestial causes. And when he says "the customs (or statutes) of the people are false," he shows all human wisdom to be futile and to have nothing useful within it.

10:3b-5: *"A tree from the forest is cut down and worked with an axe by the hands of a craftsman. Men deck it with silver and gold; they fasten it with hammer and nails so that it will not fall apart"*—or *"will not move." "They have been fashioned in the likeness of a palm tree, and they cannot speak; they have to be carried, for they cannot walk. Do not be afraid of them, for they cannot do evil, neither is it in them to do good."*

This is a description of the idols that the nations worship. "A tree from the forest," he says, "is cut down"—thus, the material out of which idols are made is cheap and perishable; "worked . . . by the hands of a craftsman"— since the craftsman is mortal, mortal also are the things that he fashions; "Men deck it with silver and gold," so that by the glow of each of these materials the simple may be deceived. This same error has been passed down to us, in that we judge people's religion by their wealth. "They fasten it with hammer and nails so that it will not fall apart," or "will not move." How great can the power of idols be, if they are not capable of standing up unless they are fastened with hammer and nails? "They have been fashioned in the likeness of a palm tree"—they have the beauty of metalwork and have been decorated through the art of painting, but they do not possess usefulness, such as would provide some benefit to the craftsman. "And they cannot speak," for there is nothing alive about them, as it is written: "They have mouths but do not speak . . . they have ears but do not hear."[232] "They have to be carried"—the one who does the carrying is stronger than the things that are carried; indeed, in the one there is the capacity to think, but in the other there is a physical form without the capacity to think. "Do not be afraid of them, for they cannot do evil, neither is it in them to do good." For most of the nations regularly worship demons, in some cases to prevent them from doing harm and in other cases to entreat some favor. Whence also is the Virgilian phrase: "a black sheep to the storm god, a white to the favoring Zephyrs."[233]

Whatever we have said about idols can also be applied to all teachings that are contrary to the truth. For false teachings promise great things and fabricate from within them an image for empty worship. They make grand claims, and they hamper the reasoning of the unskilled by their golden theories and their eloquence that glows with the splendor of silver. They are propped up by those who invent them, and they have no usefulness. The cultivation of such teachings belongs properly to the nations and to those who are ignorant of God.

---

[232]Ps 115:5-6. [233]Virgil *Aen.* 3.120 (LCL).

10:6-10: *There is none like you, O Lord; you are great, and your name is great in might. Who would not fear you, O King of the nations? For yours is beauty; for among all the wise ones of the nations and in all their kingdoms there is none like you. They are both wise[234] and foolish; the instruction of idols is but wood! Covered—or beaten[235]—silver is brought from Tarshish, and gold from Uphaz. They are the work of the craftsman and of the hands of the goldsmith; their clothing is violet and purple; they are all the work of skilled—or wise[236]—men. But the Lord is the true God; he is the living God and the everlasting King. At his wrath the earth quakes, and the nations cannot endure his indignation.*

These words are not found in the LXX but have been added mostly from the edition of Theodotion. Although they seem clear when understood literally, when taken according to anagogy[237] they hold great difficulty. None of the gods that have been invented by heretical art are like the true God. All fear him who is king of the nations, since "the fear of the Lord is the beginning of wisdom," and from this beginning we advance to love.[238] "Yours," he says, "is beauty"—beauty is found in truth, ugliness in falsehood. Even though heretics think of themselves as wise according to the wisdom of the world (which is perishing), in all

their kingdoms in which they lash out against the church "there is none like you," as the divine word says: "I will destroy the wisdom of the wise, and the cleverness of the clever I will thwart."[239] "They are wise and at the same time foolish"—their teaching, based on the natural state of their own cleverness, is either cheap and comparable to wood or else it is like silver on account of its charming eloquence. "Silver is brought from Tarshish"—either this is a region of India, as Josephus suggested,[240] or else every sea is referred to as Tarshish;[241] it has the appearance of the sky, and yet it is clouded by the artifice of words, since it would not be able to deceive if it were clear.[242] "And gold from Uphaz"—gold is called by seven names among the Hebrews, one of which is said *ophaz*, which we can identify using the term "pure gold,"[243] so that there is a bright glow to the outer surface of the idols, but on the inside they are wood and cheap material. They are covered with "violet and purple," so that they deceive the eyes with their outer surface as they take on themselves the color of heaven and heavenly kingdoms. Yet, all of these are merely the works of "wise men," who in this age appear to be wise but are fools in the eyes of God. "But the Lord" our God "is the true God"—and so all the others are lies; "he is the living God"—therefore those that have been made are dead; "and the everlasting

---

[234]The Hebrew word (*b'r*) means "stupid, brutish," and this is how Jerome translated it in his IH edition. Yet, it is clear from his comments below that Jerome accidentally wrote *sapientes* ("wise") instead of *insipientes* ("stupid") in the lemma of the commentary. [235]The alternative ("beaten") is Th as preserved under asterisk. [236]The alternative ("wise") is Th as preserved under asterisk. [237]Following Origen and other Greek fathers, Jerome uses the Greek term *anagōgē* ("elevation") to refer to the higher or spiritual sense. [238]Prov 1:7. See also Sir 25:16 (Vg): "The fear of the Lord is the beginning of love for him, and faith is the beginning of clinging to him." [239]1 Cor 1:19; cf. Is 29:14. [240]Jerome is mistaken in ascribing this opinion to Josephus, since Josephus identifies the biblical Tarshish with Tarsus in Cilicia (cf. *Ant.* 1.127; 8.181; 9.208; *J.W.* 7.238), as Jerome correctly noted in his *Comm. Jon.* 1:3a. The idea that Tarshish is in India is also reported and rejected by the commentaries on Jonah written by Cyril of Alexandria and Theodoret of Cyrus (Cyril favors Tarsus of Cilicia; Theodoret favors Carthage). Modern scholars generally locate Tarshish to the west of Israel (e.g., somewhere on the coast of Spain). [241]In his *Comm. Jon.* 1:3a, Jerome ascribes the position that Tarshish means "sea" to "the Hebrews" (cf. *Canticles Rabbah* 5.14.2; Targum to Jonah 1:3; 4:2; Targum to Isaiah 2:16; 23:1, 14; 66:19; Targum to Ezekiel 27:12, 25; 38:13). On Jerome's identification of Tarshish as "sea" according to the Hebrews, see also *Comm. Isa.* 2:16; 66:18-19. [242]The Latin word for "sky" also means "heaven"; that is, just as the sea looks like the sky but conceals danger beneath, so also heresy looks like heaven but conceals danger under its clever verbiage. [243]On the seven names for gold in rabbinic sources, see *Numbers Rabbah* 12.4, *Exodus Rabbah* 35.1, *Canticles Rabbah* 3.10.3; b. *Yoma* 44b-45a. The Hebrew word is *'ûpāz*, which Jerome explains using the Latin word *obryzum*, which comes from the Greek *obryzon* ("pure [gold]").

King"—the shadows of heretics prevail for a time but in the long run they fail. "At his wrath the earth quakes"—that is, those who have earthly works and fashion earthly images; "and the nations cannot endure his indignation"—not the people of God, but the multitude of the nations, who are not able to bear the indignation of God.

10:11: *Thus you shall say to them: "The gods who did not make the heavens and the earth shall perish from the earth and from under the heavens."*[244]

This should be said to false gods that have been put together by craftsmanship, for they did not make the heavens and the earth. Those who are "cooperators with Christ," who are called "gods" and "lords," fashion these things for the most part out of ecclesiastical teaching.[245]

10:12-16: *It is he who makes—or made*[246]*—the earth by his power, who establishes the world by his wisdom, and by his understanding stretched out the heavens. When he utters his voice, there is a tumult of waters in the heavens, and he brings up—or brings forth*[247]*—mists from the ends of the earth. He makes lightnings for the rain, and he brings forth the wind—or winds*[248]*—from his storehouses. Every man is stupid and without knowledge; every goldsmith is put to shame by his idols; for his images are false, and there is no spirit in them. They are worthless, a work worthy of laughter; at the time of their punish-ment they shall perish. Not like these is he who is the portion of Jacob, for he is the one who formed all things, and Israel is the staff*[249] *of his inheritance; the Lord of hosts is his name.*

"He who makes the earth by his power" is God the Father. Moreover, he makes it "by his power," by the Savior our Lord, for Christ is the virtue[250] of God and the wisdom of God. Christ is also his "understanding," by which he stretched out heaven. "For he spoke, and it came to be; he commanded, and it stood forth,"[251] saying to the Son, "Let us make man in our image, after our likeness."[252] "When he utters his voice there is a tumult of waters in the heavens," for all of the Lord's teaching flows down from the heavenly realm, as David says: "Rain given freely, O God, thou did set apart; thy heritage languished, but thou did restore it."[253] "And he brings up"—or "brings forth"— "mists from the ends of the earth." "Mists" or "clouds," which God has ordered not to pour rain on Israel,[254] are brought forth from the ends of the earth; one of these mists said, "For I think that God has exhibited us apostles as last of all, like men sentenced to death; because we have become a spectacle to the world, to angels and to men."[255] "He makes lightnings for the rain," for when the rain of doctrine has come and parched human hearts have been satisfied, then you will find flashes and bright lightnings of wisdom. "And he brings forth the winds from his storehouses," in which "are hid all the treasures of wisdom and knowledge."[256]

"Every man is stupid and without knowl-

---

[244]This verse is in Aramaic, which Jerome does not mention. [245]The phrase *cooperatores Christi* is ironic, and the mention of "gods" and "lords" is an allusion to 1 Cor 8:5. Jerome is trying to associate the pride of idolatry with the pride ascribed to the followers of Pelagius. By twisting the ecclesiastical teaching, they fashion for themselves the idolatrous assertion that they cooperate with Christ in salvation, thus making themselves out to be gods (as Jerome sees it). According to Jerome, to claim to cooperate with Christ in this way is like an idol claiming to have assisted God in making the world. [246]This verb and the following (Jerome: "makes . . . establishes") are participles. [247]The first option ("brings up") is not only Jerome's rendering but also matches the LXX as preserved (= MT). The alternative ("brings forth") may reflect Jerome's copy of the LXX, or else his eye may have skipped ahead (cf. "brings forth the wind"). [248]Jerome matches MT. The plural "winds" was in Jerome's copy of the LXX and is preserved in some LXX witnesses. Most LXX witnesses have "light." [249]Many modern translations: "tribe." The Hebrew *šēbeṭ* can mean "staff, scepter" and "tribe" (KB 1388-90). Aq and Th both read "staff, scepter." [250]The Latin *virtus* means "virtue" or "courage, strength"; hence the connection with "by his power." Cf. 1 Cor 1:24. [251]Ps 33:9. [252]Gen 1:26. [253]Ps 68:9. [254]Is 5:6. [255]1 Cor 4:9. [256]Col 2:3.

edge." Whether it is Paul, Peter, Moses or Abraham, in comparison with God all their wisdom is reckoned as nothing. Thus, "the foolishness of God is wiser than men."[257] "Every goldsmith is put to shame by his idols." He has fashioned images out of his own imagination, and "his images are false"; indeed, if "every man is stupid and without knowledge," then everything he makes is stupid and false. "And there is no spirit in them." It should be noted that in this passage "wind" and "spirit" reflect the same Hebrew word, *ruha*.[258] What he is referring to, however, is the spirit of sanctification, which cannot be found in the minds of heretics. "They are worthless, a work worthy of laughter." For who would not laugh when he has seen the images of heretics? For what they say is either rustic and so is like wood, or it is composed in beautiful language and so is taken to be silver; or else what they say is a counterfeit of the true concept, and so without any basis it offers the likeness of gold. "At the time of their punishment they shall perish." Heresy prevails for a time, in order to make clear who are the elect, and so that the elect may be proven true. But when the punishment of God comes and his eye looks on these foolish images, they all become silent.

"Not like these is he who is the portion of Jacob"—the portion of those who have overthrown the Jews and who daily destroy heretics. Now, the portion of the saints is God, about whom the prophet says, "The Lord is my portion."[259] "For he is the one who formed all things," who made all things and formed them both in mind and in body. "And Israel is the staff of his inheritance." Anyone who is directed to God or who perceives God with his

mind is the scepter of the inheritance of him whose name is Lord Almighty or Lord of Strength—for the word means "Lord of Armies," which in Hebrew is written Lord *sabaoth*.[260]

10:17-18: Gather up your shame from the land that you inhabit under siege. For thus says the Lord: "Behold, I am slinging out the inhabitants of the land in this turn, and I will bring distress on them, that they may be found." LXX: **He has gathered up your property from outside, which is kept in fortification.[261] For thus says the Lord: "Behold, I am overthrowing the inhabitants of this land, and I will bring distress on them, that they may be found."[262]**

He commands Jerusalem that they should gather into their fortified city whatever property they have outside and that they should make ready provisions for a long siege. For he is not, as previously, making threats about something that will occur a long time from now in the future; now he threatens their imminent captivity, which will take place very soon. He says, "Gather up from outside and from the land"—that is, from the fields—"your property, to your shame"—for whatever you have is worthy of shame. And still, although they make these preparations, take note of what the Lord says about them: "Behold, I am slinging out"—or, I will hurl as with a sling—"the inhabitants of the land in this turn"—that is, at this time. Instead of this, the LXX translated "I am overthrowing" them and causing them to fall. The Hebrew word for this is *cole*, which Aquila and Symmachus

---

[257]1 Cor 1:25. [258]The same Hebrew word, *rûaḥ*, underlies "wind" (Jer 10:13) and "spirit" (Jer 10:14). Cf. Jerome's comments at Jer 2:23c-24; 10:14; Hos 4:17-19. [259]Lam 3:24. [260]Jerome first gives the traditional rendering of the LXX, "Lord Almighty" (*pantokratōr*). Then he gives what appears to be the rendering of Sym, "Lord of Strength" (*kyrios dynameōn*; cf. Sym on Jer 11:20, 22; 19:3, 11; 20:12; 25:8, 27), which he perhaps thinks is closer to the right sense. Lastly, Jerome indicates what he understands to be the true sense of the Hebrew, "Lord of Armies," which agrees with Aq (*kyrios stratiōn*). Heb *ṣābāʾ* ("military men, troops," KB 995). [261]The LXX as transmitted reads "which is kept in choice places." The peculiar reading that Jerome gives for the LXX, "in fortification," agrees with the reading preserved for Sym. [262]Most LXX MSS read "so that your plague may be found."

translated as *sphendonisō*.[263] And the sense is this: As with a sling I will forcefully cast them out; in this way I will cause them to be besieged. I will bring distress on them and afflict them, so that they will all be found in the city and none will be able to flee the disaster.

10:19a: *Woe is me because of my hurt! My wound is grievous.* LXX: *Woe to you because of your hurt! Your wound is grievous.*

According to the Hebrew, Jerusalem itself says that it has been violently afflicted and is sustaining an incurable wound. But according to the LXX, the prophet speaks to Jerusalem and bewails it because of its hurt and its wound.

10:19b: *But I said, "Truly this is my infirmity"*—or "*wound*"[264]—*"and I will bear it"*—or "*it has taken hold of me.*"[265]

Jerusalem itself says, "Whatever I am suffering, I suffer because of my own fault. I understand my wound, which has taken hold of me." Or, "I will bear the indignation of the Lord because I have sinned against him."[266]

10:20: *My tent has been removed, and all my cords are broken—or all my skins are torn apart;*[267] *my children—or my children and my sheep*[268]—*have gone from me, and they are not; there is no one to spread my tent again—or there is no longer a place for my tent*[269]—*and to set up my curtains.*

Jerusalem laments the destruction of the city, which was overthrown so easily that you would not think that all its walls and fortifications

had been utterly demolished, but merely that a tabernacle or tent had been taken away. It says, "My tent—that is, my habitation—has been suddenly removed." "All my cords are broken"—this follows the metaphor of a tent; or, "All my skins are torn apart."

"My children and my cattle have gone from me"—the LXX added "my cattle," but this cannot stand according to *historia*. For how could sheep and cattle be carried away from Jerusalem? If there were cattle there, would they not have been eaten by those who were starving during the long siege? It says, "And they are not" or "they do not exist"—since a great number of them were not deported to Chaldea but were killed and wiped out. "There is no one to spread my tent again"—there is no one to restore me and lay the foundations of my walls, which have been thrown down to the ground.

10:21: *For the shepherds are stupid and do not inquire of the Lord; therefore they have not understood, and all their flock is scattered.*

The guilt of the leaders and the scattering of the people are described using the metaphor of shepherds and sheep. Because the leaders were stupid and did not inquire of the Lord, whom they should have sought with their whole heart, they did not see the coming calamities or understand the Lord, and so all the multitude of Jerusalem is scattered here and there.

10:22: *Hark, a rumor! Behold, it comes!—a great commotion out of the north country to make the cities of Judah a desolation, a dwelling of dragons—or a nest of sparrows—* or, as Symmachus translated, *of Sirens*—which

---

[263]The Hebrew *ql'* means "to sling" (i.e., stones); see KB 1106. The Greek word used by Aq and Sym means "I will sling," which Jerome takes as confirmation of his rendering. [264]Heb *hŏlī* ("sickness, suffering," KB 318). Jerome agrees with Aq and Sym. [265]Jerome agrees with Aq or Sym (= MT). [266]Mic 7:9. [267]Heb *mêtār* ("tent rope," KB 578-79); *ntq* (Niphal; "be torn in two, torn apart," KB 736). Jerome matches Aq. [268]Like Jerome, MT lacks "and my sheep." [269]The LXX ("there is no longer a place for my tent") continues: "nor a place for my curtains."

in Hebrew is written *thannim*.[270]

These are the words of the prophet: "Behold!" he says, "the noise and roar are heard of Babylon coming, and a great commotion or shaking of the earth is heard out of the north country. All the cities of Judah will be reduced to desolation once all of their inhabitants have been killed. And in place of the people, God will make to dwell there serpents and an array of venomous creatures"—or else, "sparrows," which are animals familiar with desolate places, since they are born and raised in deserts. Or else we can interpret the word as "Sirens," which are monsters of some kind or the apparitions of demons. All of these things that the present and previous discussions have described we refer to times when the church is persecuted, when the tents of the Lord are destroyed and every habitation of the church is reduced to desolation. And for all of these events the shepherds are to blame, who are stupid and do not inquire of the Lord, nor have they understood. This is the reason why all the flock is scattered.[271]

10:23: I know, O Lord, that the way of man is not in himself, that it is not in man to walk and to direct his steps.

Let these new preachers be ashamed who say that each person is guided by his own will, when here the prophet says "the way of man is not in himself," and David sings in his lyric song, "The steps of a man are guided by the Lord, and he will surely direct his way."[272] Or, this is the sense: "What we suffer from the Babylonians does not come from their dreadful force but from our own guiltiness and from your indignation."

10:24-25: Correct me, O Lord, but in just measure; not in your anger, lest you bring me to nothing. Pour out your wrath on the nations that do not know you and on the territories— or generations—that do not call on your name; for they have devoured Jacob;[273] they have consumed his place, and they have laid waste— or reduced to desolation—his honor—or pastures.[274]

We read this passage in the psalm: "O Lord, do not rebuke me in your anger or chasten me in your wrath."[275] This is the sense: "We deserve everything we are going through, and in fact we deserve to suffer much greater things than these. But this I beg of you: that you chasten me as a father and not as an enemy, and that you correct me as if I were a son and not an adversary. For you discipline every son whom you receive, and through every grief and chastisement you correct Jerusalem."[276] Yet, as for enemies who have not known you, and territories or regions that have not called on your name, they should experience not your measured justice but your indignation. For we were handed over so that we might be corrected, but they have made their own yoke heavy: They did not spare the old, and they afflicted the young; they consumed us and devoured us, and they reduced Jerusalem to desolation, laying waste all of the public and private structures and killing the people.

11:1-3a: The word that came to Jeremiah from

---

[270]Heb *tnym*. Jerome's "dragons" matches Th (cf. Heb *tannin*, "sea monster, serpent" [KB 1764]). The LXX put "sparrows," and both Aq and Sym are preserved as translating "Sirens." Cf. Jer 9:11. [271]Jer 10:21. [272]Ps 37:23 (LXX [36:23]). [273]MT has four verbal clauses at the end of Jer 10:25: "For they devoured Jacob, and they devoured him, and they consumed him, and they desolated his pasture." In the IH edition Jerome translated all four verbal clauses, although he rendered the first two with different Latin words ("ate . . . devoured") for the sake of variety. In the commentary he omits the second occurrence of the verb "devoured" (as does the LXX), and he gives "consumed his place" instead of "consumed him." On this last rendering, see perhaps the Targ, "They have plundered their property." [274]Jerome (agreeing with Aq) understands this to be a noun related to the verb *nwh* II, "to glorify" (KB 678). The LXX takes the word as *nāweh*, "pasture, settlement" (= MT). [275]Ps 6:1. [276]Heb 12:6; Prov 3:12 (LXX).

the Lord: "Hear the words of this pact"—or "testament"[277]—"and speak to the men of Judah and the inhabitants of Jerusalem. You shall say to them, 'Thus says the Lord, the God of Israel.'"

It does not indicate in the title during what time, under whose reign or in what year this prophecy was delivered. But we hold that these things are either joined to the previous prophecy and to that time, or else that this word of the Lord was delivered to the prophet some time after the previous prophecy. It should be noted that for the word *berith*,[278] Aquila and Symmachus always translated "covenant," whereas the LXX and Theodotion always translated "testament." Now, the message is directed to Jerusalem and to the men of the tribe of Judah.[279]

11:3b-4: "Cursed be the man who does not heed the words of this pact that I commanded your fathers when I brought them out of the land of Egypt, from the iron furnace, saying, Listen to my voice, and do all that I command you. So shall you be my people, and I will be your God."

God does not belong to Israel, and Israel to God, because of the privilege of race, the wound of circumcision or the leisure of sabbath. Here, in fact, God explains as to servants what they must do to please him. But in the Gospel, the Lord says to his disciples, "You are my friends if you do what I command you. No longer do I call you servants, for the servant does not know what his master is doing; but I have called you friends, for all that I have heard from my Father I have made known to you."[280] And after they have become friends, they are transformed from friends into children: "But to all who received him, who believed in his name, he gave power to become children of God."[281] Thus, he commands both friends and children: "You, therefore, must be perfect, as your heavenly Father is perfect,"[282] enjoining a likeness of perfection, not an equality.[283] And where you have obedience to the commandments, there you have the likeness of God. And the statement, "when I brought them out of the land of Egypt, from the iron furnace," yields this understanding: that the blazing iron furnace (or oven) signifies the magnitude of the suffering and punishment, not some place of punishment prepared with actual iron materials.

11:5a: ". . . that I may perform the oath which I swore to your fathers, to give them a land flowing with milk and honey, as at this day."

The ancestors are seen as having received the fulfillment when the children receive it, and so the promise given to Abraham is fulfilled in those who come after him. We should, moreover, understand the "land flowing with milk and honey" hyperbolically as representing an abundance of all things, as it says, "For him may honey flow and the bramble bear spices,"[284] and again, "and stayed the wine that once ran everywhere in streams."[285] Otherwise, we may certainly interpret the "land flowing with milk and honey" tropologically[286] as the church of Christ, where we, as little children and suckling babes, are trained up through faith, so that we may be able to receive solid food.[287]

---

[277]Jerome's "pact" (*pactum*) matches Aq and Sym (*synthēkē*), whereas the LXX and Th use *diathēkē*, which Jerome translates into Latin as *testamentum*. [278]Heb *bĕrit*. See Jer 31:31-34. [279]Not just to the city of Jerusalem, as previously. [280]Jn 14:14-15. [281]Jn 1:12. [282]Mt 5:48. [283]According to Jerome, the Pelagians believe that they can attain equality with God in moral perfection (i.e., absence of sin). [284]Virgil *Ecl.* 3.89 (LCL). [285]Virgil *Georg.* 1.132 (LCL). [286]The Latin word *tropologice* is taken from a Greek rhetorical term that refers to the figurative sense of a word as opposed to its literal or proper sense. In Christian exegesis after Origen it became a technical term for the spiritual sense of the text. [287]Heb 5:12-14.

11:5b: *Then I answered, "Amen, Lord"*—in place of which the LXX translated, *"So be it, Lord,"* for this is what "amen" signifies.[288]

The Lord said, "I swore to your fathers, to give them a land flowing with milk and honey,"[289] which is precisely how things are today. The prophet, because he loves his people, takes up the Lord's oath and expresses his desire that it be true and that the things given might endure forever. Thus he says, "Truly, Lord, may you fulfill what you have promised," or "So be it, Lord," that is, "May what you have given remain forever!"

11:6: *And the Lord said to me, "Proclaim"—or "Read"*[290]*—"all these words in the cities of Judah, and outside Jerusalem: Hear the words of this pact and do them."*

God, who is most merciful, often foretells things that are going to take place, so that hard hearts may in the end be softened into believing. Moreover, he foretells these things both in the city of Jerusalem and out in the countryside, so that for both of these distinct groups their repentance may be the same.

11:7-8: *"For warning I warned your fathers, in the day when I brought them up out of the land of Egypt even to this day; rising early I warned them, saying, Obey my voice. Yet they did not obey or incline their ear, but every one walked in the stubbornness of his evil heart. Therefore I brought on them all the words of this pact, which I commanded them to do"*—everything up to this point is not found in the LXX; but what follows, *"but they did not,"* was written by the LXX, although it was attached to the end of the previous passage, where it says,

"Hear the words of this covenant and do them, but they did not."[291]

How God rose early and repeatedly poured forth to them his words through the prophets, how he brought them up out of Egypt and frequently warned them, saying, "Obey my voice!" and how they followed after the stubbornness of their heart and were punished as they deserved, we have already explained above.[292]

11:9-10: *Again the Lord said to me, "There is treason among the men of Judah and the inhabitants of Jerusalem. They have turned back to the iniquities of their forefathers, who refused to hear my words; they have gone after other gods to serve them; the house of Israel and the house of Judah have broken my covenant which I made with their fathers."*

In place of "treason" (which we rendered in accordance with Symmachus), Aquila, the LXX and Theodotion translated *syndesmon*, which we could express as "conspiracy."[293] When Athaliah discovered that a plot was being made against her in the temple, she spoke with this same word: "Treason! Treason!"[294] Strictly speaking, Scripture makes use of this word when an offense comes about, not as an accidental sin of the moment but through a plot made ready ahead of time and through treason, and when the perpetrators act with one intention and singular purpose, thus despising the commands of God. And he says that both the fathers and the sons have ignored God and worshiped idols with one mind and equal intention—the "fathers" and "sons" being Israel, that is, the ten tribes, and Judah, that is, the other two, whose capital was in Jerusalem.

---

[288]Heb *'āmēn* ("surely!" KB 64).   [289]Jer 11:5a.   [290]Jerome matches Sym. Cf. Jer 2:1-2a; 3:12; 19:1-3a.   [291]Jer 11:6 (LXX).   [292]Cf. Jer 7:13-15, 21-28; 19:12-14.   [293]Sym has *synōmosia* (Jerome: *coniuratio*, "treason"). Jerome reports that the LXX, Aq and Th all have *syndesmos* (Jerome: *colligatio*, "conspiracy"), although the Syro-Hexapla gives a different reading for Aq (*tlwmwtʾ*, "calumny, oppression, iniquity" [Sok 530]).   [294]2 Kings 11:13-14; Heb *qešer* ("alliance, conspiracy," KB 1154).

They who shared the same purpose in despising God would share equal punishments in suffering captivity.

11:11-12: *"Therefore, thus says the Lord, Behold, I am bringing evil on them that they cannot escape; though they cry to me, I will not listen to them. Then the cities of Judah and the inhabitants of Jerusalem will go and cry to the gods to whom they burn incense, but they cannot save them in the time of their trouble."*

God will not listen in their time of need and trouble because they were unwilling to hear the voice of the Lord. Saul also suffered this: when Saul was greatly in fear of the Philistine army and did not deserve to receive the word of the Lord, he turned to a sorceress in order to learn from idols what he should have wrenched out from the Lord through persistence in prayer and weeping.[295] From this we learn that even if the Lord does not listen to us we should not stop praying, nor should we flee to demons for help, since they are not able to help those who worship them; rather, we should flee to the help that comes from the Lord, who, when angered, is quickly appeased and alters his judgment, provided that those against whom he was angry change their ways. All of this, of course, pertains to the tribe of Judah and the city of Jerusalem, who are facing captivity.

11:13: *"For your gods have become as many as your cities, O Judah; and as many as the streets of Jerusalem are the altars you have set up to shame, altars to burn incense to Baal."*

If we read in the books of Kings and Chronicles,[296] we will find that Judah and Jerusalem did much worse than Israel. Thus, however many cities they had, they also had that many idolatrous images; also, however many streets

and chief roads were in the city of Jerusalem, they also had that many altars to their own shame, where they offered sacrifices to the idols of Baal.

11:14: *"Therefore do not pray for this people or lift up a cry or prayer on their behalf, for I will not listen when they call to me in the time of their trouble."*

He warns Jeremiah not to petition the Lord on behalf of those against whom judgment has already been rendered, lest it seem that his prayer is ineffectual and that he is not heard on account of their evil deeds. "Do not pray for them," he says, "or lift up a cry, so as to endeavor to alter my judgment by crying and calling to mind the mercy of the old *historia* (in which I always had compassion on them).[297] For even if you did this, I would not listen to those who were forced to entreat me in their time of need." We learn from these things that it is vain for anyone to entreat God on behalf of another when that other person is not worthy to receive that for which God is entreated.

11:15-16: *"How is it that my beloved in my house has done these many wicked deeds? Will sacred flesh remove from you your evils, in which you gloried? The Lord called you a rich olive tree, fair, fruitful and lovely; but at the sound of his great speaking, fire broke forth in it and its shoots were burned up."*

He calls the people of Judah "beloved" and most pleasant—a people who set up and worshiped idols in his temple and thought that by doing this they could appease God's anger as long as they offered up many sacrificial victims. And they gloried in the multitude of their sacrifices, which cannot take away the

---

[295]1 Sam 28:5-8. [296]E.g., 2 Kings 21; 2 Chron 33. [297]By *historia* Jerome has in mind Old Testament stories about God's past mercies to Israel.

evils of their sins.[298] Furthermore, he compares Jerusalem (or, all the Jewish people) with a fair and fruitful olive tree, which was inflated with pride and did not act humbly or understand its Creator and Lord. So, because it was puffed up with pride, it was set ablaze with the fire of the Lord to such an extent that its branches or "shoots" were "burned up" and reduced to nothing—that is, all the people were destroyed by the enemy's sword. This is also the sense in another passage where it is said to Jerusalem: "I planted you as a fruit-bearing vine, wholly pure. How then have you turned into bitterness and become an alien vine?"[299]

When its walls are torn down, the boar from the forest ravages it and all the beasts devour its fruit, then we speak this passage to the leaders of the church: "How is it that my beloved in my house has done these many wicked deeds?" Or else we speak it to the wealthy who think that they deserve God's mercy even though they plunder the alien and do not remove the evils of their hearts. "Will sacred flesh remove from you your evils, in which you gloried?" As it is now, the names of those who make offerings are read aloud publicly, and the redemption of sins is turned into acclamation. They do not remember the widow in the Gospel, who conquered the donations of all the wealthy by dropping two copper coins into the treasury.[300]

11:17: *"The Lord of hosts, who planted you, has pronounced evil against you, because of the evil that the house of Israel and the house of Judah have done, provoking me to anger by burning incense to Baal."*

He says, "Your Lord planted you and called you a rich olive tree, fair and fruitful. But

since flame descended on you at the sound of God's great speaking and consumed all your branches, he who planted you now pronounces evil against you." He does not "pronounce evil" through unjust judgment or rash perverseness of speech, but " 'because of the evil that the house of Israel and the house of Judah have done,' eagerly burning incense to Baal so as to provoke me to anger." Even though God is able to do whatever he wishes, he still gives his reasons, so that it does not appear that he is acting unjustly, as it is written: "so that you are justified in your sentence and blameless in your judgment."[301]

11:18-20: *You, O Lord, made it known to me and I knew; then you showed me their intentions. But I was like a gentle lamb led to the slaughter, and I did not know; for it was against me they devised schemes, saying, "Let us throw wood into his bread,[302] let us wipe him out from the land of the living, that his name be remembered no more." But, O Lord of hosts, who judge righteously, who try the heart and the mind, let me see your vengeance on them, for to you have I revealed my cause.*

There is agreement among all churches that these things were spoken by Christ under the *persona* of Jeremiah. The Father made known to him how he ought to speak and showed him the intentions of the Jews. Like a lamb led to the slaughter, Christ opened not his mouth,[303] and he "did not know"—"sin" should be supplied, according to what was said by the apostle: "For our sake he made him to be sin who knew no sin."[304] And they said, "Let us throw wood into his bread"—that is, the cross into the body of the Savior (for he himself said, "I am the bread that came down from

---

[298]Heb 10:4. [299]Jer 2:21 (LXX). [300]Mk 12:41-44; Lk 21:1-4. [301]Ps 51:4. [302]The Hebrew text as we have it says, "Let us destroy the tree (or 'wood') with/in his (or 'its') bread." Jerome's understanding of the sentence is similar to that of the LXX. Targ: "Let us throw poison into his food." Sym: "Let us destroy his bread with wood." Aq follows the preserved Hebrew text literally. [303]Is 53:7. [304]2 Cor 5:21.

heaven"),[305] and "let us eradicate him"—or "wipe him out"—"from the land of the living." For they were contemplating this wickedness in their mind, in order to blot out his name forever. But the Son, according to the sacrament of his assumed body, speaks to the Father and invokes his justice. He praises God's righteousness and calls on God, who examines the heart and mind, to render to this people what they deserve, saying, "Let me see your vengeance on them"—on them, that is, who persist in wickedness, not on them who turn to repentance. Concerning this latter group, Christ says on the cross, "Father, forgive them, for they know not what they do."[306] And to the Father he reveals and discloses his cause, namely, that he is crucified, not because he is deserving but because of the wickedness of the people, as he says: "The ruler of this world is coming, and he finds nothing against me."[307] The Jews and our Judaizers understand these things to be spoken out of the *persona* of Jeremiah,[308] and they assert that Jeremiah suffered these evils at the hands of the people because he prophesied the future onslaught of captivity. But I do not know how they can demonstrate that Jeremiah was crucified when Scripture does not make mention of this; unless, perhaps, the people were plotting it but did not do it.

11:21-23: *Therefore thus says the Lord concerning the men of Anathoth, who seek your life, and say, "Do not prophesy in the name of the Lord, or you will die by our hand"—therefore thus says the Lord of hosts: "Behold, I will visit this on them; the young men shall die by the sword; their sons and their daughters shall die by famine; and none of them shall be left. For I will bring evil on the men of Anathoth, the year of their visitation."*

This appears to be contrary to our previous discussion, in which we wished to demonstrate that the things said were in fact spoken out of the *persona* of Christ and not out of the *persona* of Jeremiah, who properly speaking is the one who lives in the village of Anathoth, which is three thousand paces from Jerusalem.[309] But if we understand the etymology of the town Anathoth, which is interpreted as "obedience,"[310] it is clearly shown that the "men of Anathoth," who formerly attended to the Lord's precepts, represent all the Jews and especially those who live in the city of Jerusalem. It is against them that the last-stated judgment comes, in that they perish by the devastations of siege, by sword and by famine. Moreover, so that we may be free from any uneasiness about this interpretation, we will follow this rule: all the prophets dealt with most subjects in type of our Lord and Savior,[311] and whatever was fulfilled at that time through Jeremiah is prophesied in the future concerning the Lord.

BOOK THREE

The legendary Lernean serpent,[1] so they say, sprouted forth with many snakes from the midst of its head. Scylla, monster of the Sicilian Strait—with a maiden's face, to be sure, but girded with hounds[2]—smashed the wrecked ships of unfortunate sailors. Joined to the same shore was the death-bearing song of the Sirens, which the Homeric Ulysses escaped, it is said, by shutting the ears,[3] thus escaping insurmountable evil by prudent judgment. I also desired to do this and thereby

---

[305]Jn 6:51. [306]Lk 23:34. [307]Jn 14:30. [308]On the Judaizers, see also Jer 13:17c; 17:21-27; bk. 6 prol.; Jer 31:23-24, 27-30; 31:38-40. See the Introduction. [309]See Jer 1:1-3. [310]Heb 'ntwt. This was a traditional etymology found in Greek sources; see OS 201.37; Origen *Hom. Jer.* 10.4. It may perhaps be connected to 'nh I, "to respond," or 'nh II (Niphal; "to submit" [see KB 851-53]). [311]*in typum domini salvatoris.* **Book Three** [1]The Hydra. See Virgil *Aen.* 8.300; Lucretius 5.26-27; Euripides *Herc. Fur.* 1274-1275; Hesiod *Theog.* 311. [2]See Virgil *Aen.* 3.424-428; Ovid *Metam.* 13.731-734, 14.60-67; Lucretius 5.892-893; Homer *Od.* 12.85-100. [3]Ulysses (Odysseus) shut his comrades' ears (Homer *Od.* 12.165-200).

avoid the madness of heretics,[4] playing to myself and to mine like the Theban bard[5] and keeping in mind this prophetic saying: "When the sinner took his stand against me, I was hushed and kept silent from good things!"[6]

Nevertheless, the devil has not permitted that I should be able to devote myself, quietly content with my wishes, to explaining the sacred Scriptures and to transmitting to those of my language the learning of the Hebrews and the Greeks.[7] Instead, the devil presses me day and night, both openly and through deception, by mixing together falsehood with truth—or rather, besmearing complete lies with deceitful honey, so that one who hears the sweetness of the words will not fear the poison within.[8] He promises peace, so that he may wage bitter wars; he laughs, so that he may bite; he extends his hand, so that he may kill the simple Abner unexpectedly.[9] No doubt this is what the apostle means: "for we are not ignorant of his subtleties."[10] At one moment he remains silent, at another he accuses; and he sends to the whole world his papyrus letters, which previously carried gold but now speak evil.[11] Furthermore, he interprets our patience, which comes from Christian humility, as the sign of a bad conscience.

The devil, although mute, barks through his big, fat Alpine dog,[12] who is more fierce with his heels than with his teeth. For he has an offspring of the Scottish race from the region of the British, who, like Cerberus in the stories of the poets, must be struck with a spiritual club,[13] so that, together with Pluto his teacher, he may be put to rest in eternal silence. But these things are for another time. As for now, I will start in on my third book on Jeremiah, in which I will endeavor, O brother Eusebius, to fit the broad plains of interpretation into the narrow path of a commentary.

12:1-2: *You are just, O Lord, when I dispute with you—or because I will defend myself to you;*[14]*—yet I would plead my case before you. Why does the way of the wicked prosper? Why do all who are treacherous and act unjustly thrive? You plant them, and they take root; they advance—or produce children*[15]*—and bring forth fruit; you are near in their mouth and far from their heart.*

This is a disputation against all who act unjustly. The same idea is expressed briefly in the seventy-second psalm, where the prophet says, "How good is the God of Israel to those with an upright heart! But as for me, my feet had almost stumbled; my steps had well nigh slipped. For I was envious of the arrogant, when I saw the prosperity of the wicked," and so on.[16] But properly speaking this is said against heretics. They prosper despite their wickedness, and they produce as children those whom they ensnare in their heresy. They

---

[4]Ambrose *Fid.* 1.6.46, compares heresy with the Hydra and Scylla. See also *Fid.* 3.1.4, where Ambrose likens the snares of this world to the Sirens' song and recommends that the wise person escape by being bound with the chains of prudence.   [5]The Theban flute player Antigenidas was reported to have said to a well-trained pupil who had failed to win approval from the untaught masses, "Play to me and to the Muses" (Valerius Maximus 3.7 ext. 2; Cicero *Brut.* 187; Dio Chrysostom 78.18; cf. Symmachus *Ep.* 9.115.2).   [6]Ps 39:1-2 (LXX [38:2-3]).   [7]Cf. *Comm. Zach.* 6:9-15: "I formerly resolved to deliver to Latin ears the secrets of Hebraic learning and the hidden knowledge of the teachers of the synagogue, insofar as it touches on the sacred Scriptures; for this reason, I must outline the *historia* in the passages that are most obscure. Likewise, I must set forth that which I have received from the authors of the church."   [8]Cf. Ambrose *Tob.* 9.35; Prudentius *The Origin of Sin* 330-336; Augustine *Tract. Ev. Jo.* 7.6; Ovid *Am.* 1.8.104. On the use of honey to cover the foul taste of medicine, see Lucretius 1.935-50 (cf. 4.10-25).   [9]2 Sam 3:27.   [10]2 Cor 2:11.   [11]Cf. Is 18:2 (LXX) and Jerome *Ep.* 51.1, which is a Latin translation of a letter from Epiphanius to John of Jerusalem, in which Epiphanius refers to the papyrus letters of Is 18:2 in connection with a letter supposedly written against him that will come to nothing and be carried away by the sea. The devil is still the subject here, but Jerome also seems to have an individual in view (see next note).   [12]Pelagius. The mute devil who now speaks through Pelagius is Rufinus; see Jerome's comments at Jer 22:24-27.   [13]Hercules was ordered by Pluto to capture Cerberus without the use of a weapon (Apollodorus 2.5.12). Jerome must likewise counter Pelagius with a spiritual club rather than a physical one.   [14]Jerome matches Sym.   [15]MT: *hlk* ("walk, go").   [16]Ps 73:1-2. Jerome identifies this as Ps 72 following the LXX numbering.

are treacherous and act unjustly so as to plunder the church. Even as they persist in the depravity of their opinion, they boast that they have been planted by God and taken root, and that they have produced children and brought forth fruit. Although they often repeat the name of Christ, they do not have God dwelling with them, as Isaiah says: "This people honors me with their lips, but their heart is far from me."[17]

12:3: But you, O Lord, know me; you see me and try my mind toward you. Gather them together like sheep for a sacrifice, and set them apart for the day of slaughter.

It should be no cause for stumbling that the impious—or, all heretics—flourish for a time. For "you, O Lord, know me; you see me and try my mind toward you." Whom has God the Father known like his own Son? For "no one knows the Son except the Father, and no one knows the Father except the Son and anyone to whom the Son chooses to reveal him."[18]

He says, "Even though the heretics prosper, even though they produce children and bring forth fruit, and even though you are nearby in their mouth but far from their heart (that is, their conscience),[19] it is no small consolation to know that they are being fattened like cattle for a sacrifice. You will gather them together into the city of Jerusalem—or into their meeting places[20]—so that they, like sacrificial victims, may be cut up to death and then set apart, their throats having been cut with an ecclesiastical blade. For the slaying of heretics is the salvation of those who have been deceived.

12:4: How long will the land mourn and the **grass of every field wither because of the wickedness of those who dwell in it? The beasts and the birds are consumed, because men said, "He will not see our latter end"—or "God will not see our ways."[21]**

Whatever good or bad happens in the world, it does not happen apart from divine providence simply by chance; rather, it happens by the decree of God. Now the earth is barren and the grass withers: do you want to know the reason? It is the evil deeds of those who inhabit the land that are doing this, and it has reached the point where even the beasts on the land and the birds in the sky are consumed, since these things are all created for the use of people. But they have risen up in such great blasphemy that they say that God is ignorant of their ways and does not know what each one will experience. And when he says "how long," this indicates that God's anger will persist, because the mind of the sinners will not change.

12:5: "If you have raced with men on foot, and they have wearied you, how will you compete with horses? And if you are putting your faith in a safe land, how will you do in the haughtiness"—or "roaring"[22]—"of the Jordan?"

He says, "If you have been worn out by your frequent captivities to nearby nations—the Moabites, Ammonites, Philistines and Idumeans—how will you manage a distant captivity, which will lead you all the way to Chaldea?" He compares men on foot with horses, since according to *historia* all of Persia and the whole of Babylon (and the armies of those regions) took genuine delight in their cavalry. Moreover, because of the difficulty of

---

[17]Is 29:13. [18]Mt 11:27; Lk 10:22. [19]Following the lemma of Jer 12:2, the word used here is not "heart" but "kidneys," the sense of which Jerome feels obligated to clarify for his Latin readers. [20]Cf. Jer 3:3b; 4:7; 23:14. [21]Jerome essentially matches Aq, Sym and Targ, although only Aq, like Jerome, uses a plural form for "latter end," whereas Sym and Targ use a singular (Heb *'hryt*). [22]Jerome ("haughtiness") agrees with Aq. The LXX's word for "roaring" can be used metaphorically for arrogance. Heb *g'wn* ("height, pride"), but cf. *g'wh* ("roaring") in Ps 46:4.

the terrain, those nations that I mentioned above are better suited for brigandage than for open combat. And preserving the metaphor he says, "If you have failed in exhaustion racing with men on foot, what will you do if you try to match your steps with horses? And if in your own land you have some confidence, what are you going to do when you cross the Jordan and must endure its raging waters?"

12:6: "For even your brothers and the house of your father, even they have fought against you; they are in full cry after you; believe them not, though they speak fair words to you."

He says, "You will be covered with such deep surges of the Jordan, and the multitude of horsemen coming from afar will so devastate you that even your brothers (the Idumeans) and the house of your father (Moab and Ammon, who were born from the stock of Lot) will contend against you in your time of need and anguish, and they will revile you. So be careful not to trust in them or put faith in your kindred relationship, since through this relationship they will rage with more hatred for you than your enemies have." It is also possible to understand this to be about the Savior, because his brothers and the house of his father fought against him, and in full cry they said, "Crucify him! Crucify him! We have no king but Caesar."[23]

12:7-8: "I have forsaken my house, I have abandoned my heritage; I have given my beloved soul into the hands of her enemies. My heritage has become to me like a lion in the forest, she has lifted up her voice against me; therefore I hate her."

He who in the Gospel said, "Rise, let us go

hence,"[24] and again, "Your house will be forsaken, deserted,"[25] threatens the same things also in this prophet, and he says that he has done that which he is going to do.[26] For Israel is the heritage of the Lord and his allotted heritage.[27] When he says, "I have given my beloved soul into the hands of her enemies," it means this: "I have power to lay down my soul, and I have power to take it up again."[28] Moreover, the heritage (which was formerly) of the Lord, the people of the Jews, became like a lion in the forest against him when it cried out against him with impassioned voice. And since it lifted up its voice against him, he therefore regards it with hatred and casts it away, and what was formerly beloved and dear is now called hateful.

12:9: "Is my heritage to me like a speckled bird? Is she a bird dyed all over? Come, assemble together, all you beasts of the field; hasten to devour!" LXX: "Can it be that my heritage is to me like a hyena's cave, or a cave around her? Go, assemble all the beasts of the field, and let them come in order to eat her!"

He calls his heritage a speckled bird dyed all over, which according to the letter is a peacock. He says, "Israel possessed such great beauty, and Jerusalem was distinguished by such great virtues, that there was nothing good that could not be perceived in her. And so, since my heritage (rather, "formerly mine")—that is, the people of Israel—has become to me like a lion in the forest and has lifted up her voice against me, and I have renounced her with complete hatred,[29] therefore, come and assemble against her, all you beasts of the field—the multitude of various nations—and devour her who did not know her Lord!" But if, as the LXX and other translators have rendered it,[30] it is read,

---

[23]Jn 19:15. [24]Jn 14:31. [25]Lk 13:35. [26]He says here that he has already done what later in the Gospel he says that he is going to do in the future, namely, abandon them and forsake their house. [27]Is 19:25; Deut 32:9. [28]Jn 10:18. [29]Jer 12:7-8. [30]We lack clear evidence for the hexaplaric versions here, but there is evidence for other versions giving a reading similar to the LXX (Field 604-5).

"Can it be that my heritage is to me like a hyena's cave?" we may relate this to the foulness of the nocturnal beast, which lives off the corpses of dead animals and is accustomed to dig up bodies from their graves; indeed, there is nothing so foul that the hyena will not feed on it. This is how Israel has offended its Lord and so is handed over to the biting and gnawing of all beasts.

12:10-11a: *"Many shepherds have destroyed"—or "corrupted"—"my vineyard, they have trampled down"*[31]*—or "defiled"— "my portion, they have made my pleasant portion a desolate"—or "impassable"— "wilderness. They have made it"—or "it has been made"—"a desolation; and it mourns for me"—or "it perishes."*[32]

Let them hear this who desire to be leaders of the people. On the day of judgment they will have to give an account not only for themselves but also for the flocks that were entrusted to them.[33] It was because of the leaders that the Lord's portion was trampled down and defiled, so that, where formerly there had been a lodging place for God, at that spot it became a dwelling place for beasts. But others understand this to refer not to the priests and overseers of the people but to the leaders of the enemies who overthrew Jerusalem, that is, the "vineyard" of the Lord.

12:11b-12: *"And it mourns for me. With desolation the whole land is made desolate, since no man considers in his heart. On all the highways in the desert destroyers have come; for the sword of the Lord devours from one end*
of the land to the other; no flesh has peace." LXX: *"Because of me, with destruction the land is destroyed,"* and so forth.[34]

What we have translated "and it mourns for me" is joined to the previous passage according to the Hebrew, so that it says, "They have made it a desolation"—that is, my heritage— "and it mourns for me," since it has been deprived of my aid. But according to the LXX, God says that it is because of him that the land is destroyed and reduced to desolation, since no one considers in his heart and there is no flesh that has peace. For the flesh is not able to receive the peace of God. "The mind that is set on the flesh is hostile to God . . . and those who are in the flesh cannot please God."[35]

Moreover, according to the Hebrew it is "all" of Judah that is desolated, since no one considers God in his heart and there is no remnant that is able to escape. For through all the highways in the desert there come destroyers—that is, enemy armies—and the sword of the Lord devours from one end to the other. And there is no respite for those fleeing from the city, which is why it says "no flesh has peace."

12:13a: *"They have sown wheat and have reaped thorns, they have received an inheritance but it profits them nothing."*[36] LXX: *"You sowed wheat and you reaped thorns;*[37] *their allotment will profit them nothing."*

"They expected better," he says, "but worse came. They sowed prosperity, but they suffered adversity. They received from the Lord an abundance in all things, which profited

---

[31]Jerome matches Aq, Sym and Targ. [32]Jerome ("and it mourns for me") agrees with Aq, Sym and Targ, which uses the Aramaic cognate of the Hebrew word "to mourn." The LXX reads, "(a desolation) of ruin"; perhaps it is the word "of ruin" that stands behind Jerome's "it perishes"? Or else it is another Greek version? [33]Mt 12:36; Rom 14:10-12; 1 Pet 5:1-3; Jas 3:1. [34]Jerome takes the Hebrew word *'ly* (Jerome: "for me"; LXX: "because of me") with what precedes it, whereas the LXX takes it with what comes after it. Furthermore, Jerome's copy of the LXX seems to lack the word for "whole" (*pasa*) in Jer 12:11b, "the whole land." [35]Rom 8:7-8. [36]Jerome matches Aq and Sym. [37]Jerome's rendering of the LXX agrees with a few ancient witnesses; many LXX MSS have imperatives for the first two verbs of this verse.

them nothing." But according to the LXX, all heretics sow wheat, so to speak, but reap thorns, while the Lord watches to see whether they will produce fruit. And they produced not justice but an outcry.[38] Moreover, this can also be said to those in the church who spoil the words and teaching of the Lord with their malicious conversation. Concerning these people it adds, "Their allotment will profit them nothing." For how could the name of "presbyter" or "bishop" (or any other ecclesiastical office) give them aid, when they carry a greater burden because of their rank and "mighty men will be mightily tested"?[39] To whatever degree more has been entrusted to them, to that degree more is required of them.[40]

12:13b-15: *"You shall be ashamed*[41] *of your harvests"—or "boasting"—"because of the fierce anger of the Lord"—or "because of reproach before the Lord." Thus says the Lord against all my evil neighbors who touch the heritage that I have given my people Israel to inherit: "Behold, I will pluck them up from their land, and I will pluck up"—or "cast out"*[42]*—"the house of Judah from among them. And after I have plucked them up, I will change"—or "I will return"—"and have compassion on them, and I will bring them again"—or "settle them"*[43]*—"each to his heritage and each to his land."*

It is said to those whose allotment and ecclesiastical office will profit them nothing that they will be ashamed because of their boasting and their reproach before the Lord. And regarding what he adds, "against all my evil neighbors": according to the letter, those near to the holy land are Idumea, Philistia, Moab and Ammon;

but according to tropology,[44] they are all the heretics, who are reckoned under Christ's name and are thought to be nearer to Christ than those who live in the holy land but who touch the heritage of God and destroy it. It is said of them that they will be removed from their land and that the house of Judah will be taken from them. But those who have been plucked up and freed from the jaws of heretics will find God's compassion and will come again to their heritage and land.

12:16-17: *"And it shall come to pass, if they will diligently learn the ways of my people, to swear by my name, 'As the Lord lives,' even as they taught my people to swear by Baal, then they shall be built up in the midst of my people. But if they will not listen, then I will utterly pluck up that nation and destroy it, says the Lord."*

If those who have crossed over from heresy to the church will learn the ways of God's people and swear by the Lord's name and not by the name of idols, which they fashioned from their own minds, then they will be built up by the Lord and will become part of God's people. But if, having come to the church, they hold on to the remains of their perverse teachings and will not listen to the words of the Lord, then "that nation" will be utterly plucked up and eternally destroyed, so that no opportunity is left for them to repent. We perceive this happening daily, and in these matters we learn that heretics imitate the truth of the faith in order to deceive the simple. They themselves are not converted to the faith, but they drag the faithful toward faithlessness.

13:1-11: *Thus said the Lord to me, "Go and*

---

[38]Is 5:7. [39]Wis 6:6. [40]Lk 12:48. [41]I am reading *confundemini* with Jerome's IH edition and many MSS. I see *confundimini* as simply a copyist's slip. [42]Jerome matches Aq and Sym. [43]Jerome matches Aq. [44]The Latin word *tropologia* is taken from a Greek rhetorical term that refers to the figurative sense of a word as opposed to its literal or proper sense. In Christian exegesis after Origen it became a technical term for the spiritual sense of the text.

buy a linen loincloth,"—or "waistcloth"—"and put it on your loins, and do not put it in water"—or "it shall not pass through water." So I bought a loincloth according to the word of the Lord and put it on my loins. And the word of the Lord came to me a second time: "Take the loincloth"—or "waistcloth"—"that you have bought, that is on your loins, and arise, go to the Euphrates and hide it there in a cleft of the rock." So I went and hid it by the Euphrates, as the Lord commanded me. And after many days the Lord said to me, "Arise, go to the Euphrates, and take from there the loincloth"—or "waistcloth"—"that I commanded you to hide there." Then I went to the Euphrates and dug, and I took the loincloth from the place where I had hidden it. And behold, the loincloth—or waistcloth—was spoiled; it was good for nothing. Then the word of the Lord came to me: "Thus says the Lord: Even so will I spoil the pride"—or "insolence"—"of Judah and the great pride of Jerusalem. This evil people, who refuse to hear my words, who walk in the depravity"—or "uprightness"[45]—"of their own evil heart and have gone after other gods to serve them and worship them shall be like this loincloth, which is good for nothing. For as the loincloth clings to the loins of a man, so I made the whole house of Israel and the whole house of Judah cling to me, says the Lord, that they might be for me a people, a name, a praise and a glory, but they would not listen."

The waistcloth or loincloth that is joined to God's side is the people of Israel. As with linen, once they have been taken up from the ground and are filthy, they possess neither softness nor brightness, and yet they still cling to God through his mercy. After they had sinned (for this kind of linen loincloth is rational), they were led across the Euphrates—that is, to the Assyrians—and they were hidden there—that is, they were (in a sense) devoured by a multitude of great and innumerable nations and reckoned as nothing. Then, after a long time, the prophet himself (as a type of God) frees the people from captivity. Nevertheless, after they returned the people still did not obey the commands of God, but they followed other gods, and in the end they even stretched out their hands against the Son of God and so wasted away in eternal ruin.

Every holy man is also a loincloth of God; he is taken up from the ground and from the dust of the ground,[46] and he is joined to the fellowship of God. Also, with great diligence he covers up and encloses things in his church that seem (in a certain sense) filthy, lest they be exposed to the corrosion of the nations and heretics.

If this loincloth touches the water and is immersed in the flowing of the Euphrates so that it is soaked in the waters of Assyria, then it loses its original strength, rots and becomes spoiled. Although Jeremiah did return it to God's use, the loincloth did not have its original beauty or firmness from God but suffered ruin because of its own vice, since the people were unwilling to listen to God's words and "walked in the depravity of their own heart"—in other words, they did what seemed right to them. But the divine word itself explains why he has set forth this analogy, saying, "For as the loincloth clings to the loins of a man, so I made the whole house of Israel and the whole house of Judah"—namely, the ten tribes and the two tribes—"cling to me, says the Lord, that they might be for me a people, a name, a praise and a glory." "And in

---

[45]Jerome matches a Greek reading preserved under asterisk. The LXX is lacking, but Jerome's alternative rendering matches another reading preserved under asterisk and ascribed to Th. The Hebrew word in question, *šrrwt*, usually means "stubbornness," but the root *šrr* has been understood in the sense of "firm," and thus "consistent" or "truthful" (BDB 1057). Jerome follows both hexaplaric readings in adding the explanatory word *evil* to describe "their own heart"—this is lacking in MT.   [46]Gen 2:7.

spite of all these things, they did not listen to me but followed their own vices." Therefore, let him beware who is able to say, "But for me it is good to be near God,"[47] lest he somehow be separated from God's side, immersed in the Euphrates and given over to the power of the king of Assyria. Let him beware that he not be taken up into a cleft of the rock—that is, into the filth and vices of heretics—instead of being taken into that most solid Rock. He should beware lest he become so spoiled that he can never again be used as a waistcloth of the Lord.

13:12-14: *"You shall speak to them"—or "to the people"—"this word: 'Thus says the Lord, the God of Israel, "Every flask"—or "wineskin"—"shall be filled with wine." ' And they will say to you, "Do we not indeed know that every flask"—or "wineskin"—"will be filled with wine?" Then you shall say to them, 'Thus says the Lord: Behold, I will fill with drunkenness all the inhabitants of this land: those from the stock'—or 'sons'[48]—'of David who sit on his throne, the priests, the prophets and all the inhabitants of Jerusalem. And I will scatter them one from another, fathers and sons alike, says the Lord. I will not spare'—or 'long for'—'or pardon or have compassion, that I should not destroy them.' "*

For the Hebrew word *nebel*,[49] the first edition of Aquila put "flask," his second edition put the word *nebel* itself, Symmachus put "bowl," the LXX put "wineskin" and Theodotion put "vessel." All of them are filled not with oil, water, honey, milk or any other liquid substance whatsoever, but with wine and drunkenness, showing that we are a fragile vessel, as the apostle says: "But we have this treasure in earthen vessels." And it is impossible for this vessel not to be filled in us, as it is written,

"For nothing good dwells in my flesh,"[50] and again, "For I do not do the good I want, but the evil I do not want is what I do,"[51] and then, "Wretched man that I am! Who will deliver me from this body of death?"[52] Moreover, the human condition is filled with vices, sins and the drunkenness by which we forget the precepts of God, as the prophet says: "for no one living is righteous in your sight."[53] Now, "in your sight" does not mean "in comparison with God," as heretics old and new and their patrons would like, but "according to God's knowledge," since "man looks on the outward appearance, but God looks on the heart."[54] And sometimes that which seems clean to us turns out to be sordid in the eyes of God. And this is true not only for the common, ignoble and contemptible rabble but also for the kings of the church from the "stock" or "sons" of David, who, leaning back in ease, "sit" with their necks held high and their bellies stretched "on his throne." So also the priests, the second rank in ecclesiastical honor, and the prophets, who appear to have knowledge of the Scriptures ("and Judah," as the LXX added), and all the inhabitants of Jerusalem will be "filled" in punishment for their various sins. And because they have been made drunk, they are scattered from their associations; fathers are separated from sons and sons from fathers. They are polluted by various heresies, they fight fiercely among themselves under the name of Christ, and they contend against their mother who bore them, namely, the church. Therefore he says, "I will not long for them," but regard them with everlasting hatred. "I will not spare them, or pardon them or have compassion," not because of the cruelty of God's sentence but because of the truth of his judgment. For those who slaugh-

---

[47]Ps 73:28. [48]MT does not have any word corresponding to the LXX's "sons." Jerome uses the phrase "from the stock of" as an idiomatic way to express descent, even when it is not literally present in the Hebrew; see Jerome's IH translation at Jer 16:3; 35:19. [49]Heb *nēbel*. [50]Rom 7:18. [51]Rom 7:19. [52]Rom 7:24. [53]Ps 143:2. [54]1 Sam 16:7.

ter my people perish for eternity. According to *historia* this passage can also be understood straightforwardly, that the kings, priests, prophets and all the people of Jerusalem are going to be made drunk with the cup of Babylon[55] and will be overwhelmed by the evils of captivity.

13:15: *Hear and give ear; be not lifted up, for the Lord has spoken.*

Because he said above, "Every wineskin shall be filled with wine," so that kings, priests, prophets and every inhabitant of Jerusalem will be filled with drunkenness, he continues on and says, "Hear and give ear," both externally and internally, with the mind and with the body; and "be not lifted up" with pride, recognizing your frailty and acknowledging that, because of the nature of sin, there is no one who is free from this drunkenness. And so they are spoiled and ruined and unworthy of God's compassion, since they lift themselves up against God in pride.

13:16-17a: *Give glory to the Lord your God before he brings darkness, before your feet stumble on the misty—or dark—mountains! You will look for light, but the shadow of death will be there, and they will be set in darkness—or according to the Hebrew: and he will set it in the shadow of death and in mist.*[56] *But if you will not listen in secret your*[57] *soul will*

weep for your pride—or insolence.

He now calls to repentance those to whom the divine word said, "Hear and give ear; be not lifted up," so that they may give glory to God before they are led to Babylon and their feet stumble on the "dark" or "misty" mountains. Thus it is often said to sinners, "Give glory to God."[58] Furthermore, we read at the beginning of Isaiah's message against Babylon that Babylon and the whole region of the Chaldeans are called "misty" or "dark"; it is written there: "On a misty mountain raise a signal."[59] This word in Hebrew is *nesepha*.[60]

He admonished them that they should repent before they are led into captivity and experience the evils of servitude. Although they look for light, they will remain in darkness. "But if you are unwilling to listen in secret ("in darkness" according to Aquila),"[61] he says, "then (my)[62] soul"—or "your soul" according to the LXX—"will weep for your pride." Not even groaning and lamenting will be permitted openly, so as not to offend the eyes of the conquerors.

Moreover, we can interpret this passage thus: the Savior says, "You should work while it is day; night will come, when no one will be able to work any more."[63] Isaiah also prophesied concerning this time, "For the stars of heaven, Orion, and all the ornaments of heaven will not give their light; they will be dark at the sun's rising, and the moon will not give its

---

[55]Jer 25:15-29; 51:7. [56]The first option represents the LXX and the "Hebrew" translation is Jerome's IH edition. MT has two verbs for "to set": the LXX takes the first (*śāmāh*) as the adverb "there" (*śām*), whereas Jerome translates only the first verb and not the second, perhaps thinking it redundant (cf. Pesh). [57]This pronoun reflects the LXX; Jerome in the IH edition puts "my" (= MT), and his comments on this lemma and at Jer 13:17c presuppose "my," although he is not sure whether God or the prophet is the speaker. Aq has "your," and Sym has "my." [58]Ps 68:34 (LXX [67:35]). [59]Is 13:2. [60]The Hebrew word in Jer 13:16, *nešep*, is understood today as "twilight" or "darkness" (KB 730). The LXX gives "dark," Aq renders "nightly," and Sym translates "bare" as if the Niphal form of *śph*. In the passage cited by Jerome (Is 13:2), the word is *nśph*, which the LXX and most modern scholars take to be a Niphal form of *śph* ("bare") but which an anonymous Greek version used by Basil interprets as "cloudy" (Field II 453). Jerome reads both words as *nešep*, interpreted as "misty" or "gloomy." The transcription that Jerome gives, *nesepha*, represents the form found in Is 13:2. [61]Jerome's rendering in the lemma ("in secret") matches his IH edition, LXX, Sym and Targ and is closer to the Hebrew (*mistār*, "secret places" [KB 608]) than Aq is. [62]See n. 57. The Latin text of the commentary lacks a pronoun here, but Jerome's contrast with the LXX implies that he understands the sense to be "my." This pronoun was in the Hebrew text used by Jerome when he made the IH edition, but it seems to be lacking in the text he has before him when writing the commentary. [63]Jn 9:4.

light."[64] Zephaniah also assents, using the same words, "a day of distress and anguish, a day of misery and devastation, a day of darkness and gloom, a day of clouds and mist."[65] Therefore, before the time of judgment comes and our feet stumble on the dark mountains— that is, the adversarial powers,[66] which have been appointed for torment and torture[67]—let us repent, so that we, although looking for light, are not covered by the darkness of night. We should know that unless we do this, the soul—either of God or of the prophet[68]—will weep for the pride of those of us who were unwilling to listen to the words of God. Therefore, the prophet says. . .

13:17b: *My eyes will weep bitterly and run down with tears—or Jerusalem will weep bitterly and my eyes will run down with tears,*[69]

and I will not be able to hide my grief with silent groans. Moreover, the whole cause of the torment is that *the Lord's flock has been taken captive.*

We say to the Jews and to our Judaizers who follow only the simple *historia* that kills:[70] If you will not listen in "secret"[71]—that is, in "mystery" or in "darkness" (which God made his covering),[72] as is needed (according to Solomon) in order to understand a parable and a dark saying[73]—then the soul of the prophet (or their own soul) will weep for their pride, as they oppose God through their stubbornness. Then there will be eternal weeping and perpetual tears, because the Lord's flock will have been captured and destroyed by the true Nebuchadnezzar.[74]

13:18-19: *Say to the king and the ruling woman—or say to the king and to the powers: "Take a lowly seat, for your beautiful crown has come down"—or "has been removed"— "from your head." The cities of the south are shut up, with none to open them; all Judea—or Judah—is taken into exile, fully taken into exile—or into captivity.*

He enjoins the prophet to speak to king Jehoiachin and to his mother, whom he calls the "ruling woman," "mistress" or "queen," that they should take a lowly seat in the dust; for they will be ruined, and royal authority will be handed over to the king of Babylon. "The cities of the south are shut up"—that is, the cities of the tribe of Judah (and Jerusalem), which is southward near the wilderness; "with none to open them," since they are surrounded by a siege; "all Judea (or "all Judah") is taken into exile, fully taken into exile"—or else, "they got what they deserved,[75] and it was fully done to them," for thus the lxx translated. He is misguided on this passage who understands the "king" as Christ and the "powers" as angels or apostles, in that they assume a lowly body, sit in the dust and let the crown and beauty of strength slip from their head. Similarly, the "shut-up cities of the south" he interprets as the lower region, places that are open to none. And he says that all the beauty of Judah was taken into exile, which was fulfilled in the passion: "They have all gone astray, they are all alike corrupt; there is none that does good, no, not one."[76] Aquila and Symmachus translated the Hebrew word *gebira* as "ruling woman" and "mistress," which the lxx thought was *gebu-roth*, and so they translated "powers."[77]

---

[64]Is 13:10; Amos 5:8. [65]Zeph 1:15. [66]Cf. Rom 8:38 (Vg). [67]Mt 25:41. [68]The word *soul* can stand for the self and can represent the seat of one's emotions. When the text says "my soul will weep," this is an ornate way to say, "I myself will weep," the subject being either God or the prophet. [69]"Jerusalem" is not an attested reading but was probably in Jerome's copy of the lxx. [70]2 Cor 3:6. [71]See Origen *Hom. Jer.* 12.13. [72]Ps 18:11. [73]Prov 1:6. [74]The devil; cf. Jer 27:6-7a; 30:8-9. [75]Captivity. [76]Ps 14:3; Rom 3:10-12. [77]Heb *gĕbîrâ.* Jerome proposes that the lxx mistakenly took the word as the feminine plural form of *gĕbûrâ* ("strength, might"). In this case Jerome thinks that the Hebrew text rules out the proposed spiritual interpretation. Jerome sometimes uses the Hebrew to correct the "pious errors" of Christians who are not informed about the Hebrew; see *Comm. Isa.* 63:1; *Comm. Am.* 4:12-13; Jer 23:18.

13:20-21a: *"Lift up your eyes and see those who come from the north.*[78] *Where is the flock that was given to you, your beautiful flock? What will you say when he punishes you? For you instructed them against you, and you taught them at your head."*

He commands the inhabitants of Jerusalem to lift up their eyes and see the Chaldeans coming from the region of the north. The city is asked, "Where is the flock that was given to you, your beautiful flock? Where are the people that you received from God? Where is your beautiful multitude, which was so large that you would have believed that the mass of a whole province had been gathered into one place?" "What will you say when the Lord punishes you with his rod and hands you over to the Babylonian enemies? You yourself instructed them against you and taught them 'at your head' or 'from the beginning,' in that you fled to them for help and chased after their idols, and through their friendship with you they learned the route by which they might come to you." Let the negligent church hear this, since the church shows its enemies how to seize it with spiritual captivity and tear apart its flock with beastly cruelty.

13:21b-22: *"Will not pangs take hold of you, like those of a woman in travail? And if you say in your heart, 'Why have these things come on me?' it is for the greatness of your iniquity that your shameful parts are exposed, and your heels are defiled"—or "dishonored."*

"While you are unaware, sudden captivity will seize you just like unexpected labor seizes a woman. But if you want to discuss the matter and find out why you were handed over to the enemies, then listen clearly: it is the magnitude of your iniquity that has done these things to you, so that your disgrace is exposed and your fornications are displayed publicly, as when a harlot's clothes have been stripped away." Through these things we learn that, as long as our sins are minor, God bears with us patiently and looks for our repentance; but if we are going to join transgression to transgression and heap up a pile of sins, then our private parts will be exposed and our heels will be displayed to all,[79] either in the present world or in the future. "For nothing is hidden that shall not be made manifest,"[80] when this passage from Daniel is fulfilled: "These shall arise to everlasting life, and those to shame and everlasting contempt."[81]

13:23: *"If the Ethiopian can change his skin or the panther his variations, then also you can do good even though you learned evil."*

This testimony is used against the church by those who assert that people have diverse natures and that the blackness or variation of sinners is so great that they are incapable of crossing over to the brightness and beauty of a single color;[82] but those who assert this are not paying attention to what follows: "You can do good even though you learned evil." For whatever can be learned does not come from

---

[78]In Jerome's IH edition and most MSS of the commentary this verse is rendered: "Lift up your eyes and see, you who come from the north!" According to this reading, Jerome is taking *habbā'îm* ("coming ones") as vocative. Jerome's comments below, however, reflect the idea that *habbā'îm* is the object of the imperative ("see!"), which agrees with the LXX. It is most likely that Jerome in the commentary translated *habbā'îm* as the object, but this was corrupted in the MSS under the influence of the IH edition. No evidence is preserved for the hexaplaric versions. [79]The spreading of the heels betokens the spreading of the legs, which represents a posture designed to invite "fornication," either literal or metaphorical (i.e., idolatry). [80]Lk 8:17; Mk 4:22. [81]Dan 12:2. [82]This comment appears to be directed against Manichaeans, who held to a radical dualism between darkness and light and whose distinctions between the "elect" (the spiritually elite), "hearers" (regular followers of Manichaeism who may be reincarnated as "elect") and non-adherents seemed to underestimate the possibility that sinners can be brought to God. It should be noted that Jerome's theological comment works only with his particular interpretation of the verse; many modern interpreters take the verse to be saying that the people are not able to do good.

nature but from effort and the will of the individual, although a sinful will can, to some extent, be changed into a sinful nature by the regular practice and excessive love of sinning. But what is impossible for people is possible for God:[83] even if the Ethiopian and the panther appear unable to change their nature, he who works in the Ethiopian and the panther is able to do so, as the apostle says: "I can do all things in Christ who strengthens me."[84] Also in another passage he says, "I worked harder than any of them, though it was not I but the grace of God that is in me."[85] And he also says, "It is no longer I who live, but Christ who lives in me."[86] And again, we read that it is written: "What have you that you did not receive? If then you received it, why do you boast as if it were not a gift?"[87] For these reasons, let not the wise person glory in his wisdom or the mighty man in his might, or the rich person in his riches, or the chaste person in his chastity,[88] since he knows that in all these things the virtue comes from Christ, not from those who would boast in their virtues.

13:24-25a: *"I will scatter them like chaff driven by the wind from the desert. This is your lot, and the portion of your measure from me"—or "the portion of your disobedience against me"—"says the Lord."*

"Because of their regular practice of doing evil, they were not able to change their nature—not by fault of their Maker but due to their ingrained zeal for wickedness. For this reason, like chaff snatched up by the wind I will scatter them in the desert, in accordance with what is written elsewhere: 'like chaff, which

the wind drives from the face of the earth.' "[89] And he makes an *apostrophe*[90] toward Jerusalem, saying that this is its lot and the portion that it chose for itself, an abundant measure, full and overflowing[91]—or else, it is the portion of its own disobedience, according to which it was unwilling to yield to the Lord. For with what measure you give it shall be measured to you again.[92]

13:25b-27a: *"Because you have forgotten me and trusted"—or "hoped"—"in lies, I myself have stripped your thighs"—or "I will strip and reveal your hind parts"[93]—"before your face, and your shame will be seen, your adulteries, your neighings, and the wickedness"—or "alienation"[94]—"of your fornication."*

The reason for the dispersion of Jerusalem is that they forgot God and trusted—or hoped—in lies. Anyone who trusts in the things of this world more than God forgets God. Therefore, their "thighs" or "hind parts" are revealed so that their shame may be seen, and what ought to be behind them is put in front of them; as a result of this, they themselves will see what they have done, and their shame will be evident not only to them but to all. He says "your adulteries, your neighings"—they exhibit not only lust but also lustful madness, like horses that are eager to mate, as it says in Virgil: "Then, and only then, does the slimy 'horse madness,' as shepherds rightly name it, drip slowly from the groin."[95] Let us petition Jesus, that he not reveal our thighs[96] or our hind parts either in the present age or in the future, but that he may blot out our iniquities and not make evident all of our crimes.

---

[83]Mt 19:26; Lk 18:27. [84]Phil 4:13. [85]1 Cor 15:10. [86]Gal 2:20. [87]1 Cor 4:7. [88]Jer 9:23. [89]Ps. 1:4. [90]*Apostrophe* is that figure whereby the speaker turns from addressing one person, such as a judge, in order to address another individual, such as an adversary; see Quintilian 9.2.38-39. This is how Jerome deals with the shift in pronoun from Jer 13:24 to Jer 13:25. [91]Lk 6:38. [92]Lk 6:38; Mk 4:24; Mt 7:2. [93]Jerome translates the Hebrew perfect verb as past tense. The second option is Jerome's rendering of the sense of the LXX; although the LXX uses only one verb, Jerome adds a second to clarify the meaning ("will strip and reveal"). [94]Jerome's rendering is similar to Sym; Heb *zmh* ("plan, infamy," KB 272). [95]Virgil *Georg.* 3.280-281 (LCL). [96]Reading *femora* rather than *femina*.

13:27b: *"On the hills in the field I have seen your abominations. Woe to you, O Jerusalem! You will not be cleansed after me; how long will it be?"—or "Because you were not cleansed after me, how long will it be?"*

"I see your idols, not only in the city of Jerusalem but also on every hill and in all the countryside." Therefore it is said to the city: "Woe to you, O Jerusalem, because you were not cleansed after me," that is, "even though you claimed to follow in my tracks and you bandied about the confession of my name, you were in no way made clean, since you forgot me and hoped in lies." And so he rebukes the city and says, "How long will it be?" And the sense is: "For how long will I wait for you? For how long will I endure this? Will you forget me and despise my commandments forever?" For they committed fornication on the hills and in the fields, and they certainly were not cleansed, since—with their necks held high in pride—they did not humble themselves under the powerful hand of God but trusted in their crimes and vices.

14:1: *The word of the Lord that came to Jeremiah concerning the drought.*

All things participate in the anger of God. Thus, the sun goes down at noon over sinners;[97] likewise, the moon and the rest of the stars do not give their light.[98] It should be understood that in the time of the siege there was no rain, so that those who were being besieged suffered a deficiency of water. For the city is fed from one spring, the Siloam, and even this is not year-round; up to the present day, deficient rains result not only in a lack of fruit but also a lack of drinking water.

14:2-4: *"Judea"—or "Judah"[99]—"mourns and her gates collapse";—or "are emptied"[100]—they are obscured"—or "darkened"[101]—"on the land, and the cry of Jerusalem goes up. Their nobles send their lessers"—or "youths"[102]—"for water; they come to draw,"—or "they come to the cisterns"[103]—"they find no water, they return with their vessels empty; they are ashamed and distressed"—or "humiliated"[104]—"and cover their heads. Because of the desolation of the land,"—or "And the works of the land fail"[105]—"since the rain did not come"—or "there was no rain"—"on the land, the farmers are ashamed, they cover their heads."*

In this time of drought when the multitude suffers a famine of hearing and learning the word of God,[106] Judea mourns, boasting that it previously had reverence for God and a confession of the true faith. But its "gates" became "empty" or "collapsed" (we should interpret these "gates" as the senses, through which instruction is received into the soul), and then all things became obscure and covered with darkness, so that in Jerusalem neither reason nor the word of doctrine reigned, but outcry and confusion reigned instead. The nobles, who should themselves go to draw water, sent youths who lack the wisdom of age.[107] As a result, they went to the cisterns and did not find water—water that the *historia* narrates that the patriarchs

---

[97]Amos 8:9. [98]Ezek 32:7; Mt 24:29. [99]Both Jerome's IH edition and the LXX have "Judea." "Judah" is strictly speaking closer to the Hebrew form. Cf. Jer 13:18-19. [100]Heb *'ml* ("to dwindle," KB 63). [101]Jerome's rendering (*obscuratae sunt*) can also have the sense "to darken"; the second option ("darkened") is the LXX. The Hebrew *qdr* usually means "to become dark," but see Ezek 31:15, where *qdr* in the Hiphil appears to have the sense "to put into mourning" (KB 1072). [102]Jerome agrees with Aq. Heb *ṣā'ir* means "small" but also frequently means "young." KB 1041 assigns the meaning "lads, servants" to Jer 14:3 alone, supported by an Akkadian cognate. [103]The biblical Hebrew *gb* is "pit" or "cistern" (KB 170); Jerome (or his source) may be thinking of the rabbinic Hebrew verb *gbb* or *gby* ("to gather, collect"; Jastrow 203, 205). [104]The original LXX lacks these words. The first option reflects Jerome's IH edition, and the second (likely found in Jerome's copy of LXX) matches the reading of Th preserved under asterisk. The Hebrew word (*klm*) could bear any of these senses. [105]Jerome is similar to Aq (= MT). [106]Amos 8:11. [107]Sir 6:18.

found.[108] They (namely, the youths) returned with their vessels empty, not because there was no water but because they were unable to find it. They were ashamed and distressed (or "humiliated") and covered their heads, because they could not say with the apostle: "we all, with unveiled face, behold the glory of the Lord."[109] "Because of the desolation of the land"—or else, "And the works of the land fail"—works through which we proceed unto the knowledge of God. And the cause of all this is clear: "since the rain did not come on the land"—the clouds, in fact, were commanded not to pour rain on it. So also regarding the farmers, one of whom said, "you are God's field, God's building," and "we are God's fellow workers,"[110] they are ashamed and cover their heads, understanding that without God's grace and assistance it is pointless for them to exert themselves.

14:5-6: *"Even the hind"*—or *"hinds"*—*"in the field gives birth"*—or *"give birth"*—*"and forsakes"*—or *"forsake"*—*"(her or their offspring),*[111] *because there is no grass. The wild donkeys stand on the bare heights, they draw in their breath like serpents; their eyes fail because there is no herbage"*—or *"grass."*

The barrenness is indeed great when hinds, which draw snakes out of their lairs by the breath of their nostrils and kill the charmed creatures,[112] give birth in the field and forsake their offspring due to the lack of herbage or grass, since they are not making use of the food of grace. Likewise, wild donkeys (about which it is written, "Who let the wild donkey go free into the steppe?")[113] leave the flat plains and stand on the bare heights, where

they cannot run, and they draw in their breath in the manner of serpents. Their eyes fail, and they are not able to see clear light because their rational food has been taken away. This barrenness occurs often in the churches, when hinds and wild donkeys are found among the people but waste away because of the scarcity of teachers; there are found those who are able to learn, but there are not found those who are able to teach.

14:7-8a: *"Though our iniquities answer"*—or *"oppose"*[114]—*"us, act, O Lord, for your name's sake; for our backslidings"*—or *"sins"*[115]—*"are many; we have sinned against you, O hope of Israel, its savior in times of trouble."*

If we are uncertain as to why the rains do not fall on the land and why all things waste away in drought, then we should listen: "'Our iniquities have opposed us.' Therefore, O Lord, not for the sake of our works but for the sake of your holy name, conquer our many backslidings! For 'we have sinned against you,' and the secrets of our heart do not escape your notice.[116] Yet, we trust in you, who are the true hope and expectation of Israel, and you save him in times of trouble, in accordance with what is written: 'In my distress I cried to the Lord, and he answered me.'"[117] In times of drought when there is a scarcity of water we also should say, "We have sinned against you and done evil in your sight, but we await your coming—you who save Israel, not by Israel's merit but by your mercy."

14:8b-9a: *"Why should you be like a stranger in the land, like a wayfarer who turns aside to tarry for a night? Why should you be like a man*

---

[108]Gen 21:25-30; 26:18-22, 32. [109]2 Cor 3:18. [110]1 Cor 3:9. [111]I have supplied the object of "forsakes" (LXX: "forsake") based on Jerome's comments. [112]It was widely believed in antiquity that deer could draw snakes out of their lairs by charming them with their breath; see Lucretius 6.765-766; Pliny *Nat.* 8.118; 28.149; Martial *Epigrams* 12.28; Aelian *Nat. An.* 2.9; Oppian *Cynegetica* 2.233-50; Plutarch *Mor.* 976 D; cf. Josephus *Ant.* 2.246. [113]Job 39:5-6. [114]The Hebrew verb *'nh* generally means "to reply, answer," but when followed by the preposition *b* (as in this case) it often means "to testify against" (KB 852). [115]Jerome's rendering ("backslidings") is a stricter rendering of the Hebrew (*měšûbâ*). [116]Ps 44:21. [117]Ps 120:1.

confused, like a mighty man who cannot save?" LXX: *"Why have you become like a foreigner in the land, like a native resident who turns aside to tarry for a night? Shall you be like one who sleeps, like a man who cannot save?"*

The Jews understand this passage thus: "Why should you separate yourself from your people? Why should you, like a wayfarer looking for a moment's rest, not care what sort of place you lodge in? Why would you pass through to other places and not save your own people? Why would you abandon your own (formerly) glorious temple?" But we say that this passage is about the future dispensation of Christ, that he would be a stranger on the earth, that for a short time he would make his lodging on the earth and that like a powerful man passing through the land he would reach out to the multitude of the nations, so that he might cross over from one place to another, from one people to another and from temple to church.

As for what is said in the LXX, "Shall you be like one who sleeps, like a man who cannot save," this was presented not according to the truth of the matter but by way of analogy, as it is written: "Rouse yourself! Why do you sleep, O Lord?"[118] This was said not because the Lord sleeps, since it is written of him, "He who keeps Israel will neither slumber nor sleep,"[119] but because he appears to be asleep to those whom he has forsaken. Lastly, in the context it is not written "one who sleeps" or "a man who cannot save" but rather *"like* one," *"like* a man," thus showing that in each case it is expressed anthropopathically.[120]

14:9b: *"Yet you, O Lord, are in the midst of us, and we are called by your name; leave us not"—or "forget us not."*[121]

You who will be like a foreigner among the Jews, and like a stranger and wanderer who forsakes his former dwelling. But you will dwell in our midst, and "we are called by your name," so that we are called Christians. Therefore, "do not leave us or forget us," for the mouths of all the prophets have sung to us about your future coming.

14:10: *Thus says the Lord concerning this people: "Because*[122] *it has loved to move its feet"—or "They have loved to move their feet"—"and it has not desisted"—or "they have not refrained"—"and it was not pleasing to the Lord"—or "the Lord was not pleased with them"*[123]*—"now he will remember their iniquity and punish their sins."*

When the people ask, "Why have you become as a foreigner, a stranger and a wayfarer, so that you forsake your dwelling?" the Lord responds to this people, who are (formerly) his: "Do you want to know the reason? It is because the people loved to move their feet and did not take them out of the shackles of sin; or, the people did not desist and were unable to stand still. Because of this, I have forsaken them, and I take no pleasure in them." Therefore, although he delayed for a long time and in his patience was unwilling to punish their sins, because they persisted in their wickedness "he will remember their iniquity" and will punish the sins of those who are sick, so to speak, and who take no thought of God, so that they will cease from sinning any more. Moreover, it should be noted that in the sacred Scriptures the feet of sinners are always moving,[124] but to the saints it is said, "But you, stand here by me,"[125] and elsewhere it is written: "Praise the Lord, O servants of the Lord, you that stand in

---

[118]Ps 44:23. [119]Ps 121:4. [120]Jerome uses the Greek term *anthrōpopathōs*, which is an adverb meaning "in the manner of human passions or experiences." According to Jerome, the word *like* shows that God is not a man who sleeps but is described through the analogy of human experience. See also Jer 19:3b-5; 27:5; 32:35b. [121]Jerome agrees with Aq and Sym (= MT). [122]Jerome has *quia* here (for Heb *kēn*), as opposed to *qui* in the IH edition. [123]The Hebrew forms in this verse are plural (as in the LXX). Jerome translates in the singular to match the singular noun "people." [124]Prov 1:16; Is 59:7; Rom 3:15; Ps 14:3 (LXX [13:3]). [125]Deut 5:31.

the house of the Lord, in the courts of the house of our God!"[126]

14:11-12: *The Lord said to me, "Do not pray for the welfare of this people. Though they fast, I will not hear their cry, and though they offer burnt offering and sacrifice, I will not accept them; but I will consume them by the sword, by famine and by pestilence."*

It is foolish to pray for one who has sinned mortally, as John says: "There is sin that is mortal; I do not say that one is to pray for that. All wrongdoing is sin, but there is sin that is not mortal."[127] Fasts, prayers, burnt offerings and sacrifices are beneficial only when we abandon our vices and lament our former sins. But if we persist in our wickedness and think that we can buy God's favor with our prayers and sacrifices, then we are greatly mistaken, since we are supposing God to be unjust. For if someone has been appointed for the sword, for famine and for pestilence, there are no prayers by which he may be rescued. Therefore, the prophet is told that he cannot accomplish anything by praying, so as to keep him from praying in vain.

14:13-14: *Then I said, "Ah, ah, ah Lord God,"—or "You who are, Lord God"[128]— "behold, the prophets say to them, 'You shall not see the sword, nor shall you have famine, but I will give you assured peace in this place.'" And the Lord said to me, "The prophets are prophesying lies in my name; I did not send them, nor did I command them or speak to them. They are prophesying to you a lying vision, worthless divination and the deceit of their own minds."*

Let this be heeded by teachers who promise prosperity to those who sin and persist in their vices. These teachers say to the rich, "You shall not see the sword of God's torments, nor shall you have famine." You will indeed be abundantly furnished—with words from God! The Lord will give you the most assured peace in that place called the church (i.e., Jerusalem). What is said according to the Hebrew three times, "ah, ah, ah," he uttered in response to the previous statement where the Lord had threatened them, saying, "I will consume them by the sword, by famine and by pestilence."[129] Because the prophets, or rather, the "pseudoprophets,"[130] promised lies, the Lord said through Jeremiah: "Do not listen to the words of these pseudoprophets, since they were not sent by me but came of their own will. For this reason they should not be called 'prophets' but 'diviners,' who speak to the people so as to mislead them." For it is much better to amend your sins because you fear punishment than to be subject to God's judgment because you hope for prosperity.

14:15-16: *"Therefore thus says the Lord concerning the prophets who prophesy in my name although I did not send them, and who say, 'Sword and famine shall not come on this land': By sword and famine those prophets shall be consumed. And the people to whom they prophesy shall be cast out in the streets of Jerusalem because of famine and sword, with none to bury them—them, their wives, their*

---

[126]Ps 135:1-2. [127]1 Jn 5:16-17. This passage in 1 John became the basis for the distinction between mortal and venial sins. According to Thomas Aquinas, mortal sins are those in which "the will sets itself upon something that is of its nature incompatible with the charity that orients man toward his ultimate end . . . whether it contradicts the love of God, such as blasphemy or perjury, or the love of neighbor, such as homicide or adultery," whereas venial sins are those in which "the sinner's will is set upon something that of its nature involves a disorder, but is not opposed to the love of God or neighbor, such as thoughtless chatter or immoderate laughter and the like" (*STh* I-II, 88, 2, *corp. art.*; cited from the *Catechism of the Catholic Church* [New York: Catholic Book Publishing Co., 1994], 1856). [128]Jerome renders the Hebrew interjection *'āhāh* as "ah ah ah" (i.e., one sound for each consonant). The LXX takes the word as a form of the verb "to be" (*hyh*). The Syro-Hexapla preserves readings for Sym ("O Lord") and "the Hebrew" ("ahah, Lord"). [129]Jer 14:12. [130]Cf. Jer 26:7-9a; 28:10-11, 15-17.

sons and their daughters. For I will pour out their evil"—or "their evils"[131]—"on them."

Let pseudoprophets beware, who cause the people of God to stumble by promising prosperity, lest they themselves perish and the people be wiped out in a similar destruction. Let them beware lest they be cast down in the streets of Jerusalem and perish by famine and sword, with none to bury them and cover their shame with the dust of repentance, all because they trampled on the commands of God. For the prophets and the people, their wives, their sons, their daughters and the whole generation will lie in a dung pit without any undertaker. How many are cast down in the streets of Jerusalem! How many unburied we see receiving their evils, which they must suffer now because the Lord is pouring out their evils on them!

14:17: *"You shall say to them this word: 'Let my eyes'—or 'your eyes'[132]—'run down with tears night and day, and let them not be silent,'—or 'cease'[133]—'for the virgin daughter of my people is smitten with a great wound, with a very grievous blow.'"*

This passage is understood in two ways: either God laments for his people and his eyes do not cease from weeping, or else he orders the people that their eyes should weep with tears. And it is no slight thing that is being lamented, since the virgin daughter of his people has been struck with a great wound and an intolerable blow. Moreover, others think that these things are said out of the *persona* of the prophet.

14:18: *"If I go out in the field, behold, those slain by the sword! And if I enter the city,*

behold, those weakened by famine"—or "the pain of famine!"[134] "For both prophet and priest go off to a land that they do not know."

There is just cause for lamenting, since the virgin is smitten, the daughter is struck and the people are destroyed.[135] He says, "If I choose to go outside, I will see those slain. If I go into the city, I will observe those weakened and barely hanging on to their bones because of the hardship of famine." And what wonder is it to say this about the common, ignoble rabble, when also the prophets and priests, who prophesied prosperity to others but who should have been making known the commands of the law, shall themselves go to a land that they do not know and suffer the evil of captivity? Let our own prophets and priests hear this: Because of their negligence there is safety for them neither inside nor outside, since those who are outside shall stumble and those who are inside shall suffer death from famine, so that they who were the authors of these sins shall share in the torments.

14:19: *"Have you utterly rejected Judah? Does your soul loathe Zion? Why have you smitten us so that there is no healing for us? We looked for peace, but no good came; for a time of healing, but behold, terror."*

The prophet is astonished that Jerusalem and Judah (that is, the kingdom of the two tribes), where the religion of God and the temple ceremony were located, would be so suddenly rejected and struck with a blow so great that there could be no remedy for it. "We looked for peace," he says, "and for a time of healing, but no good came. Instead, there was such terror that at the very place where there had previ-

---

[131]MT, like Jerome, is singular.   [132]Jerome agrees with Aq, Sym and Targ (= MT).   [133]Jerome agrees with Aq and Targ, although some modern versions follow the LXX ("cease"). The Hebrew *dmh* can have either meaning (KB 225).   [134]Jerome agrees with Aq and Targ; Heb *thl'ym*. Both Jerome's interpretation and that of the LXX have been supported by modern scholars (KB 1717).   [135]Jer 14:17.

ously been the worship of God and tranquility, all things were filled with strife and the roaring of the enemy." Therefore, if our Zion and Judah are ever rejected and loathed by God's soul, then instead of being astonished we should say what follows:

14:20: "We acknowledge our wickedness, O Lord, and the iniquity of our fathers, for we have sinned against you."

He says, "Both we and our fathers have by the same madness despised God's precepts. The measure of our ancestors has been filled up in us,[136] so that whatever was lacking in them has been completed by what we have added."[137] For this reason it said of Judah: "May the iniquity of his fathers be remembered before the Lord, and let not the sin of his mother be blotted out! Let them be before the Lord continually; and may their memory be cut off from the earth!"[138]

14:21: "Do not spurn us, for your name's sake; do not dishonor your glorious throne; remember and do not break your covenant with us."

We ought to regard as the throne of God's glory not only the temple in Judea, which was often destroyed, but every holy one within whom, as it is written, "you have cast his throne to the ground"[139]—after which his throne is dashed to pieces and destroyed since he has offended God by the multitude of his sins. Yet, he who has perished by his own fault is preserved by the Lord's mercy, which is changed into severe judgment if the Lord should render void his pact by which he promised that we would be saved.

14:22: "Are there any among the carved

images of the nations that can bring rain? Or can the heavens give showers? Are you not he, O Lord our God, on whom we set our hope? For you do all these things."

After many and various words he returns to the title of this prophecy, in which it was written, "The word of the Lord that came to Jeremiah concerning the drought."[140] And so what he says is this: "Since the images of demons cannot give rain and the heavens cannot by themselves give showers, it is you, O Lord our God, on whom we set our hope, in whom we trust and to whom we direct our prayers, saying, 'Give us your rain!' For all things are yours, and whatever is good cannot be given apart from you, to whom it belongs." We say this also against heretics, who are unable to impart the rain of sound doctrines. Although they claim that they are the heavens, and they boast that they are the ones about whom it is written, "The heavens are telling the glory of God,"[141] nevertheless they are not able to give the showers of doctrine. For God alone is the one who instructs his people and imparts diverse kinds of grace to those who set their hope on him.

15:1a: Then the Lord said to me, "Though Moses and Samuel stood before me,"—or "against me"[142]—"yet my heart would not turn toward this people."

For we read that these men held back God's anger for the sake of the people and that long ago they averted impending judgment.[143] He says, "Even if these men were to stand before me or against me (to one of them God said, 'Let me alone, and I will destroy this people!'[144]), still I would not listen, because the crimes of this wayward people have reached their limit."

---

[136]Mt 23:32. [137]Perhaps an ironic allusion to Col 1:24? [138]Ps 109:14-15. [139]Ps 89:44. [140]Jer 14:1. [141]Ps 19:1. [142]The alternative rendering is not the LXX as preserved but may represent the reading found in Jerome's LXX. [143]Ex 32:11-14; Num 14:13-20; 1 Sam 7:8-10; 12:19-25; Ps 99:6; 106:23. [144]Ex 32:10; Deut 9:14.

15:1b: *"Cast"—or "Send"*[145]—*"them out of my sight, and let them go."*

Sinners do not depart from God in terms of place but in terms of the will, although we read that Adam and Cain were cast out from God's presence.[146]

15:2-3: *"And when they ask you, 'Where shall we go?' you shall say to them, 'Thus says the Lord: "Those who are for pestilence, to pestilence, and those who are for the sword, to the sword; those who are for famine, to famine, and those who are for captivity, to captivity."' I will appoint over them four kinds, says the Lord: the sword to slay, the dogs to tear and the birds of the air and the beasts of the earth to devour and destroy."*

The prophet Ezekiel also shows that there are four plagues to which the Jewish people are handed over: the sword, pestilence from famine, beasts and captivity.[147] Among these "beasts" you should understand both dogs and birds, to which their bodies are handed over for tearing, devouring and destroying. For when the Creator has been neglected, it is sure to happen that all created things will rise up together against the sinners.

15:4: *"And I will put them to seething"—or "commotion and distress"*[148]—*"to all the kingdoms of the earth because of what Manasseh the son of Hezekiah, king of Judah, did in Jerusalem."*

We read in the Volume of Days that Ma-

nasseh, after going into captivity and then repenting, returned to Jerusalem and ruled again.[149] But just as the merits of the saints are transmitted down to their descendants (as with David and others),[150] so also the misdeeds of sinners carry through to their descendants, if their children and grandchildren engage in similar acts. Regarding the statement "I will put them to seething" or "to commotion and distress"—this was fulfilled partly under the Babylonians, and now it is fulfilled completely, as the impious people have imitated that most wicked king who filled Jerusalem from one end to the other with the blood of the righteous.[151] From this we learn that the people are frequently destroyed because of the wickedness of kings, leaders and officials.[152]

15:5: *"Who will have pity on you, O Jerusalem, or who will bemoan you? Who will turn aside to ask about your welfare?"*

If God has been offended, it is impossible that anyone would ask about the crimes of these sinners, since no creature is as merciful as the Creator and no stranger is as sparing to others as the Lord is to his own people.

15:6a: *"You have rejected me, says the Lord, you keep going backwards."*

He gives the reason why no one has compassion on Jerusalem, bemoans them or inquires of their welfare: although they should have (following the apostle) forgotten what lies behind and strained forward to what lies

---

[145]Heb *šlḥ* (Piel; "let go," "send away," KB 1514-16). [146]Gen 3:24; 4:16. [147]Ezek 14:21-22. "Captivity" is not in Ezekiel's list of four, but Jerome counts "famine" and "pestilence" in Ezek 14:21 as one, and he may take Ezek 14:22 as a reference to captivity. [148]The first option ("seething") is Jerome, "commotion" is Sym, and "distress" is the LXX as preserved. Jerome's copy of the LXX may have contained "commotion" and "distress." [149]2 Chron 33:11-13. By "Volume of Days" Jerome means Chronicles. He elsewhere gives the title as "Words of the Days," which more closely follows the Hebrew *dibrê hayyāmîm*; see Jerome's preface to his IH translation of Samuel and Kings, where he gives the Hebrew title as *Dabreiamin*. Cf. Eusebius *Hist. Eccl.* 6.25.2; Hilary *Tract. Ps.* (CSEL 22.13). [150]1 Kings 11:12, 34; 15:4; 2 Kings 8:19; 2 Chron 21:7. [151]2 Kings 21:16; 24:4. [152]Cf. Hesiod *Op.* 260-261: "[Justice] sits down at once beside her father Zeus, Cronus' son, and proclaims the unjust mind of human beings, so that he will take vengeance upon the people for the wickedness of their kings" (LCL); Horace *Ep.* 1.2.14: "Whatever folly the kings commit, the Achaeans pay the penalty" (LCL).

ahead,[153] instead they went backwards and longed for Egyptian meat.[154]

15:6b: "So I will stretch out my hand against you and destroy you; I am weary of being petitioned"—or "of petitioning"[155]**—in place of which the LXX translated, "I will no longer forgive them."**

An outstretched hand is an indication of one who is about to strike. The slaying of sinners signifies that anger has been consummated. And what he adds, "I am weary of being petitioned" or "of petitioning," has a double sense: God has worn himself out by frequently pardoning them, and God is tired from constantly provoking them to repentance.

15:7: "I will winnow them with a winnowing fork in the gates of the land";—or "in the gates of my people"[156]**—"I have bereaved them, I have destroyed my people; they did not turn from their ways."**

"What benefit is it to me that they constantly petition me, since they do not turn from their evil ways and repent? For I have winnowed them as with a winnowing fork in order to clean out my field. I have winnowed them in the gates of the earth so that they might, in a certain sense, tread on the threshold of hell. And 'I have bereaved them, I have destroyed my people,' so that they, compelled by the disastrous circumstances, might avoid the impending disasters."

15:8: "I have made their widows more in number than the sand of the seas; I have brought against the mothers of young men a destroyer at noonday; I have made terror fall

suddenly on their cities."

God desires to save sinners by diverse remedies; thus, those who pay no attention when flattered might show fear when someone threatens them. Widows have been made more numerous than the sand of the seas, because the men have been killed. Mothers, whose children have been slaughtered, perceive the destroyer, not lurking about at night but in the clear light of day, so that the obvious strength of the powerful enemy may be exhibited. "I have made terror fall suddenly," he says, "on all their cities"—no doubt on Judah and its sinful people—"so that escape will be as difficult as the calamity was sudden."

15:9: "She who bore seven"—or "many"— "has become weak"—or "has been cast away" or else "has been made empty";[157] **"she has swooned away; her sun went down while it was yet day"—or "midday"; "she has been shamed and disgraced. And the rest of them I will give to the sword before their enemies, says the Lord."**

As we have often said, the Hebrew word *saba* means either "seven," "oath" or "many."[158] This gives rise to differing interpretations: Aquila, the LXX and Theodotion translated the word as "seven," whereas Symmachus translated it "many." Therefore, she who was rich with children is suddenly bereft; she has gone to ruin in broad daylight and is shamed because she is alone. "And the rest of the people," he says, "I will hand over to the sword, so that none of them escapes death and the anger of God."

Others refer this passage to the synagogue, which became weak so that the multitude of

---

[153]Phil 3:13. [154]Ex 16:2-3; Num 11:4-6. [155]The rendering "being petitioned" reflects Aq, whereas "petitioning" matches Jerome's IH edition. Heb *nḥm* (Niphal), "regret" or "relent." [156]Jerome matches Aq and Sym (= MT). [157]The first option ("has become weak") is Jerome's IH edition, and "has been made empty" is the LXX. The basis for "has been cast away" is not known; hexaplaric evidence is lacking. [158]Heb *šibʿâ* ("seven"), *śibʿâ* ("plenty" = "many") or *šĕbuʿâ* ("oath"). See Jer 5:22-24. Cf. Jerome *QHG* 21:30-31; 26:32-33; *Comm. Isa.* 54:1; *Tract. Ps.* 15.10.

the church might grow, as it is written: "The barren has borne seven"—or "many"—"but she who has many children is made weak."[159] Likewise her sun of righteousness (in whose wings are healing) goes down.[160] Therefore, she is covered with eternal shame, as she destroys her own people with a spiritual sword.

15:10a: *Woe is me, my mother; why did you bear me, a man of strife—or of decision*[161]—*a man of contention—or one who is judged—in the whole land?*

This can be understood as *synecdoche* with reference to Jeremiah, since he was not judged in all lands of the whole world but only in the land of Judea.[162] Yet, it corresponds perfectly to our Savior and Lord, who says in the Gospel: "I came into this world for judgment, that those who do not see may see, and that those who see may become blind."[163] And concerning him it is written: "Behold, this one is ordained for the ruin and resurrection of many in Israel, and for a sign that will be spoken against."[164] For who among the philosophers, the Gentiles and the heretics does not judge Christ when they establish laws concerning Christ's nativity, passion, resurrection and substance?[165] Nor is it surprising that Christ, according to the truth of his assumed body, should say, "Woe is me, my mother," since the following words found in another passage clearly fit his persona: "Woe is me! For I have become as one who gathers stalks at harvest time and clusters in vintage season but who has no grain, that he might eat the first fruits!"[166] And lest we think that vile grumblings are being ascribed to the word of God,

as if he is the one lamenting, it immediately goes on to say: "Woe is me, my soul, for the reverent man has perished from the earth!"[167]—not in the sense that we are dividing the persons, as the impious do, but in the sense that one and the same Son of God speaks at one moment according to his flesh and at another moment according to the word of God.

15:10b: *I have not lent, nor have I borrowed, yet all of them curse me.* LXX: *I was of benefit to none, nor was anyone of benefit to me.* Theodotion: *I have not owed anything, nor has anyone owed me.*[168]

Here is the sense for all of these out of the *persona* of Christ: No one presents himself in a manner worthy to receive my money, "nor have I borrowed" from anyone in supporting the saints and the poor, such that I would be in debt to him. Or, "I was of benefit to none, nor was anyone of benefit to me." For no one is willing to receive as much as I desire to bestow. "Nor was anyone of benefit to me." For the salvation of the creature is gain for the Creator. Or else: "I have not owed anything, nor has anyone owed me." No one has given me as much as I wanted to receive, nor has anyone made me a debtor in anything. And that which he adds, "nor has anyone owed me," has this sense: "How could someone owe usury to me, since I have not deemed it appropriate to receive interest?"[169] And he says, "All of them curse me." For who among the heretics and those that err does not curse Christ by believing perverse things and speaking even more perverse blasphemies?

---

[159]1 Sam 2:5. [160]Mal 4:2. [161]For both translation alternatives in this verse Jerome essentially agrees with Aq, Sym and Targ. [162]The Greek *synekdochē* is a figure of speech in which the whole stands for a part or a part stands for the whole; see Quintilian 8.6.19; Cicero *De Or.* 3.168; Jerome *Tract. Ps.* 109:3. [163]Jn 9:39. [164]Lk 2:34. [165]According to Jerome, heresy arises when people try to make apostolic truth conform to the precepts of philosophers (e.g., *Lucif.* 11; *Pelag.* 1.19; *Ep.* 133.2; *Tract. Ps.* 78:9; 140:9; 141:6; 144:12-15). This is probably what Jerome means by philosophers and heretics who "establish laws" for the work and person of Christ. [166]Mic 7:1. [167]Mic 7:1-2. [168]Jerome's rendering agrees with Aq and Sym (= closest to Hebrew). In many Greek witnesses the reading ascribed by Jerome to Th is given as the LXX. [169]Lev 25:37; Deut 23:19; Ps 15:5; Ezek 18:8, 13, 17; 22:12.

15:11: *The Lord said, "Your remnant shall surely be for good; I shall surely meet you in the time of affliction and in the time of distress"—or "anguish"—"against the enemy."*

These things can be interpreted according to the *persona* of Jeremiah, who was compelled to prophesy during a terrible time with captivity imminent, and who endured harsh things from the unbelieving people. In response to what was said above, "Woe is me, my mother; why did you bear me, a man who is judged and criticized in all of the land?" and so on,[170] the Lord says, "Think not about the present but the future; for your remnant and your end will be for good. In fact, even in the present circumstances, although your enemies sought to oppress you, I have been present with you and have protected you by my aid."

Moreover, this can be applied not only to Jeremiah but also to the Savior, according to the dispensation of his assumed flesh. In place of what we translated according to the Hebrew, from "all of them curse me,"[171] to this passage, where it is written, "in the time of distress against the enemy," in the common edition the following is found: "My strength failed among those who curse me. Let it be done, O Lord, while those men prosper! Surely I stood by you in the time of their affliction and in the time of their distress, for good toward the enemy."[172] And this is the sense: "My strength failed among those who curse me"—for they do not understand that my power is made perfect in weakness,[173] and that the more they curse me, the more my strength "fails" among them. And he—either the prophet or the Lord—goes on and says, "Let it be done, O Lord, while those men prosper!"—that is, "Let the curses that my enemies spoke against me come to pass, and let them prosper for good." The Lord said, "In the time of their distress and anguish, when their enemy was devastating them and hastening to capture them, I stood in your sight and petitioned you on their behalf, saying, 'Father, forgive them; for they know not what they do.'"[174] And we often find in this book that Jeremiah, too, prayed on behalf of the people.[175]

15:12: *Will iron be joined in friendship with iron from the north, and bronze?* Symmachus: *Will iron do harm to iron from the north, and bronze?* LXX and Theodotion: *Will iron know? And a bronze wrap?*[176]

The cause of the diversity is clear. The word *iare*, which is written in the present passage, can mean both "friendship" and "harm" in view of the ambiguity of its pronunciation. This same word, if the letter *daleth* is read instead of the letter *res* (which is similar to *daleth*), signifies "knowledge" or "recognition."[177] What is said should be understood in this way: "You should not be indignant that the people are hostile to you; it is not possible for the people, who are hard, to love you, since you are proclaiming to them hard things." Or, "The Babylonians, who come from the north and are like the hardest iron, cannot be joined in friendship with this people, who are hard and ungovernable like bronze." Or, "This hardest iron, that is, the people of Israel, are unworthy of the knowledge of God; they have attained such a level of evil that they have been surrounded by a hard metal, bronze."

---

[170]Jer 15:10. [171]Jer 15:10b. [172]The "common edition" (*editio vulgata*) is the OL (based on the LXX). [173]2 Cor 12:9. [174]Lk 23:34. [175]E.g., Jer 14:7-9, 19-22. [176]Most MSS of the LXX (as we have it) read: "Will iron be known? And your strength is a bronze wrap." [177]The Hebrew verb as it appears in MT is made up of three letters: *yôd*, *rēš*, *ʿāyin*. Jerome, following Aq, interprets it as a Niphal verbal form of *rēaʿ* ("friend"), meaning "to be joined to" (see r'h II, KB 1262; Jastrow 1475). Sym takes the verb to be the Hiphil of r', meaning "to do harm." The LXX and Th read a *dālet* instead of the *rēš* (which differ by only a small point, as Jerome points out in his *Comm. Isa.* 28:9), and so interpret the word as a form of *yd'*, "to know." On Jerome's handling of the confusion between similar letters in Hebrew, see Graves, *Jerome's Hebrew Philology*, 57-59.

15:13-14: "Your wealth and your treasures I will give as spoil, for free,"—or "without price"[178]—"for all your sins, throughout all your territory. I will lead forth your enemies from a land that you do not know,"—or "I will I will make you serve your enemies in a land that you do not know"[179]—"for in my anger a fire is kindled that shall burn over you."

He says, "I will hand over all of your possessions to your enemies without any price, because of the sins that you have committed throughout all your territory. For that purpose, 'I will lead forth your enemies' from the land of the Chaldeans, or 'I will make you serve your enemies' in the land of the Chaldeans, since my fire that is kindled but once in my anger will burn you without being extinguishable. For you supplied the material for your own burning, such that my fire will consume the wood, hay and stubble that are within you." And through this we see that the cause of the burning is not found in the Lord but in those who furnish the kindling wood for the fire.

15:15-16: O Lord, you know; remember me and visit me, and rescue me from my persecutors. In your forbearance take me not away; know that for your sake I bear reproach. Your words were found, and I ate them,—or I bear reproach by those who reject your words; finish them off![180]—and your word became to me—or will be to me—a joy and the delight of my heart; for I am called by your name, O Lord, God of hosts.

What we translated as "you know" is not found in the LXX. Now, he who bears reproach for God's sake has a clear conscience. This is why he says, "Your words"—which you spoke in my mouth—"were found, and I ate them"; that is, they were turned into food for me; or, according to Symmachus, "and I received them favorably," so that they who previously had been a cause for reproach became a joy to me. Thus, even the Babylonians acknowledge that things were fulfilled that Jeremiah predicted were going to take place.[181] Or else, this is the sense: "I have experienced anguish, and I have suffered afflictions from the people who persecuted me, but still I rejoice that I have submitted to your commands, and I have patiently endured hardships for the sake of your name."

15:17-18: I did not sit in the company of merrymakers, and I boasted—or but I was reverent[182]—because your hand was on me; I sat alone, for you have filled me with bitterness. Why is my pain unceasing,—or Why are those who cause me pain overcoming me[183]— my wound incurable, refusing to be healed?— or my wound is strong; how shall I be healed?'[184]—Will you be to me like the falsehood of faithless waters—or like false water that has no faith?

The Hebrews think that these things were spoken out of the *persona* of Jerusalem, because it sat alone and was filled with bitterness and its pain was unceasing.[185] And just as water passes through a city, so also the words

---

[178]Jerome's "for free" (*gratis*) is close to Sym ("for nothing"), and the alternative rendering ("without price") seems to reflect Aq. LXX: "as payment for." [179]Jerome agrees with Sym (Aq is similar), presuming the consonants *h'brty* ("cause to cross through"), as in B19a. The LXX is matched by Targ and Pesh, presuming the consonants *h'bdty* ("cause to serve"), as in many medieval Hebrew MSS and Jer 17:4. [180]Jerome agrees with Aq (= MT). [181]Jer 40:2-3. [182]Heb *'lz*, "to exult, triumph" (KB 831). Jerome and the LXX divide the clauses differently. Jerome: "and I boasted; because your hand was on me; I sat alone" (matching Aq). LXX: "but I was reverent because your hand was on me; I sat alone." [183]Jerome's "unceasing" matches Aq and Sym (MT *neṣaḥ*, "duration" [KB 716]), whereas the LXX's "overcoming" reflects *nṣḥ* in the sense of "to conquer, overpower" (Jastrow 928). [184]Jerome matches Sym on "incurable" and Aq on "refusing." [185]Jerome's report about what the "Hebrews" think may represent the view of a Jewish scholar with whom he consulted, or it may reflect Jerome's conjecture regarding how the Jews would read this passage. The identification of the speaker as the people of Israel is found in several rabbinic sources (e.g., *Sifre Deuteronomy* piska 356; *Pesikta de Rab Kahana* piska 15.2; *Lamentations Rabbah* proem 3).

of their "prophets" that promised them prosperity passed away as false. Yet, it is better that we understand these things to have been spoken out of the *persona* of the prophet, as the words of a holy man who did not sit in the company (or secret counsel) of merrymakers since he feared the hand of God hanging over him, but he boasted in the fact that he did not have fellowship with evil people.

The prophet says, "I sat alone," in accordance with what is written: "I do not sit with false men, nor do I consort with dissemblers; I hate the company of evildoers, and I will not sit with the wicked."[186] And in another passage: "I am alone as I pass through."[187] He says, "Because your hand was on me, I sat alone," "since I fear you, and I am always anticipating your hand hanging over me. I did not want to sit in the company of merrymakers, but I endured my bitterness so that I might prepare joy for myself in the future. I had no relief for my pain but was continuously weighed down with misery, so that I anticipated no cure. For my persecutors were prevailing over me, and my wound became strong. But in this I took consolation: that it was like false water that passes away. For just as waters pass away when they flow—they are seen, and then they fade away—so also every attack made by our enemies passes away because of your aid."

Would that the Lord might make it clear to us that we should not sit in the company of merrymakers and those who take no thought of the future, and that we should not give in to our enemies, but that always we should fear God's judgment and say together with the prophet: "I sat alone, for I was filled with bitterness." Therefore, let there be joy in the present time, not for the company of the wise but for the secret and hidden company of merrymakers. "But for me, it is good to be near

to God and to set my hope in the Lord"[188]—to be filled with shame but to wait for the verdict of my Judge. When the end has come, this verdict will in fact reveal that all sorrow and bitterness have vanished like flowing waters.

15:19-21: Therefore thus says the Lord: "If you will turn, I will turn you, and you shall stand before my face. If you distinguish what is precious from what is worthless, you shall be as my mouth. They shall turn to you, but you shall not turn to them. And I will make you to this people a fortified wall of bronze; they will fight against you, but they shall not prevail over you, for I am with you to save you and deliver you, says the Lord. I will deliver you out of the hand of the wicked and redeem you from the grasp of the strong"—or "of pestilence."[189]

It is clear that what was said previously was not spoken by Jerusalem but by the prophet. And so the Lord responds to him: "If you will turn the people from their sins then I will turn you from distress to joy, and you will stand before my face just as the angels stand in God's presence and see his face daily."[190] And, "If you distinguish what is precious from what is worthless, you shall be as my mouth." "You should not think," he says, "that there is no reward for good works.[191] If by your words you separate my saints from the number of sinners, then you will be as my mouth and you will be united together with my commands. For they should be imitators of you, not you of them. You should not be afraid and say, 'Why is my pain unceasing, and my wound strong (or "incurable"), so that I lack all hope of being healed?'[192] For I will make you as a fortified wall of bronze, so that you may stand against the enemy with complete firmness. I will deliver you out of the hand of the wicked (or,

---

[186]Ps 26:4-5. [187]Cf. Lam 3:28; Ps 141:10. [188]Ps 73:28 according to Jerome's *iuxta* LXX translation (72:28). [189]Jerome agrees with Aq, Sym, Targ and Pesh. Heb ʿrys, "violent, powerful" (KB 884). [190]Rev 3:5; 5:11; 8:2; 14:10. [191]2 Chron 15:7. [192]Jer 5:18.

'from pestilence'), and I will redeem you—either by my blood or in the present situation by my aid." Let us consider how great is the reward that the word of God offers, if it has power to free anyone from error and to lead anyone out from the number of sinners!

16:1-4: *The word of the Lord came to me: "You shall not take a wife, nor shall you have sons or daughters in this place. For thus says the Lord concerning the sons and daughters who are born in this place, and concerning the mothers who bore them and the fathers who begot them in this land: They shall die of deadly diseases. They shall not be lamented, nor shall they be buried; they shall be as dung on the surface of the ground. They shall perish by the sword and by famine, and their dead bodies shall be food for the birds of the air and for the beasts of the earth."*

If in a time of imminent captivity the prophet is forbidden to take a wife, lest he have troubles of the flesh and suffer not only because of his own pain but also because of the miseries of his wife and children, how much more does the apostle command, since the time is short and the end is near, that even those who have wives live as if they did not have them![193] It is therefore superfluous to repeat our censure of the new heretic, where we showed that digamy and trigamy do not come from the law but from self-indulgence.[194] For to act this way is to do *other* than what is thoroughly good, so that you are giving in to this *other* so as to avoid doing something worse! For the apostle gives the reason why he wants young widows to marry: "For some have already strayed after Satan."[195] And this teacher of continence and perpetual chastity, who blasphemously claims that he is equal to God, also praises third and fourth marriages, which I would not call marriages but consolations for misery and last testaments for those who are shipwrecked—unless perhaps he is ascribing such self-indulgence to his amazons that even in decrepit old age they enjoy the battles of lust.[196]

The reason why the prophet is prevented from taking a wife is clear: All will perish in the nearby siege by pestilence, the sword and famine; the number of the dead will be so great that the obligation of burial will not be honored, but the bodies will lie as dung for the birds and beasts to tear to pieces. And this should be noted: to waste away from disease and prolonged illness is a result of God's anger. Thus, Jehoram the son of Jehoshaphat was consumed by illness,[197] and the apostle teaches that those who dishonored holy things became sick, languished and died.[198]

16:5-8: *"For thus says the Lord: Do not enter the house of banqueting or go to lament or bemoan them; for I have taken away my peace from this people, says the Lord, my steadfast love and mercy. Both great and small shall die in this land; they shall not be buried, and no one shall lament for them or cut himself or make himself bald for them. No one shall break bread for the mourner, to comfort him for the dead; nor shall any one give him the cup of consolation to drink for his father or his mother. You shall not go into the house of banqueting to sit with them, to eat and drink."*

The apostle commands that one should not even eat with those who reject God.[199] And beyond that, "do not even greet such a person."[200] The Savior enjoins the apostles not to greet anyone on the road.[201] Elisha likewise forbids Gehazi from greeting anyone when Gehazi goes to heal the boy.[202] More-

---

[193]1 Cor 7:28-31. [194]The "new heretic" is Jovinianus, although Jerome probably also has Pelagius in mind; see Jerome *Ep.* 123.3; *Jov.* 1.14-15; bk. 1 prol. In discussing "digamy" and "trigamy," in view is remarriage (perhaps more than once) after the death of a spouse. [195]1 Tim 5:15. [196]Jerome *Jov.* 2.37. [197]2 Chron 21:19. [198]1 Cor 11:30. [199]1 Cor 5:11. [200]2 Jn 10. [201]Lk 10:4. [202]2 Kings 4:29.

over, it is a custom for those who are mourning to bring food and to prepare a banquet, which the Greeks call *perideipna* and which we usually call *parentalia*,[203] so that funeral rites may be observed for the dead relative. And elsewhere the divine Scripture says, "Give wine to those who are in mourning,"[204] obviously so that they may forget their sorrow. Therefore, he commands the prophet not to console anyone about the people, not to participate in the banquets of God's enemies and not to observe rites for the funerals of those who have departed. For it is one thing to die according to the common law of nature; it is another thing to perish by the decree of God.

He says, "I have taken away my peace from this people. They are unworthy of my steadfast love, and I will spare no age: both the great and the small will perish together, so that they will lack burial." He says, "No one shall cut himself or make himself bald for them." This was a custom among the ancients, and even today it is practiced among certain of the Jews that as a part of mourning they cut their arms and make themselves bald. We even read that Job did this.[205] And so the prophet is told that he should not break bread or proceed to offer comfort for the dead. He should not offer a cup or go into the house of banqueting. Indeed, he should not join in with those who have been prepared for God's judgment. And if this is said concerning those who mourn, what should be done about heretics, whose talk creeps along like a tumor, and who daily undermine the funerals of those who have died in the church?[206]

16:9-12a: For thus says the Lord of hosts, the God of Israel: Behold, I will make to cease from this place, before your eyes and in your days, the voice of mirth and the voice of gladness, the voice of the bridegroom and the voice of the bride. "And when you tell this people all these words, and they say to you, 'Why has the Lord pronounced all this great evil against us? What is our iniquity? What is the sin that we have committed against the Lord our God?' then you shall say to them: 'Because your fathers have forsaken me, says the Lord, and have gone after other gods and have served and worshiped them, and have forsaken me and have not kept my law, and because you have done worse than your fathers.'"

When the church sins, God makes all joy and gladness to cease from it. Concerning this the apostle says, "Rejoice; again I say, Rejoice."[207] "The voice of the bridegroom and the voice of the bride"—about whom it is written, "He who has the bride is the bridegroom."[208] He says, "But if the people ask you why they are suffering these things, and they seek the reasons for their afflictions, then you should respond to them: 'Because your fathers'—who preside over you in the churches—'have forsaken me, says the Lord, and have gone after other gods'—since their god is their belly, and their avarice, luxury and glory is in their shame[209]—'and have served them'—"for whatever overcomes a man, to that he is enslaved"[210]—'and have worshiped them'—for people honor what they love—'and they have forsaken me and not kept my law.'" It is especially important for priests not only to teach the law but to do it, so that they may teach the people subjected to them, the flock of believers, not simply by their words but their examples. And lest they say, "It is an unjust sentence, that 'The fathers have eaten sour grapes, and the children's teeth are set on edge,'"[211] he adds, "and because you have done worse than your fathers," so that just punish-

---

[203]Gk *perideipnon* ("funeral feast," LSJ 1371); Lat *parentalia* ("a festival in honor of dead relations," LS 1303). [204]Prov 31:6. [205]Job 1:20. [206]2 Tim 2:17-18. [207]Phil 4:4. [208]Jn 3:29. [209]Phil 3:19. [210]2 Pet 2:19. [211]Jer 31:29; Ezek 18:2.

ments are brought down on those who sinned worse than their fathers.

16:12b-13: *"For behold, every one of you follows his stubborn evil will, refusing to listen to me; therefore I will hurl you out of this land into a land that neither you nor your fathers have known, and there you shall serve other gods day and night, who will give you no respite."*

Once people have been forsaken by the Lord they do things that are unacceptable. Thus, they go after the desires of their evil hearts, out of which come the most wicked thoughts,[212] and therefore they become separated from the church. Thus they go to a far-off land that neither they nor their fathers knew before they sinned. In this land they serve other gods, which are not gods at all but are only thought to be gods according to the error of those who worship them. Moreover, the fact that he adds "day and night" shows the uninterrupted consistency of these sinners in doing evil, as they devote themselves to disgraceful behavior during the day and to lust at night. "Who will give you no respite" no doubt this refers to the false gods about which he said, "There you shall serve other gods." Therefore, whatever sins we commit, whatever we do in the day and at night and whatever evil deeds we accomplish, it is by the power of demons who never give us respite but always drive us to heap up transgression on transgression and make a pile of sins.

16:14-15: *"Therefore, behold, the days are coming, says the Lord, when it shall no longer be said, 'As the Lord lives who brought up the people of Israel out of the land of Egypt,' but 'As the Lord lives who brought up the people of Israel out of the north country and out of all*

the countries where I had driven them.' For I will bring them back to their own land that I gave to their fathers."

Clearly he is predicting the future restoration of the people of Israel and the compassion they will receive after their captivity. According to the letter these things were fulfilled in part under Zerubbabel, Joshua the high priest and Ezra; but according to the spiritual understanding he is describing things that were going to be completed more truly and more perfectly in Christ. "The time is coming," he says, "when it will not be said, 'this is the people who were brought out of Egypt through Moses and Aaron,' but 'this is the people who were brought out from the north country when Cyrus king of Persia set the captives free.'" He says, "and out of all the countries," which was not fulfilled in the time of Cyrus but will be fulfilled in the last time, as the apostle says: "After the full number of the Gentiles has come in, then all Israel will be saved."[213] We can also relate this passage to the persecutions that befell our people from the days of Nero (about whom the apostle writes, "I was rescued from the lion's mouth"[214]) to the time of Maximinus:[215] just as the Lord had compassion on his people and brought them back to their land, he will surely bring his people back to the church, which he gave to their "fathers," who are the apostles and apostolic men.

16:16-18: *"Behold, I am sending for many fishers, says the Lord, and they shall catch them; and afterwards I will send for many hunters, and they shall hunt them from every mountain and every hill, and out of the clefts of the rocks. For my eyes are on all their ways; they are not hid from me, nor is their iniquity concealed from my eyes. And first, I will doubly recompense their iniquity and their sin,*

---

[212]Mt 15:19. [213]Rom 11:25-26. [214]2 Tim 4:17. [215]Nero (Roman emperor, A.D. 54-68) and Maximinus (Caesar and claimant to imperial power, A.D. 305-313) are used by Jerome to represent the starting and ending points of Roman persecution against Christians.

because they have polluted my land with the carcasses of their detestable idols and have filled my inheritance with their abominations."

There are different interpretations of this section. The Jews assert that it points to the Chaldeans, who are represented under the name of "fishers," and afterwards to the Romans, who are compared with "hunters," who hunted the unfortunate people from the mountains, hills and clefts of the rocks.[216] Thus, the Lord says that he did this because he saw their ways and repaid them for their iniquities. They polluted the land by venerating images, and they corrupted the Lord's inheritance with the abominations of idols. But we [Christians] more correctly and beneficially believe that the prophet predicted these things about the future. Since earlier he said, "I will bring them back to their own land that I gave to their fathers,"[217] now he shows them how they are to be brought back: first he will send the apostles, to whom the Savior said, "Follow me, and I will make you fishers of men";[218] and afterwards he will send hunters, whom we may understand to be either ecclesiastical men or angels. When the time of consummation comes,[219] they will hunt each and every saint from the mountains of lofty dogmas, from the hills of good works and from clefts of the rocks, who are the apostles and apostolic men. For not only is Christ the "rock,"[220] but he also granted to Peter that he should be called "rock,"[221] and those who find rest in what he expressed are rightly said to be derived from the rock. And he shows that the apostles, or else those afterwards who are to be hunted, had sins and received double recompense for their iniquity. For "the servant who

knows his master's will but does not do it shall receive a severe beating."[222]

It should be known that the word *first* is found in the Hebrew but was omitted in the edition of the LXX. And when he says, *"First, I will doubly recompense their iniquity and their sin,"* he is pointing out indirectly that after they have received punishment, they will receive reward. Moreover, those who are going to be carried off "have polluted the Lord's land with the carcasses of their detestable idols and have filled his inheritance with their abominations." This shows that the whole universe is subject to God and that it is upheld not because of its own merit but because of God's compassion. What we have put here from the Hebrew, "they are not hid from me,"[223] is not found in the LXX.

16:19a: O Lord, my strength and my might, my refuge in the day of trouble—or of evils!

Without the power of God, which is Christ,[224] all human strength is reckoned as weak and as nothing.[225] Therefore one should flee for refuge to God and say, "Lord, you have been our refuge in all generations";[226] and in another passage: "He who dwells in the help of the Most High abides in the protection of the God of heaven."[227] And this "day of trouble"—or "of evils"—should be understood as that time about which the apostle says: "to deliver us from the present evil age,"[228] and "redeeming the time, because the days are evil."[229]

16:19b: To you shall the nations come from the ends of the earth and say, "Our fathers have inherited nought but lies, worthless things in which there is no profit." LXX: To you shall the nations come from the ends of the earth

---

[216]Targ translates "fishers" as "slayers" or "killers." The medieval Jewish commentators Rashi and Kimchi see this as a metaphor for the army that kills (fishers) the people and then takes the survivors captive (hunters). Joseph Kara identifies the "fisher" as Nebuchadnezzar but sees the "hunters" as the surrounding nations. [217]Jer 16:15. [218]Mt 4:19. [219]Sir 39:28; Mt 24:14. [220]1 Cor 10:4. [221]Mt 16:18. [222]Lk 12:47. [223]Jer 16:17. [224]1 Cor 1:24. [225]Is 40:17. [226]Ps 90:1 (LXX [89:1]). [227]Ps 91:1 (LXX [90:1]). [228]Gal 1:4. [229]Eph 5:16.

and say, "How have our fathers inherited false idols! And there is no benefit in them."

Israel has been cast out and carried off by fishers and hunters; as a result the multitude of the nations are called, and they confess that they and their fathers have been readily engaged in their previous errors. When they say, "How have our fathers inherited false idols! And there is no benefit in them," they are confessing the truth to which they are crossing over. This truth is protected by every defense.

16:20: "Can people make for themselves gods? Such are no gods!"

This is said by the nations who came from the ends of the earth to the Savior and who are mocking both their own ignorance and that of their ancestors. By this ignorance they believed that people could make gods, when in fact it is God's prerogative to make people.

16:21: "Therefore, behold, I will make them know this time, I will make them know my power and my might, and they shall know that my name is the Lord."

The power of God, through which all things were wrought, and the might of God, concerning which the apostle said, "Christ the might of God and the wisdom of God,"[230] are made known to the nations by means of the perfect suffering of the Son. And beautifully he said, "I will make them know *this time*"—"I will make them know clearly, and not as before through shadow and likeness and by prophecies of the future, so that once they have learned these things they might know my name and hear from the Son: "Father, I have mani-

fested your name to humanity."[231]

17:1: "The sin of Judah is written with a pen of iron, on a point of adamant; it is engraved on the tablet of their heart"—or "in the breast of their heart"[232]—"and on the horns of their platforms"—or "altars."[233]

Concerning the nations who converted to the Lord he previously said, "Behold, I will make them know this time, I will make them know my power and my might,"[234] but concerning Israel, who was cast aside, he now says, "The sin of Judah is written with a pen of iron, on a point of adamant." I do not know why the LXX translators omitted this passage,[235] unless perhaps they were sparing their people as they clearly did in Isaiah: "Therefore cease from man, whose breath is in his nostrils, for he is reckoned as lofty."[236] And there are many other passages of this kind, but to discuss all of them would require not just a book but books!

The sins of the nations were blotted out, because when they had come over to the Lord from the ends of the earth they heard this: "Praise the Lord, all nations! Praise him, all peoples! For great is his steadfast love toward us; and the faithfulness of the Lord endures forever;"[237] and concerning the nations God had said to Moses, "Let me alone, that I may kill this people; but of you I will make a great nation."[238] But the sin of Judah is permanent; on no account can it, so to speak, be wiped clean. It is written with a pen of iron, on a point of "adamant," which in Hebrew is *samir*[239]—not because there is any "point" that is called *samir* but because the "adamant" stone, which receives its name from that which is indestructible and unbreakable, is so sleek and smooth that one can write on it without

---

[230]1 Cor 1:24. [231]Jn 17:5-6. [232]Jerome's "tablet" matches Aq and Sym (= MT), whereas "breast" is the hexaplaric reading preserved under asterisk. [233]In this case the alternative translation, "altars," represents Jerome's IH edition. The basis of the first option ("platforms") is unknown. Heb *mizbēaḥ*, "altar." [234]Jer 16:21. [235]Jer 17:1-4 is not found in the LXX. [236]Is 2:22. This verse is not found in the LXX. [237]Ps 117:1-2. [238]Ex 32:10; cf. Deut 9:14. [239]Heb *šāmîr*.

difficulty with an iron pen, such that the hard substance of the iron writes on the harder adamantine writing tablet, and that which is written lasts forever. For they themselves said, "His blood be on us and on our children!"[240] Therefore it was "engraved" or cut into "the horns of their platforms" (or "altars"), so that their deeds of sacrilege might persist in eternal memory. And if this is so, where is the crazy old woman who claims that people can be without sin if they wish, and that the commands of God are easy?[241]

17:2-4: *"When their children remember their altars, their groves and their green trees on the high hills, as they are sacrificing in the open country, your wealth and all your treasures I will give for spoil; and your high places, because of your sin throughout all your territory. You shall be separated from your heritage that I gave to you, and I will make you serve your enemies in a land that you do not know, for you have kindled a fire in my anger, which shall burn forever."*

This passage is likewise not found in the LXX, for the same reason (I suspect) as I said above, namely, so that it might not remain as an eternal judgment against them.[242] He says, "You shall be separated from your heritage that I gave to you, and I will make you serve your enemies in a land that you do not know"— either under the Babylonians, or, as is even more true, under the Romans. For they themselves kindled the fire and provoked the most merciful Lord to anger, and the fire of his anger will burn forever. I am ashamed of the bickering of those on our side who denounce the Hebrew truth. The Jews read this passage

as directed against themselves, and all the while the church does not recognize what is in its own interests![243] Therefore, let us who are children of the apostles remember the sins of the former people, and let us testify that they were afflicted justly.

Moreover, the "high places," which in Hebrew are called *bamoth*,[244] can also be interpreted against the heretics, who "set their mouths to the high place, and their tongue crosses over the earth."[245] They broke forth with such insanity that they were left without the grace of the Holy Spirit, and so they destroyed the inheritance of the Lord, namely, the former truth of the faith. For this reason, there is prepared for them eternal burning and slavery to demons, who are inimical and vengeful.

17:5-6: *Thus says the Lord:* "Cursed is the man who trusts in man"*—or* "who has hope in man"*—*"and makes flesh his arm, whose heart turns away from the Lord. He is like a tamarisk in the desert and shall not see any good come. He shall dwell in the parched places of the wilderness, in an uninhabited salt land."*

If everyone is cursed who trusts in man, then Paul of Samosata and Photinus will be cursed, because, although they preached that the Savior was holy and excelled in all virtues, nevertheless they had their hope in a man.[246] But if it is argued against us that we, too, believe in one who said, "but now you seek to kill me, a *man* who has told you the truth that I heard from God; this is not what Abraham did. You do what your father did,"[247] then we will respond with this apostolic word: "If formerly we knew Christ according to the

---

[240]Mt 27:25. [241]The "crazy old woman" is Pelagius. Cf. Cicero *Tusc.* 1.48; *Div.* 2.141. [242]See Jer 17:1. [243]Jerome must have heard a Jew relate this passage to the idolatry of the Israelites (cf. *b. Sanhedrin* 63b). For Jerome, Jewish exegesis was part of the "Hebrew truth" of the Old Testament. Jerome found it shameful that some Christians were critical of the "Hebrew truth," since this "truth" could be used to condemn Jewish unbelief and thus support the church. [244]Heb *bāmôt*. [245]Ps 73:9 (OL [72:9]). [246]Both Paul of Samosata, bishop of Antioch (ca. 260-268), and Photinus, bishop of Sirmium (ca. 344-351), were charged with denying the pre-existence of the Son. [247]Jn 8:40-41.

flesh, now we no longer know him thus."[248] And again, the same apostle wrote at the beginning of his letter to the Galatians: "Paul an apostle—not from men nor through man but through Jesus Christ and God the Father, who raised him from the dead—and all the brothers who are with me."[249] For if "death is swallowed up in victory,"[250] why cannot the humble flesh that was assumed for human salvation be transformed into the majesty of divinity, so that he might make the both into one,[251] such that we do not worship a creature but the Creator, who is blessed forever.[252]

Therefore not only is one cursed "who has hope in man," but he is also cursed who "makes flesh his arm," that is, he makes flesh his strength, and so whatever he does he thinks he has done it by his own might and not by the Lord's mercy. For whoever does this, "his heart turns away from the Lord," since he claims to be capable of doing that which he cannot do. "He is like a tamarisk (which in Hebrew is *aroher*,[253] or as Symmachus translated, "an unfruitful tree") in the desert and shall not see any good come"—good that the multitude of the nations will see. "He shall dwell in the parched places of the wilderness"—this is said about the Jewish people, who dwell in the wilderness and do not produce fruit; "in a salt land"—which produces no fruit; "uninhabited"—which has neither God as a guest, nor the protection of angels, nor the grace of the Holy Spirit nor the knowledge of teachers.

17:7-8: "Blessed is the man who trusts in the Lord, whose trust"—or "hope"—"is the Lord. He is like a tree planted"—or "flourishing"[254]—"by water, that sends out its roots by the stream, and does not fear when heat comes, for its leaves remain green,"—or "its branches remain leafy"—"and is not anxious in the time of drought,"—or "does not fear in the year of drought"—"for it does not cease to bear fruit."

Let this be said concerning the Jews and heretics who have their hope in a man, namely, their own "Christ," whom they do not believe to be the son of God but a mere man who is going to come. As opposed to this, the ecclesiastical man "who trusts in the Lord" listens to this: "Know that the Lord is God!"[255] He trusts in the Lord, and so he is compared with that tree about which the first psalm sings: "He is like a tree planted by streams of water, that yields its fruit in its season, and its leaf does not wither."[256] Furthermore, "by water"—by the grace of the Holy Spirit, by diverse gifts,[257] "that sends out its roots by the stream"—it receives abundance from the Lord. Or, on another note, we can also say that we have been transferred from the drought of the Jews to the everlasting grace of baptism.

He says, "It does not fear when heat comes"—either a time of persecution or the day of judgment; and "its leaves remain green," or it will have "leafy branches"—so that it has no fear of drought but sprouts forth with the grace of all the virtues. And it is not afraid when the "time" or "year" of drought comes, when the Lord in his anger commands the clouds not to rain on Israel. And what follows, "it does not cease to bear fruit," can be used to explain that passage that is written in Mark where the Lord comes to a fig tree and does not find any fruit on it, since it was not the time for figs, and then he curses it so that it may never produce fruit.[258] For he who trusts in the Lord, and whose trust is the Lord, is not afraid even in the time of Jewish drought; instead, he always bears fruit, since he believes in him who died for us once for all and will not

---

[248]2 Cor 5:16. [249]Gal 1:1-2. [250]1 Cor 15:54. [251]Cf. Eph 2:14. [252]Rom 9:5. [253]Heb ʿarʿar ("a tree or shrub, trad. tamarisk; juniper," KB 887). [254]Jerome matches Aq and Targ. MT: šātûl ("planted," KB 1670). [255]Ps 100:3. [256]Ps 1:3. [257]Rom 12:6. [258]Mk 11:13-14.

die again[259] and who says, "I am life."[260]

17:9-10: *The heart of all is perverse and inscrutable;*[261] *who can understand it? "I the Lord search the mind and try the heart, to give to everyone according to his ways, according to the fruit of his doings." LXX: "Deep is the heart beyond all things, and it is man; who can understand him?" And the rest similarly.*

The Hebrew word *enos* is written with four letters, *aleph, nun, vav* and *sin*. If it is read *enos*, it means "man," but if it is read *anus*, it means "inscrutable" or "incurable," with the sense that no one is able to comprehend the human heart—although Symmachus interpreted the passage thus: "Inscrutable is the heart of all; what man is there who could comprehend it?"[262] We [Christians] are accustomed—with good intention, to be sure, but not according to knowledge—to use this passage against the Jews, to the effect that the Lord and Savior is a man according to his assumed flesh, and that none can understand the mystery of his nativity (as it is written: "Who will describe his generation?"[263]) except God alone, who searches out hidden things and renders to each one according to his works.[264]

It is better, however, that we simply understand that no one knows a person's secret thoughts except God alone;[265] for earlier he said, "Cursed is the man who has hope in man,"[266] and its opposite, "Blessed is the man

who trusts in the Lord."[267] And so, lest we think that human judgment is trustworthy, he adds that the hearts of almost all people are corrupt, as the psalmist says: "Cleanse me from my hidden (things), and spare your servant from the (things) of others"—no doubt he means "thoughts."[268] And in Genesis it says, "The Lord saw that the wickedness of humanity was great in the earth, and that every imagination of the thoughts of his heart was only evil continually."[269] And again, "for the mind and thought of the human heart is evil from his youth."[270] From this we learn that only God knows their thoughts.

But if it is said concerning the Savior, "But Jesus, seeing their thoughts . . ."[271] and if no one can see someone's thoughts except God alone, then Christ is God, who searches the mind and tries the heart, and renders to every person according to his works.

17:11: *The partridge warms—or gathers[272]—what he did not beget,*—and as the LXX translated, *The partridge called,[273] he gathered what he did not beget—he gets riches but not by right; in the midst of their days he will leave them,*—or *in the midst of his days they will leave him[274]—and at his end he will be a fool.*

The writers of natural history (dealing with beasts, birds, trees and plants), the principal of whom among the Greeks are Aristotle and Theophrastus, and among us, Pliny the Elder,

---

[259]Rom 6:8-10. [260]Jn 14:6. [261]The first ambiguity of the text is the Hebrew *'qb* ("uneven terrain, deceitful," KB 873), which Jerome renders as "perverse," matching Aq (LXX: "deep"). The next point of ambiguity is the Hebrew *mikkōl* ("from all"), which is either possessive ("the heart of all"—so Jerome) or comparative ("more deceitful than all"—so the LXX). On the third point of ambiguity, see Jerome's comments. [262]Jerome gives the "full" spelling of this Hebrew word (*'nwš*), as is found in more than forty Hebrew MSS listed by Kennicott, as opposed to the defective spelling found in BHS (*'nš*). Jerome is reading the word as *'ānûš* ("incurable," KB 70), which he takes to mean "inscrutable" or "incurable" (cf. Sym on Jer 15:18). Jerome seems uncertain as to the meaning of this word, since in his *Comm. Isa.* 17:11 he claims to have learned from "the Hebrews" that *'ānûš* means "strongly" (cf. *Leviticus Rabbah* 18.3). But since "strongly" does not work here, Jerome must search for a more contextually appropriate meaning among the hexaplaric versions. The LXX reads the word as *'enôš* ("man"). [263]Is 53:8. [264]Ps 62:12; Mt 16:27; Rom 2:6; Rev 2:23. [265]Ps 44:21. [266]Jer 17:5. [267]Jer 17:7. [268]Ps 19:12-13 (OL [18:13-14]). The text does not specify a noun to accompany the adjectives "hidden" (*occultis*) and "of others" (*alienis*), so Jerome explains that the psalmist is referring to his "thoughts." [269]Gen 6:5. [270]Gen 8:21. [271]Mt 9:4; Lk 9:47; 11:17. [272]Heb *dgr* ("to hatch" or "to gather," KB 214). Jerome's rendering ("warms") agrees with Aq. [273]The LXX represents a double rendering of the first word in the verse, *qr'*, which usually means "to call" but is also the word for a partridge. [274]Jerome's translation, "he will leave them," agrees with Aq. Cf. the LXX's rendering, "they will leave him," and MT, "he will leave him."

say that it is in the nature of a partridge to steal the eggs of another partridge (i.e., not his own eggs), and then sit on them and keep them warm; and later, when the young ones have hatched, they fly away from him, forsaking the parent who is not their own.[275] This is what the rich are like, who plunder the possessions of others and "get riches but not by right," without any thought of God's judgment. At some undetermined time they are struck by sudden death and lose their riches, at which point it is said to them: "Fool! This night your soul is required of you; and the things you have prepared, whose will they be?"[276] There is nothing more foolish than to fail to prepare for one's end[277] and to suppose that the here and now is everlasting.

Others,[278] however, on account of the above-mentioned *historia* and because of another whereby they say that the partridge is highly prone to fighting and so foul that it sexually defiles the bird it has defeated,[279] understand the word *partridge* to refer to the devil, since he gathered for himself the riches of others and said to the Lord, "All these I will give you, if you will fall down and worship me."[280] The devil's riches, which he gathered by evil means, will forsake him, and they will be returned to the Lord through the apostles. And he who seemed in his own eyes to be exceedingly wise will be a fool in the estimation of all. And that which is said by the LXX, "The partridge called," should be referred to the *persona* of heretics, for that "partridge" the devil "called" through the leaders of the heretics and "gathered what he did not beget"; indeed, he gathered to himself a multitude of those who were deceived. But afterwards this multitude will desert him, and he will be reckoned as the greatest fool in the estimation of all.

17:12-13: *A glorious throne set on high from the beginning is the place of our sanctification. O Lord, the hope of Israel, all who forsake you shall be put to shame; those who turn away from you shall be written in the earth, for they have forsaken the Lord, the channel—or spring—of living water.*

The partridge was forsaken because of his foolishness. But the hope of "Israel" (that is, the people of God who believe in the Lord) is the one who made all things. His glorious throne is exalted from the beginning and is the place of sanctification for all who believe. It is not that the Lord is in a certain place; but wherever he is, the place is sanctified. Conversely, those who forsake the Lord will be put to eternal shame, and those who turn away or depart from him will be written in the earth as blotted out of the book of the living.[281] For just as the one who can say with the apostle, "our commonwealth is in heaven,"[282] is written in the heavenly realms, so also those who forsake the Lord and turn away from him, with their "minds set on earthly things,"[283] are "written in the earth." And the reason why they are "written in the earth" is clear: it is because they forsook the Lord, the spring of life—or rather, the "spring of living water," who is the Lord, as he says in the Gospel: "'If anyone thirst, let him come to me and drink. He who believes in me, as

---

[275]None of the authors mentioned by Jerome state that partridges steal the eggs of other partridges. Aristotle mentions that they divide their eggs into two groups for both the male and the female to sit on (*Hist. An.* 6.8, 564a), and he elaborates in detail on the wicked character of partridges (e.g., *Hist. An.* 9.8, 613b). Pliny says that partridges deceive their mates, hiding their eggs from them so that the males do not break the eggs (*Nat.* 10.100). Jerome's account of partridges stealing eggs only to see the young fly away after hatching is repeated in Isidore of Seville *Etymologies* 12.7.63 and became commonplace in medieval bestiaries. The Targum to Jer 17:11 implies that the bird has taken eggs not his own, and that the hatchlings will leave him. This is stated explicitly by the medieval Jewish commentator Kimchi. In later times, John Calvin rejects this story about the partridge stealing eggs as an invention of the rabbis. [276]Lk 12:20. [277]Deut 32:29 (Jerome's IH edition). [278]Origen *Hom. Jer.* 17.1-3; *Hom. Exod.* 1.5. [279]Aristotle *Hist. An.* 9.8, 613b-614a; Aelian *Nat. An.* 3.16; Pliny *Nat.* 10.100-103. [280]Mt 4:9. [281]Ps 69:28; Rev 3:5. [282]Phil 3:20. [283]Phil 3:19.

the Scripture has said, Out of his heart shall flow rivers of living water.' Now this he said about the Spirit, which those who believed in him were to receive."[284]

17:14: Heal me, O Lord, and I shall be healed; save me, and I shall be saved; for you are my praise.

In the Gospel, many physicians had treated the woman who suffered from a hemorrhage, and although she had spent all her living on them, no one could cure her except him who is the true physician, whose healing is in his wings.[285] In the same way the prophet, who had suffered much disgrace at the hands of the people and was beset by their wicked plots, seeks to be healed and saved by him whose praise is true and whose remedy is true.

17:15-17: Behold, they say to me, "Where is the word of the Lord? Let it come!" But I am not troubled, following you as my shepherd,— or I am not weary, following after you[286]—nor have I desired the day of man, you know; that which came out of my lips was upright in your sight—or is before your face.[287] Be not a terror to me; you are my hope in the day of afflic-tion—or Do not be a stranger to me, sparing me in the evil day.[288]

Those who do not think that what the prophet announced will come to pass say to him, "Where is the word of the Lord? Let it come!" supposing that the delay in judgment betokens negligence in bringing it about. And while they are speaking such words, the prophet says, "I am not troubled nor am I weary as I 'follow you as my shepherd' or 'follow after you,' that is, follow along your tracks. And I was not content merely with this goal, but 'I did not

desire the day of man'—either longer life or prosperity in this world." And he calls as a witness him who is also the Judge: "You know." Then he continues, "that which came out of my lips was upright in your sight," in that he never lied, nor did he speak anything against the Lord's will.

And he says, "Be not a terror to me; you are my hope in the day of affliction," the sense of which is clear according to the Hebrew. But according to what the LXX translated, saying, "Do not be a stranger to me, sparing me in the evil day," this is the sense: "Do not spare me in the present age, which is evil, but render to me according to my sins, so that I might have eternal rest! For I know what is written: "For the Lord disciplines him whom he loves and chastises every son whom he receives."[289] Moreover, the "evil day" is either the whole age, or it is the day of judgment for those who are tortured for their sins.

17:18: Let those be put to shame who persecute me, but let me not be put to shame; let them be dismayed, but let me not be dismayed; bring on them the day of affliction; destroy them with double destruction!

The prophet prays against those who censure him for the word of the Lord and say, "Where is the word of the Lord? Let it come!"[290] He prays that those who persecute him may be "put to shame," that they may feel ashamed and return to salvation. He also prays that those who are lying, not those who are preaching the truth, may be dismayed. Finally, the prophet prays that when the day of vengeance comes, the Lord will destroy them with a double destruction, with famine and with the sword.

17:19-20: Thus said the Lord to me: "Go and

---

[284]Jn 7:37-39. [285]See Lk 8:43; Mt 9:20; Mk 5:26; cf. Mal 4:2. [286]Jerome translates the Hebrew *r'h* as "shepherd" (*rō'eh*), which matches MT (cf. Rashi, Kimchi). Aq, Sym and Pesh translate "evil" (*rā'à*). The LXX ("I am not weary, following after you") does not represent *r'h*. [287]The Hebrew word *nkh* can mean "straight, upright" or "in front of" (KB 698-99). [288]Jerome's "hope" matches Aq and Sym (Heb *mhsh*, "refuge" [KB 571]). [289]Heb 12:6. [290]Jer 17:15.

stand in the gate"—or "gates"[291]—"of the sons of the people, by which the kings of Judah enter and by which they go out, and in all the gates of Jerusalem, and say to them: 'Hear the word of the Lord, you kings of Judah, and all Judah'—or 'Judea'[292]—'and all the inhabitants of Jerusalem, who enter by these gates.'"

He says, "They despise listening to your words, and they will not come to you to inquire about the judgment of God. Therefore, you must go to a crowded place, either the gates of the temple or the gates of the city, by which the kings and all the masses enter and go out. Thus, they will be forced to listen by necessity. You shall preach the word of God in season and out of season,[293] and the excuse will not be left to them that they did not act because they did not hear."

17:21-27: Thus says the Lord: Take heed for the sake of your lives, and do not bear a burden on the sabbath day or bring it in by the gates of Jerusalem. And do not carry a burden out of your houses on the sabbath or do any work, but keep the sabbath day holy, as I commanded your fathers. Yet they did not listen or incline their ear but stiffened their neck,—and that which is not in the Hebrew: **more than their fathers—that they might not hear and receive instruction.** "**But if you listen to me, says the Lord, and bring in no burden by the gates of this city on the sabbath day, but keep the sabbath day holy and do no work on it, then there shall enter by the gates of this city kings and princes who sit on the throne of David, riding in chariots and on horses, they and their princes, the men of Judah and the inhabitants of Jerusalem; and this city shall be inhabited forever. And people shall come from the cities of Judah and the places round about Jerusalem, from the land of Benjamin, from** the flat lands, from the hill country and from the south country, bringing burnt offerings and sacrifices,"—or "incense"—"offerings"—or "manna"—"and frankincense, and bringing oblations"—or "praise"—"to the house of the Lord. But if you do not listen to me, to keep the sabbath day holy, and not to bear a burden and enter by the gates of Jerusalem on the sabbath day, then I will kindle a fire in its gates, and it shall devour the palaces of Jerusalem and shall not be quenched."

In order to avoid wrongly cutting up this command given anew by Jeremiah regarding the sabbath, it seemed good to set forth the whole passage, so that we may understand the entire thing as a whole. A person guards his own life if he does not bear the burden of sin on the day of rest and sabbath[294] and if he does not bring this burden in by the "gates of Jerusalem," which we should understand as the virtues. And he says, "Do not carry a burden out of your houses"—for the burden of sin should not be "carried" but completely thrown away—"or do any work"—that is, either servile work or the work about which it is written, "Food is meant for the stomach and the stomach for food; but God will destroy both the one and the other."[295] But there is a kind of work that should be done, about which the Savior says, "Do the work that does not perish!"[296] He says, "Keep the sabbath day holy," so that we may conduct every moment of our life in holiness, as our fathers Abraham, Isaac and Jacob did. Yet, when God commanded these things, "they did not incline their ear"—the ear of the mind, to be sure, not of the flesh—"but they stiffened their neck," throwing off the yoke of the law and (in accordance with the metaphor) behaving like wild animals.

Let us see what is the reward for those who

[291]Jerome matches Targ (= MT). [292]"Judah" is closer to the Hebrew, but Jerome's IH edition used "Judea" (= LXX). [293]2 Tim 4:2. [294]Cf. Origen *Fr. Jer.* 11. [295]1 Cor 6:13. [296]Jn 6:27.

do not bear a burden on the sabbath day but sanctify it. He says "kings shall enter by the gates of this city"—whose hearts are in the hand of God[297] and who rule over their own bodies—"and princes who sit on the throne of David"—that they might represent the pattern of Christ—"riding in chariots and on horses"—about which it is written, "The chariot of God is ten thousands, manifold thousands of those who rejoice; the Lord is among them at Sinai, in the holy place,"[298] and elsewhere, "your riding is victory"[299]—and all people who confess God and are "inhabitants of Jerusalem"—about which it is said, "His abode has been established in Salem (that is, "in peace"),[300] his dwelling place in Zion."[301] And the church of God "shall be inhabited forever."

"And people shall come from the cities of Judah and the places round about Jerusalem," which we discussed above; "from the land of Benjamin," who is the son of virtue and the right hand;[302] "from the flat lands," which in Hebrew is *sefela*[303] and indicates the plain understanding of *historia*; "from the hill country," that is, lofty doctrines; "and from the south country," about which it is written, "God will come from the south,"[304] where there is heat and abundant light and all coldness is expelled.

He says, "bringing burnt offerings," devoting themselves to God; and "sacrifices" or "incense," so that they say, "a sacrifice to the Lord is a broken spirit,"[305] and "we are the aroma of Christ everywhere,"[306] and elsewhere, "let my prayer be counted as incense before you";[307] and "offerings," in place of which the LXX put the Hebrew word *manaa*,[308] and due to the poor practice (or rather, negligence) of the scribes, it reads *manna* in our books;[309] and

"frankincense," concerning which it was said, "To what purpose does frankincense come to me from Sheba";[310] and "bringing oblations," which in Hebrew is *thoda* and can be translated "thanksgiving,"[311] and which the LXX translated as "praise"; "to the house of David,"[312] no doubt "to the church." These are the rewards for those who sanctify the sabbath and are not weighed down by any burden.

"But if you do not listen to my commands," he says, "and you do what I have commanded not to be done, then I will kindle a fire in its gates"—that is, the gates of Jerusalem, and it is said about Jerusalem, "they are all adulterers, like a heated oven is their heart."[313] "And it shall devour the 'palaces' or 'streets' of Jerusalem"—the LXX rendered this word "streets," whereas Aquila and Symmachus translated "fortified palaces," the word in Hebrew being *armanoth*.[314] "And shall not be quenched"—as the apostle says, "the fire will test what sort of work each one has done,"[315] and again, "If anyone's work is burned up, he will suffer loss, though he himself will be saved, but only as through fire."[316]

But if our Judaizers reject the figurative explanation, they are either forced to be Jews and circumcise their foreskins along with observing the sabbath, or else they rebuke the Savior who commanded the paralytic on the sabbath to carry his bed, as the Evangelist says: "This was why the Jews sought all the more to kill him, because he not only broke the sabbath but also called God his own Father, making himself equal with God."[317]

BOOK FOUR

The devil is always nearby to threaten a good work. Everywhere he sets traps for those who

---

[297]Prov 21:1. [298]Ps 68:17. [299]Hab 3:8. [300]The etymology for "Salem" as "peace" (Heb *šālôm*) was traditional in Greek sources; see Philo *Leg.* 3.79; OS 198.51; Heb 7:2. [301]Ps 76:2. [302]On the etymological meaning of Benjamin as "son of the right hand," see Jer 6:1. By including "virtue" as part of the meaning, Jerome appears to be following Origen *Fr. Jer.* 11. [303]Heb *šĕpēlâ*. The meaning "plain, flat" is found at OS 296.9. [304]Hab 3:3. [305]Ps 51:17. [306]2 Cor 2:14-15. [307]Ps 141:2. [308]Heb *mnhh*. [309]By "our books" Jerome means the OL. [310]Jer 6:20. [311]Heb *tôdâ* ("thanksgiving, sacrifice of thanksgiving," KB 1695). [312]Jerome misquotes here; he means "to the house of the Lord" (as in the lemma). [313]Hos 7:4. [314]Heb *'armĕnôt* ("[fortified] palace," KB 89). [315]1 Cor 3:13. [316]1 Cor 3:15. [317]Jn 5:18

are walking by, as the prophet describes with regard to the plots of his attendants: "By the wayside they have set a stumbling block for me."[1] And the Gospel makes this same point more fully, saying that birds of the sky snatched away and destroyed the seed that had been thrown along the path.[2] The reason why I am making reference to this principle, O brother Eusebius, the following discussion will make clear.

Although I have been occupied with a great crowd of people flowing in here from all over the world and have been busy with the cares of the holy brothers and the monastery, I am in the intervals dictating these commentaries on Jeremiah, insofar as my diligence is equal to what I lack in free time. In the meantime, the heresy of Pythagoras and Zeno, *apatheia* and *anamartēsia* (that is, impassibility and sinlessness),[3] which was silenced formerly in Origen and more recently in his disciples, Grunnius,[4] Evagrius Ponticus and Jovinianus, has suddenly begun to revive and to hiss not only in the west but also in eastern regions. On certain islands (especially Sicily and Rhodes), it is growing daily and defiling many, as they teach this heresy in secret but deny everything in public.

For a long time I remained silent and swallowed my grief quietly, but I was compelled to respond to this heresy by the repeated demands of the brothers. Still, I did not burst forth to such an extent as to reveal the names of the authors, since I wished to correct them rather than to disgrace them.[5] For I am the enemy not of people but of error.

Even so, out of revenge they smashed the jaw of their own animosity against me.[6] And by calling forth long-standing accusations made by their teachers, they proved themselves to be so ineloquent and pathetic that they could not even slander me in their own words. At that point, their little ditties were thoroughly refuted by books written against them.[7] Whoever wishes to read these books will see clearly that they are dumb dogs, as it says in Isaiah,[8] who do not know how to bark; indeed, they have the disposition and rabid zeal for lying, but they do not have the skill to bark and teach.

To these men I will speak briefly: what you are teaching is either good, or it is evil. If it is good, defend it openly. If it is evil, why do you secretly slay the wretched with error while at the same time bandying about the proper faith so as to deceive the simple? If it is true, why is it hidden? If it is false, why was it written? What is this madness, I ask? Whereas the apostle enjoins us to be prepared to make a defense to anyone who calls us to account for the hope that is in us,[9] and the prophet proclaims, "I will speak of thy testimonies before kings and shall not be ashamed,"[10] these men avoid the public, muttering in seditious corners, and they pretend that they are grieved over teachings that they are afraid to admit are their own. And when I have spoken generally against heretics and against any number of vices, they complain that they are being attacked, and in this way they announce their guilty conscience through their long-concealed indignation.

Book Four   [1]Ps 140:5. [2]Mt 13:4; Mk 4:4; Lk 8:5. [3]See Jerome *Ep.* 133.1-3; *Pelag.* 1.25; 3.4, et al. The concept of *apatheia* refers to the lack of any "passions" within a person. According to the stoic Zeno, passions may be described as excessive impulses and as movements of the soul that are irrational and contrary to nature (Diogenes Laertius 7.110; cf. Cicero *Tusc.* 4.5.11), and they cause vices, such as greed. Avoidance of the passions is also recommended in the *Golden Verses* ascribed to Pythagoras, a work known to Jerome (*Ruf.* 3.39). The stoics held that absolute perfection was possible for the sage, although they admitted that it was rare (Diogenes Laertius 7.91, 127; Cicero *Nat. D.* 2.37-39; Alexander of Aphrodisias *Fat.* 199.14-22). Jerome interprets Pelagianism as a version of stoic (and supposedly Pythagorean) teaching, on the grounds that Pelagius (and his predecessors and followers) taught that a Christian could potentially be without sin. [4]Grunting (*grunnitus*) is the sound made by swine. By "Grunter" (*grunnius*) Jerome is referring to Rufinus of Aquileia; see the Introduction. [5]See *Ep.* 133. [6]Persius *Sat.* 1.114-115, describes how Lucilius "broke his jaw" on the people of Rome while biting them with his harsh satire. [7]E.g., Jerome *Jov.*; *Jo. Hier.*; *Ruf.* See also Jerome *Pelag.* [8]Is 56:10. [9]1 Pet 3:15. [10]Ps 119:46.

If we are obligated to show caution, lest we appear to be wounding an old friendship if we cut off this most arrogant heresy with our spiritual blade,[11] then we will have to endure these torments to the faith and say along with the prophet, "I languished in misery as the thorn was driven into me."[12] But no—rather, let them hear this apostolic saying: "One should obey God rather than men,"[13] and again, "If I were pleasing men, I would not be a servant of Christ."[14] But we will pursue these matters more fully in a separate work, if these men will not keep silent. For now, let us take up the journey already begun on Jeremiah. Making brief comments in this fourth volume on the prophet, we will linger only on those parts that are obscure.

18:1-10: *The word that came to Jeremiah from the Lord: "Arise, and go down to the potter's house, and there you will hear my words." So I went down to the potter's house, and there he was working at his wheel—or stones. And the vessel he was making of clay was spoiled in the potter's hand, and changing he made it—or again he made it—into another vessel, as it seemed good to the potter to do. Then the word of the Lord came to me: "O house of Israel, can I not do with you as this potter has done? says the Lord. Behold, like the clay in the potter's hand, so are you in my hand, O house of Israel. If suddenly"—or "at last"—"I declare concerning a nation or a kingdom, that I will pluck up"—or remove—"and break down and destroy it, and if that nation, concerning which I have spoken, turns from its evil, I will repent of the evil that I intended to do to it. And if*

unexpectedly"—or "at last"[15]—"I declare concerning a nation or a kingdom that I will build and plant it, and if it does evil in my sight, not listening to my voice, then I will repent of the good that I had intended to do to it."

Information reaches our faculty of reason and discernment through all the senses: hearing, smell, taste and touch; but that which is perceived with the eyes is best retained in the mind. For this reason, he commands the prophet to go to the potter's house and to hear the words of the Lord there. He says, "And when I had proceeded to go down to the potter's house, 'he was working at his wheel,'" which the LXX, misled by the ambiguity of the word, translated as "stones." For the word *abanim*, depending on the nature of the passage and the different pronunciations, means both an instrument—in this case, a potter's wheel—and stones.[16] He says, "And while I was watching the vessel of clay being made, it was suddenly spoiled." This happened by God's providence, so that through his mistake the potter's workmanship might serve as a parable, even though the potter was not aware of it.

And again the potter, who had ruined the vessel of clay as the wheel rushed on,[17] made another one for himself as it seemed right to him. Straightway the Lord says to the prophet, "If a potter has the ability to make something again out of the same clay that had been spoiled, can I not also do this with you who, insofar as it depends on you, seem to be lost?" And in order to indicate the freedom of the will, he says that he announced evil to one nation or kingdom and good to another, but what he predicted might

---

[11]On the conflict between Jerome and Rufinus, Augustine wrote, "I have been exceedingly grieved that the mischief of such painful discord has arisen between persons once so loving and intimate, and formerly united by the bond of a friendship which was well known in almost all the churches" (*Ep.* 73.6). [12]Ps 32:4 (LXX [31:4]). [13]Acts 5:29. [14]Gal 1:10. [15]The Hebrew word here (*rega'*) is the same one used at the beginning of Jer 18:7. The LXX uses the same Greek word both times, but Jerome employs different Latin words for the sake of variety. [16]The Hebrew consonants are *'bnym*. If they are pronounced *'ăbānîm*, it is the plural form of *'bn* ("stone," KB 7-8); but if they are read as *'obnāyim*, it is a "potter's wheel" (KB 9), which may also be related to the noun *'bn* (as a dual form, i.e., a pair of wheels). Jerome's understanding of *'bnym* as "instrument" is in agreement with Sym. [17]Cf. Horace *Carm.* 3.10.10: ". . . as the wheel rushes on."

not come about; instead, the opposite might occur, since good shall come to the evil people if they repent, and evil will befall the good people if in spite of their promises they turn back to their sins. We say this, not because God is ignorant of what a certain nation or kingdom is going to do but because God gives a person over to his own will, in order that he may receive either reward or punishment according to his merit. Yet, what happens will not be entirely due to human effort but to the grace of God who gives all things bountifully. For the freedom of the will should be maintained in such a way that bountiful grace excels in all things, as this prophetic word says: "Unless the Lord builds the house, those who build it labor in vain. Unless the Lord watches over the city, the watchman stays awake in vain."[18] For "it depends not on human will or exertion but on God who shows mercy."[19]

18:11-13: "Now, therefore, say to the men of Judah and the inhabitants of Jerusalem: 'These things'—or 'Thus'[20]—'says the Lord, Behold, I am shaping evil against you and planning a plan against you. Let each one return from his evil way, and amend your ways and your doings.' But they say, 'We are hopeless!'—or 'We will be firm!'[21]—'For we will follow our own plans, and will each one act according to the depravity of'—or 'what is pleasing to'[22]—'his evil heart.' Therefore thus says the Lord: Ask among the nations: who has heard of such horrible things as the virgin Israel has done beyond measure?"

The Lord now elaborates on the parable, which he taught through visible action and words. He says, "Behold, I am shaping evil against you like the potter with the clay." Yet, it is only "evil" in accordance with what Isaiah says, "making peace and creating evil."[23] It is not that God is evil in and of himself, but rather he appears as evil to those who are being afflicted. "And I am planning a plan against you," that is, I am bringing judgment suitable to what you have done. "Change your deeds and amend your ways!" so that punishment can be changed into prosperity. "But on the contrary," he says, "they say, 'We will be firm,'" namely, in their evil deeds. Or it is as Aquila translated, "We are hopeless!" or else like Symmachus, "We are disheartened!" because each one has offended God and so either believes that it is impossible for him to be saved or else despairs that his soul can be pleasing to God. "For we will follow our own plans." Therefore, since it is deeply offensive to God to follow one's own plans and to do the will of a depraved heart, where is the power of free will or personal decision making without the grace of God? "Ask among the nations and all the countries round about: Who has done (who has even heard of doing!) service to idols as the virgin Israel has done beyond measure?" He calls Israel a "virgin" in that they served the one God, as the prophet says: "In Judah God is known, his name is great in Israel."[24]

18:14: "Shall the snow of Lebanon fail from the rock of the field? Can cold waters that burst forth and flow down be removed?" LXX: "Shall knolls[25] fail from the rock or snow from Lebanon? Shall water violently carried by the wind be diverted?"

18Ps 127:1. 19Rom 9:16. 20The phrase "thus says the Lord" is absent from the LXX but is found in all three hexaplaric versions. The two options given by Jerome are alternative ways to render this word into Latin. 21MT vocalizes the word as a Niphal participle from *y'š* ("to despair of"), agreeing with Aq, "it is hopeless." Jerome follows Sym ("we are disheartened") in reading the initial *nun* of the verb as the "we" prefix (cf. "For we will follow . . ."), although he follows Aq for the lexical meaning. The LXX ("we will be firm," lit., "we will be manly") interpreted the word *y'š* as related to *'yš* ("man"). 22Jerome agrees with Aq. Heb *šĕrirût* ("stubbornness," KB 1658). 23Is 45:7. 24Ps 76:1. 25For MT *śāday* ("field"), the LXX read *šĕdê* ("breasts"), which in Greek can also refer to "rounded hills." Sym and the Pesh agree with the LXX. Aq read *šadday* (= "sufficient"). Jerome agrees with the Targ in taking the word as "field."

Such is the sense of this Virgilian passage: "Sooner, then, shall the nimble stag graze in air, and the seas leave their fish bare on the strand . . . than that look of his shall fade from my heart";[26] and in another passage: "While rivers run to ocean, while on the mountains shadows move over slopes, while heaven feeds the stars, ever shall your honor, your name, and your praise abide."[27] He says, "Just as snow cannot fail from the summits of Lebanon or be vanquished by the heat of the sun so that it all melts, and just as streams flowing from the mountains never dry up in springs, so also my name, which is intrinsically steadfast and eternal, cannot be altered. Nevertheless, although the rest of nature preserves its order, my people have forgotten me!" For he continues:

18:15: *"Because my people have forgotten me, making offerings in vain and stumbling along in their ways, in the paths of the world,"*—or *"in everlasting paths"*[28]—*"and have walked on them on a road not trodden."*

If people forget God, forsake him who says "I am the way,"[29] and make offerings to foreign gods, then they are "stumbling along in their ways"—not God's ways, but their own—and they have abandoned the ancient and eternal paths that have been trodden by the steps of all the saints who honored God. As for this people, they walked on a road not trodden. Having forsaken the worship of God, they venerated idols. Because of this he will bring punishment, which follows:

18:16: *"so that their land may be made a desolation, a thing to be hissed at forever.*

Every one who passes by it is astonished and shakes his head."

He says, "Because they abandoned the worship of God and followed the twisted paths of idolatry, their land is reduced to desolation, something to be wondered at by all and an object of hissing. This desolation is so severe that any who see the formerly prosperous land and city, which have fallen into deserted ruin and ashes, will be shocked and astounded and will express the distress of their soul with a bodily gesture." For shaking the head shows a distressed soul, and hissing indicates a bewildered mind. We understand this to have been more fully and properly fulfilled in the time after the advent of the Lord, when the Jews were forbidden by law to enter what was formerly their land and holy city.[30] But when they did come to lament, they marveled and mourned that the predictions wrought by the prophets had been fulfilled.

18:17: *"Like a scorching wind I will scatter them before the enemy"*—or *"enemies."*—*"I will show them my back, not my face, in the day of their calamity."*

Even today the judgment of God remains against the Jews. Throughout the entire world they are scattered before their enemy, the devil—or their enemies, the demons. Although they invoke the name of God day and night in their synagogues of Satan,[31] God shows them his back and not his face, so that they may understand that he is always departing and never coming to them. Moreover, the day of the calamity of the Jews is the whole period from the passion of the Savior to the consummation of the age, so that, after the fullness of

---

[26]Virgil *Ecl.* 1.59-60, 63 (LCL). [27]Virgil *Aen.* 1.607-609 (LCL). [28]Aq and Sym agree with the LXX. Jerome gives a literalistic rendering of the Hebrew word *ʿōlām* ("world, age"). [29]Jn 14:6. [30]After the Second Jewish Revolt against Rome (132-135 C.E.), the Jews were expelled from Jerusalem and the city was destroyed and rebuilt under the name Aelia Capitolina. See Eusebius *Hist. Eccl.* 4.6.1-4. [31]Rev 2:9; 3:9.

the Gentiles has entered in, then all Israel will be saved.[32]

18:18: *Then they said, "Come, let us make plots against Jeremiah, for the law shall not perish from the priest, nor counsel from the wise nor the word from the prophet. Come, let us smite him with the tongue, and let us not heed any of his words."*

This is the plot, at that time of the Jews against Jeremiah or against the Lord Savior, and today of the heretics against the Lord's servants. They make up false charges and preempt holy people with accusations, as they plan not what truth they will speak but what falsehoods they will invent. For they boast that God's law, counsel and speech will remain with their priests, wise men and pseudoprophets, although Scripture says, "Wisdom will not enter a deceitful soul."[33]

18:19-22a: *Give heed to me, O Lord, and hear the voice of my adversaries! Shall evil be rendered for good, since they have dug a pit for my life? Remember how I stood before you to speak good for them, to turn away your wrath from them. Therefore deliver up their children to famine; give them over to the power of the sword; let their wives become childless and widowed. May their men be struck with death, their youths slain by the sword in battle. May a cry be heard from their houses!*

It was as a type of the Savior that Jeremiah endured all of this at the hands of the Jewish people, who later were destroyed when the Babylonians came. But it was fulfilled more fully and more perfectly in Christ, when the

city was overthrown and the people were massacred by the Roman sword, not because of idolatry (which was not a problem at that time), but because they killed the Son of God, when all the people cried out together: "Away, away with such a one! We have no king but Caesar!"[34] And the curse of eternal damnation against them was fulfilled: "His blood be on us and on our children!"[35] For they had dug a pit for Christ and said, "Let us remove him from the land of the living!"[36] But Christ had such great compassion toward them that he stood before the Father to speak good for them and to turn away the Father's wrath from them, so that even on the cross he said, "Father, forgive them, for they know not what they do."[37] We are only touching briefly on what is clear so that we can spend more time on obscure matters. We will not offer the absurd interpretations of some and talk about the captivity of the heavenly Jerusalem. Instead, we follow the clear *historia* and the most obvious prophecy with complete confidence in the words and the meaning.

18:22b-23: *For you shall bring the marauder suddenly on them! For they have dug a pit to take me and laid snares for my feet. Yet, you, O Lord, know all their plotting against me to death. Forgive not their iniquity, nor blot out their sin from your sight. Let them be overthrown—or made to stumble[38]—before you; consume them—or deal with them—in the time of your anger.*

If we understand this to be about Jeremiah, we should interpret the suddenly appearing "marauder" as Nebuchadnezzar. If we take it to be about the Savior, which is closer to the truth and better, we should interpret the "marauder"

---

[32]Rom 11:25-26. [33]Wis 1:4. [34]Jn 19:15. [35]Mt 27:25. [36]Jer 11:19. [37]Lk 23:34. [38]While the first option matches Jerome's IH edition, the second agrees with Aq and Sym, representing an etymologically proper translation of the Hebrew root *kšl* ("to stumble"; = MT). If the word were read as from *šlk* it could mean "thrown down," which is probably what underlies Jerome's IH edition and is reflected in the Pesh and the Targ.

as the Roman army. And lest the judgment of God appear unjust, he explains what they perpetrated against Christ, the Son of God, together with what they are going to suffer. The fact that he adds, "Forgive not their iniquity, nor blot out their sin from your sight," in no way contradicts his previous statement in which he prays to the Father on behalf of the people.[39] Indeed, after the time granted for repentance has passed, when the people have persisted in their evil, God must inflict punishment on them, not so much for their own sakes but for the sake of others, so that the unpunished sin does not harm everyone else by way of example. And what he adds, "Let them be made to stumble (or 'overthrown') before you," is similar to the statement of Isaiah and the apostle Peter: "Will you not stumble down as on a stone of offense and a rock of stumbling?"[40] The prophet in the Psalms also makes mention of this: "The stone that the builders rejected has become the head of the corner. This is the Lord's doing."[41]

19:1-3a: *Thus said the Lord, "Go, take a potter's earthen flask, and take some of the elders of the people and some of the elders of the priests, and go out to the valley of the son of Hinnom at the entry of the gate of clay"* —or *"charsith"*—*"and proclaim"*—or *"cry out" or "read"*[42]—*"there the words that I tell you. You shall say, 'Hear the word of the Lord, O kings of Judah and inhabitants of Jerusalem!'"*

In place of the potter's "flask," which in Hebrew is *bocboc*,[43] the LXX translated "small jar." In place of the gate "of clay," Aquila, Symmachus and Theodotion put the Hebrew word *harsith*,[44] whereas the LXX, according to their custom, used the Greek letter *chi* for the

Hebrew aspirant *heth*, so that they said *Charsith* instead of *harsith*, just like they put *Chebron* instead of *Hebron* and *Hiericho* instead of *Hieriho.*

Divine Scripture wants people to be taught not only by the ears but also by the eyes, since (as I said before)[45] that which reaches our intellect by seeing is retained in the mind better than that which reaches us by hearing. He says, "Take an earthen flask (or 'small jar') and take some of the elders of the people and of the priests, and go out to the valley of the son of Hinnom," where there was a Baal shrine and a wooded grove watered by the springs of Siloam—as I said earlier.[46] "That valley," he says, "is by the gate that in the Hebrew language is called *harsith*, that is, 'of clay.'" "And proclaim (or 'read') there the words that I tell you, so that the things that I am going to say will be heard there." Moreover, as I said previously, I have put "proclaim," "read" and "cry out," because the Hebrew word *carath* has these three meanings.[47] He wants his message to be heard by the "kings of Judah and inhabitants of Jerusalem," that is, those of royal lineage and the common people, so that any who refuse to listen will be without excuse.

19:3b-5: *"Thus says the Lord of hosts, the God of Israel, Behold, I am bringing such affliction"*—or *"evils"*[48]—*"on this place that the ears of everyone who hears of it"*—or *"them"*—*"will tingle. Because the people have forsaken me and have profaned this place by making offerings in it to other gods whom neither they nor their fathers nor the kings of Judah have known; and because they have filled this place with the blood of innocents and have built the high places of Baal to burn their sons in the fire as burnt offerings to Baal,*

---

[39]Jer 18:20; Lk 23:34. [40]Is 8:14; 1 Pet 2:8. [41]Ps 118:22-23. [42]Jerome's IH edition has "proclaim," whereas the LXX has "read." [43]Heb *baqbuq*. [44]Heb *hrswt* (Ketiv); *harsit* (Qere). As with the Greek versions, Jerome's transliteration matches the Qere rather than the Ketiv. The Targ translates "ruins" (cf. *heres*, "destruction"). For Jerome's suggested meaning, see KB 355. [45]Jer 18:1-10. [46]Jer 2:23a; 7:30-31. [47]Heb *qr't*. Cf. Jer 2:1-2a; 3:12; 7:1-2. [48]Heb *r'h* ("evil" or "calamity," KB 1262-63).

which I did not command"—or "consider"[49]—
"or speak, nor did it come into my mind."

Certain people foolishly interpret this passage as referring to the heavenly Jerusalem.[50] Lest I be constantly giving this warning, let it suffice for me to say only this: such an explanation, or rather heresy, should be shunned, since it subverts what is clear and tries to introduce certain deceptions into the churches of Christ. No one doubts that the people set up a Baal idol in the temple of God and that they established this idol at the shrine that was in the valley of the son of Hinnom, where there was a grove devoted to Baal and an altar on which they sacrificed and burned their sons. These are things that the Lord never "considered or decreed, nor did they come into his mind"—not that God is unaware of what will happen in the future, but rather God says that he does not know things that are unworthy of his awareness, in keeping with this Gospel statement: "Depart from me, all you workers of iniquity, I do not know you!"[51] For "the Lord knows those who are his,"[52] and "he who does not know is not known."[53] Or, undoubtedly, these things should be interpreted with respect to God according to anthropopathism,[54] as is done with other expressions.

Moreover, all heretics forsake God and profane the place where God dwells, defiling it with their deceitfulness; and they make offerings to other gods whom neither they nor their fathers—namely, the apostles and apostolic men—have known. Furthermore, the "kings of Judah," that is, the patriarchs of the heretics, fill the place that formerly belonged to God with the blood of "innocents" who have been deceived—for if these "innocents" had not been simple and foolish, they would not have been so readily subverted. And they build high places to Baal: Although they say that they are discussing lofty matters, they are really burning their sons, whom they fathered in heresy, to an idol. All these things the Lord says that he does not know, nor did it ever come into his thinking.

19:6: *"Therefore, behold, days are coming, says the Lord, when this place shall no more be called Topheth and the valley of the son of Hinnom, but the valley of slaughter."* LXX: *"For this reason, behold, days are coming, says the Lord, when this place shall no more be called Ruin and the polyandrion[55] of the son of Hinnom, but the polyandrion of slaughter."*

We have already explained the valley of the son of Hinnom, which in Hebrew is *gehennom*, from where they think that Gehenna is named.[56] Yet, I am at a loss to explain why the LXX chose to translate "Topheth" as *diaptōsis* (that is, "ruin") and "valley" as *polyandrion* (which means "a multitude of people"), unless perhaps because the people fell into ruin there and a multitude of people were slain—either spiritually though the error of idolatry or literally by the Babylonian army, which is described more clearly in what follows:

19:7-9: *"And in this place I will make void the counsel of Judah and Jerusalem and will cause their people to fall by the sword before their enemies and by the hand of those who seek their life. I will give their dead bodies for food to the birds of the air and to the beasts of the earth. And I will make this city a horror, a thing to be hissed at; everyone who passes by it will be horrified and will hiss because of all its*

---

[49]Heb *ṣwh* (Piel; "command"). Jerome's IH edition, the Targ and the MSS of the LXX that give an equivalency for this word (it is absent from many witnesses) all render this word as "command." The hexaplaric versions are lacking, but Jerome's second option may represent Aq or (more likely) Sym.   [50]Cf. Jer 18:19-22a.   [51]Lk 13:27; Mt 7:23.   [52]2 Tim 2:19.   [53]1 Cor 14:38.   [54]Jerome uses the Greek term *anthrōpopathōs*, which denotes assigning human-like emotions or mental states to something, such as God, that does not strictly possess them. See also Jer 14:8b-9a; 27:5; 32:35b.   [55]Jerome gives the Greek word used by the LXX, which refers to a place where many people assemble (LSJ 1436).   [56]Cf. Jer 7:30-31, 32-33.

---

disasters. And I will make them eat the flesh of their sons and their daughters, and everyone shall eat the flesh of his neighbor in the siege and in the distress, with which their enemies and those who seek their life afflict them."

Although we know that these things happened to the people as part of the Babylonian captivity, they refer more fully to the time of the Savior when the people were besieged by Vespasian and Titus, and to the time of Hadrian when their city collapsed into eternal ashes.[57] As a result of these disasters, those who previously had offered their children as sacrifices to idols were forced by the necessity of famine to use their children for food. Furthermore, everyone's flesh was given to the birds of the air and the beasts of the earth, so that those who had misused their divinely established offices to perform impious deeds, sacrificing their own flesh and blood to idols, made their own wombs into tombs for their children.

19:10-11a: *"Then you shall break the flask in the sight of the men who go"*—or *"go out"*[58]— *"with you and shall say to them, 'Thus says the Lord of hosts: So will I break this people and this city, as one breaks a potter's vessel, so that it can never be mended.'"*

Clearly this is said with reference not to the Babylonian captivity but to the Roman, since after the Babylonians the city was re-established and the people were led back to Judea and restored to their former affluence; but after the captivity that took place under Vespasian and Titus, and later under Hadrian, the desolation of Jerusalem persisted and will persist to the end of the age—even though the Jews think that a golden and bejeweled Jerusalem is going to be re-established and that there will again be sacrifices and offerings, marriage unions among the saints and a kingdom on earth for the Lord Savior. Although we do not follow this view, we cannot totally condemn it, because many of the ecclesiastical men and martyrs have said it.[59] Thus, "let each one be satisfied in his own mind,"[60] and let all things be reserved for the judgment of the Lord.

Now, just as a potter's earthen vessel that has been broken cannot be restored to its former appearance, so also the people of the Jews and Jerusalem, now that the city has been overthrown, will not again have their former standing. In fact, the very name of the city today has been taken away; it is called Aelia, after Aelius Hadrian. He removed the previous name together with the previous right of residence,[61] so as to cast off the haughtiness of its inhabitants.

Nevertheless, these names do not signify merely a city but rather the place of the sacred cross and of the resurrection; nor do they represent the once great wealth of the city through which the Jewish people perished but rather the glory of holiness. This glory our poor Bethlehem possesses, since it does not have gold and jewels but bread—the bread that was born in it.[62]

19:11b-13a: *"People shall be buried"*—or *"shall bury"*—*"in Topheth because there will*

---

[57]The Romans under Vespasian and Titus destroyed the temple in Jerusalem during the First Jewish Revolt (66-70 c.e.), and the Roman emperor Hadrian expelled Jews from Jerusalem following the Second Jewish Revolt (132-135 c.e.). [58]Heb *blk* ("to go, walk"). [59]Elsewhere, Jerome explicitly connects this "Judaizing" earthly kingdom with the one thousand years of Rev 20:1-10; see below at Jer 31:27-30 and Jer 31:38-40. Jerome criticizes millenarianism frequently in his commentaries, but he also acknowledges that many in the church had affirmed it. Thus in the prologue to bk. 18 of his *Comm. Isa.* Jerome says, "If we understand the Apocalypse of John literally, it is Judaizing. But if we interpret it spiritually, as it is written, then we appear to go against the opinions of many older authorities: of the Latins, Tertullian, Victorinus and Lactantius; and of the Greeks, among others, I mention here only Irenaeus, bishop of Lyons, against whom Dionysius of Alexandria, a most eloquent man and high priest of the church, wrote an excellent book, in which he ridicules the fable of the thousand years, the golden and bejeweled Jerusalem on earth, the restored temple." [60]Rom 14:5. [61]See Jer 18:16. [62]Jn 6:25-59.

be no place else to bury.[63] *Thus will I do to this place, says the Lord, and to its inhabitants, making this city like Topheth*"—or "*like a ruin.*"[64] "*And the houses of Jerusalem and the houses of the kings of Judah will be like the place of Topheth*"—or "*ruin*"—but that which is added in the LXX, "*All the houses of the kings of Judah will be like the place of Topheth,*" is not found in the Hebrew.[65] And he continues: "*All the houses on whose rooftops*"—or "*roofs*"[66]—"*they sacrificed to all the host of heaven and made offerings to other gods shall be defiled.*"

Having stated above that "this place shall no more be called Topheth and the valley of the son of Hinnom, but the valley of slaughter,"[67] he now sets forth more clearly how great the slaughter in this place will be: people will be buried there in heaps, and this place formerly devoted to religion will become a mound for the dead. The city, which adjoins this place, will be made "like Topheth"—which the LXX translated as "ruin." Both the houses of Jerusalem and the palaces of the kings will similarly be reduced to ruins. And the reason given for this is that the people were defiled and polluted with the wickedness of idolatry, since on their rooftops and roofs they made offerings and burned incense to the sun, moon and stars of heaven; nor were they content with this error, but they made offerings to demons and baked cakes for other gods.

19:14-15: *Then Jeremiah came from Topheth, where the Lord had sent him to prophesy, and he stood in the court of the Lord's house, and said to all the people: "Thus says the Lord of hosts, the God of Israel, Behold, I am bringing on this city and on all its towns all the evil that I have pronounced against it, because they have stiffened their neck, refusing to hear my words."*

When Jeremiah was at Topheth in the presence of the elders of the people whom he had brought with him there, he broke the flask (or small jar) and prophesied with the words of the Lord, so as to wear out the people and the city of Jerusalem. After this, he returned and stood in the court of the Lord's house and spoke to the whole crowd who did not want to go to the place of Topheth, telling them that the Lord was going to bring on the city of Jerusalem and on all its towns the evil that he pronounced against it. And lest we think this judgment cruel, he gives the reason why he is bringing this evil: "It is because," he says, "they have stiffened their neck, refusing to hear my words; and even after so many acts of impiety, they were unwilling to repent."

20:1-2: *Now Pashhur the priest, the son of Immer, who was appointed chief officer in the house of the Lord, heard Jeremiah prophesying these words. Then Pashhur beat Jeremiah the prophet and put him in the prison that was in the upper Benjamin Gate of the house of the Lord.*

In place of "Pashhur" the LXX translated "Phaschor," which is interpreted to mean "blackness of mouth."[68] And instead of "prison," which is what we said, the LXX and Theodotion translated "cataract," whereas Symmachus put either *basanisterion* or *streblo-*

---

[63]The first option ("shall be buried") matches Jerome's IH edition, and the second ("shall bury") is Aq and Th (= MT). Jer 19:11b is absent from the LXX. [64]See Jer 19:6. [65]This repetitive addition found in Jerome's copy of the LXX is found in some ancient witnesses to the LXX. [66]The first option matches Jerome's IH edition and agrees with the LXX. The second option is a near synonym and perhaps represents the word used by the OL version. [67]Jer 19:6. [68]Heb *pšhwr*. This meaning is based on breaking the word into the elements *ph* ("mouth") and *shwr* ("black"). Jerome has taken this etymology from Origen *Hom. Jer.* 19.14, although Jerome's interpretation of the significance of the name differs from that of Origen: for Origen, Pashhur's "blackness of mouth" comes from his being a source of false teaching, whereas for Jerome it is related to his wielding of power unjustly (see Jerome's comments at Jer 20:3).

terion, both of which signify "torments."[69] We, following the common practice,[70] put "prison," which is the kind of torment we read about in the Acts of the Apostles, when the apostles Paul and Silas were put in the confinement of prison.[71]

This Pashhur was high priest of the temple, and he made corrupt use of the priestly office granted to him, terrifying Jeremiah with torture rather than teaching and correcting him with words. Similarly, both the Savior and the apostle Paul were flogged by order of the high priest.[72] Nor is it any wonder if even today the servants of God are struck by "Phaschor," sent to prison and held in horrible confinement. For the power to do such things is granted by God, so that the faithfulness of the prophets may be demonstrated. But the one who strikes is not the greater of the two; rather, it is the one who is struck that is stronger. And the prophet accepts God's judgment patiently and does not cry out at the flogging; he merely considers the one who gave the command.

The name Immer means "word," and it is often from our words that blackness is born, not because of the parent's vice but because of the wickedness of the one who has deviated from his birth.[73] Moreover, the torment with which the prophet is tortured takes place on the "right" side of the gate, which is how "Benjamin" is interpreted,[74] and in the "upper" gate, which signifies not the truth but the unjust power of the high priest.

20:3: On the morrow when it was light, Pashhur released Jeremiah from prison, and Jeremiah said to him, "The Lord does not call your name Pashhur, but Terror on every side."

For this passage, all translated just as they did before regarding both the name of the high priest and the kind of torment.[75] But the high priest's name is now changed, so that his impending punishment may be indicated by his name. He says, "You will by no means have 'blackness of mouth' and the authority of unjust power, but you will be led captive to Babylon"—for "Terror on every side" or "Terror all around" signifies this—"so that you will look all around here and there, trembling and uncertain of your own safety, and you will dread the enemies who are coming against you." In place of "Terror," which in Hebrew is *magur*, the LXX and Theodotion translated *metoikon*, that is, "migrating," the second edition of Aquila put "foreigner," the first edition of Aquila put "looking around," and Symmachus translated "carried off" or "gathered together" and "collected."[76]

20:4-6: "For thus says the Lord: Behold, I will make you a terror, you and all your friends. They shall fall by the sword of their enemies while you look on. And I will give all Judah

---

[69]The Hebrew noun in question, *mhpkt*, is often translated today as "stocks" (KB 553). The LXX and Th translated *katarraktēs*, which can refer to a "waterfall" or "cataract" (e.g., of the Nile; cf. Heb *hpk* ["to overturn"]) but may also be used for a portcullis or sluice (LSJ 908-909). Jerome gives two possible readings for Sym, *basanistērion* and *streblōtērion*. Although it is possible that Jerome has readings in front of him for this passage from both the first and second editions of Sym (see the Introduction), Field plausibly suggested, based on corresponding MS readings, that *streblōtērion* was the Sym reading for Jer 20:2 and *basanistērion* was what Sym had for Jer 29:26, and that Jerome simply reports both options here. The meaning of *basanistērion* is "question chamber," or in the plural, "instruments of torture" (LSJ 308). *Streblōtērion* means "racking" or "torturing" (LSJ 1653). Jerome picks up from Sym the idea of "torment" in his explanation. [70]By this Jerome probably means the reading of the OL edition. [71]Acts 16:23-24. [72]Jesus is struck in the presence of the high priest (Mt 26:57-68; Mk 14:53-65; Lk 22:54-63). For Paul, see Acts 23:2. [73]Heb *'immēr* (cf. *'ēmer*, "word"). Just as Pashhur was the son of Immer, so also our words often beget evil ("blackness of mouth")—but this is not the fault of the words but of the speaker. [74]See Jer 6:1; cf. Jer 17:21-27; 31:15; 32:8a, 42-44. [75]By "all" Jerome is referring to all of the Greek versions. [76]On the first and second editions of Aq, see the Introduction. The concepts of "migrating" and "foreigner" come from associating this word with the verb *gwr* ("to dwell as a foreigner"). Jerome is independent of all the Greek versions, the Targ and the Pesh in translating *mgwr* as "Terror," although he agrees in this with the medieval commentaries of Rashi and Kimchi. See also KB 544, "fright, horror" and "atrocity."

into the hand of the king of Babylon; he shall carry them captive to Babylon and shall slay them with the sword. Moreover, I will give all the wealth"—or "strength"[77]—"of the city, all its gains, all its worth"—or "glory"[78]—"and all the treasures of the kings of Judah into the hand of their enemies, who shall plunder them, and seize them and carry them to Babylon. And you, Pashhur, and all who dwell in your house, shall go into captivity; to Babylon you shall go; and there you shall die, and there you shall be buried, you and all your friends, to whom you have prophesied falsely."

In keeping with the interpretation given above whereby the name Pashhur was changed into *magur*, all translated as they did before; thus, they gave the meaning as "terror," or "foreigner," or "removal," "transferring," and "departure."[79] The prophet threatens that Pashhur, together with his friends, will at any moment be taken captive and given into the hands of their enemies, and that all the people of the tribe of Judah will be taken into the hands of the king of Babylon, some to be killed by the sword and others to be led into captivity, with the city's wealth and the king's treasures seized by the enemy. As for Pashhur himself, he together with all his family and kindred will be led into captivity and will die in Babylon, because he deceived the people with his lies; he did not tell them what was harsh and true but instead promised prosperity falsely. At the same time, let us take note of the prophet's patience and prudence: even though he was sent to prison, he kept quiet and overcame injury with silence. Nevertheless, he did not hide the fact that he knew what was coming, since he wanted to provide some opportunity for this pseudo-prophet high priest to cease from sinning and entreat God for mercy.

20:7-8a: O Lord, you have misled me, and I was misled;—or you have deceived me, and I was deceived—you are stronger than I, and you have prevailed—or you have been powerful and have overcome. I have become a laughingstock all the day; everyone mocks me. For I have been speaking for a long time now, crying "Injustice!" and I proclaim "Destruction!"—or "For with my bitter word I will laugh, I will call on lawlessness and misery."

The prophet says that the Lord has deceived him. Because at first he heard, "I appointed you a prophet to the nations,"[80] and "See, I have set you this day over nations and over kingdoms, to pluck up and to break down, to destroy and to overthrow, to build and to plant,"[81] he did not think that he was going to speak against the people of the Jews but against the various surrounding nations—which is why he so readily accepted the task of prophesying. But it turned out quite differently in that he proclaimed the captivity of Jerusalem, and as a result he suffered difficulty and persecution. And he adds, "I have become a laughingstock all the day; everyone mocks me," because they thought that he was deluded and that everything he predicted was a lie. For even the prophet reckoned that what the Lord threatened was going to take place immediately, and the people thought that whatever did not come about immediately was not going to happen at all. "And I cry 'Babylonian destruction,' and 'the injustice of the enemy' through which my people will be subdued." But if we follow the LXX in what they said, "For with my bitter word I will laugh, I will call on lawlessness and misery," this is the sense: "I know that the present sorrow will be replaced with future joy, as it is written, 'Blessed are those

---

[77]Jerome agrees with Sym. Heb *ḥōsen* ("stronghold" or "treasure, stocks," KB 338). [78]Jerome agrees with Aq and a reading preserved under asterisk. This word is absent from the LXX. The second option ("glory") might reflect Sym. [79]See at Jer 20:3. Jerome seems unable to settle on a single Latin equivalent for Sym. [80]Jer 1:5. [81]Jer 1:10.

who weep, for they will laugh.'[82] Therefore, so willingly do I endure hardship, injustice and affliction that I even desire them and invoke them, so that I may make up for this brief suffering with eternal happiness."

20:8b-10a: *For the word of the Lord has become for me a reproach and derision all day long. I said, "I will not remember him"—or "I will not name the Lord's name"[83]—"or speak any more in his name." And there was in my heart as it were a burning fire shut up in my bones, and I was wearied,—or weakened—not enduring to bear it. For I heard the reproaches—or censure[84]—of many, and terror on every side—or of the many who were gathered all around:[85] "Persecute him! Let us persecute him!"*

"Because I was crying out and saying that the Babylonian army was coming and that the enemy sword was going to plunder everything, the word of the Lord became for me a reproach and derision, since they took the slowness of the prophecy to mean that it was a lie. Therefore, I resolved in my mind that I would no longer speak to the people with the words of God, nor would I name his name. Overcome with shame, I decided this out of modesty, to be sure, but foolishly." He said, "There was in my heart as it were a burning fire shut up in my bones, and I was wearied (or 'utterly weakened'), so that I was not able to bear it."

For the divine word, if it has been received into the soul but not brought forth through the mouth, burns within the breast. Thus the apostle Paul says, "For if I preach the gospel, that gives me no ground for boasting. For

necessity is laid on me. Woe to me if I do not preach the gospel! For if I do this of my own will, I have a reward; but if not of my own will, I am entrusted with a commission."[86] And in Athens, seeing that the city was devoted to idolatry, Paul was provoked in his spirit and agitated in his whole mind.[87] And shortly afterward in the same book we read: "When Silas and Timothy arrived from Macedonia, Paul was constrained by the word, testifying to the Jews that the Christ was Jesus."[88] Even today many of the teachers in the church suffer similar things, as they hear the censure of the multitudes gathered around against them saying, "Persecute them! Let us persecute them!"

20:10b-11a: *All the men who had been my allies, watching over my side: "Perhaps he will be deceived; then we can prevail against him and take our revenge on him." But the Lord is with me as a strong warrior.*

When our enemies rise up and our former friends and allies turn to war and desire to set traps for us, we should not be overly concerned, but let us choose to say what the prophet says: "But the Lord is with me as a strong warrior."

20:11b: *Therefore my persecutors will stumble, and they will be weak—or Therefore they persecuted me and were not able to understand.[89] They will be greatly shamed, for they did not understand the eternal dishonor—or disgrace—that will not be blotted out.*

Because they persecuted me they were not able to understand the prophetic word. Severe

---

[82]Cf. Lk 6:21. [83]Jerome's *recordabor* ("remember") is meant as a more literal rendering of the Hebrew *zkr* ("to remember"; so also Aq, Sym); but *zkr* can also mean "to name, mention" (KB 270). [84]The Hebrew word *dibbâ* ("report, rumor," KB 208) is singular. [85]On the LXX's translation of Hebrew *mgwr* as "gathered," see Sym at Jer 20:3. The Targ and the Pesh agree with the LXX against Jerome. [86]1 Cor 9:16-17. [87]Acts 17:16. [88]Acts 18:5. [89]Jerome's "will stumble" presumes the consonants * kšl* (so MT), whereas the LXX understood *śkl* ("to understand"). Jerome's "will be weak" is based on reading the word *yklw* as from *klh*, whereas the vocalization in MT presumes the root *ykl* ("to be able, overcome"; so the LXX). Jerome's translation of this verse matches Sym.

disorientation followed on their ignorance, and they did not understand the eternal disgrace that will attend them and that will not be blotted out by any forgetfulness. Therefore, let former allies who used to watch over my side say whatever they wish and even seek to entrap me, provided that after the persecution is over such great vindication and reward comes to him who is a just man and a teacher of the church.

20:12: O Lord of hosts, tester of the righteous,—or who tests righteous things[90] —who sees the heart and the mind, let me see your vengeance on them, for to you have I laid bare my cause.

Only the Lord knows how to test righteousness. Similarly, only the Lord looks at the inner parts of the heart. Therefore Jesus, who also knows the thoughts of people,[91] is God—not simply by effect, as some suppose, but by nature. Such an idea is also expressed in the Psalms: "No one living will be made righteous in your sight."[92] And if a living person is not made righteous by virtues, how much the more so for one who is dead in sins! Although the righteous person knows that he has God as his defender, the impatience of human frailty eagerly longs to see right now what it knows is going to come. And he has laid bare his cause to God, who says in another passage: "Vindication is mine, I will repay, says the Lord."[93] And it is a happy conscience whose cause is laid bare to the Lord, as the apostle says: "All that is made manifest is light."[94]

20:13: Sing to the Lord; praise the Lord! For he has delivered the life of the needy from the hand of evildoers.

He who is poor in spirit[95] and is not one of the wealthy who has received his consolation in this age[96] but is one of those concerning whom Paul spoke: "only that we might remember the poor"[97]—when he has obtained vindication from the Lord, he praises the Lord in spirit and boasts that he has been rescued from the hand of evildoers. All of this, however, is not by our merit but by the grace of him who delivers the needy person. Such a person does not have the wealth of amassed pride but the humility of a rescued pauper.

20:14-18: Cursed be the day on which I was born! The day when my mother bore me, let it not be blessed! Cursed be the man—or person[98]—who brought the news to my father, "A son is born to you," making him very glad. Let that man be like the cities that the Lord overthrew and did not relent; let him hear a cry in the morning and wailing at noon, who did not—or because he did not[99]—kill me in the womb, so my mother would have been my grave and her womb forever pregnant. Why did I come forth from the womb to see toil and sorrow and spend my days in shame?

Those who think[100] that human souls were previously in heaven and that they fell from a better state into a worse one make use of this passage and passages like it, asserting that it was better to be in heaven than to dwell on earth and assume a lowly body,[101] thereby coming up with new—or rather, already old—arguments for their heresy. But when we read this statement of the blessed Job, "Cursed be the day on which I was born, and the night on which they said, 'Behold, a boy,'"[102] and we compare it with this statement, "Cursed be the person who brought the news to my father, 'A

---

[90]Jerome agrees with Aq; Sym translates "righteous tester." [91]Mt 9:4; 12:25; Lk 6:8; 11:17. [92]Ps 143:2. [93]Deut 32:35; Rom 12:19; Heb 10:30. [94]Eph 5:13. [95]Mt 5:3. [96]Lk 6:24. [97]Gal 2:10. [98]Jerome used *vir* ("man") in his IH edition to correspond to the Hebrew *'yš*. He also gives the alternative *homo* ("person") to represent the LXX's *anthrōpos*. [99]Jerome agrees with Aq and the more common meaning of the Hebrew word *'šr*. The LXX ("because") is matched by Sym (for *'šr* meaning "because," see KB 98.B). [100]The followers of Origen. [101]Phil 3:21. [102]Job 3:3.

son is born to you,'"[103] the clear meaning is that it is better not to have existed than to live in torment, as it is written: "Death is rest for the one whose way God has shut,"[104] and "Why is light given to him that is in misery, and life to the bitter in soul?"[105] And in the Gospel we read it simply stated: "It would have been better for him if he had not been born,"[106] not in the sense that there is anyone who has not been born but in the sense that it is better not to exist than to exist wickedly. For it is one thing not to exist altogether; it is something else to exist and to be tortured without ceasing, just as we prefer a peaceful death to a miserable life. For this reason Amos calls the day of affliction a "day of darkness,"[107] and Jacob, to the extent that he lived in toil and anguish, calls the days of his life "few and evil."[108] Also, the apostle Paul says, "to deliver us from the present evil age,"[109] and again, "redeeming the time, because the days are evil."[110]

By certain inextricable and incredible arguments, the Hebrews reckon that the fifth month, in which Jerusalem was captured and the temple was destroyed, is the month of Jeremiah's birth. But I do not know if they can explain how it might be possible to interpret the passage in Job, unless perhaps they contend that his day, too, was a prefiguration and foretelling of the destruction of the temple.[111] And when he prays that they be like cities that have been overthrown, I think he is speaking about Sodom and Gomorrah.[112] All their time will be spent in grief, so that there is "a cry in the morning and wailing at noon." When it goes on to say "who did not kill me in the womb," they think that God is meant. When he says, "so my mother would have been my grave and her womb forever pregnant," this is all said using hyperbole. Finally, he explains the reason why he prefers death to life and nonexistence to wicked existence, adding, "Why did I come forth from the womb to see toil and sorrow and spend my days in shame?"

21:1-2: *This is the word that came to Jeremiah from the Lord, when King Zedekiah sent to him Pashhur the son of Malchiah and Zephaniah the priest, the son of Maaseiah, saying, "Inquire of the Lord for us, for Nebuchadnezzar king of Babylon is making war against us; perhaps the Lord will deal with us according to all his wonderful deeds, and he will withdraw from us."*

The previous high priest Pashhur (or Phaschor) who beat Jeremiah had Immer as his father, whereas this Pashhur is the son of Malchiah. I say this lest anyone think that this Pashhur is the same as the previous one.

King Zedekiah sends these men to Jeremiah but does not want the people or the officials to know, so that by a secret message delivered through lieutenants he may find out the nature of God's plan for the city of Jerusalem and the Jewish people. When he says, "for Nebuchadnezzar king of Babylon is making war against us," it shows that only now when Jerusalem is being besieged is Zedekiah seeking to learn this from the prophet. It should be noted that in the prophets, and above all in Ezekiel and Jeremiah, the order of kings and times is

---

[103]Jer 20:15. [104]Job 3:10, 17, 23; Sir 30:17. [105]Job 3:20. [106]Mt 26:24. [107]Amos 5:18, 20. [108]Gen 47:9. [109]Gal 1:4. [110]Eph 5:16. [111]On the destruction of Jerusalem in the fifth month, see Jer 1:3; 2 Kings 25:8 (cf. Jer 39:2; 52:6). This theory regarding the date of Jeremiah's birth is not found in any sources contemporary with Jerome, but the seventeenth-century *Sēder ha-Dôrôt* written by Jehiel ben Solomon Heilprin claims that Jeremiah was born on the ninth day of the month of Av (the fifth month), which is the traditional rabbinic date for the destruction of the temple (*Sēder ha-Dôrôt*, "Yĕmôt 'Ôlām," p. 122). It is possible that Heilprin was following a much older tradition. Jerome's objection is as follows: If Jeremiah's cursing the day he was born indicates that he was born in the same month as the temple's destruction, should not the same be true for Job? But what connection is there between Job and the destruction of the temple? "Unless," Jerome reasons (here he is speculating and is not claiming to follow "the Hebrews"), "Job's birth day was also a prefiguration of the temple's destruction." [112]Gen 19:24-25.

often not preserved, but, with the order reversed, what took place later according to *historia* is mentioned earlier, and that which happened earlier is mentioned later. For it is one thing to write *historia*; it is something else to write prophecy. Thus, in the present passage it is written that Zedekiah, who was captured together with the city of Jerusalem, sent a message to Jeremiah at the time when Jerusalem was being besieged; then, later on, the *historia* describes events regarding Jehoiakim his brother, who was king before him, and Jehoiachin (that is, Jeconiah) the son of Jehoiakim. These things are discussed below.

21:3-6: Then Jeremiah said to them: "Thus you shall say to Zedekiah, 'Thus says the Lord, the God of Israel: Behold, I will turn back the implements of war'—or 'battle arms'[113]—'that are in your hands and with which you are fighting against the king of Babylon and against the Chaldeans who are besieging you outside the walls; and I will gather the implements'—or 'the Chaldeans'[114]—'into the midst of this city. I myself will fight against you with outstretched hand and strong'—or 'uplifted'[115]—'arm, in anger, and in fury and in great wrath. And I will strike the inhabitants of this city, both man and beast; they shall die of a great pestilence.'"

He says, "In vain you are planning to fight against the Chaldeans who are besieging you, and in vain you are readying battle arms, the use of which you will have only inside the city in order to give the appearance of being armed. In point of fact, through those who are besieging 'I myself will fight against you with outstretched hand and strong arm,' and in my anger and fury I will strike you, so that you and everything that breathes will die within the city from famine and pestilence." And we read that this is indeed what happened. For the city was captured without any line of battle or crashing of fighters. And the siege was so great that the attackers held as prisoner not those whom they conquered but only those whom they captured. It says, "Happier were those slain by the sword than those killed by famine."[116]

21:7: "Afterward, says the Lord, I will give Zedekiah king of Judah, and his servants, and his people and those in this city who are left from the pestilence, sword and famine, into the hand of Nebuchadnezzar king of Babylon and into the hand of their enemies, into the hand of those who seek their lives. He shall smite them with the edge of the sword; he shall not be appeased, or spare them or have compassion."

That which we translated, "into the hand of Nebuchadnezzar king of Babylon and into the hand of their enemies," is not found in the LXX.[117] And in place of what we said, "he shall not be appeased, or spare them or have compassion," the LXX translated, "I will not spare them or have compassion on them." It is better according to the Hebrew, since the cruel and inflexible punishment is seen to

---

[113]Jerome offers a more literalistic rendering of the Hebrew *kĕlê hammiḥāmâ* ("instruments of war" or "vessels of war") than the LXX ("battle arms"). [114]The Hebrew text has "I will gather *them* (masculine)," which could refer either to the implements of war or to the Chaldeans, since both are masculine in Hebrew. This phrase is absent from the LXX but was supplied under asterisk in the Hexapla, where the masculine pronoun clearly refers to the Chaldeans, since "battle arms" in Greek is neuter. The first option in the lemma matches Jerome's IH edition, where he put a neuter pronoun to refer to the implements (neuter in Latin). The second option is a masculine pronoun, which represents the asterisked reading and refers to the Chaldeans. I have written the antecedents to the pronouns in the lemma above for the sake of clarity. [115]Jerome ("strong") matches MT and some LXX witnesses. Other witnesses to the text of the LXX have "uplifted," as did Jerome's copy of the LXX. [116]Lam 4:9. [117]Many witnesses to the LXX read "from death, famine and the sword, into the hands of their enemies who seek their lives." Perhaps Jerome's copy of the LXX also lacked "their enemies," or perhaps he skipped over it in reading.

belong more to the king of Babylon than to the Lord.

First he prophesied concerning the whole city.[118] Now he predicts concerning Zedekiah himself and his people who will be left alive after the pestilence, sword and famine, that he is to be captured by Nebuchadnezzar king of Babylon and cut off by the sword together with his friends, and that he should have no hope for mercy from him whose treaty and pact he abandoned through perjury.

21:8-10: *"And to this people you shall say: 'Thus says the Lord: Behold, I set before you the way of life and the way of death. He who stays in this city shall die by the sword, by famine and by pestilence; but he who goes out and surrenders to the Chaldeans who are besieging you shall live and shall have his life as a prize of war. For I have set my face against this city for evil and not for good, says the Lord: it shall be given into the hand of the king of Babylon, and he shall burn it with fire.'"*

To those who were sent by the king to the prophet in order to ask him to inquire of the Lord on their behalf, Jeremiah responded with the above statements, including those referring to King Zedekiah.[119] Now he instructs them on how they should respond to the people, and he advises that the people should surrender to the Chaldeans, even against the king's will. This was no doubt a dangerous thing for the prophet to say. For this reason he calls for his own death, saying, "Cursed be the day on which I was born,"[120] and "Why did I come forth from the womb to see toil and sor-

row?"[121] The prophet counsels the people in this way not because it is a light thing to advise those who are not yet captured to hand themselves over to captivity, as if he were ordering those about to suffer a shipwreck that before the ship wrecks they should snatch up the smashed vessel, oars and plank and hand themselves over to the water. Rather, he counsels this because, however one is captured, it is more tolerable to live than to die by sword, famine and pestilence. There are some who explain this passage according to tropology[122] in the following way: It is better to hand oneself over to secular disciplines, and especially to philosophy, than to remain in the kind of church where there is a famine of the word of God[123] and all the people are dying by the sword of heretics, by scarcity of doctrine and by heretical pestilence.

21:11-12: *"And to the house of the king of Judah: 'Hear the word of the Lord, O house of David! Thus says the Lord: "Execute justice in the morning, and deliver from the hand of the corrupt him who has been oppressed by force, lest my wrath go forth like fire,"*—or *"so that my wrath does not go forth like fire"*[124]—*"and burn with none to quench it"'"*—and that which follows, *"because of your evil doings,"* is not found in the LXX.

Since above he had said, "And to this people you shall say: 'Thus says the Lord,'"[125] he now logically continues: "And to the house of the king of Judah (with the word *say!* being understood) . . . thus says the Lord." For the clause above and this clause are joined together *apo koinou,*[126] so that the sense is: "And to this

---

[118]Jer 21:3-6. [119]The "above statements" are Jer 21:3-6, and Jer 21:7 refers specifically to Zedekiah. [120]Jer 20:14. [121]Jer 20:18. [122]The Latin word *tropologia* is taken from a Greek rhetorical term that refers to the figurative sense of a word as opposed to its literal or proper sense. In Christian exegesis after Origen it became a technical term for the spiritual sense of the text. [123]Amos 8:11. [124]Whereas the first option matches closely the wording of the IH edition, the second option as given in the lemma is a meaningless variant; what the LXX says is: "so that my wrath does not *kindle* like fire," which is no doubt what Jerome meant to say. In fact, it was probably the word *kindle* that led Jerome to report this variant in the first place, but when it was dictated (or written down) "go forth" was accidentally repeated. [125]Jer 21:8. [126]The phrase *apo koinou* in Greek (meaning "in common") refers to a figure of speech whereby

people you shall say, 'Thus says the Lord'" . . . "And to the house of the king of Judah you shall say, 'Thus says the Lord.'"

This message is specifically given to the royal house, since it is primarily the king's fault that the city is being besieged; the king is told that he must emend his error by repentance and seek out the Lord's mercy. It says, "Execute justice in the morning"—not in the darkness of iniquity but in the light of righteousness—"and deliver from the hand of the corrupt him who has been oppressed by force"—so that you are not partial in judgment,[127] but when the rich oppress the poor, God's authority rather than the oppressor's power should prevail among you. "And if you will do this," he says, "then the fire of my anger will not be kindled against you, nor will it find in you any material to consume."

The unbelievable mercy of God is shown in this passage. In view of what he said above, "For I have set my face against this city for evil and not for good . . . it shall be given into the hand of the king of Babylon, and he shall burn it with fire," with the Lord's judgment already breaking out against them, he now tries to provoke them to salvation, not because he is unaware that the city will be captured but in order to preserve human free will, so that they may be seen as perishing, not out of ignorance of what was going to happen but by their own choice. In the same way, the Savior knew that the people were going to reject him and that he was going to be crucified; in fact, he predicted this often to the apostles.[128] Nevertheless, he would still admonish them, wanting to restore

them to repentance, so that whatever they suffered later would come about, not because of the sternness of the one giving the warning but because of their own vice.

21:13-14: *"Behold, I am against you, O inhabitant of a firm and flat valley, says the Lord, you who say, 'Who shall strike'—or 'terrify'[129]—'us, or who shall enter our habitations?' I will punish you"—and that which follows, "according to the fruit of your doings, says the Lord," is not found in the LXX.[130] "And I will kindle a fire," he says, "in her forest, and it shall devour all that is round about her."*

In place of "O inhabitant of a firm and flat valley," the LXX translated, "Behold, I am against you, who inhabit the valley of Sor, the plain." In place of "Sor," Symmachus translated "rock," Theodotion put "enclosed," the first edition of Aquila translated "firm," and his second edition put "Tyre." For *sor* or *sur* in the Hebrew language can mean "Tyre," "stone" or "constrained."[131] And so he speaks against Jerusalem, which has been "enclosed" by a blockade or is surrounded by the Babylonian army just as "Tyre" is surrounded by the Great Sea, or else thinks itself strong and impregnable like the hardest "rock" in view of its large, "firm" defenses.

Jerusalem says, "Who will be able to terrify us, or who shall enter our habitations?" God, on the contrary, says, "I will punish you. You will not be able to escape my notice. Indeed, I will punish you with destruction. I will render to you the fruit of your evil deeds. I will kindle

---

two different clauses share a single word or phrase in common. In this case, Jerome is suggesting that "you shall say" can be supplied in Jer 21:12 on the grounds that it is shared "in common" with the similar sentence in Jer 21:8. [127]Deut 1:17; 16:19; Lev 19:15. [128]Mt 16:21; 17:22-23; 20:17-19; 26:2; Mk 10:32-34; Lk 18:31-33. [129]Both Jerome and the LXX are reading this word (*yht*) as a Hiphil form of *htt*, which could mean either "to shatter" or "to terrify" (KB 365). The Targ and the Pesh both interpret the word as a form of *nht* ("to descend"; cf. the RSV: "Who shall come down against us?"). [130]The LXX as preserved lacks not only the text indicated by Jerome but also the first phrase of the verse: "I will punish you." All of this was supplied in the Hexapla under asterisk from Aq and Th. [131]The Hebrew letters in question are *ṣwr*. The LXX and Aq's second edition interpreted the word as *ṣôr/ṣōr* ("Tyre," KB 1053). Sym understood *ṣûr* ("rock"). This same vocalization (*ṣûr*), with the same basic sense, was in many contexts interpreted by Aq as "solid" or "firm" (Deut 8:15; 32:31; 2 Sam 2:16; Ps 27:5 [26:5]; 28:1 [27:1]; 61:2 [60:3]; 62:7 [61:8]; Is 8:14; 30:29; Hab 1:12). Jerome follows Aq in the lemma and in the IH edition. Th's "enclosed" probably derives from reading a past participle of the verb *ṣwr* ("to surround," KB 1015).

a fire in your forest. My anger—not the Babylonians, as you think, or the king of the Chaldeans—shall accomplish all these things." He calls Jerusalem and all the surrounding region a "forest" that lacks trees bearing the fruit of good deeds, so that it is prepared for burning.[132] And beautifully he calls the valley "flat," so that it is accessible to the enemies, as it says in Isaiah: "a vision of the valley of Zion";[133] it is not a "high mountain,"[134] which would be difficult to ascend.

Whatever was prophesied to the royal house and the chief city we refer to the ecclesiastical order and the leaders of the churches—those, at least, who have given themselves over to pride, wealth and lewdness.[135] It will not be spared from ruin simply because it is the royal house. Consider: Of all those who were from the line of David, very few were found who pleased the Lord, such as David himself, Hezekiah and Josiah; the vast majority of the leaders from the royal line provoked the Lord's anger against the whole people.

22:1-5: *Thus says the Lord: "Go down to the house of the king of Judah, and speak there this word, and say, 'Hear the word of the Lord, O king of Judah, you who sit on the throne of David, you, and your servants and your people who enter these gates. Thus says the Lord: Do justice and righteousness, and deliver from the hand of the corrupt him who has been oppressed by force. Against the alien, the fatherless and the widow do no harm and do not act unjustly,'—or 'act impiously'[136]—'nor shed innocent blood in this place. For if you will indeed obey this word, then there shall enter the gates of this house kings from the stock of David who sit on his throne, riding in chariots and on horses, they, and their servants and their people. But if you will not heed these words, I swear by myself, says the Lord, that this house shall become a desolation.'"*

This vision—or rather this word—of the Lord came to the prophet either before Zedekiah sent messengers to him or else after he told the messengers what they should reply to the king.[137] The Lord bids Jeremiah not to speak to the king through messengers but to go to the palace himself and speak to the king there. We should give heed to the divine wisdom in this: Through messengers the Lord commands that miseries be announced, with only some prosperity mixed in if the king is willing to repent; but here, when the prophet himself is ordered to go, Jeremiah does not announce miseries and approaching captivity, but instead he warns the king what the king should do in order to avoid God's impending judgment.

Moreover, it is proper for a king to do justice and righteousness, to deliver from the hand of the corrupt those who have been oppressed by force and to offer assistance to the alien, the fatherless and the widow, who are easily oppressed by the powerful. And so as to inspire in them a greater concern for God's commands, the prophet adds, "do no harm," so that not only should you rescue them but also you should not even allow them through your negligence to be harmed by others; "nor shed *innocent* blood in this place," for to punish murderers, profaners and poisoners is not shedding blood but administering the law.

The prophet says, "If you will do these things, O kings of Judah, then you will possess your former power and will enter the gates of Jerusalem with splendor. But if you will not do these things, O royal house, then severity will befall you, not so much from the Lord as from your own choice, so that the entire city is reduced to desolation." Whatever was said to

---

[132]Mt 7:19; Lk 3:9.   [133]Is 22:1.   [134]Is 40:9.   [135]Cf. *Comm. Jer.* 30:18-22; *Comm. Ezech.* 13:1-3a: "Whatever was said at that time to the Israelite people now is referred to the church, so that 'holy prophets' become 'apostles and apostolic men,' and 'lying and frantic prophets' become 'all the heretics.'"   [136]Heb *hms* ("to treat violently," KB 329).   [137]Jer 21:1, 3-7.

the royal house, let the bishops and their associates, the presbyters and deacons and every ecclesiastical order understand: If they will do what was commanded and (together with the other commands) not shed innocent blood by causing any of the least ones to stumble[138] or wounding the conscience of any individual,[139] then they will fulfill the office granted to them by the Lord; but if they will not do what was commanded and despise their office, then they themselves will reduce the church to desolation.

Yet, from the stock of David they shall enter the gates of Jerusalem, and they shall sit on the throne of him who is interpreted "strong of hand."[140] Moreover, when they restrain their own passions and the passions of the people, they shall ride in chariots and on horses, and they shall enter the church with well-ordered steps and with a chorus of the many virtues harmonizing together in every way. And so that we will believe that this is true, he swears by himself, since according to the apostle he has no one greater by whom he can swear.[141]

22:6-9: *For thus says the Lord concerning— or against—the house of the king of Judah: "You are as Gilead to me, as the head"—or "beginning"[142]—"of Lebanon, yet surely I will make you a desert, an uninhabited city. I will consecrate a destroyer against you, the man and his arms; and they shall cut down your choicest cedars and cast"—or "throw"—"them into the fire. And many nations will pass by this city, and every man will say to his neighbor, 'Why has the Lord dealt thus with this great city?' And they will answer, 'Because*

they forsook the pact of the Lord their God and worshiped other gods and served them.'"

Scripture recounts that Gilead, which was occupied by the half tribe of Manasseh, was beyond the Jordan.[143] On this mountain Laban pursued Jacob as he fled,[144] and according to Genesis this mountain received the name *sōros*, that is, "mound of witness," because there Jacob and Laban swore an oath by stones piled up in a heap.[145] In addition, there is the "head" or "beginning" of Lebanon, a high mountain that was thick with cedar trees, as David sings: "The Lord breaks the cedars of Lebanon";[146] and elsewhere: "I have seen the wicked exalted, and towering like the cedars of Lebanon";[147] and in Zechariah we read, "Open your doors, O Lebanon, so that fire may devour your cedars!"[148] Therefore, since Jeremiah had been speaking against the royal house, in the present passage he speaks through metaphor against the temple (or the "house" of Judah's line), because it is itself on a high place and because the people expected from the sacred temple a remedy for all their sins. Thus, this same prophet relates, "Is there no balm in Gilead? Is there no physician there? Why then has a cure for the daughter of my people not arisen?"[149]

Therefore, he threatens the royal house, the city of Jerusalem and the temple (which he calls the "head of Lebanon"), that they will be reduced to desolation together with all of their towns, not by the power of the king of Babylon but by the command of the Lord who says, "I will consecrate a destroyer against you." Nebuchadnezzar and all his army are called "consecrated" because they are carrying out God's decree. He says, "And they shall cut

---

[138]Mt 18:6; Mk 9:41; Lk 17:2. [139]1 Cor 8:12. [140]This etymological interpretation of the name David (Heb *dwyd*) is based on seeing the element "hand" (*yd*) plus some word for "strong" (*'addîr*? KB 13). This meaning was known in the Greek onomastica (OS 202.64) and was taken over by Jerome in his *Nom. Hebr.*, although Jerome adds the meaning "beloved" as an alternative (OS 35.11; 61.9-10; 68.13; 77.29; 79.5) or else gives "beloved" instead of "strong of hand" (OS 74.3; 80.16; 81.11). On the meaning "beloved," cf. Heb *dôd* (KB 215). In this instance, Jerome uses the traditional etymology as found in the older Greek tradition. [141]Heb 6:13. [142]Heb *r'š* (lit., "head" [thus Jerome's *caput*]), although the sense in this context is "summit." Cf. Aq and the LXX on *br'šyt* at Gen 1:1; Jerome *QHG* 1:1. [143]Deut 3:13; Josh 13:29-31; 1 Chron 27:21. [144]Gen 31:23. [145]Gen 31:46-48. Jerome gives the Greek word *sōros* ("heap," LSJ 1750); perhaps this is Aq. [146]Ps 29:5. [147]Ps 37:35 (LXX [36:35]). [148]Zech 11:1. [149]Jer 8:22.

down your choicest cedars"—the officials and leaders of the city—"and throw them into the fire"—so that the consuming flame will devour all of them. And when everything has been destroyed, many nations will pass by the city and the temple, which they were formerly forbidden to enter, and each one will say to his neighbor, "Why has the Lord dealt so sudden and complete an overthrow to this great and illustrious city?" "And those who were asked will give answer," he says, "and they will explain the causes of the devastation, saying, 'It is because they forsook the pact of the Lord their God and worshiped idols instead of God.'" Let this be heard by the royal house of our city, its leaders and its "cedars," who lift up their "summit" to the clouds and say with pride, "Who will not see us?" For the flame of the Lord devours quickly those who are unwilling to yield to his commands. It is one thing for God to consecrate a destroyer and his army; the consecration of priests and those who serve the Lord is something totally different.

22:10-12: *Weep not for him who is dead, nor bemoan him; but with tears lament him who goes away, for he shall return no more to see his native land. For thus says the Lord concerning Sellum the son of Josiah, king of Judah, who reigned instead of Josiah his father and who went away from this place: "He shall return here no more, but in the place where I have carried him captive, there shall he die, and he shall never see this land again."*

The righteous king Josiah had three sons, Jehoahaz, Jehoiakim and Zedekiah. Jehoahaz was led captive to Egypt by Pharaoh Neco the king of Egypt, where he died. In place of him Pharaoh Neco appointed his brother Eliakim as king, and he changed his name to Jehoiakim.[150] When Jehoiakim died, his son Jehoiachin became king, but he was led into captivity together with his mother and some officials by Nebuchadnezzar king of Babylon. Zedekiah, Jehoiachin's uncle, became king in place of Jehoiachin.[151] Zedekiah was led to Babylon when Jerusalem was captured.[152] We must ask, therefore, who is this king for whom one should not weep and who will be led into captivity never to return, since there were three kings who were captured and led away. The Hebrews think that this refers to all of them combined together, that is, Jehoahaz, Jehoiachin and Zedekiah,[153] and that all the sons of Josiah are called Sellem or Sellum, which is translated "consummation" or "completion,"[154] because the kingdom of Judah was brought to an end with these kings.[155] Yet, it seems more correct to me that this was spoken concerning Zedekiah, since both this prophecy and the previous one are about him, the kingdom of Judah truly came to an end with him, under him the city was captured, and it is written that he was led to Babylon and died there. He is "'Sellum' (that is, 'consummation' or 'completion') the son of Josiah, king of Judah, who reigned instead of Josiah his father." Besides, Jehoiachin was not the son of Josiah; he was Josiah's grandson, the son of Jehoiakim. Thus, we should understand everything—from the beginning of this vision, when King Zedekiah sent him Pashhur the son of Malchiah and

---

[150]2 Kings 23:33-34; 2 Chron 36:3-4. [151]2 Kings 24:6, 12, 15, 17; 2 Chron 36:8-10. [152]2 Kings 25:6-7; Jer 39:7; 52:11. [153]Jerome is confused here. He means the three sons of Josiah (as listed above), Jehoahaz, Jehoiakim (not Jehoiachin) and Zedekiah. This confusion between Jehoiakim and Jehoiachin gives rise to a needless comment at the end of the discussion ("Besides, Jehoiachin was not the son of Josiah"). [154]Heb *šallum*; cf. *šlm* ("to be completed, ready," KB 1533). [155]The idea that the name Sellum (*šallum*) refers to all three sons of Josiah is not found in any rabbinic sources. Rabbinic texts regularly identify *šallum* as Zedekiah, on the grounds that "the kingdom of David was 'completed' (*šlmh*) in his days" (see *p. Sheqalim* 6:1, 49b; *b. Horayot* 11b; Targum to 1 Chron 3:15). Most modern commentators (so also Theodoret) identify *šallum* with Jehoahaz. Ironically, Jerome changes his mind on this passage in his comments at Jer 22:18-19.

Zephaniah the priest, the son of Maaseiah,[156] up to this section—as spoken against or about King Zedekiah.

22:13-17: *"Woe to him who builds his house by unrighteousness and his upper rooms by injustice; who oppresses his friend without cause and does not give him his wages; who says, 'I will build myself a great house with spacious upper rooms,' and opens for himself windows, making roofs with cedar and painting it with red ochre. Do you think you are a king because you compare yourself with cedar? Did not your father eat and drink and do justice and righteousness? Then it was well with him. He judged the cause of the poor and needy for his own good. Is not this to know me? says the Lord. But your eyes and heart are set on greed, shedding innocent blood, trickery and the path of evil work."* LXX: *"O you who build your house not with righteousness and your upper rooms by injustice; his neighbor works for him for nothing, and he does not give him his wages. You built for yourself a measured house with airy upper rooms adorned with windows, furnished with cedar and anointed with red ochre. Are you a king because you contend against Ahaz, your father? They will not eat and drink; it was better for you to do justice and noble righteousness. They did not know; they did not perform justice for the lowly or justice for the poor. Is this not a case of them not knowing me? says the Lord. Behold, your eyes are not right and your heart is not good, but they are set on your greed and iniquity, so that you may shed innocent blood."*

I have put each edition as a whole, so that both the Hebrew truth and the difficulty of the popular edition may be easily recognized.[157]

The message is against Jehoiakim, the son of Josiah king of Judah, about whom we spoke above.[158] Pharaoh Neco king of Egypt set Jehoiakim up as king in place of his brother Jehoahaz, whom the pharaoh led bound in chains to Egypt. We read of it in both Kings and Chronicles,[159] and the *historia* narrates that Jehoiakim son of Josiah reigned cruelly for eleven years in Jerusalem, lived an impious life and afterwards died. Yet, his burial is not narrated, even though holy Scripture has this custom whereby it states that all the kings died and were buried. But Scripture narrates the death of this king but not his burial; we will speak about this later on.[160]

And so he offers this lament over the aforementioned king, that he trusts in injustice, thinks that his royal honor is everlasting, makes for himself upper rooms, oppresses friends, does not render the proper wage to those who work and regards the edifice of his palace as eternal. "Will you be able to rule forever," says the divine message, "because you think you are comparable to a lofty cedar, namely, your father Josiah,[161] who was a righteous king?" "Your father," he says, "ate and drank and enjoyed royal wealth. Yet, it did not offend God that he had riches; rather, he pleased God because he did righteousness and justice, and for this reason it was well with him in the present age and will be well with him in the future." He says, "He judged the cause of the poor and needy," both for the benefit of those whom he helped and "for his own good." And all these favorable things came to him because "he knew me, says the Lord." "But your eyes, O Jehoiakim, are bent on greed, trickery and the path of evil work, so as to shed innocent blood!"

As for the LXX, I cannot understand what sense this might make. For, although the rest

---

[156]Jer 21:1. [157]The "popular edition" (*editio vulgata*) is the OL based on the LXX. The "Hebrew truth" (*hebraica veritas*) is reflected in Jerome's translation based on the Hebrew text. [158]Jer 22:10-12. [159]The book "of Kings" (*Regum*) and the book "of Things Omitted" (*Paralipomenon*—in Greek, *paraleipomenōn*), which is the Greek title of Chronicles. On the titles of biblical books, see Jerome's preface to his IH translation of Samuel-Kings. [160]Jer 22:18-19. [161]The Targ also takes the "cedar" to be a reference to Josiah.

of the passage fits together at least in some way, the statement "Are you a king because you contend against Ahaz, your father?" makes no sense at all. (In place of "Ahaz," in the Hebrew it is written "araz," which means "cedar."[162]) And that which follows, "They will not eat and drink, etc." is so tangled up and confused that without the truth of the Hebrew reading it would be unintelligible.

At the same time, we can take this passage according to anagogy[163] as against heretics, who build for themselves a house that is measured, not great and wide with the richness of the church. Moreover, they do not build with righteousness and justice, since they desire to plunder other people's things. Thus it says, "You built for yourself a measured house with airy upper rooms," which are carried about with every wind of doctrine.[164] And they are "adorned with windows," since they do not have a lasting structure or firm stability. They are "furnished," he says, "with cedar." Indeed, they appear to have a most beautiful array of beams, but when the rains and storms of persecution come they quickly rot and collapse. Lastly, they are "anointed with red ochre." For they claim to adhere to the suffering and blood of the Lord,[165] but their rule is not lasting because they contend against and provoke to anger "araz," that is, "Cedar," their father. For every heretic is born in the church, but when heretics are cast out from the church they fight against their parent. And when it says, "They will not eat and drink," one should understand "the body and blood of the Savior." And so on with the rest of the passage.

He says that all their error comes from the fact that they do not know God and do not have right eyes; instead, they have a heart that is prone to greed, so that they plunder other people's things and shed the blood of those who have been deceived. For this is what it means to commit murder. Obscure matters should be discussed more extensively.

22:18-19: *Therefore thus says the Lord concerning Jehoiakim the son of Josiah, king of Judah: "They shall not lament for him, saying, 'Ah my brother!' or 'Ah sister!' They shall not mourn for him, saying, 'Ah lord!' or 'Ah his majesty!' With the burial of a donkey he shall be buried, rotten and cast forth outside the gates of Jerusalem."*

That which we put from the Hebrew, "They shall not lament for him, saying, 'Ah my brother!' or 'Ah sister!'" is not found in the LXX.[166] This is said exclusively against Jehoiakim king of Judah, so the enigma is cleared up that formerly appeared hidden and the ambiguity among the three brothers is resolved. The message is not about Jehoahaz or Zedekiah but is strictly about Jehoiakim, who, as the Hebrew *historia* narrates, was killed by bands of Chaldeans, Syrians, Ammonites and Moabites.[167] In *Malachim* his death is recorded but his burial is passed over in silence. And in the Book of Days we read that he was bound in chains and led to Babylon, and beyond this mention is not made of him.[168] And beautifully it says that he is to be buried "with the burial of a donkey," so as to indicate through different words that he will go unburied, that is, that he is to be torn apart by wild animals and birds; for this is the burial of a donkey.

---

[162]Heb *'rz* ("cedar"). The LXX read *'hz*, ("Ahaz"). Both Sym and Aq read "cedar" as Jerome does, but in this case Jerome agrees with Sym (not Aq) in his reading of the syntax of the sentence.   [163]Following Origen and other Greek fathers, Jerome uses the Greek term *anagōgē* ("elevation") to refer to the higher or spiritual sense.   [164]Eph 4:14.   [165]Cf. Origen *Fr. Jer.* 13.   [166]According to our best witnesses to the LXX, only the expression "Ah sister!" is absent from the LXX, although in the next clause the expression "Ah his majesty" is also absent.   [167]2 Kings 24:2. See Jerome's comments at Jer 22:13-17.   [168]2 Kings 24:5-6; 2 Chron 36:6. *Malachim* is the Book of Kings (Heb *mĕlāchîm*), and the Book of Days reflects the Hebrew title of Chronicles (Heb *dibrê hayyāmîm*, "Words of Days"). See Jerome's preface to his IH translation of Samuel-Kings and n. 159.

22:20-23: *"Go up to Lebanon, and cry out and lift up your voice in Bashan; cry out to those who pass by, for all your lovers are destroyed. I spoke to you in your prosperity, but you said, 'I will not listen.' This has been your way from your youth, that you have not obeyed my voice. The wind shall feed all your shepherds,"*—or *"lovers"*[169]—*"and your lovers"*—or *"friends"*[170]—*"shall go into captivity; then you will be ashamed and confounded because of all your wickedness. You who sit in Lebanon and make your nest among the cedars, how you groaned when pain came on you, pain as of a woman in travail!"*

Through the metaphor of Lebanon (a mountain) and Bashan (a region beyond the Jordan) the message is delivered to Jerusalem that it has trusted in Egypt to no purpose; or else it is delivered to Jehoiakim himself, who was ruling in Jerusalem at that time and had been established as king by the Egyptians,[171] that he has trusted in Egyptian aid to no purpose, and that the Egyptians also shall be overcome by the Babylonian king and led into captivity. And when he says, "I spoke to you (that is, God spoke through the prophets; or else 'they spoke to you,'[172] so that 'my prophets' is understood) in your prosperity, but you said, 'I will not listen,'" he charges Jerusalem with pride and with misusing their great wealth in contempt of God. He also explains how, not only at this time but even from the beginning when they were first led out of Egypt, they would not listen to God. For this reason their shepherds and leaders will be scattered here

and there and their necks will be bowed down to Babylonian captivity. And when he adds, "You who sit in Lebanon and make your nest among the cedars," he is scoffing at their arrogance that sprang from their abundance in all things. He also says that sudden pain and unexpected captivity will come on them as on a woman who is giving birth.

What we said as, "cry out to *those who pass by*," which in Hebrew is written *meabarim*, the LXX and Theodotion translated as "across the sea" and Symmachus translated as "over against the sea,"[173] so as to signify that the voice of the prophet ought to reach from Jerusalem all the way to Mount Lebanon and Bashan.

22:24-27: *"As I live, says the Lord, even if Jeconiah the son of Jehoiakim, king of Judah, were the ring on my right hand, yet I would tear him"*—or *"you"*[174]—*"off and give you into the hand of those who seek your life, into the hand of those of whom you are afraid, even into the hand of Nebuchadnezzar king of Babylon"*—which is not found in the LXX[175]—*"and into the hand of the Chaldeans. I will cast"*—or *"hurl"*—*"you and your mother who bore you into another country, where you were not born, and there you shall die. But to the land to which they will long to return, there they shall not return."*

Earlier he said, "to the house of the king of Judah thus you shall say,"[176] and then, "Go down to the house of the king of Judah";[177] and again, "Thus says the Lord concerning the house of the king of Judah."[178] In reverse

---

[169]The first option ("shepherds") is Jerome and the LXX (Targ *prns*, "manager," is related to this interpretation); the second option ("lovers") is Aq and Sym. The Hebrew word could be either from *rēaʿ* ("friend, lover") or from *rōʿeh* ("shepherd"); cf. Jer 6:2-4a. [170]Again, the first option ("lovers") matches both Jerome's IH edition and the LXX. Although hexaplaric evidence is lacking, the second option ("friends") is probably Aq and/or Sym. [171]2 Kings 23:34; 2 Chron 36:4. [172]This is the reading of the LXX according to several MSS. [173]The Hebrew consonants are *mʿbrym*. The RSV interprets these letters as the preposition *mn* ("from") plus the place name *ʿbrym* ("from Abarim"; see KB 783). Jerome takes the word to be a plural participle (with "m" prefix) from the verb *ʿbr* ("to pass through") meaning, "those passing through." The LXX, Th and Sym see the preposition *mn* ("from") combined with the preposition *ʿbr* ("beyond"), plus the noun *ym* ("sea"). Jerome may be in unstated agreement with Aq. [174]Jerome ("him") may be trying to follow the sense of the passage. The LXX and the preserved Hebrew text read "you." [175]The phrase "even into the hand of Nebuchadnezzar king of Babylon" is lacking in the LXX. [176]Jer 21:11-12. [177]Jer 22:1. [178]Jer 22:6.

order, first he spoke about Zedekiah, who was the last king of Jerusalem, and then he went back to Jehoiakim his brother who ruled before him. With that prophecy completed, he now speaks against Jehoiakim's son (Josiah's grandson) Jeconiah, king of Judah, who is otherwise called Jehoiachin. Jehoiachin, together with his mother, the officials, the craftsmen and many nobles, was led to Babylon and died there. Therefore, this is said: "Even if Jeconiah were on my hand like a ring that does not easily come off the hand of its bearer and only with difficulty slips from his finger, still I would pull him off and hand him over to the king of Babylon, and there he will die together with his mother and his comrades, and he will never again see the land of Judah that he desires."

Wretched Grunnius,[179] who opened his mouth in order to slander holy men, taught to the people of his own language the lies of Sextus the Pythagorean (a thoroughly heathen man) by translating into Latin his one book, which he divided into two volumes.[180] He had the audacity to publish them under the name of the holy martyr Xystus,[181] bishop of the city of Rome, even though these volumes make no mention of Christ, the Holy Spirit, God the Father, patriarchs, prophets or apostles! With his customary rashness and insanity he called this book "The Ring," and it is now read throughout many provinces, especially by those who preach *apatheia* and sinlessness.[182] Therefore, just as the Lord threatened Jeconiah that he would hurl him

like a ring from his hand and finger, I admonish the reader that he should likewise cast off this impious book; if he wishes to read it, he should read it as any other book written by a philosopher and not as a volume of the church.

In commentaries and expositions where it is customary to set forth diverse opinions from different interpreters, I regularly make use of phrases such as "certain people say this," "others argue that," and "several hold the following opinion."[183] But the wretched Grunnius, and now after many years his (and Jovinianus's) disciple,[184] have criticized me for doing this, accusing me of having set forth their opinions under other people's names—something that I did out of goodwill, so as not to appear to be maligning anyone by using a specific name. Therefore, since my kindness has resulted in accusation, I now say this, both to him who is dead and to him who lives and is trying to renew the former's heresy:[185] their teacher Origen referred this passage to Christ, because he was torn from the hand of God the Father like a ring, and he was sent to a land of captivity through the Valley of Weeping,[186] having been handed over to the cross. Likewise Christ's mother—no doubt the synagogue—was captured and sent away. Origen does not fear to say such things, since he contends that what follows, "O land, land, land, hear the word of the Lord! Thus says the Lord: Write this man down as detestable (or 'childless'),"[187] and so forth, is meant to refer to the Lord of majesty. By the way, in case his disciples

---

[179]Rufinus. See the prologue to bk. 4. [180]The *Sentences of Sextus* was a Greek collection of ethical and spiritual sayings that was widely read in the early church (see Origen *Cels.* 8.30; *Comm. Matt.* 15.3). Rufinus translated the work into Latin believing that its author was the Christian bishop and martyr Sixtus II. The work was used by Pelagius in order to argue that one could live a sinless life (see Augustine *Nat. Grat.* 77). Jerome countered that the work was written by a pagan philosopher named Sextus. Augustine (*Retractions* 2.68) eventually followed Jerome's lead in reckoning the work as pagan (see also Jerome *Ep.* 133.3; *Comm. Ezech.* 18:5-9). That the *Sentences of Sextus* was essentially a Christian work was defended by Henry Chadwick, *The Sentences of Sextus* (Cambridge: Cambridge University Press, 1959). [181]Sixtus II (d. 258). See Eusebius *Hist. Eccl.* 7.5-7, 9, 27. [182]In the preface to his translation of the *Sentences of Sextus*, Rufinus likens the work to a ring, in that it is small (i.e., concise) and precious. In addition, Rufinus calls the work a handbook (Gk *encheiridion*, lit., "at hand"), which can be rendered into Latin as "ring" (*anulus*). On *apatheia* and sinlessness, see *Comm. Jer.*, bk. 4 prol. [183]On the "laws" of commentary writing, see *Comm. Jer.*, bk. 1 prol. [184]Pelagius. [185]The dead enemy is Rufinus and the living is Pelagius. See *Comm. Jer.*, bk. 3 prol. [186]Ps 84:6. [187]Jer 22:29-30.

should dare to deny it, Origen wrote this in the fifth book of his *Stromateis*.[188]

22:28: Is this man Coniah a clay, broken vessel? Is he a vessel without any delight?"—or "use?"[189] "Why are he and his seed hurled and cast into a land that they do not know?"

In place of what we said, "Is he a clay, broken vessel?" Symmachus translated, "Is he vile, rejected refuse (or 'waste')?" The LXX did not put anything for this but simply translated, "Has Jeconiah been dishonored, like a vessel without any use?" Since this is said concerning Jeconiah son of Jehoiakim, would anyone dare to identify this as a type of Christ and take the apostle's statement that the Lord Savior is the image of the invisible God and the firstborn of all creation[190] (that is, wisdom, word, truth, life and righteousness), to mean that Christ is the one called "ring," who was "cast away" or "removed" from the hand of the Lord and given over to king Nebuchadnezzar? "He and his seed," he says, "are hurled and cast into a land that they do not know." No one doubts that this happened in the case of Jeconiah. The name Jeconiah means "preparation for the Lord."[191] In the present passage the first syllable (that is, the word for "Lord") is removed, and it is simply Coniah, so that preparation "for destruction and ruin" is understood.

22:29-30: O land, land, land, hear the word of the Lord! Thus says the Lord: "Write this man down as childless, a man who shall not succeed

in his days; for none of his seed shall sit on the throne of David and rule again in Judah."

If I wanted to indicate for each individual detail how many things the LXX either left out or changed, it would take a long time, especially since the diligent reader can perceive out of each edition what has been changed, what has been added and what has been subtracted.[192] In place of "childless" in the Hebrew is written *ariri*, which the first edition of Aquila translated as "childless," the second edition as *anauxēton* (that is, "without increase"), Symmachus as "empty" and the LXX and Theodotion as "outcast" and "detestable."[193]

The question arises: How can the prophecy stand that none will be born from his line who will sit on the throne of David and rule again in Judah, when our Lord and Savior was born from his seed and Gabriel said to Mary concerning his birth: "Behold, you will conceive in your womb and bear a son, and you shall call his name Jesus. He will be great and will be called the Son of the Most High; and the Lord God will give to him the throne of his father David, and he will reign over the house of Jacob forever; and of his kingdom there will be no end"?[194] Well, since what is lacking in the LXX, "In his days he shall not succeed (or 'increase')," has given rise to this question among those who do not understand, we are able to say the following: The LXX translated, "Write this man as an outcast person; for none of his seed shall increase, sitting on the throne of David and ruling again in Judah." The phrase "none shall increase" was put twice in the Hebrew.[195] But

---

[188]This work is lost. It consisted of ten books (Eusebius *Hist. Eccl.* 6.24.3) and supported Christian teachings by appealing to pagan philosophers (Jerome *Ep.* 70.4). Origen *Fr. Jer.* 14 treats this passage but does not refer it to Christ.   [189]Heb *ḥepeṣ* is frequently "delight" but can also be "matter" or "business" and so perhaps "use" (KB 340). The Targ (*srwk*) and the Pesh (*ḥšḥw*) agree with the LXX ("use"). Evidence for the hexaplaric versions is lacking.   [190]Col 1:15.   [191]Jerome is interpreting the Hebrew name *yknyhw* such that the initial *yod* is the divine name *yhwh*, and the remainder of the name is related to the verb *kwn* ("to prepare") This etymology is found in his *Nom. Hebr.* (OS 62.3). In reality, the divine name is represented by the end of the word (*yhw*). But according to Jerome's interpretation, the shorter form of the name in this passage indicates the removal of the "Lord" so that one may assume that "destruction" is being prepared.   [192]Deut 4:2 and Josephus *Ant.* 1.17 list two categories of textual deviation, adding and subtracting. *Let. Aris.* 311 and Philo *Mos.* 2.34 mention adding, subtracting and changing, as Jerome does here.   [193]Heb *'ryry* ("childless," KB 884).   [194]Lk 1:31-33.   [195]The Hebrew text of Jer 22:30 uses the phrase "shall not succeed or increase" (*l' yṣlḥ*) twice. The verse reads: "Write this man down as

those who first wrote in the Greek books, supposing that it had been added, removed it.[196]

Let us respond, therefore, that *in the days of Jeconiah* there was no man to succeed him, sitting on his throne; but after much time there would be born a man from his seed who would possess his seat. Moreover, it is also possible to resolve the question this way: There will not be a "man" or "human" who will sit on the throne of David, but God will sit on the throne; and God's rule will not be earthly and brief as was David's rule but heavenly and eternal, as Scripture says: "He will reign over the house of Jacob forever; and of his kingdom there will be no end."

And so Jeconiah was born from Jehoiakim, Shealtiel from Jeconiah, Zerubbabel from Shealtiel, until in succession it comes to Christ.[197] But in the days of Jehoiachin,[198] his son did not succeed him as king as he had succeeded his father, but Shealtiel and Zerubbabel lived in captivity, and all the way down to Christ none obtained royal power. This is why in the Hebrew it is written, "In his days"—in that very time when he lived—"none shall sit on the throne of David." For all of them were captives, and thereafter no one from David's line held royal authority in the land of Judah. As Josephus reports, leaders at that time were taken from the priestly line and from the tribe of Levi. These were succeeded by Herod the son of the proselyte Antipater. And afterwards under Vespasian even this kind of rule (or better, semblance of sovereign power) was utterly destroyed.[199]

23:1-4: *"Woe to the shepherds who destroy and tear the flock of my pasture!"—or "O, the shepherds who scatter and destroy the sheep of my pasture!"*[200]*—says the Lord. Therefore thus says the Lord, the God of Israel, concerning the shepherds who care for my people: "You have scattered my flock and have driven them away, and you have not attended to them. Behold, I will attend to you for your evil doings, says the Lord. Then I will gather the remnant of my flock out of all the countries where I have driven them, and I will return them to their fields,"—or "I will restore them to their pasture"—"and they shall be fruitful and multiply. I will set shepherds over them who will care for them, and they shall fear no more, nor be dismayed, neither shall any of their number be missing, says the Lord."*

This prophetic message is addressed to, or is about, the "shepherds." We read about Jeconiah, the second-to-last king of Judah and descendant of David, that it is written: "O land, land, land, hear the words of the Lord! Write this man down as outcast (or 'childless'); none of his seed shall sit on the throne of David."[201] In other words, all hope for Jewish rule was cut off. For this reason, he transitions over to the leaders of the church. Since the synagogue and its "shepherds" were forsaken and condemned, the message addresses the apostles, about whom it is said, "I will set shepherds over them who will

---

childless, a man who *shall not succeed* (*l' yslḥ*) in his days; for *none* of his offspring *shall succeed* (*l' yslḥ*), sitting on the throne of David and ruling again in Judah." Jerome's reasoning is hard to follow if one is not looking at the Hebrew text because Jerome deleted the second occurrence of this phrase in the lemma (as in the IH edition), presumably for stylistic reasons. But here, Jerome points out that the Hebrew text has the phrase twice. According to Jerome, the LXX deleted the first occurrence of this phrase along with the following words, "in his days"; this was a mistake, since it is precisely in these words ("who shall not succeed in his days") that the theological problem of the passage is resolved. Only recourse to the Hebrew provides the solution. [196]These Greek writers (Jerome probably has in mind the original translators of the LXX) thought that the repetition was due to a previous copying error, and so they deleted the first occurrence, which they believed had been wrongly added. Cf. Jer 30:12-15. [197]Mt 1:12-16. [198]Jeconiah. [199]Josephus *Ant.* 14.490-491; 20.249-251. [200]The Hebrew text begins with *hôy* ("Woe!") and continues with verbs that usually mean "to destroy" and "to scatter." Jerome's rendering differs slightly from his IH edition in that he uses *lacerant* for "tear" instead of *dilacerant* (as in the IH edition). The LXX reverses the order of the verbs vis-à-vis the Hebrew text, probably to express the presumed logical order of events: first the sheep are scattered, then they are destroyed. [201]Jer 22:29-30.

care for them, and they shall fear no more, nor be dismayed, neither shall any of their number be missing, says the Lord." For boldly and without any fear the apostles will feed the ecclesiastical flock, and the remnant of the people of Israel will be saved from all lands and returned to their fields or pastures, and they will be fruitful and multiply. And the Lord will attend to the evil shepherds—that is, the scribes and Pharisees—for their evil doings. We can also understand this according to tropology[202] in relation to leaders of the church who are unworthy to govern the Lord's sheep. When these leaders have been cast aside and condemned, the people are delivered when they are handed over to others who prove to be worthy, and thus the "remnant" are saved. The "shepherds" who destroy the sheep are the teachers of heresy. The ones who "tear" and "scatter" are those who create schisms. The ones who "drive" the sheep away are those who separate from the church unjustly. The ones who do not attend to the sheep are those who shut their hand against the penitent.[203] But the Lord will show compassion on all of the penitent, restoring their former pastures while removing the evil shepherds.

23:5-6: *"Behold, the days are coming, says the Lord, when I will raise up for David a righteous branch,"—or "a righteous sunrise"[204]— "and he shall reign as king and will be wise"— or "will understand"—"and shall execute justice and righteousness in the land. In his days Judah will be saved, and Israel will dwell securely. And this is the name that they"—or "he"[205]—"will call him: 'Our righteous Lord'—or 'The Lord is our righteousness.'"*

This name in Hebrew is *sadecenu*. And that which the LXX has badly added, "among the prophets," should be cut out.[206] In fact, after this section there is another that was left out by the LXX, and at the end of this omitted section we find the title "Concerning (or 'Against') the Prophets."[207] But we will speak about this title in its place.

Therefore, after the "shepherds" of the synagogue—namely, the scribes and Pharisees—have been cast away, the remnant of Israel has been saved, and the apostles of the gospel have been set up in place of the former leaders,[208] the Shepherd of shepherds is introduced: the Leader of leaders, the King of kings and the Lord of lords,[209] namely, Christ our Savior, who in the strictest sense is the "righteous branch" or the "righteous sunrise." About him we read: "In his days righteousness shall arise,"[210] and in another passage: "Behold, the man whose name is sunrise, and beneath him he shall arise and build the temple of the Lord."[211] Just as in Isaiah he is called *Emmanuhel*, that is, "God is with us,"[212] in Jeremiah he receives the name "our righteousness." Thus the apostle also says, "who has been made our wisdom from God, our righteousness and sanctification and redemption."[213] Contrary to the Savior, the antichrist (and the devil who indwells him) in Zechariah is said to be a "foolish shepherd."[214]

---

[202]The Latin word *tropologia* is taken from a Greek rhetorical term that refers to the figurative sense of a word as opposed to its literal or proper sense. In Christian exegesis after Origen it became a technical term for the spiritual sense of the text. [203]Deut 15:7. [204]Heb *ṣmh* ("sprout, branch"). Jerome matches Aq and Sym. The LXX seems to presuppose the root *zrh* ("to rise, shine"; cf. *mizrāh* ["sunrise"]); but cf. Zech 3:8; 6:12; Ezek 16:7; 17:10, where the LXX translates *ṣmh* as "sunrise" (perhaps equating it with a form of *zrh*). [205]Heb *yqr'w*, which is vocalized in MT as a singular verb with an objective suffix (i.e., "he will call him"), as translated by the LXX. In contrast, Jerome takes the final *waw* as the sign of a plural verb (i.e., "they will call"—with "him" being assumed), as does the Targ. Evidence for the hexaplaric versions is lacking. [206]The LXX added the phrase "among the prophets" to the end of the verse. See n. 207. [207]The LXX does not have Jer 23:7-8 of MT. The title "Concerning the Prophets" appears at the beginning of Jer 23:9 in MT. The LXX goes straight from the end of Jer 23:6 to the beginning of Jer 23:9, only it takes the title of Jer 23:9 (as seen by MT and Jerome) and connects it with the end of Jer 23:6 ("among the prophets"). [208]Jer 23:1-4. [209]1 Tim 6:15; Rev 17:14; 19:16. [210]Ps 72:7 (LXX [71:7]). [211]Zech 6:12 (LXX). [212]Is 7:14; Mt 1:23. [213]1 Cor 1:30. [214]Zech 11:15.

He says, "and shall execute justice and righteousness in the land." For "the Father judges no one but has given all judgment to the Son."[215] In those days the two and ten tribes, Judah and Israel, will be restored together; and in accordance with Ezekiel, from the two sticks one stick will be made.[216] And if the Lord names him according to the LXX, then his name will be called *Iosedec*, that is, "righteous Lord." But if he is named according to the Hebrew, which says, "*they* will call his name," then the name is "the Lord is our righteousness." For this is the meaning of *adonai sedecenu*, in place of which Symmachus translated, "O Lord, make us righteous!"[217]

23:7-8: "*Therefore, behold, the days are coming, says the Lord, when they shall no longer say, 'As the Lord lives who brought up the people of Israel out of the land of Egypt,' but 'As the Lord lives who brought up and led the seed of the house of Israel out of the north country and out of all the countries where I had driven them.' Then they shall dwell in their own land.*"

This whole section is not found in the LXX. This is the sense: The people of God were not made free by Moses from Egypt, but by Jesus Christ from all countries to which they had been dispersed in the whole world. This is being fulfilled partially in the world now, and it will be fulfilled completely when they come from east and west, from north and south, to sit at table with Abraham, Isaac and Jacob;[218]

thus, after the fullness of the Gentiles has entered in, then all Israel will be saved.[219]

23:9a: *Concerning the Prophets (or "among the prophets" or "Against the Prophets").*

As we said earlier, this title was placed in the edition of the LXX at the end of the previous unit, where we read, "And this is the name that the Lord will call him: 'Iosedek among the prophets.'"[220] But most interpreters, being ignorant of this fact, invent various absurdities in order to explain it. It would have been much better for them to admit their lack of knowledge, rather than to make others the heirs of their ignorance. In reality, the message is directed "against the prophets," or rather, against the pseudoprophets of Jerusalem and Samaria,[221] whom he calls by the common and popular name "prophets," about whom it is written later on: "and in the prophets of Samaria I saw lawlessness," and right after: "and in the prophets of Jerusalem I saw a horror."[222] By using the conjunction "and" in these later texts, he shows that what was said previously had to do with the prophets of the Lord,[223] who showed themselves to be similar to pseudoprophets.

23:9b: *My heart is broken within me,—or in me—all my bones tremble—or are shaken;*[224] *I am like a drunken man, like a man drenched—or overcome*[225]*— with wine, before the face of the Lord and before the face of his holy word— or and before the face of the beauty of his glory.*[226]

---

[215]Jn 5:22. [216]Ezek 37:15-25. [217]The Hebrew text has *yhwh ṣdqnw*, which in MT is vocalized as the divine name plus the noun *ṣedeq* ("righteousness") with a first person plural suffix: "The Lord is our righteousness." This is how Aq translated the name, and this is the correct meaning of the Hebrew according to Jerome. The LXX transliterated the name as *Iōsedek*, which Jerome interprets as "righteous" (i.e., *ṣaddîq*) "Lord" (*Yw*). This was the translation given by Jerome in the IH edition. Jerome also reports Sym, who took *ṣdq* to be a Piel imperative addressed to the Lord. [218]Mt 8:11. [219]Rom 11:25-26. [220]Jer 23:5-6. [221]The Targ at Jer 23:9 refers to them as "prophets of falsehood." [222]Jer 23:13, 14. [223]Since Jer 23:13-14 refer to prophets of Baal (see Jer 23:13), by introducing them with the conjunction "and" he shows that they are additional to the first prophets mentioned in Jer 23:9, who are the Lord's own prophets, albeit false ones. [224]The Hebrew word (*rhp*) occurs only here (in the Qal) and in Gen 1:2 and Deut 32:11 (in the Piel), where it is often translated "hovering" or "moving" and "flutters." [225]The Hebrew idiom is "like a man whom wine passes over," which is translated literally by Aq and Sym, whereas Jerome is idiomatic: Jerome's *madidus* ("drenched") is often used for "intoxicated." [226]Jerome matches MT. The LXX read *hdr* ("beauty") in place of MT's *dbr* ("word").

Before the countenance of Almighty God, that is, the Father, and before the countenance of his Son, who is called by the apostle the "splendor of God" and the "form of God's substance,"[227] the prophet shudders both in mind and body and reckons himself as nothing, as it is said in another passage: "I was like a beast before you";[228] or he is offering to God the sacrifice of his conscience and humility, as it is written in the Psalms: "The sacrifice of God is a broken spirit; a broken and humble heart God will not despise."[229] As for the bones that "tremble" or "are shaken," let us understand them just as the same David sings: "All my bones shall say, 'O Lord, who is like you?'" He is like a drunken man and like a man "drenched" or "overcome" with wine, possessing no understanding and no wisdom, for "the Lord knows the thoughts of human beings, that they are empty."[230] And if this is so, where are those who preach that righteousness can be perfected in a human being?[231] But if they respond by saying that they are not talking about themselves but about the saints, I would think that there are none more saintly than Jeremiah, who, as a virgin, a prophet and one sanctified in the womb, prefigures by his very name our Lord and Savior. For Jeremiah is interpreted "exalted of the Lord."[232]

23:10: *For the land is full of adulterers; because of cursing—or oaths[233]—the land mourns, and the fields—or pastures—of the wilderness are dried up. Their course is evil, and their might is deceptive.*

That which we translated from the Hebrew, "For the land is full of adulterers," is not found in the LXX, which put "oath" instead of "curse." He gives the reasons why the produce of the land has been rendered barren: because of adultery and "cursing" or unnecessary "oaths"—or rather, perjuries. Whatever you understand literally in connection with the land of Judea, refer it to the congregation of the believers: There is a barrenness of virtue and divine favor in the churches because of adultery and because of lying or perjury.

23:11-12: *"Both prophet and priest are defiled; even in my house I have found their wickedness, says the Lord. Therefore their way shall be like a slippery path in the darkness, into which they shall be driven and fall; for I will bring"—or "bring in"—"evil on them, the year of their punishment, says the Lord."*

When wickedness is found in the church of God, and especially in its leaders, we should understand this to have been fulfilled: "Both prophet and priest are defiled; even in my house I have found their wickedness, says the Lord." The house of Christ is the church, about which Paul writes to Timothy, "so that you may know how you ought to behave in the household of God, which is the church of the living God, the pillar and bulwark of the truth."[234] Take the "prophet" as a teacher and the "priest" as the ministerial office. If they should conspire together with depraved minds, their way will be like a slippery path in the darkness, and they will not have the Lord saying to them, "I have come as light into the world, that whoever believes in me may not remain in darkness."[235] Therefore the saint, escaping all darkness, says, "The light of your countenance is imprinted on us, O Lord; you have put joy in my heart."[236]

When these "prophets" and "priests" were in darkness and on the slippery path—namely, in

---

[227]Heb 1:3. [228]Ps 73:22. [229]Ps 51:17. [230]Ps 94:11. [231]Jerome is referring to the Pelagians. [232]On this interpretation of "Jeremiah," see Jer 1:10. [233]Heb *'lh* ("curse," KB 51). Jerome ("cursing") matches Aq. The second option ("oaths") represents Jerome's copy of the LXX. The best witnesses to the LXX read "these things" instead of "curse" or "oath," but the reading known to Jerome is found in some LXX witnesses. [234]1 Tim 3:15. [235]Jn 12:46. [236]Ps 4:6-7.

heretical error—they were driven about and fell down at the slightest movement. And the Lord brings in "evil" on them—not evil in the sense that the Lord brings evil, but it is "evil" to those who are enduring God's punishment. Besides, the same circumstances can be both evil and good: evil for those whom they torment but good for those whom they correct. And this should be noted: The "year of their punishment" from the Lord refers to the correction of sinners. The torment is in line with that which is written: "I will punish their transgression with the rod and their iniquity with scourges; but I will not remove from him my steadfast love."[237]

23:13: "And in the prophets of Samaria I saw foolishness"—or "lawlessness:"[238] "they prophesied by Baal and led my people Israel astray."

According to the mystical understanding, I think that the "prophets of Samaria" refer properly to heretics and to all who boast by a deceptive name about their knowledge. Just as with the prophets of Samaria, in whatever they say they prophesy by Baal (that is, by an idol dedicated to demons), so also with heretics, in whatever they say within the church or outside the church they speak by demons, in order to trip up the people of Israel who formerly perceived God. Therefore, what he says is full of meaning: "And in the prophets of Samaria I saw foolishness." For they do not have the one about whom it is said, "Christ is the strength of God and the wisdom of God."[239]

23:14: "And in the prophets of Jerusalem I

saw an example"—or "a horror:"[240] "adultery and the way of lying; they strengthen the hands of evildoers, so that no one turns from his wickedness"—or "from his wicked way"; "all of them have become like Sodom to me, and its inhabitants like Gomorrah."

He says, "These things are indeed found in the assemblies of the heretics; but also among the prophets of Jerusalem (that is, the teachers of the church) I have seen examples (or the horror) of people committing adultery against the word of God and walking along the way of lying, in that they gave their assent to the deceptions of heretics. They strengthened the hands of evildoers, adding their own crimes to the heretics' wicked deeds, and they led to destruction those whom they should have corrected. Let the perpetrators of these crimes not reckon themselves safe from punishment! For they and their supporters—all of them—will become like Sodom, and those who will not separate from them—but are inhabitants with them—will be like Gomorrah." Therefore, let him boast as much as he likes, and let the prophets of Jerusalem glory in their evil teaching. Because they have prevailed through lying and have strengthened the hands of evildoers, their end will be like Sodom and Gomorrah.

23:15: Therefore thus says the Lord of hosts concerning the prophets: "Behold, I will feed them with wormwood"—or "pain," and according to Symmachus, "bitterness"[241]— "and give them poisoned"—or "bitter"[242]— "water to drink; for from the prophets of Jerusalem defilement has gone forth into all the land."

---

[237]Ps 89:32-33. [238]Heb *tplh* ("tastelessness, offensiveness," KB 1776). In the IH edition Jerome had used *fatuitas* ("folly, foolishness"), whereas here he gives *stultitia* (a near synonym to *fatuitas*). Jerome agrees here with Sym. Aq put "saltless." "Lawlessness" is the LXX. [239]1 Cor 1:24. [240]Heb *š'rwrh*. Jerome agrees with Aq. [241]Jerome ("wormwood") matches Aq and the literal sense of the Hebrew. The LXX gave "pain," and Sym translated "bitterness" (cf. Targ). [242]Heb *r'š*. There is a common word with these letters (*r'š* I, KB 1164) that means "head," and a less common word (*r'š* II, KB 1167) that refers to a "poisonous plant." Aq and the reading of "the Hebrew" (see the Introduction) use a form of the word *head*. The LXX translates "bitter" (cf. Sym above). Jerome understands the word as "poison," as does the Targ.

Let us use this testimony against those who send letters into all the world filled with lies, deception and perjury, in order to defile the ears of those who listen and wound the reputation of the innocent. This text is fulfilled in them: "From the prophets of Jerusalem defilement has gone forth into all the land." For they are not content to feed on their own iniquity and attack those nearby. Throughout the whole world, they try to slander those whom they have come to hate, spreading their insults everywhere.

23:16-17: *Thus says the Lord of hosts: "Do not listen to the words of the prophets who prophesy to you and deceive you; they speak a vision of their own minds, not from the mouth of the Lord. They say to those who despise me"—or "who reject my word"[243]—"the Lord says, 'There shall be peace for you;' and to everyone who walks in the depravity of his own heart, they say, 'No evil shall come on you.'"*

Lest the people think that they are free from any guilt because they simply acquiesced to the corrupt teachers, the prophet says, "Do not listen to the words of the prophets who prophesy lies to you and deceive you." There will be equal punishment for the teacher and the student. "They do not speak what comes from the mouth of the Lord, but they make up things in their own mind." "They say to those who despise me" (or "who reject my word")— namely, the heretical and the corrupt—what do they say? "The Lord says, 'There shall be peace for you.'" They say this so that you will not fear the harsh punishments or be terrified

by "empty" threats. "There shall be peace and tranquility for you," and whatever we say and announce to you is what "the Lord says." "No evil shall come on you," which you fear because of your guilty conscience; rather, good will come to you, as "the Lord says."

23:18: *For who has stood in the counsel of the Lord to perceive and to hear his word, or who has given heed to his word and listened?*

Where we have translated, "in the *counsel* of the Lord," and in the Hebrew is written *bassod*, Aquila translated "secret," Symmachus "speech," and the LXX and Theodotion translated "substance" or "essence."[244] This is the sense: "O you ignorant mob, do not believe the prophets who are announcing lies to you, who say, 'The Lord says: there shall be peace for you; no evil shall come on you.'[245] For how could they know the secrets of God? Or, by what conversation could they have learned of the Lord's counsel? How did the speech of the divine arrangement come to them?" Certain of our interpreters think that they have found in this passage a place where the "substance" of God is addressed.[246]

23:19-20: *Behold, the whirlwind—or storm and shaking[247]—of the Lord's wrath goes forth, and an erupting storm will come on the head of the wicked. The anger of the Lord will not turn back until he has executed and accomplished the intent of his mind. In the latter days you will understand his plan.*

The people stated above, "The Lord says to us: there shall be peace for you,"[248] and the

---

[243]Depending on how one vocalizes the Hebrew text, it could mean: "to those who despise me: the Lord says . . ." (so MT and Jerome); or it could be vocalized as "to the despisers (or 'rejecters') of the word of the Lord . . ." (so the LXX). The hexaplaric versions are lacking, but the Targ and the Pesh both interpret like MT and Jerome. The second option given by Jerome is his paraphrase of the LXX. [244]The Hebrew word is *bĕsôd*, made up of the preposition *b* ("in") and the noun *sôd* ("confidential discussion" or "secret, scheme," KB 745). Jerome gives all of the hexaplaric evidence. The Targ and the Pesh both agree with Aq ("secret"). Jerome's meaning ("counsel") matches the meaning of the word in rabbinic Hebrew (Jastrow 961). [245]Jer 23:17. [246]Jerome refers to Christians who saw in this passage, as it appears in the LXX and in the OL, a reference to God's "substance" in the trinitarian sense. Cf. Jer 13:18-19. [247]Heb *s'rh* ("high wind"). The first option is Jerome (*turbo*, "whirlwind"), and "storm" may be a further explanation of the sense of the word. "Shaking" represents the LXX. [248]Jer 23:17.

prophet charged them with not being able to understand the future or fathom the judgment of God.[249] Now, by announcing to them the opposite of what they expected, the prophet shows them to be completely misinformed. Instead of peace and security, the Babylonian storm is coming, and it comes not just on anybody but on the "heads of the wicked"— either on the whole people or on those who proclaimed lies to the people. Nor will God's anger and fury be appeased as in times past, but that which he has predicted and so often threatened will be fully accomplished, and his intention and judgment will be confirmed by his punishing the wicked. He says, "When the final moment of captivity arrives, the exulting conqueror prevails over you and he binds your hands with the rattling of chains, then "you will understand his plan," which now you can only boast that you know—but in vain.

23:21-22: *"I did not send the prophets, yet they ran; I did not speak to them, yet they prophesied. But if they had stood in my counsel and had proclaimed my words to my people, then I would have turned them from their evil way and from their wicked schemes."*

The apostle explains this idea to the Romans: "And since they did not see fit to acknowledge God, God handed them over to a base mind and to improper conduct. They were filled with all manner of wickedness, evil, badness, malice, covetousness" and so forth.[250] For once false teachers have handed themselves over to lies, perjury and the death of those they have deceived, they do not move cautiously or in measured steps, but hastily they run to their own destruction and to the destruction of the deceived. The Lord does not speak to them, but they speak on their own as if from the mouth of the Lord. He says about them, "If

they had stood in my counsel"—that is, if they had been willing to yield to my will—"and had proclaimed my words to my people"—instead of flattering them and ruining them with false praise, saying, "You have no sins! You possess perfect righteousness! Holiness, modesty and righteousness are abundantly present among you, and I will not hand you over to uncleanness and disgrace, to improper conduct and to following your own wicked schemes." Let us consider how heretics, once they relinquish a healthy palate, hand themselves over to delicacies, feast on flesh, frequent baths, reek with musk, and, drenched in various perfumes, seek to beautify their bodies. For they set no hope on future things and do not believe in the resurrection. Although they do not reveal this with their words, they show it by their deeds. For if they did believe, they would not do these things. And in this passage, where it is written, "If they had stood in my counsel," Aquila, Symmachus, Theodotion and the LXX translated just as they did above.[251]

23:23-24: *"Am I a God at hand, says the Lord, and not a God afar off? Can a man hide himself in secret places so that I cannot see him? says the Lord. Do I not fill heaven and earth? says the Lord."* LXX: *"I am a God who is near, says the Lord, and not a God afar off. Can a person be concealed in secret places so that I cannot see him? says the Lord.[252] Do I not fill heaven and earth? says the Lord."*

Aquila and Symmachus translated similarly: "Am I a God nearby (or 'at hand'), and not a God afar off?" But the LXX and Theodotion put the opposite meaning, saying, "I am a God who is near, says the Lord, and not a God afar off." The former[253] affirm that God knows not only what is at hand but also what is far off and understands not simply the present but

---

[249]Jer 23:18. [250]Rom 1:28-29. [251]Jer 23:18. [252]This first instance of "says the Lord" in Jer 23:24 is absent from the best witnesses to the LXX, but it is found in MT and the hexaplaric versions and was present in Jerome's copy of the LXX. [253]Aq and Sym.

also the future, whereas the latter[254] declare that God is everywhere and that there is no place where God is not present. For God is near to all things, and especially to the saints, just as clothing clings to the skin. Sinners, by contrast, will perish far from God. We read this same idea in the Psalms: "Where shall I go from your Spirit? Or where shall I flee from your presence? If I ascend to heaven, you are there! If I go down to Sheol, you are there! If I take up my wings of the morning and dwell in the uttermost parts of the sea, even there your hand shall lead me, and your right hand shall hold me."[255] Amos also agrees with these words, saying, "Though they go down to Sheol, from there shall my hand take them; though they climb up to heaven, from there I will bring them down. Though they hide themselves on the top of Carmel, from there I will search out and take them; and though they hide from my sight at the bottom of the sea, there I will command the serpent, and it shall bite them."[256] And again in the above psalm it says, "Because the darkness is not dark to you, and the night is bright as the day; the darkness is as the light."[257] Moreover, in the prophets it frequently says, "Thus says the Lord." This is always being added in, so that what the prophets say will not be despised as merely the words of prophets but will be continuously acknowledged as God's message.

23:25-27: *"I have heard what the prophets have said who prophesy lies in my name, saying, 'I have dreamed, I have dreamed!'— or 'I have dreamed a dream!'[258] How long shall this be in the heart of the prophets who prophesy lies and who prophesy the delusions"—or "desires"—"of their own heart, who wish"—or "think"[259]—"to make my people forget my name by their dreams that they tell one another, even as their fathers forgot my name for Baal?"—or "in Baal?"*

There are many kinds of prophesying, one of which is prophesying by dreams, which is the kind of prophecy found in Daniel. As the above title was "Concerning the Prophets" or "Against the Prophets"[260]—whom we clearly understand to be pseudoprophets—this prophetic message is directed at those prophets who trust in their dreams and regard all of their thoughts as divine revelation, even though revelation is made known exclusively to the saints and servants of God. But if we read that impious kings such as Pharaoh and Nebuchadnezzar dreamed dreams that were true,[261] this was not because of the merit of the dreamers, but so that through the opportunity provided by them the holy men Joseph and Daniel might become distinguished, and so that the harsh and savage hearts of the tyrants might perceive the majesty of the Lord in their own consciences.

There are also dreamers today in the church—and especially in our flock—who claim that their errors are prophecies from the Lord and who frequently repeat, "I have dreamed, I have dreamed!" The Lord rebukes these people, saying, "How long shall this be in the heart of the prophets who prophesy lies, and who prophesy the delusions of their own heart?" These dreamers act this way so that, just as the ancient people who were led out of Egypt forgot God's name, the descendants of the ancient people might forget God as well. Prophecy of this kind is not in the name of the Lord but in the name of Baal, which properly speaking is an idol of the Sidonians; or, it is an idol of the Babylonians and is called by the similar name Bel.[262]

---

[254]LXX and Th. [255]Ps 139:7-10. [256]Amos 9:2-3. [257]Ps 139:12. [258]Heb *ḥlmty ḥlmty*, which in MT and Jerome (agreeing with Aq and Sym) is interpreted as two verbs ("I have dreamed, I have dreamed!") but in the LXX and the Pesh is taken to be a verb and its cognate noun ("I have dreamed a dream"). [259]The Hebrew word is *ḥšb*, which most often means "to regard" or "to think" (KB 360). In this case, Jerome ("wish") is idiomatic, and the LXX is more literal. [260]Jer 23:9a. [261]Gen 41; Dan 2; 4. [262]Heb *b'l*. Baal is best known in Scripture as the Phoenician deity whose worship in Israel was promoted especially from the time of King Ahab and his Sidonian wife

23:28-29: *"Let the prophet who has a dream tell the dream, and let him who has my word speak my word faithfully. What has chaff in common with wheat? says the Lord. Are not my words like fire, says the Lord, and like a hammer"—or "an axe"*[263]*—"that breaks the rock in pieces?"*

To expound a dream is the privilege of those who are worthy to have God's message and to say, "Thus says the Lord." To these people the Lord has spoken, and in them there is truth and not deceptive falsehood. What does the chaff of heretics have to do with the wheat of the church? John the Baptist speaks more fully about this: Christ will clear his threshing floor, and with his winnowing fork he will leave the chaff to be scattered by the blowing winds and to be burned with fire, whereas the wheat he will gather up into the granary,[264] in order to make heavenly bread, and so that everyone who believes might say, "Taste and see that the Lord is sweet!"[265]

Beautifully, corrupt doctrine is compared with chaff, which has no kernel and cannot nourish the people who believe but is broken off from empty stubble. Heretics are always promising prosperity and extending the rule of heaven to sinners, saying, "The rule of heaven has been prepared for you. You are capable of imitating God's majesty, in that you can be without sin; for you have received the power of free will and the knowledge of the law, through which you can obtain whatever you wish." These heretics use flattery to deceive the worthless, and especially "weak women burdened with sins and carried about with every wind of teaching, who will listen to anybody and can never arrive at a knowledge of the truth."[266] And since heretics deceive all

their listeners by fawning on them, the Lord, contrasting his own words with the chaff of heretics, says, "Are not my words like fire, says the Lord, and like a hammer which breaks the rock in pieces?" "My message," he says, "is to announce impending punishment, so as to deter people from sinning." He threatens the chaff of sinners with burning, so that the hard heart of the heretics and the stone-like inflexibility of their words may be broken in pieces with a hammer. Then, taking away their heart of stone he will replace it with a heart of flesh,[267] that is, a heart that is soft and tender and therefore able to receive and appreciate God's commands. This is also what the Lord says through Ezekiel: the pseudo-prophets daub the people's wall with untempered mortar, that is, with flattery, which later is destroyed by a deluge of rain and the truth of God's judgment; and women pseudo-prophets sew pillows under every elbow,[268] so as to cause sinners to be at rest rather than to appease God's anger with tears. In place of "hammer" the LXX translated "axe"—this is the axe about which John the Baptist spoke: "Even now the axe is laid to the root of the trees."[269] This axe cuts down trees that do not bear fruit, and this hammer breaks in pieces the hardest rock. As Nahum the prophet also says, "His (no doubt, 'God's') wrath destroys dominions, and the rocks are broken in pieces by him."[270] This is written against heretics. As for the rest, it was written about ecclesiastical men, that the hammer and the axe have not been heard in the house of God.

23:30-32: *"Therefore, behold, I am against the prophets, says the Lord, who steal my words from one another. Behold, I am against the prophets, says the Lord, who use their*

Jezebel (1 Kings 16:31). Bel refers to a Babylonian deity (Is 46:1; Jer 50:2; 51:44). Bel is spelled differently in Hebrew (*bl*) but is probably mentioned by Jerome because of Jeremiah's Babylonian context. [263]Heb *ptyš* ("blacksmith's hammer," KB 924). Jerome agrees with Aq and Targ. [264]Mt 3:12; Lk 3:17. [265]Ps 34:8. [266]2 Tim 3:6-7; Eph 4:14. [267]Ezek 11:19; 36:26. [268]Ezek 13:18. [269]Mt 3:10. [270]Nah 1:6.

tongues and say, 'He says'—or 'and sleep their sleep.'[271] *Behold, I am against those prophets who dream falsehood, says the Lord, and who tell them and lead my people astray by their lies and their wonders"—or "astonishments," "terrors"[272]—"when I did not send them or charge them; so they do not profit this people at all, says the Lord."*

Falsehood always imitates the truth; unless it had some likeness to what is right, it would not be able to deceive the innocent. Therefore, just as among the former people prophets would lie and say, "Thus says the Lord," or "I saw the Lord," or "The word of the Lord that came to so-and-so," so also heretics take up the testimonies of Scripture from the Old and New Testaments and "steal the words" of the Savior "from one another"—from the prophets, apostles and evangelists. They "use their tongues," so that with their mouths they might speak poison of the heart, and they "sleep their sleep," about which it is truly written, "They slept their sleep and found nothing"[273]—or, according to the Hebrew, "And they say, '[he] says,' "—with "the Lord" being understood, or else "the divine message." And so the Lord warns that he himself is going to come against teachers of this kind, who lead his people astray by their lies and their astonishments and wonders. For they promise great, fantastic and remarkable things so as to deceive the wretched. And "they do not profit this people at all," thus fulfilling the apostolic saying,

"teaching for base gain what they have no right to teach."[274] These teachers regularly announce prosperity to the wicked and injury to the righteous.

23:33-36a: *"Therefore, if this people, or a prophet or a priest asks you, 'What is the burden'—or 'argument'—'of the Lord?' you shall say to them, 'You are the burden,'[275]—or 'argument'—'and I will cast you off,'—or 'I will smash you'—'says the Lord.' And as for the prophet, priest or people who says, 'The burden'—or 'argument'—'of the Lord,' I will visit"—or "take vengeance on"—"that man and his household. Thus shall you say, everyone to his neighbor and everyone to his brother, 'What has the Lord answered?' or 'What has the Lord spoken?' But 'the burden'—or 'argument'—'of the Lord' shall be mentioned no more, for the burden"—or "argument"—"will be every man's own word."*

Aquila translated the Hebrew word *massa* as "burden" or "weight," whereas Symmachus, Theodotion and the LXX translated it as "argument."[276] Whenever the Lord threatens some solemn matter that is difficult to bear and is full of weight and hardship, the word *arma* (that is, "weight") is used in the title.[277] But whenever the Lord pledges to bring prosperity or promises that better things will come after judgment, he calls it either a "vision" or the "word of the Lord." Thus, it was clear based on the title of the prophecy—

---

[271]The Hebrew has *wyn'mw n'm* ("and [they] say, 'says'"; both words are from the root *n'm*). In the IH edition, Jerome added the word *Lord* in order to fill out the sense ("and [they] say, 'the Lord says'"). Here, Jerome sticks more closely to the Hebrew. The LXX understood the two words in question to be from the root *nwm* ("to sleep"). Sym differs from Jerome and the LXX, and Aq has "saying." The closest to Jerome is Targ ("and [they] say, 'Thus he says'"). [272]The first option ("wonders") is Jerome's IH translation, and the two words given as alternatives represent Jerome's attempt to give the sense of the word used by Aq and Sym, *thambēsis* (see LSJ 783). As Field has suggested, it is also possible that what the MSS have as *terroribus* ("terrors") should be *erroribus*, which would match the LXX (*tois planois*, "errors"). [273]Ps 76:5 (LXX [75:6]). [274]Tit 1:11. [275]Here in the commentary Jerome gives "You are the burden" for the Hebrew consonants *'tmhmś*, reading *'attem hammaśśā* as the LXX does. In the IH edition Jerome translated "Why do you have a burden?" reading *'et-mah-maśśā'* as does MT. The hexaplaric versions are lacking. [276]Heb *maśśā'*. The word derives from *nś'* ("to carry, lift up") and commonly refers to a "load" or "burden" (KB 639). It is also occasionally used in prophetic literature to introduce oracles, perhaps with the sense "to raise one's voice" (KB 639; cf. Hab 1:1; Is 13:1; Lam 2:14; Nah 1:1; Zech 9:1; 12:1; Mal 1:1). The LXX rendered it *lēmma* ("something taken or received"), which could be material gain, an assumption or premise, or a thesis or argument (LSJ 1045). [277]The Greek word *arma* ("burden, load") is the rendering of Aq (cf. Aq at Num 4:27; Deut 1:12; Hos 8:10).

whether it said "weight," "vision" or "word of the Lord"—what sort of prophetic message would follow. Since the prophets were accustomed to announce dismal tidings to the sinful people and threaten punishments so as to restore the people to repentance, the people, who had been deceived and led astray by the lies of the pseudoprophets, thought that what the Lord threatened would not come about. They turned a serious matter into a game and joke, and while the real prophets were prophesying they would say, as if laughing, "Again he sees the weight and burden of the Lord!" And in this way it came about that it was no longer called a "vision," but because of the joking and derision it was called a "burden" and "weight."

Therefore, the Lord commands Jeremiah that, if one of the people, a prophet or a priest should ask him, "What is the weight (or 'argument') of the Lord?" he should answer them and say, "You are the burden and you are the argument"—for I will seize you and "cast you off," and I will "smash" you and put you to ruin. Then, if anyone from among the people, the prophets or the priests dares to mention the "burden" or "weight" of the Lord, "I will punish that man and his household," he says, "and I will wipe him out forever." Consequently, they will no longer say, "What is the burden of the Lord?" but everyone will say to his neighbor and to his friend, "What has the Lord answered?" or "What has the Lord spoken?" He says, "You will forget what went before, and the 'burden' or 'weight' or 'argument' of the Lord will never again be heard coming from your mouth, because for each person individually his own words and deeds will be taken into account as his weight and burden, as it is written: 'Out of your mouth you will be justified, and out of your mouth you will be condemned.'"[278]

23:36b-40: *"And you pervert the words of the living God, the Lord of hosts, our God. Thus you"*—or *"you (plural)"*[279]—*"shall say to the prophet, 'What has the Lord answered you?' or 'What has the Lord spoken?' But if you say, 'The burden of the Lord,'"*—everything up to this point is not found in the LXX;[280] and he continues: *"thus says the Lord, 'Because you have said this word, "The burden"*—or *"premise"*—*"of the Lord," even though I sent to you, saying, "You shall not say, 'The burden'*—or *'premise'*—*'of the Lord,'" therefore, behold, I will surely lift you up'*—or *'take you'*—*'and abandon you and the city that I gave to you and your fathers away from my presence. And I will bring on you everlasting reproach and perpetual shame, which shall not be forgotten.'"*

The Lord commands that the word "burden" or "weight" (or "premise") should no longer be spoken among the people, but they should ask for an "answer" or "word" from God. But because the people had contempt for fulfilling God's word, the word itself is interpreted against them and says, "Because you said what I did not wish you to say, even though I often sent prophets to you and ordered you not to say it, therefore I will fulfill against you in action your own word of 'premise,' 'burden' and 'weight.' In fact, I will 'take you' and 'lift you up,'[281] and then I will carry you and smash you to the ground from high up, putting you to ruin. This will happen not only to you but also to this city that I gave to your ancestors."

---

[278]Mt 12:37; 15:18. [279]Jerome (singular) agrees with MT and Targ. The second option (plural) represents the hexaplaric reading preserved under asterisk, which was likely in Jerome's copy of the LXX. [280]According to our copies of the LXX, Jer 23:36b and Jer 23:37a are lacking in the LXX, but Jer 23:37b is represented in the LXX by the question "And what has the Lord our God spoken?" The beginning of Jer 23:38 is also lacking from the LXX, but after this the LXX matches up again essentially with MT, as Jerome suggests. [281]As a fitting response to their own statement about the "argument" ("thing taken up") of the Lord, God will "take" them and smash them.

"And I will bring on you," he says, "everlasting reproach and perpetual shame, which shall not be forgotten." We know that this took place during the time of the Babylonian captivity. But it was fulfilled more fully and more perfectly after the suffering and resurrection of the Savior, when the Lord said, "Your house is forsaken."[282] And his judgment will remain all the way to the end. We can also explain it differently according to the LXX: the word *lēmma* means not only "argument" but also "gift" and "present." Because the people were promising themselves prosperity, he tells them that they should no longer say this, since they are not worthy of the "gifts" and "presents" of God; rather, they are worthy to be cast away from God and utterly abandoned away from God's assistance.

The substance of a matter is often made known through words and through the interpretation of names. Thus, as in the cases of Abraham, Sarah, Peter and the sons of Zebedee, alterations in the names of things can signify changes in substance.[283] So also in this very prophet, Pashhur is called "terror," "transferring" and "colonist" or "foreigner."[284] It should be noted that the Greek and Latin codices do not have the words "of the living God, the Lord of hosts, our God." Let the Hebrews read this against themselves in their own scrolls, because this properly signifies the mystery of the Trinity.

BOOK FIVE

The fifth book of our commentary on Jeremiah, O brother Eusebius, will begin with two baskets: one will show the sweetness of right faith and the other will show the bitterness of the heretics' treachery. Hananiah the son of Azzur may oppose Jeremiah,[1] Shemaiah of Nehelam may desire that the prophet be sent into prison,[2] and Zephaniah the priest may join in with the words of the pseudoprophets.[3] Yet, although truth can be tied up and imprisoned, it cannot be overcome.[4] Truth is content with the smallness of its own forces, and it is not frightened by the vast numbers of the enemy. So raise up your hands to heaven together with Moses,[5] and lift up that ancient serpent in the wilderness,[6] and immediately Amalek will be destroyed and the poisonous bites will lose their power. Then, free from danger, the people of the Lord will cross over the flowing Jordan with Jesus, and on the other side of the vast wilderness they will eat the bread that was born in our little town of Bethlehem.[7]

24:1-10: *The Lord showed me: Behold, two baskets—or, according to Symmachus, containers[8]—of figs placed before the temple of the Lord, after Nebuchadnezzar king of Babylon had taken into exile from Jerusalem Jeconiah the son of Jehoiakim, king of Judah, together with the princes of Judah, the craftsmen and the engravers, and had brought them to Babylon. One basket had very good figs, like first-ripe figs, but the other basket had very bad figs, so bad that they could not be eaten. And the Lord said to me, "What do you see, Jeremiah?" I said, "Figs, the good figs very good, and the bad figs very bad, so bad that they cannot be eaten." Then the word of the Lord came to me: "Thus says the Lord, the*

---

[282]Lk 13:35. [283]Gen 17:5, 15-16; Mk 3:16-17; Mt 16:17-18; Jn 1:42. [284]Jer 20:3. **Book Five** [1]Jer 28. [2]Jer 29:24-28. [3]Jer 29:29. [4]As Jerome has Critobulus say in *Pelag.* 1.25, "For the truth can be hard pressed but never suppressed." See also Augustine *Enarrat. Ps.* 61:16: "Truth may be obscured for a while, but it cannot be defeated" (on Ps 62:10 according to the Latin Bible [61:11]). Cf. Livy 22.39.19: "Truth, they say, is all too frequently eclipsed but never extinguished." On the enduring power of truth in spite of challenges, see Polybius 13.5.5-6. The same sentiment is expressed with respect to "the good" in Publilius Syrus 76: "The good may be suppressed, but it is never extinguished." [5]Ex 17:11. [6]Num 21:9; Jn 3:14. [7]Josh 1:2, 11; 3:17; 5:11; Mt 2:1-6; Jn 6:35-59. The names of Jesus and Joshua are closely related and are written the same in Greek. Crossing the Jordan River under Joshua's leadership is likened to crossing into the land with Jesus. [8]The word that Jerome reports for Sym, *kophinos*, is another word for "basket."

God of Israel: Like these good figs, so I will regard the exiles from Judah, whom I have sent away from this place to the land of the Chaldeans, for their good. I will set my eyes on them for good, and I will bring them back to this land. I will build them up and not tear them down; I will plant them and not uproot them. I will give them a heart to know that I am the Lord; and they shall be my people and I will be their God, for they shall return to me with their whole heart." "But like the bad figs that are so bad they cannot be eaten, thus says the Lord: so will I give up"—or "hand over"—"Zedekiah the king of Judah, his princes, the remnant of Jerusalem who remain in this city and those who dwell in the land of Egypt. I will give them to vexation and to affliction"—or "to dispersion"[9]—"before all the kingdoms of the earth, to be a reproach, a parable, a byword and a curse in all the places where I shall drive them. And I will send sword, famine and pestilence on them, until they shall be consumed from the land that I gave to them and their fathers."

Some interpret the two containers or baskets of good and bad figs in terms of the law and the gospel, the synagogue and the church, the Jewish people and the Christians, Gehenna and the kingdom of heaven, one of which refers to the punishment of sinners and the other to the dwelling place of the saints.[10] But we, following the apostle Paul, know that the law is good and holy, the commandment is good and holy,[11] and the God of both Testaments is one. Therefore, we refer these figs instead to those who did believe and did not believe in the coming of our Lord and Savior. Thus, those who were stirred up by the scribes and

Pharisees and cried out, "Crucify, crucify him!"[12] are the basket of bad figs, but those from among the people who believed in him after his ascension are likened to good figs and the noble basket and container. Furthermore, we may also follow the simple and true *historia*, according to which he said that the basket of good figs is Jeconiah, who handed himself over to the king of Babylon in accordance with the counsel and authority of Jeremiah, and to whom the Lord promises prosperity; but the basket of bad figs is Zedekiah, who opposed God's decree and so was captured, blinded in his eyes and led to Babylon, where he died.[13] God set his eyes for good on those who yielded to his authority: he brought them back to their land, he built them up and did not tear them down, he planted them and did not uproot them, and he gave them a heart to know that he is the Lord. They became his people, and he was their God. And he set his eyes on them for good to such an extent that even in captivity his eyes were on them, and he permitted them while in the region of Babylon to work the land, build houses and plant orchards;[14] Daniel, having suddenly been taken captive, was made a leader by means of miraculous signs;[15] the three youths were gloriously rescued from the burning of the furnace;[16] and when the seventy years had been completed,[17] under Zerubbabel and Joshua the high priest, and under Ezra and Nehemiah, the greater part of the people returned to Jerusalem. The number of returnees was recorded in the book of Ezra.[18]

And this also should be noted: this vision came to the prophet in the time of Zedekiah after Jeconiah was led away in "exile," for it does not say "captivity," since Jeconiah handed

[9]Where Jerome (matching MT) has "to vexation and to affliction," the LXX has merely "to dispersion." Aq and Sym represent both of the Hebrew words found in MT, but their rendering of the second term as "evil" is a more literalistic translation of the Hebrew (r'h) than Jerome's "affliction." [10]Cf. Origen *Fr. Jer.* 22, where there is a contrast between those who were formerly strangers to God by nature but who became good figs by faith, and those living after the captivity who are from the circumcision and are bad figs. See also Caesarius of Arles *Sermon* 106.4 (FC 47.128). [11]Rom 7:12. [12]Lk 23:21. [13]Jer 39:4-7; 52:8-11; 2 Kings 25:5-7. [14]Jer 29:5. [15]Dan 2:48; 5:29; 6:3. [16]Dan 3. [17]Jer 25:11-12; 29:10; Dan 9:2. [18]Ezra 2:2; 3:2, 8; 5:2; Neh 7:7; 12:1.

himself over. We ought to understand the "craftsmen" and "engravers" either as interpreters and teachers of the law or as artisans and fashioners of gold and precious stones, whose skills are highly valued among the barbarian nations. In place of "engravers" the LXX translated "prisoners," so as to point to the misery of captivity, and on their own the LXX added, "and the rich," which is not found in the Hebrew.[19]

He compares the very good figs with "first-ripe figs," which in Greek are called *proima*[20]—namely, with Abraham, Isaac and Jacob, and with Moses, Aaron and Job, and with the rest of the holy men, about whom one of the twelve prophets says, "Like grapes in the wilderness I found Israel. Like the first figs on the fig tree I found their fathers."[21] Therefore, we also are called children of Abraham,[22] whereas to the Jews it is said, "If Abraham were your father, you would do his works."[23] Moreover, these baskets that contained good and bad figs were not out in the open and outside of the church but "before the temple of the Lord," since all things lie exposed to his judgment. The figs that are outside have less bitterness than the figs that, after a confession of faith, were mutated through apostasy. Likewise, there is less sweetness in the good figs that are not in sight of God's temple— such as the philosophers of the world, who, based on natural goodness and awareness of their Creator, are seen to praise virtues more than to follow them—than there is sweetness in the figs that are in God's temple, some of which were prophets and apostles. One such fig said about these matters, "I gave to you milk, not solid food,"[24] and, "My little children, whom I am again bringing forth until Christ be formed in you!"[25] This is why it is said that in the sight of God's temple the good figs were "very good" and the bad figs were "very bad."

And to keep us from supposing that we can attach our own meaning to this, Scripture offers its own explanation: "Like these good figs, so I will regard the exiles from Judah, whom I have sent away from this place to the land of the Chaldeans, for their good." This refers to Jeconiah and the princes who were captured with him. Concerning the basket of bad figs it says, "But like the bad figs that are so bad they cannot be eaten, so will I give up Zedekiah the king of Judah, his princes, those who fled to Egypt and those who remain in this city to vexation and to affliction before all the kingdoms of the earth." This took place when they were captured in Egypt and Nebuchadnezzar set his throne over Tahpanhes.[26] The Lord sent against them the sword, famine and pestilence,[27] until they were consumed from the land that the Lord had given to their ancestors.

Moreover, what he says about the good figs, "I will give them a heart to know that I am the Lord," is similar to this apostolic saying, "God is at work in you, both to will and to work,"[28] because not only our works but also our wills depend on God's aid. He who always interprets allegorically goes astray in this passage.[29] Seeking some greater import for the historical truth, he speaks in terms of the heavenly Jerusalem about those who were captured, carried off to the land of the Chaldeans and brought back to their original land (such as Jeremiah and the other holy prophets); and he relates that others, who were sinners, will die in this land and in the Valley of Tears.[30] I have set forth the whole *pericope* of this vision at once, so as not to divide up the meaning in my exposition.

---

[19]The Hebrew word *masgēr* was translated by Jerome as "engraver" (*masgēr* II, KB 604: "metal worker") and by the LXX as "prisoner" (cf. *masgēr* I, KB 604, "prison"). As Jerome states, the LXX also adds "and the rich" after "the engravers" as another category of people taken to Babylon. [20]Gk *prōimos* (or *proimos*) can refer to "early" fruits (LSJ 1543). [21]Hos 9:10. [22]Gal 3:7; Mt 3:9; Lk 3:8. [23]Jn 8:39. [24]1 Cor 3:2. [25]Gal 4:19. [26]Jer 43:8-13. [27]Jer 42:15-17. [28]Phil 2:13. [29]Origen. Cf. *Princ.* 4.3.8-10; see Jerome's comments at Jer 27:2-4; 27:9-11. [30]Ps 84:6.

25:1a: *The word that came to Jeremiah concerning all the people of Judah—or over all the people of Judah—in the fourth year of Jehoiakim the son of Josiah, king of Judah.*

This transpired prior to the previous vision, for the previous vision took place under Zedekiah after Jeconiah was taken to Babylon, whereas this vision happened under Jehoiakim the son of Josiah and father of Jeconiah. As I said earlier,[31] it was not the concern of the prophets to preserve the chronology of events, as the laws of history require, but to write in whatever way they knew would be useful for their hearers and readers. Likewise in the Psalter, certain people wrongly expect to find that the order of the psalms is given according to the structure of history, even though this kind of order is not followed in lyric poetry.[32]

25:1b-2: *This was the first year of Nebuchadnezzar king of Babylon*—which is not found in the LXX; it continues: *which the prophet Jeremiah spoke to all the people of Judah and all the inhabitants of Jerusalem, saying:*

In the fourth year of the reign of Jehoiakim, the son of Josiah and father of Jeconiah, Nebuchadnezzar took up supreme power in Babylon, so that Nebuchadnezzar's first year in Babylon was Jehoiakim's fourth year as king in Jerusalem. And so it was in the eighth year of his reign that Nebuchadnezzar led into captivity Jeconiah (who reigned for only three months after the death of his father Jehoiakim) together with his mother and his princes.[33] Jehoiakim was killed in the eleventh year of his reign in Jerusalem.[34]

25:3: *"From the thirteenth year of Josiah the*

son of Amon, king of Judah, to this day—this is the twenty-third year—the word of the Lord has come to me, and I have spoken to you, rising at night and speaking, but you have not listened."

In the thirteenth year of the reign of Josiah, who ruled in Jerusalem for thirty-one years,[35] Jeremiah began to prophesy, and he prophesied under Josiah for nineteen years; after this, Josiah's son Jehoahaz succeeded his father as king. But Jehoahaz was immediately led into captivity by Neco, the king of Egypt, and so Jehoiakim, the brother of Jehoahaz, attained royal power.[36] It was in the fourth year of the reign of Jehoiakim that this word of the Lord came to Jeremiah. This was now the twenty-third year after Jeremiah the prophet had begun speaking to the people. He never ceased proclaiming to them, but rising each day in the night and at dawn he would speak to the people. "But you have not listened," he says.

If, as the new heretics (descended from the old) wish to think,[37] the law was given as a one-time-only aid for us, such that commands were established that we can either do or not do based on our own free will, why is it that the prophet constantly repeats himself and daily reiterates God's commands? Why aren't these commands, once given, sufficient for those who received them? Is it not rather the case, as this passage shows, that we are always in need of God's help, and that it is impossible for what was once given to be sufficient for us, unless we are daily renewed by the Lord's correction?

25:4a: *"And the Lord sent to you all his servants the prophets, rising at dawn and sending, but you have not listened."*

---

[31]Jer 21:1-2; 26:1-3. [32]E.g., see Diodore of Tarsus, "Preface to the Psalms," on the expectation that the psalms were originally arranged in chronological order. Notice how Jerome explains the nonchronological nature of the book of Psalms by appealing to the genre of lyric poetry. [33]2 Kings 24:8-15. [34]2 Kings 23:36; 2 Chron 36:5. [35]2 Kings 22:1; 2 Chron 34:1 (ca. 640-609 B.C.E.). [36]2 Kings 23:30-34; 2 Chron 36:1-4. [37]The Pelagians, descended from Origen and his followers.

Not through one prophet alone, but through all of the prophets, God constantly admonished his people. As if he were stationed at his post and keeping his watch, God rose at dawn in order to warn them. He says, "But you have not listened"; thus, the more frequent the admonitions became, the greater were the sins of those who despised those admonitions.

25:4b-5: *"Nor did you incline your ears to hear, when I said, 'Turn now, every one of you, from his evil way and from your wicked thoughts, and you shall dwell on the land that the Lord has given to you and your fathers from the age and to the age.'"*

So great was the hardness of the people that they did not even take on a posture of listening and incline their ears, even when the Lord implored them that each one should turn from his evil ways and wicked thoughts. O the infinite mercy of God, who does not simply inflict punishment when people sin but provokes people to repentance! And he does this, not only for evil deeds, which are signified by "evil ways," but also for "wicked thoughts," which are reckoned as sin even apart from the deeds. And he offers them a reward if they will do what they are told: they may dwell on the land, which was given to their ancestors but was taken away because of the vices of the children. As for what he says, "from the age and to the age," or "from eternity and to eternity," this shows that the gifts of God are eternal if those to whom they are given show themselves to be worthy.

25:6-7a: *"Do not go after other gods to serve and worship them, or provoke me to anger with the work of your hands. Then I will do you no harm. Yet you have not listened to me."*

He says, "In addition to the above admoni-

tions, I warned you not to serve other gods and worship them and by doing this provoke me to anger because of the work of your hands, so that I must do what I do not want to do, namely, do you harm." "Yet you have not listened to me." And that which follows: "says the Lord, that you might provoke me to anger with the work of your hands to your own harm," is not found in the LXX.

25:8-9a: *"Therefore thus says the Lord of hosts: Because you have not listened to my words, behold, I will send for and take all the tribes of the north, says the Lord, and for Nebuchadnezzar the king of Babylon, my servant."*

"Because you provoked me to anger," he says, "and did evil to your own destruction, and you arrogantly trampled on the one who was provoking you to repentance, I will send for all the tribes (or nations) of the north, and I will bring their leader, Nebuchadnezzar king of Babylon, my servant." Either the Lord sends angels to stir up the nations, or else he inspires within the nations the thought of stirring, so that they do the Lord's will. As to the fact that he calls Nebuchadnezzar "my servant:" he is not called a "servant" in the same way as the prophets and all the saints are called "servants," since they truly served the Lord. Rather, Nebuchadnezzar is called the Lord's "servant" in the sense that he serves the Lord's will by overthrowing Jerusalem, in a manner similar to what the apostle says: "whom I have delivered to Satan, so that they may learn not to blaspheme."[38] Based on the location of Jerusalem, the area of the "north" is without doubt the area of the Chaldeans.

25:9b: *"And I will bring them against this land and its inhabitants, and against all these nations round about; I will destroy them, and*

---

[38]1 Tim 1:20.

make them an astonishment, a hissing and an everlasting desolation."

These are the rewards given to those who despise God's words and refuse to listen to them. Therefore, it is our own sins that cause whatever calamity is brought against us. Just as all the nations at that time were brought against Jerusalem, so also today they are brought against the indifferent church. In this way God destroys them, and he makes them into an astonishment, a hissing and an everlasting desolation, so that they become an example and an object of wonder to all others. Hissing is a sign of astonishment and wonder. And everlasting desolation is realized in those who do not have God as their protector.

25:10-11a: *"And I will banish from them the voice of mirth and the voice of gladness, the voice of the bride and the voice of the bridegroom, the sound of the millstone and the light of the lamp. And this whole land shall become a desolation and an astonishment."*

This is attested even today in the assembly of evildoers, in that their teachers do not teach the word of God but hiss like serpents. The "voice of mirth and the voice of gladness" will perish among them, so that they never hear this saying of the apostle: "Rejoice; again I will say, Rejoice."[39] Also to perish will be "the voice of the bride," the ecclesiastical faith, and "the voice of the bridegroom," our Lord and Savior—for "he who has the bride is the bridegroom";[40] and "the sound of the millstone," since grain will not be ground by it and nothing will be provided for the people to eat; and "the light of the lamp," namely, the teaching and knowledge of the prophets—indeed it is said concerning John the Baptist, "He was a shining lamp,"[41] and another prophet says, "Your word, O Lord, is a lamp to

my feet and a light to my path."[42] He says, "The whole land of the heretics shall become a desolation and an astonishment," since its end is shown to be foolish.

25:11b-13: *"And all these nations shall serve the king of Babylon seventy years. Then after seventy years are completed, I will punish the king of Babylon and that nation, the land of the Chaldeans, for their iniquity, says the Lord, and I will make it an everlasting desolation. I will bring on that land all my words, which I have uttered against it, everything written in this book, which Jeremiah prophesied against all the nations."*

After seventy years Jerusalem regained its former inhabitants, and once its punishment was completed it enjoyed its former prosperity since it yielded to God's judgment. But the king of Babylon was destroyed by the coming of the Medes and the Persians because he was puffed up with pride and believed that he had conquered the nations by his own power and not by the Lord's will. And even today only the ruins of the city of Babylon remain. The Lord has made it an eternal desolation and has fulfilled all the words that are contained in the book of this very prophet. For later on in the book the word of Jeremiah describes the disasters that Babylon will suffer.

25:14: *"For they served them, even though they were many nations and great kings; and I will recompense them according to their deeds and the work of their hands."*

This is not found in the LXX.[43] It shows that Jeremiah prophesied not only against Babylon but also against the rest of the nations that served in the Babylonian army and fought against the people of the Lord. Accordingly, in

---

[39]Phil 4:4. [40]Jn 3:29. [41]Jn 5:35. [42]Ps 119:105. [43]At this point in the text the LXX has the oracles against the nations that are found in Jer 46-51 of the Hebrew text. Jerome follows the Hebrew order in his commentary.

later passages he speaks against Egypt, the Philistines, Moab, Ammon, Idumea, Damascus, Kedar, the kingdoms of Hazor and Elam, and in the end against Babylon and the land of the Chaldeans.[44]

25:15-17: *For thus the Lord, the God of Israel, said to me: "Take from my hand this cup of the wine of wrath"—or "this cup of unmixed wine"[45]—"and make all the nations to whom I send you drink it. They shall drink and become inebriated"—or "shall vomit"[46]—"and be crazed because of the sword that I am sending among them." So I took the cup from the Lord's hand and made all the nations to whom the Lord sent me drink it"*

The drinking of a cup of wine that is "unmixed" or "undiluted" (which in Greek is *akratos*) is a sign of the Lord's wrath, such that every nation that waged war against God's people will drink from the cup of the wrath of the Lord. Isaiah also writes about this cup against Jerusalem: "You have drunk and emptied out the goblet of wrath and the cup of ruin; now, rouse yourself!"[47] This cup, however, is drunk by every nation, to the point where they vomit and become crazed.

A certain perverse interpreter[48] takes this in a good sense, that this cup, like a cleansing potion, forces out of the body whatever choleric liquid, phlegm or noxious fluid is in the chest and restores the person to his former health. This interpreter also takes Jeremiah to stand for the Savior, since it was the Savior who gave this potion to all the nations, to whom he was sent, so that after they had set aside idolatry they might devote themselves to the worship of God. But the following passage will show this to be contrary to the holy

Scriptures. For it is not as a remedy, as he would like to think, but as a punishment that they are made to drink this unmixed cup.

25:18: *"Jerusalem and the cities of Judah, its kings and princes, to make them a desolation and an astonishment, a hissing and a curse, as at this day"*

The prophet says, "I thought that I would make only the nations drink this cup, and so I offered myself gladly to this ministry. But along with the other nations, or rather before the other nations, I gave the cup to 'Jerusalem and the cities of Judah, its kings and princes, to make them an astonishment and a desolation, a hissing and a curse,'" as is demonstrated in the present case. Thus he also said earlier: "O Lord, you have misled me, and I was misled. You have prevailed and overcome."[49]

25:19-20a: *"Pharaoh king of Egypt, his servants, his princes, all his people, and all in general"*

After Jerusalem, Pharaoh king of Egypt drank. His associates, princes and all his people also drank, as well as all those who are not even Egyptian but who dwell in the area around Egypt. The LXX identified them as *symmiktous*, that is, "mixed people"—not native to the Egyptian region but resident aliens and foreigners.

25:20b: *"all the kings of the land of Ausitis"*

"Ausitis" in Hebrew is *Us*.[50] The *historia* recounts that Job was from this place: "There was a man in the land of Ausitis, whose name

---

[44]Jer 25:19-26; 46:1–49:22; 49:23-39; 50:1–51:58. [45]Heb *hmh* ("heat," "wrath," KB 326). Jerome agrees with all of the hexaplaric versions. The LXX may be reading a passive participle of *hmh* ("to be fit, worthy," Jastrow 476), or perhaps *hmr* ("wine," Jastrow 480). [46]The first option ("become inebriated") is Jerome's idiomatic rendering of the Hebrew. In the IH edition he translated "be disturbed" or "agitated" (similar to Aq and Targ). The LXX ("shall vomit") is similar to Sym ("to retch," *sparassō* 4a [LSJ 1624]). [47]Is 51:17. [48]Cf. Origen *Princ.* 2.10.6. [49]Jer 20:7. [50]Heb *ʿuṣ*.

was Job."[51] Yet, it should be known that this phrase is not found in the LXX, and Theodotion translated *Us* as "island."

25:20c: *"and all the kings of the land of the Philistines (Ashkelon, Gaza, Ekron, and the remnant of Azotus)"*

He refers in a general way to the land of the Philistines, that is, the Palestinians, and specifically he refers to their cities, Ashkelon, Gaza, Ekron and Azotus. He passes over only the city Gath, which is included in the word *remnant*. For this is what is written: "and the remnant of Ashdod." The region of the city of Gath is near to Azotus, which in Hebrew is *Esdod*.[52] Moreover, Isaiah also writes that the Palestinians were captured and destroyed by the Babylonians.[53]

25:21-22a: *"Idumea, Moab, and the sons of Ammon; all the kings of Tyre, all the kings of Sidon"*

"Idumea"—where the mountains of Seir are found, and which in Hebrew is called "Edom." Moab and Ammon are both sons of Lot;[54] the regions are near the Dead Sea. Tyre and Sidon are leading cities on the Phoenician shore. They were overrun by the Babylonian invasion. Carthage was a colony of these cities, and through corruption of the word the *Phoeni* came to be known as *Poeni*. Their language is for the most part akin to the Hebrew language.[55]

25:22b: *"and the kings of the islands that are across the sea"*

He passes over Cyprus and Rhodes and mentions the islands that are called the Cyclades.[56] For even these were captured by the Babylonians.

25:23: *"Dedan, Tema, Buz, and all who have shaved heads"*

These nations are in the desert, near to and dispersed within the region of the Ishmaelites, whom nowadays they call Saracens and about whom it is said, "who shave their heads."

25:24a: *"and all the kings of Arabia"*

After Dedan, therefore, and Tema, Buz and the Ishmaelites, he follows the order of the regions.

25:25a: *"and all the kings of Zimri"*[57]

This also is not found in the LXX.

25:25b: *"and all the kings of Elam, and all the kings of the Medes"*

Because Elam and the kings of the Medes follow Zimri, we suspect that "Zimri" is the land of Persia—unless perhaps, because Zimri comes after Arabia, the "kings of Zimri" should be understood as desert kings. Elam and the land of Persia are beyond Babylon. It was by Elamites, Persians and Medes that Babylon was captured and destroyed. But they also drank the unmixed cup when the king of the Macedonians made them drink it.[58]

---

[51]Job 1:1. Jerome has taken over this information from the Greek tradition; see Eusebius *Onom.* (OS 286.67); Jerome *Nom. Hebr.* (OS 158.26). [52]Ashdod. On the five Philistine cities, see 1 Sam 6:17. On the proximity of Gath to Ashdod, see 1 Sam 5:6-8, which is alluded to in OS 246.73-74. [53]Is 14:29-32. [54]Gen 19:37-38. [55]The *Phoeni* (Phoenicians) came to be known as *Poeni* (Punics, i.e., Carthaginians). Jerome also appeals to the similarity between Hebrew and "Punic" at *Comm. Isa.* 7:14, where he asserts that the Punic cognate of the Hebrew *'lmh* means "virgin." For other appeals to Punic, see *QHG* 36:24; *Comm. Gal.* 2 prol.; *Comm. Jon.* 4:6. [56]The Cyclades ("encircling") islands were in the Aegean Sea encircling the island of Delos; see Herodotus 5.31; Thucydides 1.4. [57]Jerome has accidentally omitted Jer 25:24b, which in the IH edition he translated, "and all the kings of the west that dwell in the desert." [58]Babylon fell in 539 B.C.E. to the forces of the Medes and the Persians. The period of Persian rule in the ancient Near East ended with the conquests of Alexander the Great in 332 B.C.E.

25:26a: *"and all the kings of the north, near and far"*

Having enumerated the regions of Persia, Babylon, Elam and the Medes, he now makes a general reference to all the kings of the north, who are near and far. In place of "north," which in Hebrew is *safun*, the LXX translated *aphēliōtēs*, which we would translate as the "east wind."[59]

25:26b: *"each one against its brother, and all the kingdoms of the earth that are on the face of the earth."*

Lest the detailed enumeration of all the regions in the eastern territory become tedious, he refers generally to all the kingdoms of the earth, which dwell on the earth. As for the phrase "each against its brother," one must understand the words "I have given the unmixed cup." That is, they all raged, vomited, were crazed and contended in battles one with another.[60] As for that which he adds:

25:26c: *"and after them the king of Sesach shall drink"*

This is not found in the LXX. It has this sense: "All the surrounding nations will submit to Babylonian rule and all will be subject to Babylon's power, so that every nation that has been spoken of previously will serve Babylon and drink from its cup." Thus also in the vision against Babylon it is written: "Babylon is a golden cup making all the earth drunken."[61] But the last king of Babylon will drink this potion when Cyrus the king of the Medes and the Persians, who is the rider of horses in pairs, camels and donkeys,[62] makes him drink it.

Babylon, which in Hebrew is "Babel," should be understood as the referent for "Sesach." One who has even a little knowledge of the Hebrew language will not have to labor hard to explain how this is so. Consider how among us the Greek alphabet is read in order all the way to the last letter, that is, *alpha*, *beta*, etc., all the way to the letter *o*. Then, in order to help little children memorize the alphabet we are accustomed to reverse the order of the reading and mix up the last letters with those at the beginning, so that we read *alpha*, *o*, *beta*, *psi*, etc. It is the same thing among the Hebrews: the first letter is *aleph*, the second is *beth*, the third is *gimel*, and so on until the twenty-second and final letter, *thau*, with the second-to-last letter being *sin*. And so in the reverse order we read *aleph*, *thau*, *beth*, *sin*, etc., and when we come to the middle, the letter *chaph* is paired with the letter *lamed*. Thus, if we read in the normal order, it is "Babel," but if we read in the mixed-up order, it is "Sesach." Furthermore, the vowel letters between *beth*, *beth* and *lamed*, and between *sin*, *sin*[63] and *chaph*, are not indicated in this word, in accordance with the idiom of the Hebrew language.[64]

I think that it was prudent for the holy prophet to hide the name of Babylon, lest he openly stir up against himself the madness of those who were besieging Jerusalem and who were ready to seize him at any moment. We

---

[59]Heb *ṣāpôn* ("north"). [60]Jer 25:15-17. [61]Jer 51:7. [62]Is 21:7-9. [63]The second-to-last letter of the Hebrew alphabet can have two different pronunciations, *sin* and *shin*, as indicated by the medieval practice of placing a dot in different locations above the letter to mark the different pronunciations. Jerome does not regularly distinguish between these two different pronunciations (MT marks this letter as a *shin*). On Jerome's understanding of the "s" sounds in Hebrew, see *Comm. Tit.* 3:9; *Nom. Hebr.* (OS 10.1-11); *Comm. Isa.* 11:1-3. [64]In rabbinic literature the procedure whereby one pairs together the first and last letters of the alphabet, and then the second and second to last, and so on, is called *atbash* (i.e., *aleph, tav, bet, shin*). The story about Rabbi Akiba's education in *Avot of Rabbi Nathan* 6.2 illustrates how the *atbash* order was used in teaching the alphabet. The name Sheshach in Jer 25:26 is identified as an *atbash* for Babylon in midrash *Numbers Rabbah* 18.21 and in the medieval commentators Rashi and David Kimchi. Jerome points out that the vowels are not actually written in Hebrew in order to explain why this name alteration can work by simply switching the consonants (i.e., there are no written vowels to change).

read that the apostle did this same thing against the Roman Empire, writing about the antichrist:

> Do you not remember that when I was still with you I told you this? And you know what is restraining him (understand: "the antichrist") now so that he may be revealed in his time. For the mystery of lawlessness is already at work; only he who now restrains it will do so until he is out of the way. And then the lawless one will be revealed, whom the Lord Jesus will slay with the breath of his mouth and destroy by the appearance of his coming.[65]

By "he who now restrains" he means the Roman Empire. For until the Roman Empire is destroyed and taken "out of the way," the antichrist will not yet come, as it says in the prophecy of Daniel.[66] But if he had chosen to say this openly, he would have foolishly stirred up the frenzy of persecution against Christians and the nascent church.

We have spoken about this passage longer than the brevity of commentaries allows; the Greeks and Latins might not like this,[67] especially because this passage is not found in their codices. Yet, it would be pointless to doubt this interpretation, since in a later passage this same prophet says, "How Sesach is taken, the praise of the whole earth seized! How Babylon has become an astonishment among the nations!"[68]

Allegorical interpreters refer this whole passage to all the nations that the devil has made drunk with the purely unmixed cup of sins. For in the end he himself will drink punishment and torment, about which the apostle writes, "whom the Lord Jesus will slay with the breath of his mouth,"[69] and in another passage he says, "The last enemy to be destroyed is death."[70] It is possible that the names of the diverse nations represent through their etymologies the names of great powers, and that particular vices match up with particular designations.

25:27: *"And you shall say to them, 'Thus says the Lord of hosts, the God of Israel: Drink, be drunk and vomit, fall and do not rise, because of the sword that I am sending among you.'"*

The prophet says, "After you have made all the nations drink and have fulfilled the Lord's decree, you shall again command these things by the words of the Lord, and you shall say, 'Drink, be drunk and vomit, fall and do not rise.'" If "to drink," "to be drunk," "to vomit" and "to fall" are symbols of salvation, such that noxious fluids are being expelled as by a cleansing potion, then why does it go on to say, "And do not rise"?[71] Moreover, he specifies clearly what sort of potion this is that causes them to fall forever, namely, "because of the sword that I am sending among you."

25:28-29a: *"And if they refuse to accept the cup from your hand to drink, then you shall say to them, 'Thus says the Lord of hosts: Drinking, you shall drink. For behold, I begin to work evil at the city that is called by my name; and shall you, as if innocent, be exempt? You shall not be exempt'—or 'and shall you be cleansed with cleanness? You shall not be cleansed.'"*[72]

---

[65]2 Thess 2:5-8. [66]Cf. Jerome *Expl. Dan.* at Dan 7:23-27; 9:24-27; 11:24-45. [67]On the "laws" of commentary writing, see *Comm. Jer.*, bk. 1 prol. [68]Jer 51:41. The fact that Sheshach is used in parallel with "Babylon" in Jer 51:41 indicates to Jerome that the two words refer to the same thing. [69]2 Thess 2:8. [70]1 Cor 15:26. [71]See Jer 25:15-17. Jerome is countering an interpretation of Origen. [72]The question "Shall you be exempt?" is expressed in Hebrew with the infinitive absolute used in conjunction with the finite verb of the same root (*nqh* ["be free, without blame," KB 720]) to express some kind of emphasis. Jerome translates the infinitive absolute as a separate phrase ("as if innocent"), as does the LXX ("with cleanness"). Yet, the LXX actually reads, "And you were not cleansed with cleansing" (past tense), omitting the final clause, "you shall not be cleansed." What Jerome gives as his second option in the lemma is Aq, Sym and

He makes known in private that those who refuse to do willingly what God commands will eventually take it up by necessity, hearing, "Drinking, you shall drink." "Whether you wish it or not," he says, "God's decree shall be fulfilled. For if the city of Jerusalem, which is called by God's name (as the prophet says, 'In Judah God is known, his name is great in Israel'[73]), will drink this unmixed cup of wrath, how much the more so will you who worship idols, instead of God's name, not be cleansed!"

25:29b: "For I am summoning a sword against all the inhabitants of the earth, says the Lord of hosts."

This is the purely unmixed potion, this is the cup of the Lord's wrath, which is summoned not only against Jerusalem but also against the whole earth and all the surrounding nations. He spoke about this above: "I will send for Nebuchadnezzar the king of Babylon, my servant. And I will bring them against this land and its inhabitants, and against all these nations round about."[74]

25:30-31: "And you shall prophesy to them all these words, and say to them: 'The Lord will roar'—or 'will give answer'[75]—'from on high, and from his holy habitation utter his voice; roaring, he will roar over his ornament,'—or 'he will give answer over his place'[76]—'and the shout, as of those who tread grapes, will resound against all the inhabitants of the earth. The clamor reaches to the ends of the earth,'—or 'destruction comes on part of the earth'[77]— 'for the Lord is holding court with the nations;

he is entering into judgment with all flesh, and the wicked he will hand over to the sword, says the Lord.' "

First of all, let us say that the truth of our interpretation demonstrated here. "You shall prophesy to all the nations," he says, "and you shall say to them that the Lord roars from on high," that is, he gives an indication of his wrath, as it is written: "The lion roars; who will not fear? The Lord has spoken; who can but prophesy?"[78] "And from his holy habitation he utters his voice," so that he frightens all who hear. Moreover, "he will roar over his ornament," that is, over his temple. And when he roars, the shout sounds forth as if it were from those who tread grapes in a press. Amid the shedding of everyone's blood there resounds a mournful song, which Symmachus calls a "dirge" and Aquila a "lament." The clamor of this shout and song reaches to the ends of the earth, for the Lord is holding court with the nations.

Now, if the Lord is holding court with the nations, then they each must be receiving different recompense. In order to make sense of this passage (as certain people wish), we must cite "he who does not believe is condemned already"; indeed, he is condemned "because he has not believed."[79] But among those who do not believe, they may be inflicted with diverse punishments.[80] "He is entering into judgment with all flesh," so that no one goes away unjudged. Lastly, the "wicked," that is, those who do not believe the Lord, "he will hand over to the everlasting sword."

Allegorical interpreters treat this passage according to the LXX, construing what is

---

Th (who like the LXX translate *nqh* as "to cleanse") with the addition of the LXX's handling of the infinitive absolute. Jerome agrees with the Targ (*zkh*, "to be acquitted") in his interpretation of the Hebrew word *nqh*. [73]Ps 76:1. [74]Jer 25:9. [75]Jerome agrees with Aq, Sym and MT. [76]Jerome agrees with Aq and Th. For Jerome's "ornament" or "beauty" (Lat *decor*), the Hebrew has *nāweh* ("grazing place," KB 678); but cf. *nāweh* used for *nā'eh* ("beautiful, suitable") in postbiblical Hebrew (Jastrow 865, 884). [77]Jerome agrees with Aq and MT. [78]Amos 3:8. [79]Jn 3:18. [80]The issue Jerome is addressing is this: Why would God need to hold court with the nations if they are all going to receive the same punishment? Therefore, it must be that each will potentially receive different judgments. Jerome is willing to accept this, but he also wants to make clear that all of the nations will indeed be punished, since they did not believe.

clearly a threat made by the Lord in a positive sense. They say, "The Lord will give answer from on high" to those, namely, whom he is going to save; "from his holy place he will utter his voice, and he will give a word in answer over his place." "And they will respond" to his decree "like grape gathers" who are filled with fruit. "Destruction comes against all the inhabitants of the earth"—not for the whole earth but "on part of the earth," namely, on those who do not believe. "For the Lord is holding court with the nations; he is entering into judgment with all flesh, and the wicked will be handed over to the sword, says the Lord."

25:32-33: *"Thus says the Lord of hosts: Behold, affliction"—or "evil"*[81]*—"is going forth from nation to nation, and a great tumult"—or "tempest"*[82]*—"is stirring from the summits"—or "farthest parts"—"of the earth!" "And the slain of the Lord"—or "those wounded by the Lord"—"on that day shall be from one end of the earth to the other. They shall not be lamented, or gathered or buried; they shall lie in a dung pit on the face of the ground."*

Let them be ashamed who attempt to construe the meaning of holy Scripture in a positive sense when they are discussing matters that are filled with threats! I think that the Lord even said about this passage, "Nation will rise against nation, and kingdom against kingdom,"[83] which is found within a decree of judgment in the Gospel. Let us understand these events according to *historia*, when all the nations in the whole area were subjugated by the king of Babylon and experienced his cruel authority; or according to prophecy, regarding

events a long time afterwards in the future consummation of the world. And some are said to be "slain by the Lord," not because the Lord himself killed them but because by the destruction of these wicked people the will and authority of the Lord are fulfilled.

25:34-35: *"Howl,"—or "Shout"*[84]*—"you shepherds, and cry, and sprinkle yourselves with ashes, you leaders of the flock,"—or "beat yourselves, you rams of the sheep"*[85]*—"for the days of your slaughter and dispersion have come, and you shall fall like costly vessels"—or "like choice rams."*[86] *"No refuge will remain for the shepherds or escape for the leaders"—or "rams"—"of the flock."*

It should be noted in this passage that only the LXX put "shout" (in the negative sense), in place of which the other translators gave "howl," as it is written in the Hebrew. The difference between the "shepherds" and the "leaders (or 'rams') of the flock" is that the shepherds are those endowed with reason, whereas the "leaders" or "rams" represent the wealthy who are themselves identified as part of the flock. As for that which he adds, "the days of your slaughter and dispersion have come," at that time the day will come when their sins will be complete, and they will be scattered and will fall like "costly vessels," so that they will be broken beyond repair. However costly they were before, their damage will be even greater when they break. Or, they will be like "choice rams," in that they will be like a fattened sacrifice for those who desire to consume them. "No refuge will remain for the shepherds" once they have failed to repent. Indeed, it is said to the Pharisees, "You brood of vipers! Who warned you to flee from the

---

[81]Heb *rʿh* ("evil" or "calamity, disaster," KB 1262-63). [82]Heb *sʿr* ("heavy gale," KB 762). [83]Lk 21:10. [84]Heb *yll* (Hiphil; "to howl, lament," KB 413). Jerome matches the hexaplaric versions. [85]Whereas Aq and Sym translate the verb *plš* (Hitpael) as "draw back," Jerome (agreeing with Targ) understands it to refer to covering oneself in ashes and so (like Targ) adds the words "with ashes" to complete the sense. As for Jerome's "leaders" (LXX: "rams"), Jerome is in agreement with MT (*ʾaddîr* ["mighty, prominent people," KB 13-14]). [86]Jerome ("vessels") agrees with Aq, Sym and Targ (MT: *kly*, "vessel").

wrath to come?"[87] And in the Psalms we read, 'No refuge remains to me.'[88] And he says, "or escape for the leaders (or 'rams') of the flock"—with the words "will remain" to be supplied *apo koinou*.[89]

25:36-37: "The voice of the cry of shepherds and the howl of the leaders of the flock!"—or "the shout of the rams of the flock!"[90] "For the Lord is devastating their pasture, and the fields of peace"—or "the good things of peace"[91]—"have become silent, because of the fierce anger of the Lord."

It should be noted here that "shout" was put instead of "howl" by the LXX. The difference between the "shepherds" and the "rams" is this: the "shepherds" are those within the church who are regarded as presiding over the flock with wisdom, knowledge and doctrine, whereas the "rams" are those who are indeed seen as leaders of the people but who do not have wisdom and doctrine within them and are kindred to fools due to their excessive simplicity.

When we have enjoyed peace but have not understood the benefits or "good things" of peace, and when we have given ourselves over to luxury, leisure and pleasure, then the benefits of peace cease or "become quiet," and they are taken away from us on account of the "fierce anger of the Lord." In this way, we see

fulfilled what is written: "When people say, 'There is peace and security,' then sudden destruction will come on them,"[92] and at this destruction all things become quiet.

25:38: "Like a lion he has left his covert,"—or "lair" or, as is even more accurate, "tabernacle" (since this is what the Hebrew *soccho* means)[93]—"for their land has become desolate"—or "impassible"[94]—"because of the anger of the dove"—or "because of the powerful sword"[95]—"and because of the Lord's fierce anger."[96]

The Lord about whom it was said above, "He will roar from on high, and from his holy habitation he will utter his voice; roaring, he will roar over his ornament"[97]—he himself leaves his tabernacle, about which it is written: "His place has been made in peace (or, in 'Salem'), and his habitation in Zion."[98] He abandons his seat, and thus he fulfills what was said through this same prophet: "I have forsaken my house, I have abandoned my heritage."[99]

Moreover, "like a lion he has left his lair," so as to grant a free hand to all the beasts that are intent on ravaging his land. For when the land had a lion as guardian and protector, no one dared to attack it. He says, "For their land (no doubt, 'the land of the Jewish people,' or else 'the land of all the nations') has become

---

[87]Lk 3:7. [88]Ps 142:4. [89]The phrase *apo koinou* in Greek (meaning "in common") refers to a figure of speech whereby two different clauses share a single word or phrase in common; see Jer 21:11-12. [90]See Jer 25:34-35. [91]Jerome is in basic agreement with Sym and the Targ (Heb *nāwâ* ["grazing place," KB 678-79]). Most preserved witnesses to the LXX have "lodgings" here, but Jerome's copy of the LXX had "beautiful things" (so also the LXX text in Theodoret's *Comm. Jer.*). On the translation "beautiful things" (*nā'eh* in postbiblical Hebrew), see Jer 25:30-32. [92]1 Thess 5:3. [93]In the IH edition Jerome had used the Latin word *umbraculum*, which can have the sense "covert," whereas the LXX used the Greek word *kataluma* ("lodging"), which Jerome interpreted as *cubile* ("place of rest" or "lair"). Yet, Jerome also suggests that a strictly accurate translation of the Hebrew *sukkô* would be "tabernacle" (cf. Heb *sukkâ* ["thicket," but more often "hut" or "tabernacle," KB 753]). Although Sym is not preserved for this verse, Jerome may be following him here (see Sym, "tabernacle," at Ps 27:5; 42:5). [94]Jerome matches Aq and Sym. [95]The Hebrew text as we have it reads "because of *ḥărôn hayyônâ*," which could be taken to mean "because of the anger (*ḥărôn*) of the oppressor" (from *ynh* ["to be violent, oppress," KB 416]). Jerome, agreeing with Aq and Th, translates, "because of the anger of the dove" (*yônâ*, "dove"). The LXX translates "because of the powerful (cf. "oppressive"?) sword (reading *ḥereb* instead of *ḥărôn*)." The Targ also reads "sword" instead of "anger." [96]The Hebrew text says "and because of his fierce anger," but Jerome explicitly identifies this as the Lord's fierce anger. [97]See Jer 25:30, where Jerome identified the "ornament" as the temple. [98]Ps 76:2. The Hebrew text and the IH edition say that "his tabernacle" is "in Salem"—this is apparently the connection that brought the verse to Jerome's mind. In Hebrew "Salem" means "peace." [99]Jer 12:7.

desolate and impassible, because of the anger of the dove" (instead of which the LXX translated, "because of the powerful sword"). One should not be surprised that Nebuchadnezzar is understood as the Lord's "dove," since above we read that he was called the Lord's "servant."[100] Yet, we can also interpret "dove" through the *persona* of Jerusalem, since Jerusalem became angry and bitter when it lost the protection of the lion and became desolate.

26:1-3: *In the beginning of the reign of Jehoiakim the son of Josiah, king of Judah, this word came from the Lord: "Thus says the Lord: Stand in the court of the Lord's house, and speak to all the cities of Judah, out of which they come to worship in the house of the Lord, all the words that I command you to speak to them; do not hold back a word. Perhaps they will listen, and every one turn from his evil way, that I may repent of"—or "cease from"[101]—"the evil that I intend to do to them because of their evil doings."*

This prophecy is earlier than the previous one, even though it came under the same king. For that one came "in the fourth year of Jehoiakim the son of Josiah, king of Judah,"[102] whereas this one came at the beginning of the reign of the same king, as Scripture says: "In the beginning of the reign of Jehoiakim the son of Josiah, king of Judah, this word came from the Lord." Therefore, as we have already said often, the order of *historia* in the prophets must be reconstructed, since, as in the present passage, things that took place earlier under the same king may be mentioned later, and things that took place later may be mentioned earlier.[103]

He who is going to speak the word of the Lord ought to stand along with Moses[104] and together with the psalmist hear: "you that stand in the house of the Lord, in the courts of the house of our God!"[105] The Lord commands him to speak to all the cities of Judah—although the LXX did not translate the word *cities*, out of concern that it might seem inappropriate for him to stand in the court of the Lord's house and speak to cities that are not present. But he is indeed speaking to the cities when he speaks to the people and the citizens. Furthermore, it is excellent how he stands in the court and vestibule of the Lord's temple, so that, on the occasion of their praying to the Lord and worshiping him, they are forced to hear the words of the prophet.

The prophet says, "Do not hold back a word." "Even if it is unpleasant, and even if the madness of those who hear is stirred up against you, you must nevertheless say all that is commanded to you. You must fear not the persecution of those who will be stirred up against you but the authority of the Lord who gives the order!" He says, "Perhaps they will listen and turn." The word expressing uncertainty, "perhaps," cannot be reflective of the Lord's majesty, but rather is said for the sake of our mental disposition, in order to preserve human free will. The human will is not compelled by necessity either to do anything or not to do anything simply because of the Lord's foreknowledge. For things do not happen *because* God knows that they will happen; rather, because they are going to happen God knows about them, since he knows the future.

And yet it should be known that, according to this same Jeremiah, if God announces calamities but the people repent, then God will repent concerning the things that he threatened to do. Also, if God promises prosperity but the people behave recklessly, then God will change his sentence and bring calamity instead of good.[106] A similar issue is

---

[100]Jer 25:9; 27:6; 43:10. [101]Jerome agrees with Aq, Targ and MT. [102]Jer 25:1. [103]See Jer 21:1-2; 25:1a. [104]Deut 5:31. [105]Ps 135:2. [106]Jer 18:5-10.

also addressed in this Gospel passage: "I will send my beloved son; perhaps they will respect him,"[107] which is obviously spoken out of the *persona* of God Almighty. And so in the present passage he says, "Perhaps they will listen, and every one turn from his evil way," that is, "because they have turned, I will repent of the sentence that I rendered and I will not do that which I intended to do to them." Indeed, he speaks of "the evil that I intend to do to them *because of their evil doings*." "If their 'evil doings' are changed, then my sentence can be reversed." Let us read the *historia* of Jonah and Nineveh.[108]

26:4-6: "*You shall say to them, 'Thus says the Lord: If you will not listen to me, to walk in my law that I have given to you and to heed the words of my servants the prophets whom I, rising at night and directing,*[109] *sent to you, though you have not heeded, then I will make this house like Shiloh, and I will make this city a curse for all the nations of the earth.'*"

Therefore, it has been put into our power either to do things or not to do them—provided, however, that we ascribe to God's grace whatever good work that we intend, strive after or accomplish; for it is God, as the apostle says, who has granted us both to will and to work.[110] But if it is sufficient for a person to walk just once in the law that was given to us through Moses, as the foolish heresy supposes,[111] then why did he add, "to heed the words of my servants the prophets," since they were sent after the law, not just once but frequently, and not in a quiet and easy manner but persistently and with alarm? He says, "I, rising at night, sent to you my servants daily; if you are unwilling to heed them, then I will

make this house (that is, the temple of God) like Shiloh, where the tabernacle was located.[112] And as soon as the temple is destroyed, the city will become a curse for all the nations of the earth."

The temple was built on the threshing floor of Ornan and on Mount Moriah (that is, "Vision"),[113] where it says that Abraham offered his son Isaac. When this temple was built, the worship at Shiloh ceased and sacrifices were never again offered there. In the same way, when the church was built and spiritual sacrifices came to be offered, the ceremonies of the law ceased and the city of the Jews was made a curse for all the nations of the earth. But the Lord has freed us from this curse, as the apostle says: "Christ redeemed us from the curse of the law, having become a curse for us."[114]

26:7-9a: *The priests and the prophets—or pseudoprophets—and all the people heard Jeremiah speaking these words in the house of the Lord. And when Jeremiah had finished speaking all that the Lord had commanded him to speak to all the people, then the priests and the prophets—or pseudoprophets—and all the people laid hold of him, saying, "Let him be put to death! For he has prophesied in the name of the Lord, saying, 'This house shall be like Shiloh, and this city shall be desolate, without inhabitant.'"*

The priests and prophets (which the LXX translated more clearly as "pseudoprophets"[115]) are angry at Jeremiah because he is proclaiming the truth and because once the temple is overthrown and the city is deserted then the religion—and the profits that come from the religion—will cease. So they lay hold of him,

---

[107]Lk 20:13. [108]Jon 3:10. [109]See Jer 25:3. [110]Phil 2:13. [111]The followers of Pelagius. [112]Josh 18:1; 1 Sam 4:3; Jer 7:12. [113]The Hebrew for Moriah, *mryh*, is being expounded through the Hebrew word *mr'h* ("vision"). On Mount Moriah, see Gen 22:2; 2 Chron 3:1. [114]Gal 3:13. [115]In numerous places within the book of Jeremiah where false prophets are in view (Jer 6:13; 26:7, 8, 11, 16; 27:9; 28:1; 29:1, 8), the LXX translates the Hebrew word "prophet" with the Greek term "pseudoprophet" in order to make clear that the prophet is false. See Jerome's comments at Jer 14:13-14; 28:10-11, 15-17.

and with the people's consent they intend to put him to death, since he said, "This house shall be like Shiloh, and this city shall be desolate, without inhabitant." Therefore, if ever the priests, pseudoprophets or deceived people become angry at us because of the Lord's command or because of the truth of the faith, we should not be overly concerned but should follow God's decree, keeping in mind not the present evils but the future good.

26:9b-10: *And all the people were assembled against Jeremiah in the house of the Lord. When the princes of Judah heard these words, they came up from the king's house to the house of the Lord and took their seat in the entry of the New Gate of the house of the Lord.*

Jeremiah prophesied these words of the Lord within the temple: "I will make this house like Shiloh, and I will make this city a curse for all the nations of the earth,"[116] and immediately with a turbulent uproar an entire mob was assembled by the prophets, priests and people against Jeremiah in the temple, where the prophet was being held by force of the priests, the prophets and the mob. And when the princes of the city who live in the royal house heard this, they went or "came up" from the king's house to the house of the Lord. It should be noted that going to the house of the Lord is always an ascent upwards. "And they took their seat in the entry of the New Gate of the house of the Lord." For it was the responsibility of the princes to sit at the gate of the Lord's house and to ascertain the truth of any difficult or contentious matter. Moreover, it is called the "New" Gate because those who sat at this gate and presided in judgment resisted the wicked schemes of the priests and pseudoprophets.

26:11: *Then the priests and the prophets said to the princes and to all the people, "This man deserves the sentence of death, because he has prophesied against this city, as you have heard with your own ears."*

While the princes of the city, who had rushed from the royal palace to the temple in order to calm the uproar of the people, were sitting at the gate of the temple and at the New Gate, and while the assembly of the people was gathered together, the priests and the pseudoprophets made their accusation. And the prophet would have perished, so far as it concerned the priests and prophets, if the accusers had possessed the power to execute judgment. From this we see that those who appeared to be devoted to religion, because of their hatred of the prophet's sanctity, were more fiercely opposed to him than were those who governed over public affairs.

26:12-15: *Then Jeremiah spoke to all the princes and all the people, saying, "The Lord sent me to prophesy to"—or "over"—"this house and this city all the words you have heard. Now therefore make good your ways and your doings, and hear the voice of the Lord your God, and the Lord will repent of the evil that he has pronounced against you"—or "the Lord will cease from the evils that he has pronounced against you."[117] But as for me, behold, I am in your hands. Do with me as is good and right in your eyes"—or "as is expedient for you."[118] "Only know and understand that if you put me to death, you will bring innocent blood on yourselves and on this city and its inhabitants, for in truth the Lord sent me to you to speak all these words in your ears."*

While the princes of the city were sitting at

---

[116]Jer 26:6. [117]Heb *nhm* (Niphal; "regret, be sorry," KB 688). Jerome matches Aq, Sym and Targ. [118]Jerome gives a literal rendering of the Hebrew (= Aq and Targ). The full reading of the LXX says, "as is expedient and as is better for you."

the gate in the presence of the people and the priests and prophets were accusing the prophet Jeremiah and threatening him with the death penalty, Jeremiah spoke with prudence, equity, humility and persistence to the princes and to all the people who were being stirred up by the factions of the priests and pseudoprophets. With prudence, because he said that he was sent by the Lord to speak against the temple and the city and to advise them that if they would listen to his counsel and repent, then the Lord also would commute the sentence of judgment against them. With humility, since he says, "Behold, I am in your hands. Do with me as is good and right in your eyes." And with persistence: "In truth the Lord sent me to you to speak all these words in your ears." In other words, he says, "If you are angry that I have spoken against the temple and the Lord's city, and if you are concerned about the welfare of the city and the temple, then why do you pile up sins on sins and make both the city and its inhabitants guilty of my blood?" Therefore, if the difficulties of our circumstances ever require of us humility, let us take on this humility in such a way that we do not abandon truth and perseverance. For it is one thing to be insulting in an arrogant and judgmental way, which is a sign of foolishness; but it is something else to warn of an impending danger so that you take nothing away from the truth.

26:16: *Then the princes and all the people said to the priests and the prophets, "This man does not deserve the sentence of death, for he has spoken to us in the name of the Lord our God."*

The people, who previously had been tripped up by the priests and pseudoprophets, join now with the princes of the city and speak in favor of Jeremiah, saying that they do not wish to be liable for Jeremiah's death, since Jeremiah has prophesied in the name of the Lord and by the Lord's mouth. For once they have accepted an argument, the untaught mob quickly changes its opinion. The indignation of the accusers, primarily the priests and pseudoprophets, cannot be changed. But the people did change, in spite of the priests and pseudoprophets accusing Jeremiah and persisting in their accusations, because the prophet gave the people hope for God's clemency. If they made good their ways and listened to the voice of the Lord their God, then the Lord would turn away from his sentence of judgment.[119]

26:17-19: *And certain of the elders of the land arose and spoke to all the assembled people, saying, "Micah of Moresheth prophesied in the days of Hezekiah king of Judah and said to all the people of Judah: 'Thus says the Lord of hosts, Zion shall be plowed as a field; Jerusalem shall become a heap of ruins and the mountain of the house a wooded height.' Did Hezekiah king of Judah and all Judah put him to death? Did he not fear the Lord and entreat the favor of the Lord, and did not the Lord repent of the evil that he had pronounced against them? But we are about to bring great evil on ourselves."*

The princes of the city and the people understand the truth about this dispute. Now, certain elders whose responsibility it was to know the old traditions recall the *historia* and the prophecy of Micah of Moresheth, who prophesied under King Hezekiah. They liken Micah's prophecy to the prophecy of Jeremiah, who was being threatened with the death penalty. They show that Micah said things that were even more severe than what Jeremiah said, and yet the righteous King Hezekiah did not in any way persecute Micah. Instead, Hezekiah and the people turned to repen-

---

[119]Jer 26:13.

tance, so that the Lord's negative sentence was changed into a favorable one. For Micah said, "Zion shall be plowed as a field; Jerusalem shall become a heap of ruins and the mountain of the house a wooded height,"[120] whereas later on Jeremiah says, "I will make this house like Shiloh, and I will make this city a curse for all the nations of the earth."[121]

So the elders gave their advice, thinking that what Micah predicted would never come to pass, since due to the people's repentance it had still not happened even after a long time. Likewise, these elders thought that what Jeremiah pronounced would not take place, if (as Jeremiah advised) they made good their ways and their doings and listened to the voice of the Lord their God, so that the Lord might not bring against them the evil that he had threatened.[122] In this way the elders subdued the madness of the accusers, and at the same time they included themselves along with the accusers, saying, "But we are about to bring great evil on ourselves." The elders say this not because they think that they should kill the prophet but because if they were to kill him, they would not be harming the accused but themselves. But they could rescue themselves by changing their verdict.

26:20-24: *There was another man who prophesied in the name of the Lord, Uriah the son of Shemaiah from Kiriath-jearim. He prophesied against this city and against this land in words like those of Jeremiah. And when King Jehoiakim, with all his powerful men and princes, heard his words, the king sought to put him to death; but when Uriah heard of it, he was afraid and fled and went to Egypt.* And that which follows, *"Then King Jehoiakim sent to Egypt certain men, Elnathan the son of Achbor and other men with him to Egypt,"* is not found in the LXX. But then the

LXX resumes: *And they fetched Uriah from Egypt and brought him to King Jehoiakim, who slew him with the sword and cast his dead body into the burial place of the common people. But the hand of Ahikam the son of Shaphan was with Jeremiah so that he was not given over to the people to be put to death.*

It may be asked: If Uriah the son of Shemaiah from the town of Kiriath-jearim—who prophesied the same things as Jeremiah—fled in great fear to Egypt, was brought back from there and was put to death, then how was Jeremiah able to escape, considering that Jeremiah did not flee but boldly persisted in his initial message? How is it that Jeremiah was set free by the common judgment of the princes and by the counsel of elders, in spite of his accusers, the priests and pseudoprophets? To this question one may respond briefly: when for the same reason and the same message one person is punished and another is set free, the judgment of God cannot be known—unless perhaps we can say that Uriah was slain under the condemnation of his accusers and the people, whereas Jeremiah was preserved alive in accordance with God's judgment so that he might preach to the remaining unfortunate people and draw them back to repentance. This is indeed what we read in the Acts of the Apostles, when the apostle James immediately suffered Herod's punishment and was crowned with martyrdom, whereas Peter and the other apostles were preserved alive in order to teach the doctrine of the Lord.[123]

Take special note of the prophet's consistency: not even when he was brought back from Egypt did Uriah change his message, but although he saw that they intended to kill him, he still spoke what the Lord commanded. The fact that he was afraid, fled and went to Egypt

---

[120]Mic 3:12. The "mountain of the house" in Micah is Mount Zion, on which the house of the Lord (i.e., the temple) sits.   [121]Jer 26:6.   [122]Jer 26:13.   [123]Acts 12:1-11.

is not a sign of faithlessness but of prudence, in that we should not expose ourselves to danger needlessly. Moreover, we read that even our Lord and Savior slipped away from the hands of those who persecuted him,[124] and he commanded the apostles: "When they persecute you in one town, flee to another!"[125]

It may also be asked how Jehoiakim king of Judah, which was a small and weak state that was in the process of falling apart, had the power to send people to Egypt and bring Uriah back from there. This question is easily resolved, once we consider that Jehoiakim was set up as ruler by Neco king of Egypt, and this prophecy took place at the beginning of his reign.[126]

Although Jeremiah was set free by the Lord's help, credit is still given to the one through whom the Lord set the prophet free, namely, Ahikam the son of Shaphan. We will read about a similar thing later on, when Jeremiah is rescued out of a muddy cistern from the peril of death by the counsel and aid of the eunuch Ebed-melech.[127]

27:1: *In the beginning of the reign of Jehoiakim the son of Josiah, king of Judah, this word came to Jeremiah from the Lord.*

This is not found in the edition of the LXX. Many think that it is the beginning of the following section, but this is not the case.[128] Rather, it should be joined to what was said above, so that we may believe that the words and deeds reported in the previous section took place at the beginning of the reign of Jehoiakim. Thus, he had the power to send

men to Egypt since he was sending them to an allied king. It seems to me that the LXX omitted this notice so that they would not appear to be saying the same thing twice, for already at the beginning of this section they put "In the beginning of the reign of Jehoiakim the son of Josiah, king of Judah, this word came from the Lord."[129]

27:2-4: *Thus the Lord said to me: "Make yourself bonds and fetters"—or "kloious," which in Hebrew are called "mutoth," and in common speech we call "collar,"[130]—"and put them on your neck, and send them to the king of Edom, the king of Moab, the king of the sons of Ammon, the king of Tyre and the king of Sidon by the hand of the envoys who have come to Jerusalem to Zedekiah king of Judah. And give them this charge to convey to their masters: 'Thus says the Lord of hosts, the God of Israel: This is what you shall say to your masters.'"*

The previous vision came to the prophet in the beginning of the reign of Jehoiakim the son of Josiah, king of Judah.[131] But this vision came under Zedekiah, who was the last one to rule in Jerusalem, and under whom the city was captured and overthrown. Jeremiah is ordered to put on his neck "fetters," or wooden pillories, which (as we said) in Hebrew are called *mutoth*, and to send them to the kings of Edom, Moab, the sons of Ammon, Tyre and Sidon, by means of legates who had come to Zedekiah. Jeremiah is commanded to charge these legates to announce to their masters that they must serve king Nebuchadnezzar and

---

[124]Lk 4:30; Jn 8:59. [125]Mt 10:23. [126]2 Kings 23:34; 2 Chron 36:4; Jer 26:1. [127]Jer 38:7-13. [128]Jer 27:1-22 in the Hebrew text is found at Jer 34:2-22 in the LXX, except that the present verse is absent from the LXX. The problem is that, although this clearly appears to be a section heading (contra Jerome), the following chapter relates to Zedekiah, not Jehoiakim (see Jer 27:3, 12; 28:1). Many modern commentators consider this verse to be a late and misplaced addition to the text. The RSV simply changes the name of the king to "Zedekiah." As for the "many" who take this verse to be the beginning of the next section, Theodoret interprets the passage this way, and he may represent an Antiochene commentary tradition (e.g., Diodore or Theodore) known to Jerome. [129]Jer 26:1. [130]Jerome first gives the Latin word *catenas* ("fetters") in the lemma, which he used in the IH edition. But he clarifies the meaning of the word by citing the Greek term used by the LXX (*kloios*, "collar") and the underlying Hebrew word (*mwṭh* ["yoke," KB 555]). [131]Jer 26:1–27:1.

that they must heed the word of the prophet that is about to follow. And so that the legates and kings of the other nations cannot respond, "Why don't you give this command to your own people?" Jeremiah says similar things to King Zedekiah and to the priests and prophets. He who always interprets allegorically,[132] fleeing the truth of the *historia*, interprets this passage with reference to the heavenly Jerusalem, saying that the inhabitants of the heavenly Jerusalem should willingly assume bodies and descend into "Babylon,"[133] that is, the "confusion" of this world, which has been given over to the evil one,[134] and they should serve the king of Babylon, who is (no doubt) the devil. And if they are not willing to do this, then (he says) they will not bear heavy bodies but will die by the sword, famine and pestilence, and they will not be human beings but demons. This he has indeed said, so let none of his defenders make false charges against us. But all that aside, let us follow the simple and true *historia*, lest we entangle ourselves in clouds and illusions.

27:5: *"It is I who have made the earth, with the people and beasts that are on the face of the earth, by my great power and by my outstretched arm, and I give it to him who is pleasing in my eyes."*

Even though this Scripture is speaking anthropopathically,[135] in such manner as we human beings speak and are able to understand, nevertheless there is a "power" and "arm" of God about which the apostle speaks: "Christ the strength of God and the wisdom of God";[136] and Isaiah says, "Lord, who has believed what we have heard, and to whom has the arm of the Lord been revealed?"[137] John the Evangelist also writes, "All things were made through him, and without him nothing was made."[138] And David says in his song, "By the word of the Lord the heavens were made, and all their strength by the breath of his mouth."[139] The fact that he says, "I give it to him who is pleasing in my eyes," shows that it is by the grace of God that all things are granted to humankind. Moreover, he says, "It is I who have made the earth, with the people and beasts." The order is reversed, for in Genesis, animals are made first and humanity is made at the end, but here he names humanity first and afterwards names the animals that are subject to humanity.

27:6-7a: *"Now I have given all these lands into the hand of Nebuchadnezzar, the king of Babylon, my servant, and I have given him also the beasts of the field to serve him. All the nations shall serve him, and his son, and the son of his son."*

How unfortunate it is for Israel when in comparison with Israel Nebuchadnezzar is called the "servant of God"! It is written in the Gospel, "The world was made through him, yet the world did not know him. He came to his own home, and his own people did not receive him."[140] Therefore, justly does the Maker hand over his creatures to whomever he wishes. Consequently, the devil, of whom Nebuchadnezzar serves as a type, acknowledges, "All these things have been handed over

---

[132]Origen. See Jer 24:1-10; 27:9-11.   [133]"Confusion" is a traditional etymological meaning for "Babylon" (Heb *bbl*); see Gen 11:9 (Heb *bll*, "to confuse"); OS 174.91-92; Origen *Hom. Jer.* 19.14.   [134]1 Jn 5:19.   [135]Jerome uses the Greek adverb *anthrōpopathōs* ("with human feelings"). Compare Jerome's application of this concept with that of Hermogenes (second century C.E.) *On Types of Style* 2.10: "All mythical thoughts are typical of poetry, such as the stories about Cronos and the Titans and the Giants and Zeus himself and the other gods, narrated as if they had human feelings (*anthrōpopathōs*) and describing how they were born and what they have done or do, either among themselves or in their dealings with human beings, and their love-affairs and wars and friendships and their births and how they live and other such aspects of their existence" (Cecil W. Wooten, *Hermogenes' On Types of Style* [Chapel Hill: University of North Carolina Press, 1987], 116). See also Jer 14:8b-9a; 19:3b-5; 32:35b.   [136]1 Cor 1:24.   [137]Is 53:1.   [138]Jn 1:3.   [139]Ps 33:6.   [140]Jn 1:10-11.

to me."[141] Moreover, as for what he adds, "And I have given him also the beasts of the field to serve him," we may either understand this simply as referring to every kind of animal (for things subject to a person are handed over together with that person), or else we may take the "beasts" as referring to the untamed nations, because he was served even by those nations that had not previously learned to serve. And he calls Belshazzar and Evil-merodach "his son" and "the son of his son" (according to the Hebrew).[142] Daniel writes about these things.[143]

27:7b: "until the time comes of his land and of he himself"

Lest it be thought that Nebuchadnezzar's rule will be everlasting, beautifully it says that Nebuchadnezzar himself will be captured by the Medes and the Persians. For this is what is indicated by "until the time comes of his land and of he himself." But this is not found in the LXX.

27:7c: "And many nations and great kings shall serve him."

The prophet did not say "all nations," for this properly belongs to the rule of Christ—although according to Symmachus it does not read, "Many nations and great kings shall serve him," but "many nations and great kings shall subject him to servitude,"[144] so that Nebuchadnezzar, to whom all nations were previously subject, will himself be subject to the Medes and Persians. That which we have put based on the Hebrew, "I have given these to him to serve him. All the nations shall serve him, and his son, and the son of his son, until the time comes of his land and of he himself;

and many nations and great kings shall subject him to servitude," is not read in the edition of the LXX, as we already said.[145]

27:8: "But if any nation or kingdom will not serve this Nebuchadnezzar king of Babylon and put its neck under the yoke of the king of Babylon, I will punish that nation with the sword, with famine and with pestilence, says the Lord, until I have consumed them by his hand."

Not only does the Lord subject sinful nations to Nebuchadnezzar, but the apostle also says concerning sinners, "whom I have delivered to Satan that they may learn not to blaspheme";[146] and in another passage: "I have delivered such a man to Satan for the destruction of the flesh, so that his spirit may be saved."[147] Thus, he warns that we must be subject to these powers, not only to avoid God's wrath but also for the sake of our own conscience,[148] so that these powers do not condemn us.

27:9-11: "So do not listen to your prophets, your diviners, your dreamers, your soothsayers or your sorcerers, who are saying to you, 'You shall not serve the king of Babylon.' For it is a lie that they are prophesying to you, to remove you far from your land and to drive you out, and you will perish. But any nation that will bring its neck under the yoke of the king of Babylon and serve him, I will leave on its own land, says the Lord, to till it and dwell there."

He who gives an allegorical interpretation of this passage goes astray[149] when he urges those who are stationed in the heavenly Jerusalem not to listen to their prophets, diviners, dreamers, soothsayers and sorcerers, but rather to

---

[141]Lk 4:6; Mt 4:9.   [142]In other words, "the son of his son" is a Hebrew idiom for "grandson."   [143]Dan 5; Jer 52:31; 2 Kings 25:27.
[144]Jerome matches MT. Sym agrees with Targ.   [145]See Jer 27:7b.   [146]1 Tim 1:20.   [147]1 Cor 5:5.   [148]Rom 13:5.   [149]Origen; see Jer 24: 1-10; 27:2-4.

serve Nebuchadnezzar and assume a humble body,[150] namely, the state of infancy, as a crying child wrapped in swaddling clothes. For if they will do this, then once their servitude (that is, the condition of their human mortality) is finished, they will be able to return to their land and dwell in it and do the work that they previously did. And this interpreter supposes (as he says) that those who despise God's commands are weighed down with human bodies and will become demons and unclean spirits, and that they will not regain their previous position.

But we expound this passage straightforwardly, and we say that there were "prophets" among the nations who pretended that they could, by means of a divine spirit, predict what was going to happen; and there were "diviners," about whom is this popular saying, "They say that wise men can divine what will be";[151] and there were "dreamers," who imitated Joseph and Daniel; and there were "soothsayers," who by the flight of birds and the voices of song birds declared what should be done or what should not be done; and there were "sorcerers," whom we can identify either as potion makers or as servants of demonic apparitions, who in Hebrew are called *chassanae*.[152] "All of these are deceiving you," the prophet says, "and they are causing you to stumble by making you not serve the king of Babylon." For it is much better to accept servitude willingly, to serve someone friendly to you and to cultivate a fruitful land, than to be captured and to serve by necessity and compulsion.

27:12-15: To Zedekiah king of Judah I spoke according to all these words: "Bring your necks

under the yoke of the king of Babylon, and serve him and his people, and live. Why will you and your people die by the sword, by famine and by pestilence, as the Lord has spoken concerning the nation that will not serve the king of Babylon? Do not listen to the words of the prophets who are saying to you, 'You shall not serve the king of Babylon,' for it is a lie that they are prophesying to you. I have not sent them, says the Lord, but they are prophesying falsely in my name, with the result that I will drive you out and you will perish, you and the prophets who are prophesying to you."

After addressing all the nations he turns to Zedekiah, speaking to him with the same words with which he threatened the nations. For he who has sinned as much as (or more than) the rest of the nations is not worthy of the privileged status of the Israelite nation. And so, because the villainous people despised listening to Jeremiah, they were consumed by the sword, fire and pestilence. It should be observed that in holy Scripture those who prophesy falsely in the name of the Lord are called "prophets" instead of "pseudoprophets."[153] "Because you do this," he says, "I will drive you out and you will perish, you and the prophets who are prophesying to you." Therefore, the destruction of those who are deceived is similar to the destruction of those who deceive.

This which we have put from the Hebrew:

under the yoke of the king of Babylon, and serve him and his people, and live. Why will you and your people die by the sword, by famine and by pestilence, as

---

[150]Phil 3:21. [151]This saying was also quoted by Jerome's teacher, Aelius Donatus (Terence *Hecyra* 696). [152]The Hebrew text as we have it has *kaššāpêkem* ("your sorcerers"; see *kaššāp*, KB 503). Jerome seems to be reading *nun* in place of *pe*, and so once he has removed the "your" suffix, he is left with *kaššānê*. Since the confusion between *nun* and *pe* is based on their similarity in the early Hebrew script, this confusion probably occurred early in the textual tradition underlying Jerome's Hebrew MS, and he is simply reporting what he has in his text. Otherwise, Jerome's eyes fail him here (cf. *Comm. Ezech.* bk. 7 prol.: "With my eyes dim with old age and suffering something of the infirmity of blessed Isaac [cf. Gen 27:1], I am not able to reread the Hebrew scrolls by candlelight, since even in the brightness of the daytime sun they are obscure to me due to the extreme smallness of the letters"). [153]See Jer 26:7-9a.

the Lord has spoken concerning the nation that will not serve the king of Babylon? Do not listen to the words of the prophets who are saying to you . . .

is not found in the LXX.[154] I am bringing this to your attention, so that the prudent reader may be aware of how much is lacking in terms of individual details from the Greek and Latin codices.

27:16-17: *Then I spoke to the priests and to this people, saying, "Thus says the Lord: Do not listen to the words of your prophets who are prophesying to you, saying, 'Behold, the vessels of the Lord's house will now shortly be brought back from Babylon,' for it is a lie that they are prophesying to you."* This which we have put, "now shortly," is not found in the LXX; nor does the LXX have what follows: *"Do not listen to them; serve the king of Babylon, so that you may live. Why should this city become a desolation?"*[155]

After addressing the nations and the king he now speaks to the priests and the people, since he already announced destruction to the prophets: "I will drive you out and you will perish, you and the prophets who are prophesying to you."[156] Again, he says the same things that he had said to the king and to the nations, that they should not listen to the words of their prophets and claim that the vessels that had been carried off together with Jeconiah, his princes and his mother,[157] will soon be brought back to the Lord's temple. He advises them that they should serve the king of Babylon and thereby live, and that the city that subjects itself willingly will not be given over

to burning. The Lord's mercy is found in surrendering to the lighter punishment, so as not to suffer the heavier one.

27:18-22: *"If they are prophets, and if the word of the Lord is with them, then let them meet"*—what follows, and what we will put all the way to the end of the chapter, is not found in the LXX[158]—*"with the Lord of hosts, that the vessels that are left in the house of the Lord, in the house of the king of Judah and in Jerusalem may not go to Babylon. For thus says the Lord of hosts in regard to the pillars, the sea, the stands"*—which in Hebrew is written *mechonoth*[159]—*"and the rest of the vessels that are left in this city, which Nebuchadnezzar king of Babylon did not take away, when he took into exile from Jerusalem to Babylon Jeconiah the son of Jehoiakim, king of Judah, and all the nobles of Judah and Jerusalem—thus says the Lord of hosts, the God of Israel, in regard to the vessels that are left in the house of the Lord, in the house of the king of Judah and in Jerusalem: They shall be carried to Babylon and remain there until the day when I give attention to them, says the Lord. Then I will bring them back and restore them to this place."*

As we said, these things are not present in the LXX but have been translated from the Hebrew truth. Instead of what we have translated, the LXX put something else, which was not written in the Hebrew, saying, "Let them meet me. For thus the Lord said: Some of the remaining vessels that the king of Babylon did not carry away when he exiled Jeconiah from Jerusalem shall enter into Babylon, says the Lord."[160] The

---

[154]For Jer 27:12-15 (LXX 34:10-12), the LXX jumps from "Submit your neck (Heb v. 12) and work for the king of Babylon" to "for they are prophesying unjust things to you" (Heb v. 14), omitting the intervening text. [155]The LXX lacks "now shortly" from Heb v. 16 (LXX 34:13) and all of Heb v. 17. [156]Jer 27:15. [157]2 Kings 24:12-15; 2 Chron 36:9-10. [158]For Jer 27:18, the LXX (34:15) has, "If they are prophets, and if the word of the Lord is among them, then let them meet me." The LXX also has some words that correspond to parts of Heb vv. 19, 20 and 22, but they are different enough that Jerome simply says that the LXX lacks "what we will put." [159]Heb *mĕcônâ* ("under-support, kettle stand," KB 579). Jerome's understanding of this word agrees with Aq and Sym. Th transliterated it, which may have inspired Jerome to give the Hebrew form. [160]LXX 34:16-18.

LXX has given the sense rather than the words, perhaps thinking that it would be irrational for God to be speaking to "the pillars, the sea, the stands and the rest of the vessels that are left in this city"[161]—as if we did not also read that early one morning God gave orders to a worm,[162] and he said to the sea, "Peace! Be still!"[163]

The fact that he says, "Let them meet with me" or "Let them meet with the Lord of Hosts," shows that the true prophet is able through his prayers to put up resistance to the Lord, just as Moses stood in the breach against the Lord in order to avert the fury of his wrath.[164] Samuel did this, too.[165] As for Moses, the Lord said to him, "Let me alone, that I may destroy this people!"[166] When he says, "Let me alone," the Lord shows that he can be held back by the prayers of the saints. He says, "Let the prophets meet with the Lord, and when they can show that whatever they predicted has come about, then their prophecy will be confirmed as true." As for the pillars, the sea, the stands and the rest of the vessels, we read about them in *Malachim*[167] and at the end of the book of this prophet,[168] where it is listed which vessels were taken to Babylon when Zedekiah was captured, the city was burned and the temple was destroyed.

28:1-3a: *And it came to pass in that year, at the beginning of the reign of Zedekiah king of Judah, in the fifth month of the fourth year, Hananiah the son of Azzur, the prophet from Gibeon, spoke to me in the house of the Lord, in the presence of the priests and all the people,* *saying, "Thus says the Lord of hosts, the God of Israel: I have broken the yoke of the king of Babylon. Within two years I will bring back to this place all the vessels of the Lord's house."*

Some who in the Hebrew text are called "prophets," that is, *nebeim*,[169] the LXX translates as "pseudoprophets," in order to make the sense more clear. Indeed in the present passage, Hananiah is called a "prophet," that is, *nebia*, and not a "pseudoprophet."

This message from the Lord came to Jeremiah in the fifth month of the fourth year of King Zedekiah. This was before Ezekiel started prophesying to them in Babylon, since Ezekiel had been taken captive with Jeconiah.[170] Speaking against the prophet Jeremiah, Hananiah places his trust in the Lord's temple. Hananiah promises prosperity to the people, who are well pleased to listen to lies, especially lies that promise good fortune. Jeremiah had said that the rest of the vessels—of the temple, or of the royal house or of all the people—that Nebuchadnezzar had left previously would also be taken to Babylon. Hananiah, however, promises that even those vessels that had been taken will be returned.

28:3b-4: *". . . which Nebuchadnezzar king of Babylon took away from this place and carried to Babylon. I will also bring back to this place Jeconiah the son of Jehoiakim, king of Judah, and all the exiles from Judah who went to Babylon, says the Lord, for I will break the yoke of the king of Babylon."*

---

[161]The prepositions used in Hebrew (esp. the first, "to the pillars") could be taken to mean either that the Lord spoke directly to these objects or that he spoke in regard to them. Jerome suspects that the LXX thought that the Lord was speaking directly to the objects, which would be irrational, with the result that they omitted these details in their paraphrase. Jerome corrects the LXX not by pointing to the idiom "in regard to" but by providing examples of the Lord speaking to inanimate things.   [162]Jon 4:7.   [163]Mk 4:39.   [164]Ps 106:23.   [165]1 Sam 8:6, 21.   [166]Ex 32:10.   [167]In the Books of Kings (*Mēlākim*, "Kings"). On the Hebrew titles for Old Testament books, see Jerome's preface to his IH translation of Samuel and Kings.   [168]2 Kings 25:13-17; Jer 52:17-23.   [169]The Hebrew text here calls Hananiah a "prophet" (singular *nābi'*), but Jerome supplies the plural form in Hebrew (*nĕbî'îm*) when he makes his general observation. See Jer 26:7-9a.   [170]Zedekiah was made king and Jeconiah was exiled to Babylon in 597. The events of this chapter took place in the fourth year of Zedekiah's reign (593), whereas Ezekiel began to prophesy in the fifth year (592) of the exile of Jeconiah (i.e., Jehoiachin); see Ezek 1:2.

In place of this the LXX translated, "and also Jeconiah and the exiles from Judah, because I will break the yoke of the king of Babylon,"[171] putting briefly the sense rather than the words of the Hebrew truth. Hananiah the "prophet" (as he seemed to the people at that time) promises that not only the vessels but also King Jeconiah will be brought back to Jerusalem. He also promises that the yoke of the king of Babylon is going to be broken, that is, his rule will be overthrown. Furthermore, he says that this will take place before two years are completed, so that the near time of the promise will increase the magnitude of their delight.

28:5-6: *Then the prophet Jeremiah spoke to Hananiah the prophet before the eyes of the priests and all the people who were standing in the house of the Lord; and the prophet Jeremiah said, "Amen! May the Lord do so; may the Lord make the words that you have prophesied come true, so as to bring back to this place from Babylon the vessels of the house of the Lord and all the exiles."*

He wishes that what the pseudoprophet spoke falsely might come to pass—for this is what is signified by the word *amen*, which the Lord often uses in the Gospel: "Amen, amen, I say to you."[172] Jeremiah desires to speak favorable things rather than speak the truth, just as another prophet also testifies, saying, "Would that I were not a man who has the spirit, and that I were speaking lies instead!"[173] Jonah, by contrast, is grieved over the fact that he has lied, and he is rebuked by the Lord on the grounds that a false statement by a prophet is more advantageous than the destruction of so great a multitude.[174] As for Jeremiah, lest he

appear to be confirming the prediction of the pseudoprophet, he sets aside the wrongdoing of a liar and delivers the truth through the example of others.

28:7-9: *"Yet hear now this word that I speak in your hearing and in the hearing of all the people. The prophets who preceded you and me from the beginning prophesied war, affliction and famine against many countries and great kingdoms. As for the prophet who prophesies peace, when the word of that prophet comes to pass, then it will be known that the Lord has truly sent the prophet."*

Jeremiah could have said to Hananiah, "You speak falsely, and you are deceiving the people. You are not a prophet but a pseudoprophet." But if he had said that, the pseudoprophet could have said the same things in return to Jeremiah. Therefore Jeremiah avoids causing insult and speaks to him as if he were a prophet. "Not only are you and I prophets," he says, "but before us there were many other prophets, such as Isaiah, Hosea, Joel, Amos, and others. They prophesied against many countries and against not small kingdoms but great ones, announcing to them war, adversity and the deprivation of all things. There were others, of course, who promised peace and prosperity. But the veracity of each message is confirmed not by the adulation that accompanies the lie but by the outcome of the events." Thus, through the examples of others Jeremiah speaks about himself and about Hananiah, asserting that the truthfulness of a prophet is shown when the final outcome of events has come to pass. The Lord also said this same thing through Moses: that a prophet is proven by the end result of his prophecy.[175] And this

---

[171]LXX 35:4. [172]Heb *'āmēn*. For the repetition of *amēn* (Gk) in the New Testament, see especially the Gospel of John (e.g., Jn 1:51; 3:3, 5, 11; 5:19, 24, 25; 6:26, 32, 47, 53; 8:34, 51, 58; 10:1, 7). [173]Mic 2:11 according to Jerome's IH edition. [174]Jon 4:1-3, 11. Cf. Jerome *Comm. Jon.* 4:2b-3, where Jonah is said to have fled from the Lord so as to avoid deceiving people or preaching what is not true of God. [175]Deut 18:21-22.

should be noted: he rebukes the liar not with fierce threats but with the assurance that comes from the truth. He defers to the future, so that those who hear may wait to see how things turn out.

28:10-11: *Then the prophet Hananiah took the fetter—or yoke, which in Hebrew is said muthoth[176]—from the neck of Jeremiah the prophet and broke it. And Hananiah spoke in the presence of all the people, saying, "Thus says the Lord: Even so will I break the yoke of Nebuchadnezzar king of Babylon from the neck of all the nations within two years." But Jeremiah the prophet went his way.*

The LXX did not translate the phrase "within two years," and they also did not say that Hananiah was a prophet, lest (no doubt) they appear to be calling someone a prophet who was not a prophet, as if there were not many things in sacred Scripture that are said in accordance with the opinion of the time in which the events took place, rather than in accordance with the actual truth of the matter.[177] Thus, Joseph in the Gospel is called the "father" of the Lord,[178] and Mary herself, who knew that she had conceived by the Holy Spirit and replied to the angel, "How shall this be, since I have no husband?"[179] says to her son, "Son, why have you treated us so? Behold, your father and I have been looking for you anxiously."[180]

At the same time, one should consider Jeremiah's prudence, humility and patience. The pseudoprophet does physical harm to Jeremiah and destroys the yoke that had been ripped from his neck—which, by the way, he

could not have done if it had been made of iron—while Jeremiah remains silent and conceals his pain. For the Lord had not revealed to him what he should say. Thus, by Jeremiah's silence holy Scripture shows that prophets do not speak merely by their own decision but by the will of God, especially regarding matters of the future, which are known to God alone. And so Jeremiah departed and "went his way," as if he had been defeated and was fulfilling this prophetic statement: "I am like a man who does not hear and in whose mouth are no rebukes."[181]

28:12-14: *After the prophet Hananiah had broken the fetter—or yoke[182]—from off the neck of Jeremiah the prophet, the word of the Lord came to Jeremiah, saying, "Go, tell Hananiah, 'Thus says the Lord: You have broken a wooden fetter,'—or 'yoke'—'but you will make'—or 'I will make'[183]—'in their place a yoke'—or 'fetters'—'of iron. For thus says the Lord of hosts, the God of Israel: I have put on the neck of all these nations an iron yoke, so that they will serve Nebuchadnezzar king of Babylon'*—and that which follows is not found in the LXX: *'and they shall serve him, for I have given to him even the beasts of the field.'"*

In the present passage according to the LXX it is not written that Hananiah is a "prophet."[184] This is also the case with what follows, since, as I said before, the LXX did not want to appear to be calling someone a prophet who is really a pseudoprophet.

But what about the Hebrew truth? After the prophet Jeremiah went on his way and

---

[176]As at Jer 27:2-4, Jerome first gives "fetter" (*catenam*) from the IH edition but then improves it according to the Hebrew. The LXX uses "collar," just as in the earlier passage. The Hebrew form here is singular (*môṭâ* ["yoke," KB 555]), but Jerome gives the plural, as it is written at Jer 27:2. Whereas at Jer 27:2 Jerome used the LXX ("collar") in order to clarify the meaning of the Hebrew, in this case he gives the sense of the Hebrew as "yoke" (matching Targ, *nyr*'). [177]See Jer 26:7-9a; cf. Jer 28:15-17. [178]Lk 2:33, 48. [179]Lk 1:34. [180]Lk 2:48. [181]Ps 38:14. [182]Jerome used "fetter" in the IH edition, but here he gives "yoke" as an option. See Jer 27:2-4; 28:10-11. In Jer 28:14, the word for "yoke" is *'ōl* (not *môṭâ*), and so Jerome uses *iugum* (not *furcam* as before). [183]Jerome matches MT and Targ. The hexaplaric versions are lacking. [184]See Jer 28:10-11.

swallowed his injury in silence, the word of the Lord came to him, so that the prophet would not have to speak with his own words to the pseudoprophet who boasted in falsehood, but he could say to the pseudoprophet, "Thus says the Lord." Of course, when Hananiah broke the wooden yoke, he spoke in the presence of the Lord by the same authority, "Thus says the Lord"; this is because falsehood always imitates the truth. And that which Jeremiah adds, "You have broken a wooden yoke, but you will make (or 'you have made') in their place fetters of iron," shows that by rejecting the lesser penalty the people brought even greater punishments on themselves.

He who interprets allegorically[185] goes astray in this passage when he identifies the wooden yoke and fetters as ethereal and airy bodies, that is, the bodies of demons and adversarial powers, and the iron yoke or chains as our more dense bodies that are woven together with tendons, bones, flesh and veins. According to this interpreter, some souls were unwilling (on account of their sinful nature) to descend from the heavenly Jerusalem and submit to lesser torments. Because of this, these unwilling souls were condemned to the fetters of our bodies and were made to endure the chains and squalor of an infant's cries and swaddling clothes. Moreover, they were made to serve the devil, who is the king of Babylon, that is, the king of this world (as Scripture says, "the whole world has been given over to the evil one"[186]), along with the beasts of the field, which have been bound within the bodies

of irrational animals. That unlearned massager and follower of the treachery of Grunnius has forced me to make public the vices of another, which formerly I would speak about discreetly so as to leave the matter to the prudence of the reader.[187]

28:15-17: *And Jeremiah the prophet said to the prophet Hananiah, "Listen, Hananiah, the Lord has not sent you, and you have made this people trust in a lie. Therefore thus says the Lord: 'Behold, I will cast you out'—or 'expel you'[188]—'from the face of the earth. This very year you shall die.'" And that which follows, "'because you have spoken against the Lord.' In that same year, in the seventh month, the prophet Hananiah died,"* is not found in the LXX; in place of this, the LXX simply put *"And he died in the seventh month."*

Here also the LXX does not say that Hananiah is a prophet, even though holy Scripture—according to the Hebrew—calls him a prophet.[189] Yet, when Jeremiah actually condemns him, saying, "Listen, Hananiah, the Lord has not sent you," he makes no mention of Hananiah being a prophet. For how could Jeremiah call him a "prophet" while denying that the Lord had sent him? But the truth and proper order of the *historia* are preserved, as we said above, not according to what was but according to that which was thought at that time.[190]

"You have deceived my people with falsehood," he says, "so that they will not accept God's command. Because of this, you should

---

[185]Origen. Cf. Jer 24:1-10; 27:2-4, 9-11. According to Jerome, Origen taught that when, as a result of sin, souls fell from their original spiritual state into states of bodily existence, the souls that were willing to submit to God's punishment adopted ethereal bodies and became demons, whereas those unwilling to accept God's punishment were forced to adopt more dense material form (i.e., a harsher punishment) and become humans. This is indeed reminiscent of Origen's belief in two creations (a spiritual and a material) and in a fall into the material world. It is unclear whether Jerome's description is accurate on every detail. On Origen's views, see *Princ.* 1.5.5; 1.6.2-3; 1.8.1-4; 2.9.6; *Philoc.* 21.21. [186]1 Jn 5:19. [187]Jerome refers to Pelagius, identifying him as a disciple of Rufinus (Grunnius; see bk. 4 prol.). Pelagius and Rufinus have forced Jerome to publicize and explicitly condemn this piece of Origen's exegesis. In the past, Jerome could have reported the exegesis and left it to the reader to make the condemnation; see the prologue to bk. 1. [188]Heb *šlḥ* (Piel; "dismiss, send away, expel," KB 1515). [189]See Jer 26:7-9a. [190]See Jer 28:10-11, 15-17. In the present passage, the narrative frame of Jer 28:15 (in Hebrew) refers to Hananiah as a prophet, but Jeremiah himself does not. According to Jerome, the narrator is following the opinion of the day, whereas Jeremiah has a specific rhetorical reason for not using the word.

know that you are going to die this very year!" If death frees us from the prison of our bodies (in accordance with this testimony, "Bring my soul out of prison,"[191] which the heretics interpret badly), why now is death being imposed on the pseudoprophet as a punishment? And this also should be noted: When Jeremiah had been wounded by the pseudoprophet but had not yet received the word of the Lord, he remained silent; but after he had been sent by the Lord, Jeremiah boldly condemned the liar and announced his impending death. As to the fact that he died in the "seventh" month: there are some who suggest that this number always indicates "rest."[192] These interpreters wrongly propose that he may have died in the "seventh" month because he was being freed from the evils of the body, citing as proof that which has been written: "Death is a person's rest."[193] We, however, know that the bodies of believers are temples of God—if, that is, the Holy Spirit dwells within them.[194]

29:1-7: *These are the words of the book that Jeremiah the prophet sent from Jerusalem to the remnant of the elders of the exile, and to the priests, the prophets and all the people, whom Nebuchadnezzar had taken into exile from Jerusalem to Babylon. This was after King Jeconiah, and the queen mother,—or queen[195]—the eunuchs, the princes of Judah and Jerusalem—or the princes of Judah from Jerusalem or else the nobles[196]—and the skilled workers[197] had departed from Jerusalem. The book was sent by the hand of Elasah the son of Shaphan and Gemariah the son of Hilkiah, whom Zedekiah king of Judah sent to Babylon to Nebuchadnezzar king of Babylon. It said: "Thus says the Lord of hosts, the God of Israel, to all the exiles whom I have sent into exile from Jerusalem to Babylon: Build houses and live in them; plant gardens"—or "orchards"[198]—"and eat their fruit. Take wives and have sons and daughters; take wives for your sons, and give your daughters to husbands, that they may bear sons and daughters; multiply there, and do not be few in number. But seek the peace of the city"—or "of the land"[199]—"to which I have sent you into exile, and pray to the Lord on its behalf, for in its peace will be your peace."*

This letter, or rather, short book of the prophet Jeremiah is sent to Babylon through Elasah and Gemariah, legates of Zedekiah, to those who were taken captive along with Jeconiah and his mother by Nebuchadnezzar. The prophet's aim is to take the opportunity afforded by a royal legation in order to complete his work and explain to those people who had been exiled what the Lord was commanding them to do. And beautifully it says, "after king Jeconiah, and the queen mother, the eunuchs, the princes of Judah, etc., had departed . . . thus says the Lord of hosts, the God of Israel, to all the exiles whom I have sent into exile from Jerusalem to Babylon." Thus, they are shown to have been taken into exile not by the power of the king of Babylon but by the will of the Lord. God's message is addressed first to the elders, then to the

---

[191]Ps 142:7. [192]E.g., Gen 2:2; Ex 16:30; 20:11; 31:15. [193]Sir 22:11; 30:17. [194]1 Cor 3:16; 6:19; 2 Cor 6:16. [195]Heb *gĕbîrâ* ("mistress," "queen mother" or "queen," KB 173). Jerome takes this to be a reference to Jeconiah's mother (see Jer 13:18-19), whereas the LXX uses the specific word for "queen." [196]The first option ("the princes of Judah and Jerusalem") is Jerome's IH translation and matches MT. The second option ("the princes of Judah from Jerusalem") is the reading under asterisk in the Hexapla taken from Th. The third option ("the nobles") represents the LXX (Jer 36:2), which reads "and all the free men." [197]The Hebrew text gives two categories of skilled workers, "craftsmen" and "metal workers." In the IH edition Jerome translated both terms (*faber et inclusor*), but here he collapses both words into the single term *artifices*. The preserved versions (LXX, Sym and Targ) all translate both words. Perhaps Jerome's eye slipped? Or perhaps he felt that the list, with all of its variant readings, was getting too long and needed to be abbreviated? [198]Heb *gannâ* ("garden," but also "paradise," KB 199). The LXX ("orchards") uses the Greek term *paradeisos*. Cf. Rev 2:7. [199]Jerome agrees with Aq, Sym and Targ (= MT).

priests, third to the prophets, and fourth to all the people, so that the letter might reach those who were being warned according to the order of their age, even for the prophets.

The prophet instructs them, not by his own words but by the words of the Lord, that they should build houses and live in them, plant gardens (or orchards) and eat their fruit, take wives and have sons and daughters, multiply in their place of exile and not be few in number, seek the peace of the city (or land) to which the Lord has sent them into exile and pray to the Lord on its behalf. And he gives the reason why they should do this: "for in the peace of this land will be your peace." Because the captivity of Jerusalem was going to take place in a short time, Jeremiah was commanded not to take a wife or to have sons.[200] Thus it is also said to us through the apostle, "The time has grown short; it remains that those who have wives should live as if they did not have them."[201] And if, on account of the difficulties of the time, the usage of wives is taken away from those who have them, how much more is it imperative for those without wives not to take them!

Yet, Jeremiah issued this whole prophetic oracle so that the exiles would not give their assent to the pseudoprophets who were promising them that after a short time they would be returned to Jerusalem. On the contrary, the exiles should know that they are going to tarry for a long time in Babylon, and so they ought to take wives, plant gardens, sow orchards, build houses and have children. And regarding what he adds, "Seek the peace of the city (or 'of the land')," and again, "for in its peace will be your peace," this confirms the apostolic saying whereby it is commanded: "First of all, then, I urge that supplications,

prayers, intercessions and thanksgivings be made for all people, for kings and all who are in high positions, that we may lead a quiet and peaceable life in all piety and chastity."[202]

Furthermore, according to the mystical understanding: When because of our sins we have been thrown out of Jerusalem, that is, the church, and handed over to Nebuchadnezzar (concerning this the apostle says, "I have handed this man over to Satan for the destruction of the flesh, that his spirit may saved in the day of the Lord," and again, "whom I have handed over to Satan, that they may learn not to blaspheme"[203]), we should not be so careless or numb with idleness that we utterly despair of salvation. Instead, we should build houses—not on the sand but on the rock[204]—of such kind as the midwives built in Exodus, because they feared the Lord;[205] then, we should plant gardens or orchards, as the Lord planted Paradise in Eden and put within it the tree of life, about which it is written, "She is a tree of life for those who lay hold of her; those who hold her fast are called blessed";[206] and third, we should take wives, one of which is wisdom, about which Solomon writes, "Love her, and she will guard you . . . encompass her, and she will exalt you,"[207] and in another passage: "I desired to take her for my bride, and I became a lover of her beauty."[208] Nor is it enough for us to have one spouse, wisdom, unless we also have the rest: fortitude, temperance and justice,[209] so that from these we may have children.

And let us also give our daughters to husbands, so that the true faith (which is represented in the sons) may be united with good works (to which the daughters refer). In this way good works may be joined with soundness of faith. And bearing such sons and

[200]Jer 16:2. [201]1 Cor 7:29. [202]1 Tim 2:1-2. [203]1 Cor 5:5; 1 Tim 1:20. [204]Mt 7:24-27; Lk 6:48-49. [205]Ex 1:21, which says (lit.), "And so, because the midwives feared God, he built for them houses." [206]Prov 3:18. [207]Prov 4:6, 8. [208]Wis 8:2. [209]"Wisdom" or "Prudence" (*sapientia*), "Fortitude" (*fortitudo*), "Temperance" (*temperantia*) and "Justice" (*iustitia*) are the four traditional cardinal virtues. See Plato *Prot.* 330b; 349b; 359a (five virtues: the four plus "piety"); *Resp.* 4.427e; 433a-c; *Leg.* 1.631c-d; 12.965d (four virtues); Wis 8:7; Cicero *Fin.* 5.23.67; *Off.* 1.2.5; Ambrose *Exp. Luc.* 5.62-68; Augustine *Mor. Eccl.* 15; *Ep.* 167.2; *Trin.* 6.4; 13.20; Jerome *Ep.* 66.3.

daughters let us multiply in number, so that as we tear down what is childish and grow into maturity we may be worthy to hear, "I am writing to you, fathers, because you know him who is from the beginning,"[210] and together with the apostle we may say to our children, "For in Christ Jesus through the gospel I fathered you."[211] Let us also seek the peace of the church, which is our city and land, so that we might be worthy to return to it after we have been taken into exile by the Lord's judgment and made to live in the error of "confusion."[212] For if it will receive us, we will live in peace. Moreover, we should take note of the Lord's mercy: He commands us to pray for our enemies and to do good to those who persecute us,[213] so that we should not be content only with our own salvation but should seek also the salvation of our enemies.

29:8-9: *"For thus says the Lord of hosts, the God of Israel: Do not let your prophets who are in your midst and your diviners deceive you, and do not listen to your dreams that you dream, for it is a lie that they are prophesying to you in my name; I did not send them, says the Lord."*

By writing against them,[214] the prophet Ezekiel attests to the fact that there were prophets or rather pseudoprophets among the people in Babylon whom Nebuchadnezzar had carried off along with Jeconiah and his mother. Jeremiah likewise admonishes that these pseudoprophets should not be trusted. Of course, at the time when this letter was sent, Ezekiel had not yet begun to prophesy in Babylon. For this message is sent at the beginning of the reign of King Zedekiah,[215]

whereas Ezekiel started to prophesy in the fifth year of the exile of Jeconiah,[216] which was also the fifth year of Zedekiah's reign.

Furthermore, according to tropology[217] we should understand as "pseudoprophets" those who interpret the words of Scripture in a manner different from what the Holy Spirit signifies. We should understand as "diviners" those who proclaim the conjectures of their minds and doubtful matters about the future as if they were true without the authority of divine words. And we should understand as "dreamers" those who do not heed what has been written: "Do not give sleep to your eyes or slumber to your eyelids."[218] The apostle Jude also speaks about them: "In like manner these men in their dreaming defile the flesh and reject authority."[219] Their minds are not watchful. Rather, they are weighed down with the heavy slumber of presumption and error, and they are surrounded by night terrors. The apostle Paul says to them, "Awake, O sleeper, and arise from the dead, and Christ shall give you light."[220]

29:10-14a: *"For thus says the Lord: When the seventy years have come to be completed in Babylon, I will visit you, and I will raise up over you my good word, that I will bring you back to this place. For I know the thoughts that I think about you, says the Lord, thoughts of peace and not of affliction, to give you a goal and patience"—or "and hope."[221] "And you will call on me, and you will come,"—or, according to Symmachus, "you will find"[222]— "and you will pray to me, and I will hear you. You will seek me and find me, when you seek me with all your heart; I will be found by you"—or "I will appear to you."[223]*

---

[210]1 Jn 2:13. [211]1 Cor 4:15. [212]"Confusion" is the traditional etymological meaning of "Babylon" (see Jer 27:2-4). [213]Mt 5:44; Lk 6:27-28. [214]Ezek 13. [215]Jer 28:1. [216]Ezek 1:2. [217]The Latin word *tropologia* is taken from a Greek rhetorical term that refers to the figurative sense of a word as opposed to its literal or proper sense. In Christian exegesis after Origen it became a technical term for the spiritual sense of the text. [218]Prov 6:4. [219]Jude 8. [220]Eph 5:14. [221]Heb *tqwh* ("expectation, hope," KB 1782). The first option ("patience") is Jerome, and the second matches Aq and Th (preserved under asterisk) and the Targ. [222]Jerome matches Aq and Th (preserved under asterisk), which agrees with MT. [223]Jerome matches MT; the second option is the LXX.

The prophet says, "Do not believe your pseudo-prophets, diviners and dreamers, who promise that you will soon return to Jerusalem. For until the seventy years are completed (when Cyrus king of the Persians sets the captives free), you will never return to your homeland. But after the seventy years I will fulfill my promises: "I will bring you back to this place. For I know the thoughts that I think about you, says the Lord." He says that he knows what he is thinking, whereas they do not know, in spite of their prophets, diviners and dreamers; thus, knowledge of the future belongs to God alone. "To give you an end and patience"—an end to captivity and patience in the present suffering (or "hope" for the future). Then "you will call on me, and you will come"—to Jerusalem—"and you will pray, and I will hear you." To be sure, the Lord was able to fulfill what he promised without the invocations and prayers of the captives; but he urges them to make entreaties so that they may be worthy to receive what has been promised. "You will seek me and find me, when you seek me with all your heart." This accords with the Gospel saying: "Ask, and you will receive; seek, and you will find; knock, and it will be opened to you."[224]

According to *anagōgē*,[225] we dwell for a long time in the "confusion" of this age,[226] until we are worthy to receive the "rest" of the number seven.[227] When our repentance has been accepted, God fulfills what he promised, and we are brought back to our place, the church. For this is the reason why the Lord appears to wound us, so that he may heal us and bring an end to our suffering and patient waiting.[228] When we will call on him, return to the church and pray, then we will be heard. We will seek and find him when we have sought him with all our heart, and then he will appear

to us. Some interpret the "seventy years" according to what is written: "The days of our years, they contain seventy years."[229] And after these years have been completed, we may return to the Lord with all our heart and be heard by him, and there will be an end to our suffering and patient waiting; for now we possess all things in shadow and shade.[230]

29:14-20: *"I will be found by you, says the Lord, and I will restore your captivity and gather you from all the nations and from all the places where I have driven you, says the Lord, and I will bring you back from the place to which I sent you into exile." "Because you have said, 'The Lord has raised up prophets for us in Babylon,' Thus says the Lord concerning the king who sits on the throne of David and concerning all the people who dwell in this city, your kinsmen who did not go out with you into exile: 'Thus says the Lord of hosts, Behold, I am sending on them sword, famine and pestilence, and I will make them like bad figs that are so bad they cannot be eaten. I will pursue them with sword, famine and pestilence, and I will make them a vexation to all the kingdoms of the earth, to be a curse, an astonishment, a hissing and a reproach among all the nations where I have driven them, because they did not heed my words, says the Lord, that I sent to you by my servants the prophets, rising at night and sending,[231] but you would not listen, says the Lord.' Hear the word of the Lord, all you exiles whom I sent away from Jerusalem to Babylon!"*

Everything that I have noted with asterisks is not contained in the LXX. As for the rest, where individual verses or a few words have been omitted by the LXX, I have chosen not to annotate all of this since I am overcome by

---

[224]Mt 7:7; Lk 11:9. [225]Following Origen and other Greek fathers, Jerome uses the Greek term *anagōgē* ("elevation") to refer to the higher or spiritual sense. [226]We dwell in Babylon, which means "confusion" (see Jer 27:2-4). [227]The number seven signifies "rest" (see Jer 28:15-17). [228]Deut 32:39; Job 5:18; Hos 6:1; Is 19:22. [229]Ps 90:10. [230]Job 8:9; 14:2; Pss 144:4; 39:6; 1 Cor 13:12. [231]Jer 25:3; 26:4-6.

weariness and I do not want to annoy the reader.

The Lord promises those in exile that after seventy years of captivity he will bring them back from every nation and from all the places to which he expelled them, and that once their captivity is undone he will restore them to their former position and to their homeland. "And since I am going to do these things of my own accord," he says, "and I will restore you at a specified time, it is pointless for you to be deceived and to suppose that you have prophets in Babylon who make false promises to you. Thus, you should know that you ought not to hope for immediate restoration, but you should build houses, plant orchards, take wives, have sons, multiply in number and wait for the promised time.[232] Hear what the Lord says to Zedekiah, who presently reigns in Jerusalem, and to all the inhabitants of this city, that is, all your kinsmen who were unwilling to submit to my judgment and depart with you to Babylon: there is no way that they can escape captivity, but they will die by the sword, famine and pestilence." And he will make them like "bad figs," which Theodotion translated as *sudrinas*, the second edition of Aquila as "very bad" and Symmachus as "very recent." In Hebrew they are called *suarim*, but the Greek letter *delta* crept in by a mistake of the scribes in place of the middle syllable (or letter) *alpha*, so that *sudrim* was written instead of *suarim*.[233] And just as a basket or wicker bin that has good figs is said to contain "first fruits," so also another basket that has bad figs is described as containing "very recent" figs.

The Lord says, "I will pursue those who now dwell in the city of Jerusalem with sword, famine and pestilence. Thus, having first been consumed by the siege,[234] those who are able to survive and flee will be scattered into all lands and will become an example of cursing, astonishment, hissing and reproach to all places where I will drive them. This will happen because they did not heed my words, says the Lord, which I spoke to them through my servants. Rising at night and sending, I never ceased admonishing them that they should imitate you who are now enjoying safety and ease in exile until the promise of the Lord is fulfilled. But you who obeyed my decree and handed yourselves over to the king of Babylon, hear the words that I am going to say."

In this passage, that interpreter who goes astray[235] dreams up the fall of the heavenly Jerusalem. He supposes that this prophecy is directed at those who dwell in the "Babylonian region" (that is, this world), and he contends that they did well to descend willingly into bodies, build houses in the land of the Chaldeans, plant orchards, take wives and have sons. And because of their good deeds (so this interpreter argues), those who dwell in this world will be restored after seventy years to their former place in the heavenly Jerusalem.

On the other hand (according to this interpreter), those who were unwilling to descend to the earthly domain will suffer what the Lord threatens to Zedekiah and to those people who refused to imitate their brothers and go to Babylon. The Lord will send to them sword, famine and pestilence, that is, the lack of all things, and he will make them like very bad figs, which certainly cannot be eaten.

---

[232]Jer 29:5-6. [233]The Hebrew word is *šō'ārîm* (meaning "difficult"; see KB 1618; RSV: "vile"). In Jerome's copy of Th, the word appeared transcribed into Greek as *sudrinas*, with a "d" sound in the middle of the word instead of an "a." Jerome takes this to be an error in the copying of Th's Greek text (as shown by his giving the letters in Greek, not Hebrew), and he corrects it by going back to the original Hebrew to show how the word should be transcribed (notice how he replaces the Greek ending -*as* with the Hebrew -*im*). For my "second edition of Aquila," the Latin text merely has "second." This difficulty in the Latin caused Reiter to suggest that the first edition of Aquila was also mentioned in connection with the faulty transcription. But I think it unlikely that the same copying error would have arisen in both Th's and Aq's "first edition," so I am taking Jerome's "second" to refer on its own to Aq's "second edition." [234]I am reading *confecti* in place of *confestim*, following Vallarsi. [235]Origen; see Jer 24:1-10; 27:9-11; 28:12-14.

Moreover, the Lord will pursue them with an everlasting sword and will make them a vexation to all the kingdoms of the earth, in order that they may become not humans but demons—airy powers[236]—and that they may be a curse, an astonishment, a hissing and a reproach among all the nations, in the presence of all the angels who preside over the various individual territories. They will suffer these things because in the heavenly Jerusalem they would not listen to the words of the prophets, who told them that they should descend to the earthly domain and assume a lowly body,[237] and that once they had repented and their true sabbath rest[238] was over, they could take possession of their former place.

This interpreter has indeed said these things. When his disciples and the excrement of Grunnius's[239] household hear them, they think that they have heard divine mysteries. Moreover, they regard us who despise such things as irrational beasts, calling us "Pelusians,"[240] on the grounds that we are stuck in the mud of this body and cannot perceive heavenly things.

29:21-23: *"Thus says the Lord of hosts, the God of Israel, concerning Ahab the son of Kolaiah and Zedekiah the son of Maaseiah, who are prophesying falsely to you in my name: Behold, I will deliver them into the hand of Nebuchadnezzar king of Babylon, and he shall slay them before your eyes. On account of them this curse shall be used by all the exiles from Judah in Babylon, saying, 'The Lord make you like Zedekiah and Ahab, whom the king of Babylon roasted in the fire,' because they have committed foolishness"—or "lawlessness"[241]— "in Israel, they have committed adultery with the wives of their friends"—or "fellow citizens"[242]—"and they have spoken falsely in my name a word that I did not command them. I am the judge and the witness, says the Lord."*

The Hebrews[243] say that these men who "committed foolishness in Israel" and "committed adultery with the wives of their fellow citizens" are the elders to whom Daniel spoke, saying to one, "You old relic of wicked days!" and saying to the other, "You offspring of Canaan and not of Judah, beauty has deceived you and lust has perverted your heart! This is how you have been dealing with the daughters of Israel, and they were conversing with you through fear; but a daughter of Judah would not endure your wickedness."[244] As for what the prophet says now, "they have spoken falsely in my name a word that I did not command them," the Hebrews believe that it points to this: these elders deceived wretched and weak women, who were carried about with every wind of doctrine,[245] by telling them that they were from the tribe of Judah and that the Christ was to be born from their seed. And these women, beguiled by desire, offered their bodies so as to be the future mothers of Christ. But what is said in the present passage, "whom the king of Babylon roasted in the fire," appears to contradict the *historia* of Daniel, which asserts that the elders were stoned to

---

[236]Eph 2:2. [237]Phil 3:21. [238]Heb 4:9. [239]*Grunnius* means "grunter," referring to Rufinus; see the Introduction. On the phrase "excrement of Grunnius's household," see Cicero *De Or.* 3.164. [240]Residents of Pelusium in Egypt. The Greek word *Pelusian* (Jerome gives the word in Greek) is related to the Greek word for "mud" (*pēlos*); see Strabo 17.1.21. On Origen's exegesis, see Jerome *Jo. Hier.* 19. [241]Heb *něbālâ* ("stupidity" or "willful sin," KB 664). [242]Heb *rēaʿ* ("friend, neighbor," KB 1254; Aq: "companions"; Sym: "neighbors"). [243]Jerome has taken over this Jewish tradition from Origen, who reported two separate Jewish interpretations, one that identified the wicked elders of Susanna with Ahab and Zedekiah (Jer 29:21-23), and another that describes how Ahab and Zedekiah committed adultery by claiming that they would father the Messiah (Origen *Ep. Afr.* 7-8). Jerome has combined these two interpretations (see also Jerome *Expl. Dan.* 13:5). Rabbinic sources do not offer exact parallels, but *b. Sanhedrin* 93a describes the adulteries of Ahab and Zedekiah and tells how they were condemned by Nebuchadnezzar with the aid of the three youths from Dan 3, and *Tanḥuma Vayyiqra* 6 reports that Ahab and Zedekiah committed adultery by promising women that they would father prophets through them. [244]Dan 13:52, 56-77 (i.e., Sus 52, 56-57). [245]2 Tim 3:6-7; Eph 4:14.

death by the people as a result of Daniel's judgment,[246] whereas here it is written that the king of Babylon roasted them in the fire. For this reason, this story is rejected as a mere fable by many of us and by almost all of the Hebrews; nor do they read it in their synagogues.[247] "For how could it be," it is argued, "that captives had the authority to stone their own leaders and prophets?" And more important than this, they affirm the truth of what Jeremiah writes: that the elders were indeed convicted by Daniel but that judgment was brought against them by the king of Babylon, who as conqueror and lord had supreme power over those whom he had captured.

How many of our own flock, like Ahab and Zedekiah, prophesy falsehood in the name of the Lord, commit foolishness in Israel and commit adultery with the wives of their fellow citizens who were born of the very same city, the church! The true Nebuchadnezzar[248] will roast them in the fire of sin, as Hosea the prophet says: "They are all adulterers, like an oven heated by the baker."[249] Fortunate is the one who bears the yoke in his youth and who sits alone because he is filled with bitterness;[250] he is able to say with David, "I do not sit in the council of the wicked, and with workers of iniquity I do not walk."[251] And as for what the prophet now adds, "I am the judge and the witness, says the Lord," it has this sense: "Regarding these things that I am saying about the two pseudoprophets who speak falsely in my name a word that I did not

command them, I did not come to know these things by conjecture, but I myself know them to be true. No one can hide anything from me or escape the truth of my judgment."

29:24-29: To Shemaiah of Nehelam you shall say,—And that which follows is not found in the LXX: *"Thus says the Lord of hosts, the God of Israel: Because you sent books in your name to all the people who are in Jerusalem,"*—and yet the LXX added of themselves: *"I did not send you in my name"*—and then continuing properly: *"and to Zephaniah the son of Maaseiah the priest"*—and again from the Hebrew: *"and to all the priests, saying,"*—then, the *historia* is put forward: *" 'The Lord has made you priest instead of Jehoiada the priest, so that you might be leader'*—or 'ruler' or 'overseer'[252]—*'in the house of the Lord over every madman who prophesies, to put him in fetters and in prison'*—or 'in confinement and in a sluice.' In place of "sluice,"* Symmachus translated *mochlon,* and Aquila put the Hebrew word itself, *sinac.*[253] *'Now why have you not rebuked Jeremiah of Anathoth who is prophesying to you? For he has sent to us in Babylon, saying, "It will be long; build houses and live in them, and plant gardens and eat their fruit." ' "* And so Zephaniah the priest read this book in the hearing of Jeremiah the prophet.

Shemaiah from the place called "Nehelam" (which is interpreted as "torrent")[254] was taken to Babylon together with king Jeconiah, and he

---

[246]Dan 13:61-62 (i.e., Sus 61-62). [247]Jerome accepts the tradition that identifies the elders mentioned in Susanna as Ahab and Zedekiah, but he rejects the story of Susanna itself as a fable, since it is unlikely that the Jews under foreign rule would have had the authority to execute people, and, more importantly, because (based on the given identification) the book of Jeremiah gives a different and more plausible account of the deaths of Ahab and Zedekiah. In the *Expl. Dan.* 13:60, Jerome suggests that either the identification of Ahab and Zedekiah is incorrect or Sus 62 should not be taken literally but means that the people handed the wicked elders over to the king of Babylon to be put to death. [248]The devil; see Jer 27:6-7a. [249]Hos 7:4. [250]Lam 3:27, 28, 15. [251]Ps 26:4; see also the LXX (25:4). [252]Heb *pāqîd* ("overseer," "leader," KB 960). The first option is Jerome, the second represents the LXX, and the third is Sym. [253]The Hebrew words are *mahpeket* ("stocks" or "block," KB 553) and *ṣînōq* ("difficult," but KB 1023: "neck iron"). The first option is Jerome's version. The first alternative ("in confinement and in a sluice") is the LXX. Jerome also reports that Aq transliterated the second Hebrew word (*ṣînōq*), and he gives the Greek word used by Sym for *ṣînōq* (*mochlon* ["iron bar," LSJ 1149]). [254]Heb *nhlm*. In *Nom. Hebr.* (OS 55.1) Jerome had reported "someone's inheritance" as the meaning of this name (cf. Heb *nhlh*, "inheritance"). Here, he gives the meaning as "torrent" (cf. Heb *nhl*, "torrent" or "river valley"). See also Jer 29:30-32.

prophesied falsely to the people, saying that they would quickly return to Jerusalem. The following words of Jeremiah show that he was a pseudoprophet: "Thus says the Lord concerning Shemaiah of Nehelam: Because Shemaiah prophesied to you when I did not send him . . ."[255]

Jeremiah sent a letter to those who were in Babylon, saying, "Build houses and live in them; plant gardens and eat their fruit. Take wives and have sons!"[256] and after some other things he added, "Do not let the prophets who are in your midst and your diviners deceive you!" and then, "for it is a lie that they are prophesying to you in my name; I did not send them, says the Lord."[257] Because Jeremiah wrote this, Shemaiah, who understood that under the general term "pseudoprophet" Jeremiah was writing against him, sent a letter in opposition to Jeremiah to the priest Zephaniah the son of Maaseiah and the rest of the priests in Jerusalem, asking why the priest Zephaniah had not rebuked Jeremiah, since it was Zephaniah's duty to discern among the prophets which ones spoke by the Holy Spirit and which by a contrary spirit. Furthermore, Shemaiah ordered that Jeremiah be locked up in prison to make him suffer the penalty for his lies and cease from disturbing the people any further.

Now, Jehoiada was the priest who handed over ruling power to Joash after Athaliah was slain, and he had the priest of Baal put to death.[258] This, in effect, is what Shemaiah wrote: "Why didn't you imitate the priest Jehoiada and have the pseudoprophet Jeremiah put to death? For the Lord has set you in the place of Jehoiada so that you may have responsibility for the temple and so that you may discern who is speaking by the Holy Spirit and

who is speaking by a demonic spirit." Indeed, the apostle mentions "discerning between spirits" as a gift given by the Lord.[259] "Why have you not rebuked Jeremiah of Anathoth?" Shemaiah said. Shemaiah proposed that what he himself deserved as a pseudoprophet be done to the prophet Jeremiah, thereby hindering truth with a lie.

Thus, those who show discretion are regarded as children of darkness by those who are the "children of light" in this generation.[260] While we conduct ourselves patiently and hope for the salvation of these lamentable persons, the heretics hinder us and call us by their own name, even though they are blind men leading the blind into a pit.[261]

Shemaiah said, "For he has sent to us in Babylon, saying, 'It will be long'"—that is, all the hardship will be long. Jeremiah wrote the truth in opposition to Shemaiah's lie, saying that the return of the exiles would take a long time and that only after seventy years were they going to return to Jerusalem. And for this reason they should build houses, plant orchards and eat their fruit, take wives and have sons, as the previous message described.[262]

When Zephaniah the priest (to whom this letter was specifically written) received the letter, he read it to Jeremiah, beating up on him in a certain sense and rebuking him by the very reading itself for daring to write such things to Babylon.

29:30-32: *Then the word of the Lord came to Jeremiah: "Send to all the exiles, saying, 'Thus says the Lord concerning Shemaiah of Nehelam: Because Shemaiah has prophesied to you when I did not send him and has made you trust in a lie, (therefore thus says the Lord:*

---

[255]Jer 29:31.   [256]Jer 29:5-6.   [257]Jer 29:8, 9.   [258]2 Kings 11:17-21; 2 Chron 23:12-21.   [259]1 Cor 12:10.   [260]Lk 16:8.   [261]Mt 15:14; Lk 6:39. See bk. 4 prol., where Jerome refers to his attempts to remain silent and show caution in the context of his dispute with Rufinus and others whom Jerome associates with Pelagianism. Jerome believes that he has shown discretion in his conflict with these "heretics," and he feels that they have maligned him falsely.   [262]Jer 29:1-7.

Behold, I will visit Shemaiah of Nehelam and his seed; he shall not have anyone to sit in the midst of this people, and he shall not see the good that I will do to my people, says the Lord, for he has talked rebellion against the Lord.' "

Shemaiah the pseudoprophet, truly from "Nehelam" since he drew alien and turbid waters from a "torrent,"[263] becomes angry over the fact that Jeremiah wrote the truth in opposition to his own lie. He writes a letter to the priest Zephaniah asking why the prophet dared to write the truth, and he desires that the prophet be locked up in prison so that he will not speak. Zephaniah also condemns the prophet, but Zephaniah does so subtly as he reads the liar's epistle and makes known Shemaiah's accusation against Jeremiah. How very much they participate in the crime, they who defend pseudoprophets, encourage liars and make things that have been wrongly contrived by others into their own sins!

Therefore, let the pseudoprophet hear and let the priest understand what he himself deserves to hear through the prophet: "Thus says the Lord: Behold, I will visit Shemaiah." The Lord says this, not the prophet. The Lord will visit Shemaiah of Nehelam, not to restore but to punish the liar, as it is written: "I will visit their crimes with the rod and their sins with scourges."[264] And the Lord visits not only the pseudoprophet but also his seed, that is, all his disciples whom he has deceived by his error. The Lord says, "He shall not have anyone to sit in the midst of this people." May the wicked lineage of Shemaiah the pseudoprophet be cut off from the assembly of the saints and have nowhere to sit in the midst of those who are at rest. Indeed, he was not able to stand with those who stood,[265] and he did not heed this statement: "If he had stood in my counsel."[266] Although the Lord promises to give us perfection in all the virtues after the seventy years is completed, Shemaiah will not see the good that he already claims for himself in the present time.

Lastly, all of this will come about "because he has talked rebellion against the Lord," in that Shemaiah said that the people of Judah had already been freed from the captivity of sins[267] and were about to return to Jerusalem. The apostle chides them in this way: "Already you are filled! Already you have become rich! Without us you have become kings! And would that you did reign, so that we might share the rule with you!"[268]

BOOK SIX

The vastness of the book of Jeremiah the prophet overcomes our resolution, so that, however briefly we speak, we nevertheless speak many words. Thus, the present sixth book of our commentary on Jeremiah will contain mystical promises that the Jews and our Judaizers think will be fulfilled at the consummation of the world. For they have not yet been able to demonstrate that these promises were fulfilled under Zerubbabel. But we, following the authority of the apostles and evangelists—and above all the apostle Paul—will show that whatever was promised carnally to the people Israel has been fulfilled spiritually in us and is being fulfilled today. Between Christians and Jews there is no other conflict than this: although both we and they believe that Christ the son of God has been promised,[1] we say that the future things pertaining to Christ have already been fulfilled, whereas they say that they are yet to be fulfilled. If,

---

[263]See Jer 29:24-29. [264]Ps 89:32. [265]Ezek 1:21. [266]Jer 23:22; cf. Jer 23:18. [267]Jn 8:34. [268]1 Cor 4:8. **Book Six** [1]It is true that there were Jews in Jerome's day who believed in a promised messianic figure based on the Hebrew Bible, but Jerome's comment here should not be taken to mean that he knew of Jews who expected the Messiah to be the "son of God." Rather, in all likelihood Jerome refers to Christians whose views he regarded as "Judaizing." See Michael Graves, " 'Judaizing' Christian Interpretations of the Prophets As Seen by Saint Jerome," *Vigiliae Christianae* 61 (2007): 142-56.

therefore, we believe that Christ has already come, it is necessary that we teach that all the future things that were said pertaining to Christ have been fulfilled and that we are the children of Abraham. About these children it is written: "God is able from these stones to raise up children of Abraham."[2] And to Abraham the promise was made: "And in your seed all nations will be blessed."[3] Moreover, the "chosen vessel"[4] teaches us that this blessing was fulfilled in Christ, when he says, "He did not say, 'in seeds,' but 'in the seed,' who is Christ."[5]

Therefore, O brother Eusebius, pray to the Lord Jesus Christ that we may be enabled to explain the promises of this prophecy by the same effort and grace of the Spirit by which we interpreted the promises of the other prophets, especially Isaiah. However much Jeremiah seems simple and easy in his words,[6] by so much is he deeply profound in the majesty of his thoughts.

30:1-3: *The word that came to Jeremiah from the Lord: "Thus says the Lord, the God of Israel: Write in a book all the words that I have spoken to you. For behold, days are coming, says the Lord, when I will restore the restoration of my people, Israel and Judah, says the Lord, and I will return them"—or "I will seat them"[7]—"in the land that I gave to their fathers, and they shall take possession of it."*

While the pseudoprophets in Babylon and Hananiah the son of Azzur in Jerusalem were promising the people who had been taken captive with Jeconiah that they would be coming back soon,[8] Jeremiah the prophet maintained that this would not happen within two years, as the others were falsely claiming, but at the end of seventy years. Now Jeremiah is commanded to write in a book and transmit to posterity the things that will take place, which the Lord announced beforehand. From this it is clear that the time of the prophecy is not near; rather, these things will be fulfilled after a long time, when Israel and Judah will have returned to their land and when Ezekiel's prophecy will have come to pass that the two sticks shall be joined together and David shall rule as king,[9] as is written of him: "My servant David shall be king over them, and they shall all have one shepherd."[10] Therefore, whatever we said concerning that prophecy[11] should also be understood with regard to the present passage, especially since Ezekiel in Babylon and Jeremiah in Jerusalem prophesied the same things at the same time.

30:4-6: *These are the words that the Lord spoke concerning Israel and Judah: "Thus says the Lord: We have heard a voice of terror";— or "fear"—"there is dread and not peace. Ask now, and see, can a man bear a child? Why then do I see every man with his hands on his loins like a woman in labor? Why has every face turned yellow?"*

Sorrowful things are announced first, so that after the abundance of calamity joyous things may follow. Health is indeed more pleasing after illness has been expelled and the abundance of grief turns into an abundance of gladness. What Jeremiah says is this: Their

---

[2]Mt 3:9. [3]Gen 22:18; 26:4; 28:14; Acts 3:25. [4]The "chosen vessel" is the apostle Paul; see Acts 9:15. [5]Gal 3:16. [6]In the prologue to Jerome's IH edition of Jeremiah, Jerome states that Jeremiah's style in Hebrew is rustic and simple owing to his small-town origins in Anathoth. In the IH prologue to Isaiah, Jerome says that Isaiah was a noble man who spoke with eloquence and urbanity, with no rusticity mixed in. In the IH prologue to Ezekiel, Jerome represents Ezekiel as a middle ground between urbanity and simplicity. This threefold division of grand, simple and middle styles goes back to a standard model in Roman times for describing the kinds of speaking used in rhetoric; see Dionysius of Halicarnassus *Dem.* 1-3; Quintilian 12.10.58-65; Cicero *Or. Brut.* 21.69-70; Aulus Gellius *Noct. Att.* 6.14.1-11. See Graves, *Jerome's Hebrew Philology*, 62-68. [7]Whereas the first option is Jerome, the second matches the reading of Aq as preserved in the Syro-Hexapla. Jerome (like MT, LXX and Targ) understands the word as a Hiphil of *šwb* ("to cause to return"), whereas Aq interpreted it as a Hiphil of *yšb* ("to cause to sit"). [8]Jer 27:16; 28:1-4. [9]Ezek 37:16-25. [10]Ezek 37:24. [11]In his *Comm. Ezech.*

fear and dread will be exceedingly great because peace will be driven away and all things will be filled with war and blood. Even men—whose responsibility is to fight against enemies—will be seized with womanly terror, and they will clasp their hands together to take hold not of their weapons but of their stomachs, like a woman giving birth holds her loins. As a result of this everyone's face will turn yellow, each one showing the terror of his heart by the paleness of his face.

Some people interpret this passage according to tropology[12] by citing this testimony: "Out of fear of you, O Lord, we have conceived and been in labor and given birth; the Spirit of your salvation we have wrought on the earth."[13] They also cite as a parallel the apostolic testimony where he says, "My little children, with whom I am again in travail until Christ be formed in you."[14] But these testimonies clearly pertain not to terror but to gladness, whereas the present Scripture points to a time of ruin and devastation for Israel.

30:7: *"Alas, for that day is great, nor is there anything like it; it is a time of distress for Jacob; yet he shall be saved out of it."*

He predicts a time of misery so that he may introduce a time of joy. Even though such great evils have taken place that the suffering of all the men is compared with the suffering of a woman giving birth, nevertheless the distress of Jacob (that is, of the people of God) will be changed into prosperity, and "he shall be saved out of it" (one should understand "out of the time"—that is, the time being described in this discourse). Understand "Jacob" as the twelve tribes, which were not saved under Zerubbabel

as some persons falsely think, but were saved by the calling of the gospel.

30:8-9: *"And it shall come to pass in that day, says the Lord of hosts, that I will break his yoke from off your neck, and I will burst his bonds, and strangers shall no more rule over them. But they shall serve"*—or *"work for"*[15]— *"the Lord their God and David their king, whom I will raise up for them."*

This is the David who is also mentioned in the Gospel: "to grant us that we, being delivered from the hand of our enemies, might serve this one without fear, in holiness and righteousness before him all the days of our life."[16] For just as the first Adam and the second Adam are described according to their bodily reality,[17] so also with "David" our Lord and Savior, for everything of the flesh within him came from David. He received from holy Mary whatever was from the stock of David, and he possessed his origin and conception from the Holy Spirit. As for what he says, "I will break his yoke from off your neck, and I will burst his bonds," it should no doubt be interpreted under the type of Nebuchadnezzar as a reference to the devil.

30:10-11: *"Then fear not, O Jacob my servant, says the Lord, nor be dismayed, O Israel; for lo, I will save you from a far-off land and your seed from the land of their captivity. Jacob shall return and have quiet and abound in all things, and there shall be none whom he shall fear. For I am with you to save you, says the Lord; I will make a full end of all the nations among whom I scattered you, but of you I will not make a full end. But I will chastise"*—or *"instruct"*[18]— *"you in judgment, so that you do not seem to*

---

[12]The Latin word *tropologia* is taken from a Greek rhetorical term that refers to the figurative sense of a word as opposed to its literal or proper sense. In Christian exegesis after Origen it became a technical term for the spiritual sense of the text. [13]Is 26:18 (LXX). [14]Gal 4:19. [15]Heb *'bd* ("to work," "to work for someone, serve," KB 773). Jerome agrees with Sym. [16]Lk 1:74-75. [17]1 Cor 15:44-45, "according to their bodily reality" (*iuxta corporis veritatem*). [18]Heb *ysr* (Piel; "chastise, rebuke" or "teach," KB 418-19). The first option is Jerome and the second agrees with Aq, Sym and Th (but Jerome's statement below is the only evidence for Aq).

yourself to be innocent"—or "and cleansing, I will not cleanse you."[19]

This pericope is not found in the LXX, and in several codices of the common edition it has been added under asterisk from Theodotion.[20] The divine word makes a promise to them and calls Jacob and Israel by the intimate name "my servant" (Moses and the other prophets also boasted in this title, as did the apostle Paul at the beginning of his epistles),[21] so that the two and ten (that is, twelve) tribes might know that they will be saved from a far-off land. Furthermore, their captivity will be ended, peace will be restored to them, and they will be filled with abundance in everything, as it says in the psalm: "May peace be within your walls and abundance within your towers!"[22] This will happen because they will enjoy the Lord's presence when the enemy nations that captured them go to ruin and they are freed from these nations. They were handed over not for punishment but for instruction, and he teaches them so that they may be judged as his own, not destroyed as strangers. For "he who does not believe is condemned already,"[23] that is, he has been sentenced beforehand to destruction.

As for what he adds, "so that you do not seem to yourself to be innocent"—or, according to Symmachus, "and cleansing, I will not cleanse you," or, according to Aquila, "(Although I will instruct you through judgment), by no means will I render you innocent"—it signifies this: the whole world is in need of God's compassion; there is no one, however holy he may be, who proceeds securely up to the Judge. This may be taken against the new

heresy, derived from an old one,[24] which supposes that in this age and in this mortal flesh—even before this perishable nature puts on the imperishable and this mortal nature puts on immortality[25]—anyone can attain perfection and the just person is able to fulfill all the virtues at the same time.

30:12-15: "For thus says the Lord: Your break is incurable, and your wound is grievous. There is none to judge your case in order to bind it; there is no remedy of healing for you. All your lovers have forgotten you; they do not seek you out; for I have struck you with the blow of an enemy, with cruel"—or "strong"[26]—"chastisement; because of the vastness of your iniquity, your sins have become hardened"—or "have multiplied."[27] "Why do you cry out over your hurt? Your pain is incurable. Because of the vastness of your iniquity, because your sins have become hardened, I have done these things to you."

He speaks as if to a beautiful woman, to whom he said above: "I will chastise you in judgment, so that you do not seem to yourself to be innocent."[28] And metaphorically he speaks to Jerusalem,[29] in that Jerusalem was badly wounded by the judgment of God. Moreover, there is no way that she can be cured by any healer other than by the very one who struck her: "There is none," he says, "to judge your case"—nor is there any to cover over the scarred skin of your deep wound. "Wherever you turn, 'there is no remedy for you,' since you have offended God, who is the only true physician. 'All your lovers have forgotten you,' either your

---

[19]The first option is Jerome and the second is Sym. Jerome agrees with neither Aq ("by no means will I render you innocent") nor with Th ("And holding guiltless, I will not hold you guiltless"); Heb *nqh* (Piel; "to leave unpunished, declare free from punishment," KB 720). The Hebrew construction is the infinitive absolute plus finite verb, which Th and Sym render in a literalistic way. Aq gives the sense of the Hebrew idiom, whereas Jerome offers a loose paraphrase suited to the context. [20]This passage is absent from the LXX but is found in some Greek MSS under asterisk, as Jerome reports. [21]Ex 4:10; 14:31; Num 11:11; 12:7; Deut 34:5; Josh 1:1-2, passim; Rom 1:1; Phil 1:1; Tit 1:1; Philem 1. [22]Ps 122:7. [23]Jn 3:18. [24]Pelagianism derived from Origen; cf. Jer 20:14-18; 23:9b; 25:3. [25]1 Cor 15:53. [26]Heb *'akzārî* ("cruel," KB 45). "The Three" (i.e., Aq, Sym and Th) have "merciless." [27]Heb *ʿṣm* ("be powerful, be countless," KB 868). [28]Jer 30:11. [29]Cf. Jer 6:2-4a.

priests and leaders, or else the angelic guardians who protected you before you offended the Lord. 'They do not seek you out,' acting contrary to the apostle, who sought out the believers, not what belonged to the believers.[30] 'For I have struck you with the blow of an enemy, with cruel chastisement.'" It is one thing to be struck by a friend; it is something else to be struck by a foe. It is one thing to be struck by a father; something else by an enemy. The one beats in order to correct; the other strikes in order to kill. Therefore the prophet mournfully says, "O Lord, do not rebuke me in your anger or discipline me in your wrath!"[31] This happened, however, for the following reason: "because of the vastness of your iniquity, your sins have become hardened."

And that which follows, "Why do you cry out over your hurt? Your pain is incurable. Because of the vastness of your iniquity," is not found in the LXX. Evidently, since the phrase "because of the vastness of your iniquity . . . your sins have become hardened" is said a second time, those who wrote at first thought that it had been added.[32] This is the sense: "The vastness of your iniquity and your hard-hearted sins caused me to strike you with the blow of an enemy and beat you with cruel chastisement. Your sins could not be cured except through biting dust, a fiery branding iron and sharp metal, with which I could amputate the rotting and incurable flesh. Still, it is because of the vastness of your iniquity and your hardened sins that I have done these things to you—not because I wanted to, but because my concern for healing you compelled me.

30:16-17: *"Therefore all who consume you*

shall be devoured, and every one of your foes shall go into captivity; those who ravage you shall be ravaged, and all who prey on you I will make a prey. For I will heal your scar, and from your wounds I will cure you, says the Lord, because they have called you an outcast":—or "dispersed"[33]*—" 'Zion, she who has no one seeking after her!' "*

We know that these things took place under Zerubbabel. When the Babylonians and Chaldeans ravaged the Assyrians (that is, Nineveh), and after that the Medes and Persians conquered the Babylonians and Chaldeans, destroying Babylon, then Zion began to have the Lord seeking after her; the scar of her wound was healed, and she was cured from her blows. This was fulfilled more fully and more perfectly in Christ.

30:18-22: *"Thus says the Lord: Behold, I will restore the restoration of the tents of Jacob and have compassion on their dwellings";—or "captivity"*[34]*—"the city shall be rebuilt on its mound, and the temple shall be founded according to its order. Out of them shall come praise and the voice of those who celebrate. I will multiply them, and they shall not be few."* And that which follows, *"I will glorify them, and I shall not diminish them,"* is not found in the LXX.[35] It says, *"Their sons shall be as in the beginning, and their congregation shall remain before me; and I will punish all who oppress them. Their leader shall be one of themselves, their ruler shall come forth from their midst; I will make him draw near, and he shall approach me, for who is this who sets his heart to draw near to me? says the Lord."* And again, that which follows in the Hebrew is not

---

[30]2 Cor 12:14.   [31]Ps 38:1.   [32]Jerome seems to have in mind the original translators of the LXX as those who deleted the verse because they thought it had been wrongly added, since it repeats phrases from Jer 30:14 (cf. Jer 22:29-30).   [33]Jerome agrees with Sym (and perhaps also Aq and Th). Heb *ndh* (Niphal participle; "scattered," KB 673, or "banished, outcast," BDB 623).   [34]Jerome agrees with Aq, but the IH edition, like MT and Aq, has "his dwellings."   [35]The missing clause was available in the Hexapla under asterisk (from Th), but Jerome's rendering of the first verb ("glorify") is closer to the Hebrew. The Hebrew has *kbd* in the Hiphil (cf. *kābôd*, "glory"), whereas Th has "pour out."

found in the LXX: *"And you shall be my people, and I will be your God."*

A type of these things took place previously in Zerubbabel and Ezra when the people returned, the city began to be rebuilt on its mound, the ceremonies of the temple started to be observed, and so forth. These events are found in Ezra's own book. But this has been fulfilled more fully and more perfectly in our Lord and Savior and in the apostles, when the city was rebuilt "on its mound"—the city about which it is written, "A city set on a hill cannot be hid."[36] And the temple was founded "according to its order" and ceremonies, such that whatever took place carnally among the former people is fulfilled spiritually in the church.[37] Then there came forth "praise" or "thanksgiving"—for this is what *thoda* means[38]—so that all the apostles could say, "Grace to you and peace."[39] And there came forth "the voice of those who celebrate"—not the sort of celebration with which the people ate and drank and rose up to play,[40] but the kind with which David celebrated before the ark of the Lord.[41] They were "multiplied" and were "not few," so that the whole world might believe in God our Savior. And they were "glorified," so as to fulfill what is written: "Glorious things are spoken of you, O city of God."[42] "Their sons"—that is, the apostles— "were as in the beginning," that is, as Abraham, Isaac and Jacob, rulers of Israel's offspring. Then, the Lord "punished all who oppressed" God's people; that is, he punished the adversarial powers.[43] "Their leader" was "one of themselves"—no doubt this is our Lord and Savior, who according to the flesh is one of the offspring of Israel. And "their

ruler" was "brought forth from their midst." The Father "made him draw near" to himself, and he "approached" the Father, so that the Son could say, "I am in the Father and the Father in me."[44] For no one is able to "set his heart" on the Lord like this, nor can anyone be joined to the Father as the Son is joined to the Father. As for what he says according to the Hebrew but not the LXX, "And you shall be my people, and I will be your God," we perceive that this was indeed fulfilled partially in Israel, but it was fulfilled fully in the multitude of nations.

30:23-24: *"Behold the whirlwind of the Lord! Wrath has gone forth, a rushing tempest; it will settle on the head of the wicked. The Lord will not turn back the wrath of his anger until he has executed and accomplished the intent of his heart. In the latter days you will understand this."*

The whirlwind of the Lord's wrath, a rushing tempest and storm, will settle on the head of the "wicked," who are either demons or else those who have blasphemed the Son of God. He "will not turn back the wrath of his anger until he has executed and accomplished the intent of his heart," that is, until Jerusalem is surrounded by an army and thoroughly wiped out. And just as an artist cannot be understood until his work is completed, nor can the effectiveness of medicine be understood until good health has been restored, so also it was only after the overthrow of Jerusalem and the expulsion of the prior people that the believers could understand that the rejection of the Jews is the occasion for our salvation.

---

[36]Mt 5:14. [37]See *Comm. Jer.* 21:13-14, bk. 6 prol.; *Comm. Ezech.* 13:1-3a. [38]Heb *tôdâ* (properly "thanksgiving," or more generally "praise," KB 1695). Jerome may have learned this from Aq (see Aq's *eucharistia* for *tôdâ* at Lev 7:12). [39]Rom 1:7; 1 Cor 1:3; 2 Cor 1:2; Gal 1:3; Eph 1:2; Phil 1:2; Col 1:2; 1 Thess 1:1; 2 Thess 1:2; Philem 3; 1 Pet 1:2; 2 Pet 1:2; Rev 1:4. The Latin expression for "thanksgiving" (*actio gratiarum*) contains within it the idea of grace (*gratia*). This is how Jerome connects the "thanksgiving" of Jer 30:19 with the apostolic "grace." [40]Ex 32:6. [41]2 Sam 6:5. [42]Ps 87:3. [43]Demonic powers; see Jer 1:10; 2:14b-15; 4:16-17; 8:17; 13:16-17a; 28:12-14. [44]Jn 14:11.

31:1: *"At that time, says the Lord, I will be the God of all the families of Israel,"—or "of the race of Israel"*[45]*—"and they shall be my people."*

Unless the Lord's intention is accomplished and his wrath settles on the head of the wicked, he cannot be the God of all the families of Israel. This, however, is said to the remnant that will be saved. And if the phrase "I will be the God of the race (or 'all the families') of Israel" is quoted against us, let us take up this example: "If you were Abraham's sons, you would do the works of your father."[46] Likewise the apostle writes, "Consider fleshly Israel."[47] This teaches that there is another Israel that is spiritual. Therefore, he is Israel who perceives God with his mind or who is upright of the Lord;[48] it is this kind of Israel that will be the people of God.

31:2: *Thus says the Lord: "The people left remaining from the sword found grace in the wilderness; Israel shall go to his rest." LXX: The Lord said thus: "I found heat in the wilderness with those who perished by the sword; go, and do not slay Israel!"*

In this passage the Latin codices gave the absurd translation "lupines" in place of the word *heat*, due to the ambiguity of the Greek word. For the Greek word *thermon* can signify either.[49] Yet, even this is not what is found in the Hebrew. For in the Hebrew it is written *hen*, which Aquila, Symmachus and Theodotion translated *charin*, that is, "grace." Only the LXX put "heat," since they thought that the final letter was an "m." For if we read *hen* with the letter "n," it means "grace," but if we read with an "m," it means "heat."

This is the sense according to the Hebrew: The Jewish people left remaining from the Roman sword, who were indeed able to evade the anger of the Lord's fury, "found grace in the wilderness" of the Gentiles, so that amid the throng of nations they might be saved in the church. Thus Israel shall go and find his rest, in which he had always hoped and which the oracles of the prophets had promised to him. And now, this is the understanding according to the LXX: The Lord found the apostles and their associates, who were filled with heat and life, in the wilderness of the Gentiles, among those who had been slain because they lacked faith and the heat of life. This is why he commands the angels and those in God's service not to slay everyone or to wipe out Israel completely. He says to them, "Go, and do not slay Israel." There are some who are alive, who are hot with the ardor of faith and who have shunned the coldness of infidelity and death. These are the ones whom the Lord will find in the wilderness!

31:3-6: *"The Lord appeared to me"—or "to him"*[50]*—"from afar. I have loved you with an everlasting love; therefore I have drawn you, showing compassion. Again I will build you, and you shall be built, O virgin Israel! Moreover, you shall adorn yourself with your timbrels"—or "you shall take up your*

---

[45]Jerome matches Aq (= MT). [46]Jn 8:39. [47]1 Cor 10:18. [48]A common etymology for "Israel" (*yśr'l*) in the Greek tradition was "seeing God" (*r'h 'l*), e.g., OS 181.82; Philo *Congr.* 51; *Somn.* 2.173; *Fug.* 208; *Q.G.* 3.49; 4.233; Origen *Princ.* 4.3.11. A variation on this, which took the first two letters into account, was "the man who sees God" (*'yš r'h 'l*) or, by inference, "the mind that sees God" (e.g., OS 170.90; 203.92; Origen *Hom. Num.* 11.4; Philo *Somn.* 2.173 expounds the name as "the mind that contemplates God"). Jerome gives "seeing God, or else the man (or mind) that sees God" in *Nom. Hebr.* (OS 13.21), but he explains this more fully in *QHG* 32:28-29, where he criticizes the traditional etymology and suggests as other options "upright of God" [(*yśr 'l*) cf. Jerome *Comm. Hos.* 12:2-6; *Comm. Isa.* 12:44] and "prince of God" (*śr 'l*). For an attempt to follow the etymology given in Gen 32:29, see Josephus *Ant.* 1.333. [49]The ambiguity of the Greek is a question of accent. For the Greek *thermos*, if the accent is on the first syllable it means "lupine," but if on the second it means "heat." But the LXX represents a misunderstanding of the Hebrew *hn* ("grace"; Gk *charis*), which the LXX interpreted as *hm* ("heat"). [50]Jerome matches Sym and Pesh (= MT).

timbrels"[51]—"*and shall go forth in the dance of the merrymakers. Moreover, you shall plant vineyards on the mountains of Samaria; Plant the plantings and gather the vintage!*[52] *For there shall be a day when watchmen will call on mount Ephraim: 'Arise, and let us go up to Zion, to the Lord our God.'*"

Israel offended the Lord, saying, "We have no king but Caesar,"[53] and "Come, let us kill him, and the inheritance will be ours."[54] Thus they withdrew far from the Lord. For this reason "the Lord appeared to him" after a long time, and not in the time of Zerubbabel and Ezra when they were captives again. Yet, the Lord loved Israel "with an everlasting love" that will never be removed, drawing Israel near and showing compassion on him. For Israel is saved not at all by his own merit but by the Lord's mercy. "Again I will build you," he says, "and you shall be built, O virgin Israel!" We should understand this exclusively with reference to the church. For they go astray who long for a golden and bejeweled Jerusalem, consecrating their own greed in the mystery of the Lord's city.[55] "Moreover, you shall adorn yourself with your timbrels," so that you may make music to the Lord in the churches after all the flesh of evil works within you has been destroyed; and together with the throng of the Gentiles "you shall go forth in the dance of the merrymakers." Furthermore, "you shall plant vineyards on the mountains of Samaria"—not in the valleys and low places but "on the mountains of Samaria," which after the captivity of the people of Israel were possessed by foreign nations, to whom it is said, "Plant the plant-

ings and gather the vintage!" Then the day of the Lord came, when watchmen—namely, apostles and apostolic men—called out on the mountain of "Samaria" and on mount "Ephraim"—the first of which means "watching"[56] and the other "richness"[57]—indeed, what do the watchmen of Samaria say? Or rather, what do they cry on mount Ephraim? "Arise," you who are lying down, leave behind what is lowly and put away animal sacrifices, for the sacrifice acceptable to the Lord is a broken spirit.[58] "And let us go up to Zion," that is, to the church, where there is observation and contemplation of God.[59] And once we have come to Zion—or rather have ascended to it—we shall ascend likewise "to the Lord our God."

31:7: *For thus says the Lord:* "*Rejoice with gladness, O Jacob, and neigh against the head of the nations; proclaim, sing and say, 'Lord, save your people, the remnant of Israel!'*"

It is significant that not all Israel is saved but only a remnant of Israel. The Lord commands and says, "Rejoice with gladness," O you who are from Jacob, "and neigh" at "the head of the nations," referring to all nations, since what was formerly the tail has been turned into the head. "Proclaim, sing and say!" What is it that they are ordered to say? "Lord, save your people!" What people? Undoubtedly "the remnant of Israel," who were saved according to election, about which Paul also speaks, taking up the testimony of Isaiah: "If the Lord of Hosts had not left us a seed, we would have fared like Sodom and been made like Gomorrah."[60]

---

[51]Jerome matches Aq, Targ and Pesh, whereas Sym essentially followed the LXX. Heb *'dh* ("adorn oneself," KB 789). [52]Jerome here differs considerably from the IH edition, which reads, "the planters shall plant and shall not gather the vintage until the time comes." The lemma here is closer to the Hebrew in terms of the number of words, but the IH edition has some similarity to the vocalization of MT (e.g., "planters"). Both translations have some similarity to readings preserved in Greek. Nothing matches anything exactly! [53]Jn 19:15. [54]Mk 12:7. [55]Jerome refers to millenarians; see Jer 19:10-11a. [56]Heb *šmrwn* (cf. *šmr*, "to keep, watch over"). This is a traditional etymology; see Jer 4:15. [57]On this etymology, see Jer 4:15. [58]Ps 51:17. [59]Jerome has already identified Zion as a "fortress" or "watchtower" (Jer 6:2-4a). The concept of a "watchtower" (*specula*) leads to the idea of "observation" or "speculation" (*speculatio*) and therefore "contemplation" of God. For Zion as the church, see Origen *Fr. Jer.* 32. [60]Rom 9:29; Is 1:9. Cf. Rom 11:5.

31:8: *"Behold, I will bring them from the north country and gather them from the farthest parts of the earth."* And that which follows, *"at the feast of Phase, and he shall beget many sons,"* is not found in the Hebrew but is read only in the LXX. In place of this among the Hebrews is written: *"Among whom are the blind and the lame, the woman with child and her who is in travail together, a great company of those returning here."*[61]

The remnant of the people of Israel are gathered by means of the apostles and apostolic men, about whom we read above, "watchmen will call on the mountain,"[62] and who are commanded to "proclaim, sing and say,"[63] so that the remnant of Israel may be saved. The Lord promises that he will return them "from the north country" ("which is a harsh wind and is called by a fitting name"),[64] that is, from a state of coldness with respect to the love of the Lord. And he will "gather them from the farthest parts of the earth," not in some other time, but in the feast of *Pascha*, that is, in the celebration of the Lord's passion,[65] when the Lord was crucified and that which he himself promised in the Gospel was fulfilled: "When I am lifted up, I will draw all people to me."[66] Then he begat a vast people, so as to fulfill this passage of Isaiah: "A nation was brought forth at once,"[67] for in the span of one day three thousand men and five thousand men came to believe.[68]

And that which is written in the Hebrew, "Among whom are the blind and the lame, the woman with child and her who is in travail together, a great company of those returning here," although it was fulfilled literally in that the blind saw and the lame walked,[69] it can better be understood according to *anagōgē*,[70] in that they who previously were blind with treachery later believed in the Savior, and they who were lame, to whom Elijah said, "How long will you go limping with both feet?"[71] afterwards walked. The people who sat in darkness and in the shadow of death saw a great light,[72] the lame hastened along, and the woman with child gave birth to sons, "a great company of those returning" to faith.[73] The Jews think this was fulfilled under Ezra when the people set out from Babylon to return to Jerusalem after the day of the Passover;[74] but in this there was only a type, not the truth. For they have not been able to show that all the things about which we have read and are going to read were fulfilled at that time.

31:9: *"With weeping they shall come,"*—or *"they shall go out"*—*"and with compassion*[75] *I will lead them back, and I will lead them through torrents of water in a straight path in which they shall not stumble,"*—or *"wander"*[76]—*"for I am a father to Israel, and Ephraim is my firstborn."*

If we read according to the Hebrew, "With

---

[61]The LXX of Jer 38:8 ends: "at the feast of Phasek, and he (some MSS 'you') shall beget a great multitude, and they shall return here." Jerome neglects to mention the last clause since it also appears in the Hebrew ("those returning here"). The "feast of Phasek" refers to the Passover (see Soph 863). Jerome renders this as *in solemnitate Phase* (for *sollemnitas* as the eucharistic service and the Passover, see Sout 381). [62]Jer 31:6. [63]Jer 31:7. [64]See Prov 27:16 (LXX). [65]*Pascha* is the Greek form of the Aramaic word *pashā'* (Heb *pesah*), traditionally understood as Passover (but see KB 947). It was common in the church to associate Pascha with the (unrelated) Greek word *paschein* ("to suffer"), thereby creating a link between the Passover feast and the suffering ("passion") of Christ; see Melito of Sardis *On the Passover* 46; Irenaeus *Haer.* 4.10.1; *Epid.* 25; Tertullian *Adv. Jud.* 10; Hippolytus, as cited in the *Chronicon Paschale* [P. Nautin, ed. *Homélies pascales*, vol. 1, SC 27 (Paris: Éditions du Cerf, 1950), 52-53]. Origen had already learned that *pashā'* did not mean "to suffer" [P. Nautin, ed. *Homélies pascales*, vol. 2, SC 36 (Paris: Éditions du Cerf, 1953), 34-35]. Jerome says the same and gives the meaning "to pass over" at *Comm. Isa.* 31:5. But this does not hinder Jerome from making use of this traditional Christian etymology as part of his spiritual exposition. [66]Jn 12:32. [67]Is 66:8. [68]Acts 2:41; 4:4. [69]Mt 11:5; Lk 7:22. [70]Following Origen and other Greek fathers, Jerome uses the Greek term *anagōgē* ("elevation") to refer to the higher or spiritual sense. [71]1 Kings 18:21. [72]Is 9:2; Ps 107:10. [73]Jerome's word for "company" (Heb *qāhāl*) is *ecclesia*, thus "a great church." [74]1 Esd 7:10-15. [75]*misericordia* ("compassion" = Aq, Sym) for IH edition's *precibus* ("prayers," "supplications"). Heb *thnwn* ("pleading," KB 1719). [76]Heb *kšl* ("stumble, stagger," KB 502).

weeping they shall come"—for this is what *iabu*[77] means—then we will say that weeping may sometimes be a sign of great joy, as in "I weep for joy!"[78] But if we read according to the LXX, who said, "With weeping they shall go out, and with compassion (or "encouragement"[79]) I will lead them back," then we will give this sense, which is also described in the Psalms: "Going, they go and weep, carrying their seed; but coming, they come with rejoicing, carrying their sheaves."[80] For they wept when they were led captive, and they received great encouragement when by the Lord's compassion they were led back. The Lord "led them through" the apostles and apostolic men, who are filled with bountiful rivers of water, "in a straight path," namely, in the path of faith, and not in the falsehood of the Jews. He says, "They shall not stumble in it," since they cease to be blind, whereas formerly it was said to them, "If you were blind, you would have no guilt; but now that you say, 'We see,' your guilt remains."[81] We can also understand the "straight path" as Christ; whoever walks on this path will not stumble. He says, "For I am a father to Israel," who was led back, "and Ephraim is my firstborn." For "where sin (formerly) abounded, grace abounded all the more."[82] Scripture speaks of "Ephraim" as a type of the people gathered in from the nations.[83] For the younger son of Joseph stole the birthright from Manasseh, who was the firstborn by nature. But in the mystery of the cross Jacob's hands crossed, and he who stood at Jacob's left hand received the blessing of his right hand, and he who stood at Jacob's right hand was blessed by the left and was reduced to the second rank.[84] Just as Jacob stole the birth-right from Esau,[85] Ephraim stole it from Manasseh. Thus, all the people of the ten tribes are called "Ephraim," since Jeroboam the son of Nebat, who was from this tribe, was the first to rule in Samaria.[86]

31:10-14: *"Hear the word of the Lord, O nations, and declare it in the islands far away; say, 'He who scattered Israel will gather him and will keep him as a shepherd keeps his flock.' For the Lord has ransomed Jacob and has redeemed him from the hand of ones more powerful"—or "stronger"[87]—"than he. They shall come and give praise on the height of Zion, and they shall flow together to the good things of the Lord, over the grain, the wine and the oil, and over the young of the flock and the herd; their soul shall be like a watered garden,"—or "like a fruitful tree"[88]—"and they shall hunger no more. Then shall the virgin"—or "virgins"[89]—"rejoice in the dance, the young men and the old together. I will turn their mourning into joy; I will comfort them and give them gladness out of sorrow. I will saturate the soul of the priests with fat,"—or "of the sons of Levi"[90]—"and my people shall be filled with my good things, says the Lord."*

The calling of the Gentiles is indicated clearly when Scripture says, "Hear the word of the Lord, O nations, and declare it in the islands far away; say . . ." What do they declare in the islands far away? That the Lord "who scattered Israel will gather him." So when they were scattered, it was due not to the enemies' power but to the Lord's will. "And he will keep him as a shepherd keeps his flock." For "the good shepherd lays down his life for his sheep."[91] "For the Lord has ransomed Jacob," at the price

---

[77]MT: *yābō'û*, from *bw'* ("to come to" or "to come in"). See Jer 32:26-29. [78]Terence *Ad.* 409. [79]The LXX has "encouragement" for Jerome's "compassion." [80]Ps 126:6 (LXX [125:6]). [81]Jn 9:41. [82]Rom 5:20. [83]Gen 48:19. [84]Gen 48:13-16. [85]Gen 25:29-34. [86]1 Kings 11:26; 12:20. [87]Heb *hzq* ("firm, hard," "strong," KB 304). Jerome's IH edition has "more powerful." The LXX translates "stiff, firm." [88]Jerome matches Aq, Sym and Pesh (= MT). [89]Jerome matches Aq and Pesh (= MT). The LXX reads, "Then virgins shall rejoice in the assembly of (presuming *bqhl* instead of *btlh*) young men, and old men shall rejoice." [90]Jerome matches the asterisked reading in the Hexapla and the Pesh (= MT). The LXX gives "the soul of the priests, sons of Levi." [91]Jn 10:11.

of his own blood, "and has redeemed him from the hand of ones more powerful (or 'stronger') than he." This shows that the adversarial powers[92] are stronger than humanity's frail nature. However strong each may be, although the adversarial powers are stronger than our nature, they are not stronger than our faith, provided that we merit to be redeemed by him who is able to bind the strong man and plunder his house.[93]

The prophet says, "They shall come"—no doubt, those redeemed from the hand of ones more powerful than they—"and give praise"—to the one who redeemed them—"on the height of Zion"—that is, in the church—"and they shall flow together to the good things of the Lord"—abundance in all things, which is experienced not in the fruit and nourishment of this flesh but in the diversity of virtues. He says "over the grain, the wine and the oil," according to which a type of the Lord's bread is completed and a type of his blood is fulfilled, and the blessing of sanctification is shown, "God, your God, has anointed you with the oil of gladness beyond your fellows."[94] He says "and over the young of the flock," who are the simple ones in the church, "and the herd," which have horns to gore adversaries.[95]

So that we may know that these blessings pertain not to the body but to the soul, he continues, "their soul shall be like a watered garden"—or "like a fruitful tree" that is planted by channels of water,[96] even in the delights of the Paradise of the Lord.[97] "And," he says, "they shall hunger no more"—not in regards to that hunger about which it is written, "Blessed are those who hunger and thirst for righteousness," but only regarding that hunger that comes from the lack of all

things and can be made better with plenty.

"Then shall the virgin rejoice in the dance," about which the apostle writes, "For I betrothed you to one husband so as to present you as a pure bride to Christ";[98] "the young men," to whom John says, "I am writing to you, young men, because you have overcome the evil one";[99] "and the old," to whom this same John declares in mystical language, "I am writing to you, fathers, because you know him who was from the beginning."[100] "I will turn," he says, "their mourning into joy," such that those dismayed by the cross will be made glad by the resurrection. "I will comfort them and give them gladness out of sorrow," in accordance with what the Lord says, "Blessed are those who mourn, for they shall be comforted."[101] And "I will saturate the soul of the priests," who have knowledge of God, from whose mouth people seek the law of the Lord,[102] who believe in the Lord and to whom the prophet sings, "You are a priest forever after the order of Melchizedek."[103] But that which follows in the LXX, "of the sons of Levi," is not found in the Hebrew; and clearly this was not said with regard to those priests who are the sons of Levi, but with regard to those of whom Melchizedek served as a type. Moreover, the "saturation" of the priests is confirmed in the apostles when they were aglow with faith and filled with new wine.[104] So also, the place where the Lord was seized is called *Gessemani*, which in our language means "valley of fat."[105] And when the priests are fat with the Lord's teaching and drunk in the company of Joseph,[106] and they say, "Your cup is so very saturating,"[107] then shall come to pass what the Lord promises: "My people shall be filled with my good things." All these things are being

---

[92]Cf. Jer 30:18-22. [93]Mt 12:29. [94]Ps 45:7. [95]Ps 44:5 (LXX [43:6]). [96]Ps 1:3. [97]Ezek 28:13; Gen 13:10; see also Jerome *QHG* 2:8, where he says that "Eden" means "delights." [98]2 Cor 11:2. [99]1 Jn 2:13. [100]1 Jn 2:13. [101]Mt 5:4. [102]Mal 2:7. [103]Ps 110:4; Heb 5:6; 7:17. [104]Rom 12:11; Acts 2:13. [105]Jerome reported this etymology for Gethsemane in *Nom. Hebr.* (OS 61.22). It presumes the Hebrew *gy'* ("valley") *šmny* (of "fat" or "grease"). Another possibility is *gt* ("press") *šmny* (of "fat" or "grease"), or rather, "oil press." [106]Gen 43:34. [107]Ps 23:5 (LXX [22:5]). Jerome's word for "saturation" or "to saturate" is *ebrietas* or *inebrio*, which also refers to drunkenness.

bestowed now in part, but then they shall be given fully, when we see face to face and our lowly body is changed by the glory of resurrection.[108]

31:15: *Thus says the Lord: "A voice is heard on high of lamentation, wailing and mourning, Rachel weeping for her sons; she refuses to be comforted for her sons, because they are not."* LXX: *The Lord said thus: "A voice was heard in Ramah, of lamentation, wailing and mourning; Rachel weeping for her sons; she refuses to cease, because they are not."*[109]

Matthew cites this testimony neither according to the Hebrew nor according to the LXX. For we read in Matthew after the description of the death of the infants: "Then was fulfilled what was spoken by the prophet Jeremiah: 'A voice was heard in Ramah, wailing and much crying; Rachel weeping for her children; she refused to be consoled, because they are not.'"[110] From this it is clear that the evangelists and apostles did not follow any particular person's interpretation of the Hebrew, but as Hebrews born of Hebrews[111] they expressed in their own words what they read in Hebrew.

When Joseph's mother, Rachel, came to Bethlehem she went into labor suddenly, and seized with pain she gave birth to a son. Since the mother was dying, the midwife called him Ben-oni, that is, "son of my sorrow." But his father, Jacob, changed the word and called his name Benjamin, that is, "son of the right hand."[112] So the question is asked: How could the Evangelist Matthew transfer the testimony of the prophet to the slaying of the infants, when this testimony was clearly written with regard to the ten tribes (the chief of which was Ephrathah), and the slaying of the infants was not in the tribe of Ephraim but in the tribe of Judah?[113] In fact, Ephrathah and Bethlehem are dyonymous;[114] thus, even the names of both of them are in agreement: Bethlehem means "house of bread," and Ephrathah means *karpophoria*, which we can translate as "richness."[115] Since therefore Rachel was laid to rest in Ephrathah, that is, in Bethlehem—just as holy Scripture and the inscription on her tomb even today testify[116]—it is said[117] that she weeps for her sons who were killed near her and in her territory.

Certain of the Jews interpret this passage thus: when Jerusalem was captured under Vespasian,[118] countless thousands of captives were led through this way by Gaza and Alexandria to Rome. But others say that in the final captivity under Hadrian when the city of Jerusalem was overthrown, innumerable people of diverse ages and both sexes were sold at the marketplace of Terebinthus.[119] For this reason, it is an accursed thing among the Jews to visit this acclaimed marketplace. Let these people say what they want. We say that the Evangelist Matthew has rightly taken up this testimony because it is the place where Rachel was

---

[108]1 Cor 13:12; Phil 3:21. [109]Many LXX MSS read, "Rachel weeping; she refuses to cease for her sons, because they are not." Jerome's copy of the LXX has been influenced by the Hexpla. As for Jerome's "to be comforted" (Heb *lhnhm*) and the LXX's "to cease" (Heb *lhdl*?), Jerome matches Aq and Targ (= MT). [110]Mt 2:17-18. [111]Phil 3:5. [112]Gen 35:16-18. On the etymology of Benjamin, see Jer 6:1. On Ben-oni, see Jerome *Nom. Hebr.* (OS 3.23). [113]Jerome sees Ephrathah as a form of Ephraim, the chief tribe of the northern kingdom. [114]Gen 35:16-19; Ruth 4:11; 1 Chron 4:4; Mic 5:2. Jerome gives the Greek term *diōnymos*, which means "having two names" (see LSJ 441; LS 622; cf. *Comm. Isa.* 51:17-19, where Jerome identifies Jerusalem and Zion as dyonymous). Jerome is saying that Ephrathah can refer not only to Ephraim as chief of the ten tribes (as in Jeremiah) but also to Bethlehem, as it does in Matthew. [115]This etymology of Bethlehem [Heb *bêt* ("house of") *lehem* ("bread")] was known in Greek sources, but other options were available. Thus, "house of bread" is given by itself in OS 182.93; 201.55; but OS 188.78 has "house of bread or life," and OS 73.57 gives "house of life, house of the holy, house of bread." On Ephrathah, see Jer 4:15 (*karpophoria* means "fruit-bearing" in Greek). [116]Gen 35:19-20. Cf. Origen *Cels.* 1.51; Eusebius *Onom.* 82; Jerome *Ep.* 108.10. [117]"It is said" in Matthew. The quotation can be applied to the slaying of the infants because Rachel died near to where the infants were slain. [118]During the First Jewish Revolt against Rome (66-70 C.E.). [119]During the Second Jewish Revolt against Rome (132-135 C.E.); see Jer 19:10-11a; Jerome *Comm. Zach.* 11:4-5. On Terebinthus, see Sozomen *Hist. Eccl.* 2.4.

buried, and she wept for the sons of those nearby in the surrounding houses as if she were weeping for her own sons.

31:16-17: *Thus says the Lord: "Let your voice cease from weeping and your eyes from tears; for there shall be a reward for your work, says the Lord, and they shall come back from the land of the enemy"—or "enemies." "There is hope for your end, says the Lord, and your sons shall come back to their own borders."*

According to the letter this has not happened yet, for we do not read that the ten tribes, who lived in exile in the Median and Persian states, came back to the land of Judah. But according to the spirit this was fulfilled in the passion of the Lord and is being fulfilled up to the present, when Israel is being saved from out of the whole world, and to Rachel it is said, "Let your voice cease from weeping and your eyes from tears." The sense is: "Cease from weeping, for the Lord has looked favorably on your prior works. Your sons shall come back from the land of the enemy. You shall not continue in your present sorrow. For there is hope for your end, says the Lord, and your sons shall come back to their own borders, which their fathers Abraham, Isaac and Jacob possessed."

Moreover, we can better understand this with regard to the infants:[120] they whose blood was shed in place of Christ shall have the reward for their blood; instead of the land of their enemy Herod, they shall possess the kingdom of heaven;[121] and they shall come back to their former station when in return for their lowly body each one receives a glorious body.[122] And this is their end hope: the righteous will shine like the sun,[123] and these infants who were formerly babes and sucklings[124] will rise again without increase of age, injury or bodily distress. Thus they will attain mature manhood, the measure of the fullness of Christ.[125]

31:18-19: *"Hearing, I heard Ephraim being removed"—or "lamenting"[126]—"you have chastened me, and I was trained, like an untamed young bull"—or "like a calf, I did not learn."[127] "Convert me, and I shall be converted, for you are the Lord my God. For after you converted me,"—or "after I was captured"[128]—"I repented; and after I recognized"—or "and after you showed me"[129]— "I struck my thigh";—or "groaned"[130]—"I was ashamed, and I was confounded, because"—or "(groaned) from the day of shame, and I showed to you that"[131]—"I bore the disgrace of my youth."*

God speaks what he heard Ephraim saying and lamenting. No one doubts that he is referring to the ten tribes, whose first ruler, Jeroboam the son of Nebat, made golden calves at Dan and Bethel, so that when the people had been led astray by this error they would cease from honoring and worshiping God.[132] "You chastened me," he says, "and I was chastened."[133] Every reproach profits us for salvation, seeming harsh at the time but afterwards bringing

---

[120]Mt 2:16. [121]Mt 18:3-4. [122]Phil 3:21. [123]Mt 13:43. [124]Ps 8:2; Mt 21:16. [125]Eph 4:13. [126]Jerome agrees with Aq. Heb *mtnwdd*, Hitpolel from *nwd*, which in the Qal means "be aimless, homeless" (= basis for Jerome and Aq) and in the Hitpolel (for this passage only) is taken by KB 678 to mean "pity oneself." The Targ has them weeping and exiled, giving both senses. [127]Jerome agrees with Sym (against Aq). [128]The first option is Jerome, but the second is not the LXX as preserved. The source of the second option is not clear. [129]In this case, the first option is the LXX, which essentially agrees with all of the hexaplaric versions, and the second is Jerome's IH edition. Neither the Targ nor the Pesh matches Jerome. The Hebrew consonants are *hwd'y* (from *yd'* ["to know," plus first person suffix]), which MT and the versions take as a Niphal ("I came to know"), whereas Jerome reads it as a Hiphil ("[you] caused me to know"). [130]Jerome agrees with Aq and Sym (= MT). [131]Jerome agrees with Aq (= MT). The reading of the LXX is, "I groaned from the day of shame, and I showed to you that I bore the disgrace of my youth." [132]1 Kings 12:20, 28-29. [133]Jerome uses the same word ("to chastise") twice in this quotation, as does the Hebrew and the LXX. In the IH edition Jerome uses a different word ("to train") the second time for variety's sake.

about peaceable fruits. As for what he says, "like an untamed young bull," or "like a calf, I did not learn," it means this: although he was trained with much effort and with many floggings so as to turn him to repentance, he did not profit by it. "Convert me," he says, "and I shall be converted." Therefore, even the very act of repenting we are not able to accomplish, unless we rely on God's help. "For after you convert me and I become converted to you, then I will know that 'you are the Lord my God,' and I will no longer know my errors and sins." "After you converted me, I repented." See this: God's aid is so great, and the human condition is so weak, that we are not strong enough to repent unless the Lord converts us beforehand. He says, "And after you showed me repentance (or 'knowledge of you')—or else, "And after I recognized you"—"I struck my thigh." It is a sign of grief, bewailing and weeping over former sins to strike one's thigh with the hand and to confess that one has previously been a fool. "I was ashamed," he says, "and I was confounded"—or else, "from the day of shame." For is it not a time for us to be ashamed when we call to mind our past sins and recollect the memory of all that we have done wrong? As for what the LXX said, "And I showed to you," it means this: After he has groaned and recognized his faults, then he achieves such a level of progress that he can even show the right way to those who do not know God, as David says in his repentance: "Then I will teach transgressors your ways, and sinners will return to you."[134] He says, "Because I bore the disgrace of my youth." He says that he sinned because of the ignorance of his age; thus, he may readily follow along with the petition that David also sings: "Remember not

the sins of my youth, or my acts of ignorance."[135] So also in what follows the Lord calls him a child and one who is flowing with delights.[136] He says this on account of the great riches and fertile land in which the tribe of Ephraim so greatly abounded.

31:20: *"Is Ephraim my honorable"—or "beloved"[137]—"son? Is he my delicate child? For because I spoke about him,"—or "my words were in him"[138]—"I will remember him still. Therefore my heart is in turmoil over him; compassionate, I will have compassion on him, says the Lord."*

After Ephraim repents, saying at first, "You have trained me, and I was trained, like an untamed young bull," and at the end, "I bore the disgrace of my youth,"[139] the Lord responds and thoughtfully encourages the convert with this oracle: "Ephraim is my beloved son, whom I loved so much from the beginning that I preferred him to his brother Manasseh."[140] He is an "honorable son," who against the order of nature received the honor of the firstborn because the Lord deemed him worthy. He is a "delicate child," about whom it is written, "The sons of Ephraim, who bend and shoot the bow, turned back on the day of battle."[141] The whole book of the prophet Hosea is written to and against Ephraim,[142] and Jacob blesses him.[143] Moreover, we can interpret "delights" in this passage according to what is said in the psalm: "Take delight in the Lord, and he will give to you the petitions of your heart,"[144] in place of which in Greek and in Hebrew it has, "Abound with delights!"[145] Thus also the paradise in Eden is called a paradise of delights.[146]

---

[134]Ps 51:13. [135]Ps 25:7 (LXX [24:7]). [136]Jer 31:20, 22. [137]Heb *yqyr* ("precious, dear," KB 431), but cf. Aramaic *yqyr* ("important, honored," Sok, *DJPA* 244; Jastrow 591). Jerome matches Aq and Sym. [138]Jerome, like MT, reads *dbry* as a verb ("I spoke"), whereas the LXX reads it as a noun ("my words"). [139]Jer 31:18-19. [140]Gen 48:19. [141]Ps 78:9. [142]Hos 4:17; 5:3, 5, 9, 11, 12, etc. [143]Gen 48:20. [144]Ps 37:4. The Latin word *deliciae* ("delights") is related to the word *delicate* (*delicatus*). Heb *š'š'ym* ("desire, delight," KB 1619). [145]Heb Hitpael of *'ng* ("pamper oneself, take one's pleasure in," KB 851). LXX: *katatruphaō* ("delight in"; emphatic word formation). [146]Cf. Jer 31:10-14; Jerome *QHG* 2:8.

"Because my words were in him," he says, "I will still hold him in my remembrance." Lest it be thought that this blessing was gratuitous and was conferred more out of the indulgence of the bestower than out of the merit of him on whom it was conferred, it says, "I will remember him because my words were in him—not in his mouth, not on his lips, but in the innermost affections of his heart. For this reason, 'my heart is in turmoil over him.'" The Lord also says this to him through Hosea: "What shall I do with you, O Ephraim? What shall I do with you, O Israel? How can I make you like Admah and like Zeboiim? My heart recoils within me, my heart is in turmoil. I will not execute the fury of my anger, and I will not destroy Ephraim."[147] "Compassionate, I will have compassion on him, says the Lord." He says, "My words were indeed in him; he received all my commandments with an eager spirit and kept them in his heart. But even still, 'compassionate, I will have compassion on him.'" He does this in order to show that all the righteousness of humanity is still in need of God's compassion.

31:21-22: *"Set up for yourself watchtowers, make yourself bitterness; direct your heart into the straight way, on which you walked. Return, O virgin Israel, return to these your cities. How long will you dissolve in delights, O wayward daughter? For the Lord has created a new thing on the earth: a woman encompasses a man."* **LXX:** *"Set up for yourself watchmen, make punishment; give your heart into your shoulders. Return to the way on which you walked, O virgin Israel, return to your cities*

in mourning. How long will you turn away, O dishonored daughter? For the Lord has created you salvation for a new planting; in your salvation people will go around."

Where we have said, "How long will you dissolve in delights?" Symmachus put, "How long will you sink to the depths?"[148] I have given both editions in full in order to show that this passage, which is very obscure and contains the sacraments of the church, has been ignored or omitted by the LXX—or whoever else translated this prophet. The Hebrew word *sionim* can be rendered as "watchmen" or as "watchtowers," as Aquila and Symmachus translated.[149] And so I marvel at what the popular edition was thinking when instead of *sionim* (that is, "watchmen") it put "Zion" and thereby confused the meaning of the text, since it thought that after addressing Ephraim God's message suddenly switches now to addressing Zion and the tribe of Judah.[150] But really the oracle continues addressing Ephraim. Above it was said to Ephraim, "Hearing, I heard Ephraim," and "Ephraim is my honorable son" or "my delicate child."[151] Now he says to Ephraim, "Set up for yourself watchtowers," or "watchmen," that they may announce to you that abundant good fortune in all things is coming.

As for what follows, "bitterness," which in Hebrew is *themrurim*,[152] and which Symmachus translated as "conversion," it means this: Either Ephraim should weep over its old sins, or else with great joy Ephraim should be converted to God with its whole heart. Moreover, Ephraim ought to set or direct its

---

[147]Hos 6:4; 11:8-9. [148]Heb *hmq* (Hitpael; "to turn hither and thither, to waver," KB 330). [149]MT: *siyyumim* ("stone monument, road marker," KB 1022). Jerome's copy of the LXX read "watchmen," whereas other witnesses to the LXX merely transliterated the word into Greek. Jerome's "watchtowers" (following Aq and Sym) presumes the association with "Zion"; see Jer 6:2-4a; 31:3-6. [150]Some LXX witnesses transliterate the word into Greek (*siōnim*), and some even give a shortened transliteration (*siōn*), which was taken by the OL as "Zion." Jerome does not know about the LXX transliteration tradition, so he is at a loss to explain the origin of the OL's rendering. [151]Jer 31:18, 20. [152]Heb *tmrwrym*. RSV: "guideposts" (cf. KB 1758, *tmrwr* II). Jerome and Aq: "bitterness" (cf. KB 1758, *tmrwr* I; cf. *mar*, "bitterness"). The LXX transliterated the word as *timrōrim*, which was corrupted in some LXX MSS, including Jerome's, to *timōrian* ("punishment").

heart into the way through which it has traveled. For it is from there that Ephraim will return. In place of this the LXX put, "Give your heart into your shoulders." This means that Ephraim ought to join its thoughts to its deeds, or else that they ought to contemplate the shoulders of those who are carrying them and leading them back from captivity. Isaiah describes this more fully when he declares that they will be led back on camels and in chariots and litters.[153] "Return," he says, "O virgin Israel, return to your cities, which you forsook when they were captured. How long will you dissolve in negligence and wander about in the depths of error? Pay attention to what I am about to say, and carefully consider from where this great blessedness for which you hope is going to come. Hear something that you have never known before! The Lord has created a new thing on the earth: Apart from the seed of a man and apart from any sexual union or conception, "a woman encompasses a man" in the bosom of her womb. This man will appear to increase in wisdom and stature,[154] at least in accordance with the stages of life regarding crying and infancy. Yet, when the accustomed months have passed a perfect man will be contained within this woman's womb. Thus both Symmachus and Aquila have translated, in agreement with our edition.

What the popular edition was thinking on this passage I might be able to say, and thereby find some sense in it, except that it would be sacrilegious to draw a conclusion about the words of God based on a human meaning. Theodotion translated, "For the Lord has created a new salvation; in salvation a person will go around," agreeing with the popular edition, except that Theodotion put the singular instead of the plural.[155] Lastly, this should be noted: the birth of the Savior and the conception of God is formally called a "creation."

31:23-24: *Thus says the Lord of hosts, the God of Israel: "Once more they shall say this word in the land of Judah and in its cities, when I return their captivity: 'The Lord bless you, the beauty of righteousness, the holy mountain!' And Judah and all its cities shall dwell on it together, and the farmers and those who drive their flocks."* LXX: *The Lord of hosts, the God of Israel said thus: "Once more they shall say this message in the land of Judah and in its cities, when I bring back its deportation: 'Blessed be the Lord on his righteous, holy mountain!' And they shall dwell in the land of Judah and in all its [or his] city*[156] *together with the farmer; and he shall be lifted up in the flock."*

According to the Hebrew it is clear that in the restoration of Israel and in the return of their captivity to their land they shall dwell in the cities of Judah. It shall be said to each one individually, "May you be blessed by the Lord, who is truly the beauty of righteousness and the holy mountain"; whoever dwells on him shall fear no treachery. Judah will dwell without iniquity in its cities, and there shall be farmers and a multitude of cattle. This is seen to have been fulfilled partially under Zerubbabel and Ezra; but the fullness of the prophecy refers to the times of Christ, either in his first advent when these things took place spiritually, or in his second advent when all things will come to completion—according to us spiritually, but according to the Jews and our Judaizers carnally.[157]

Moreover, according to the LXX this is the sense: "Once more this message shall be said in the land of Judah and in its cities, when I return its captivity." What shall be said?

---

[153]Is 60:6. [154]Lk 2:52. [155]Th: "a person will go around." LXX: "people will go around." [156]Most LXX MSS read "in the cities of Judah and in all its [or his] land." [157]On the Judaizers, see Jer 11:18-20; 13:17c; 17:21-27; 19:10-11a; 31:27-30; 31:38-40.

"Blessed be the Lord on his righteous, holy mountain!" The mountain that is worthy to receive the names of "righteousness" and "holiness" is none other than the Savior. Otherwise, it is foolish to believe, following the Jewish error, that an irrational and senseless mountain is "righteous" and "holy." The Savior is the very one about whom the following phrase is written: "and in all his (meaning 'the Savior's') city together with the farmer." No doubt the "farmer" signifies God, about whom it is written in the Gospel: "I am the vine, you are the branches; my Father is the farmer."[158] Thus the apostle also says, "You are God's field, God's building."[159] As for what follows, "and he shall be lifted up in the flock," it means this: in each flock the righteous and holy one—even the farmer himself, the Lord—is lifted up, and among his servants and those who believe he ascends on high.[160]

31:25-26: "For I have inebriated the weary soul,"—or "For I have inebriated every thirsty soul"[161]—"and every hungry soul I have satisfied"—or "I have filled."[162] Therefore I was awakened, and I saw, and my sleep was sweet to me.[163]

The changing around of the speakers makes understanding the prophets difficult.[164] The Lord said, "Once more they shall say this word in the land of Judah and in its cities, when I return their captivity." What, then, do they say? No doubt, that which follows: "The Lord bless you, the beauty of righteousness, the holy mountain!" and so forth.[165] And when they have said these things, the Lord responds, "For I have inebriated the weary (or 'thirsty') soul, and every hungry soul I have satisfied." And then the people who had come back from captivity reply to this by saying, "Therefore I was awakened and I saw, and my sleep was sweet to me." For the Lord inebriates the weary or thirsty soul, saying in the Gospel: "If anyone thirst, let him come to me and drink," and "He who believes in me, as Scripture says, out of his heart shall flow rivers of living water,"[166] so that every hungry and thirsty soul is satisfied. Concerning this thirst and this hunger the Lord testifies in the Gospel: "Blessed are those who hunger and thirst for righteousness, for they shall be satisfied."[167]

It should be noted that "inebriation" is used here in a good sense, just as in the Song where it is said, "Eat, O friends, and drink; be inebriated, O lovers!"[168] Joseph was also inebriated with this inebriation together with his brothers at noon.[169] Those who are inebriated and satisfied, who had been weary and hungry, give thanks and reply, "I was awakened and I saw the Lord," namely, the one arouses and says, "Rise, O sleeper, and arise from the dead, and Christ shall give you light."[170] "And my sleep," he says, "was sweet to me," so that I emulate the words of my Lord, who says, "I lie down and sleep; I rise again, for the Lord sustains me."[171]

31:27-30: "Behold, the days are coming, says the Lord, when I will sow the house of Israel and the house of Judah with the seed of humanity and the seed of beast. And just as I have watched over them to pluck up and break down, to overthrow, destroy and shatter, so I will watch over them to build and to plant, says the Lord. In those days they shall no longer say, 'The fathers have eaten a sour grape, and the children's teeth are set on edge.' But everyone shall die for his own sin; any person who eats a sour grape, his teeth shall be set on edge."

---

[158]Jn 15:1, 5. [159]1 Cor 3:9. [160]Ps 68:18; Eph 4:8. [161]Heb 'yp ("tired, exhausted," KB 820). [162]Heb ml' (Piel; "to fill," KB 583). [163]IH edition: "Therefore I was aroused as from sleep, and I saw, and my sleep was sweet to me." [164]Cf. Expl. Dan. 11:1: "It is the custom of the prophets to introduce new speakers (personae) suddenly, without any introductory words." Cf. Comm. Jer. 8:14-15. [165]Jer 31:23. [166]Jn 7:37-38. [167]Mt 5:6. [168]Song 5:1. [169]Gen 43:25, 34. [170]Eph 5:14. [171]Ps 3:5.

The words "house" and "house"—that is, the "house" of Israel and the "house" of Judah—are not found in the LXX, but only "Israel" and "Judah," so that it has: "I will sow Israel and Judah." As for what he adds, "with the seed of humanity and the seed of beast," we should refer this to those endowed with reason and those that are simple. Just as at the beginning of Jeremiah it was said to him, "See, I have set you this day over nations and over kingdoms, to pluck up and to break down, to destroy and to overthrow, to build and to plant," and "I am watching over them to perform what I have threatened,"[172] so also now he says, "I will watch over them to build and to plant," for "you are God's field, God's building."[173]

According to the Jews and our Judaizers, all promises of this kind are going to be fulfilled in the thousand-year reign.[174] But since the apostle says, "I planted, Apollos watered, but God gave the growth,"[175] and since Isaiah the prophet speaks of the Savior as a builder of enclosures and houses,[176] we maintain that these things were fulfilled spiritually in the first advent of Christ—and fulfilled in part, not in whole, "for now we see in a mirror through enigmas" and we do not know as we ought to know;[177] "but when the perfect comes, that which is partial will pass away"[178]—or else, we believe that they will be fulfilled in the second advent, when the Lord will appear in glory and the fullness of the Gentiles will come in, so that all Israel is saved. This will happen not in part individually; rather, God will be all in all.[179]

As for what he adds, "In those days they shall no longer say, 'The fathers have eaten a sour grape, and the children's teeth are set on edge,'" and so forth, we discussed this more fully in our exposition of Ezekiel, when we interpreted this passage: "Son of man, what have you to do with this proverb spoken among the sons of Israel, 'The fathers have eaten a sour grape, and the children's teeth are set on edge'? As I live, says the Lord, this proverb shall no more be used in Israel. For all souls are mine, the soul of the father as well as the soul of the son: the soul that sins shall die."[180] From this text we learn that death is caused not by the Lord but by sin, for "the soul that sins shall die." And in the present passage it is said that Israel shall not fail forever because of the sins of their ancestors; rather, after a long time they shall be saved through their own merit and through faith in Christ. It should be observed that vices and sins are called "sour grapes," such that the teeth of those who eat them are set on edge and they cannot taste the Lord's sweetness, concerning which it is said, "Taste and see that the Lord is good!"[181] Whoever does not understand the Scriptures in this way, as the truth of the matter has it, eats a sour grape. Therefore none of the heretics, who believe perverse things, are able to eat the bread that comes down from heaven.[182] On the contrary, their teeth are set on edge—not because of the harshness of the bread but because of the wickedness of the teeth.

31:31-34: *"Behold, the days are coming, says the Lord, when I will make"—or "establish"[183]—"a new pact"—or "testament"[184]—"with the house of Israel and the house of Judah, not like the pact"—or "testament"—"that I made with their fathers*

---

[172]Jer. 1:10; cf. Jer 1:12. [173]1 Cor 3:10. [174]On the Judaizers, see Jer 11:18-20; 13:17c; 17:21-27; 19:10-11a; 31:23-24; 31:38-40. On Judaizers and the thousand-year reign, see *Comm. Hos.* 2:14-15; *Comm. Joel* 3:7-8; 3:16-17; *Comm. Zach.* 14:10-11; 14:18-19; *Comm. Isa.* 23:18; 54:1; bk. 18 prol.; *Comm. Ezech.* 37:15-28; 38:1-23; *Comm. Jer.* 31:38-40. [175]1 Cor 3:6. [176]Is 58:12. [177]1 Cor 13:12; Rom 8:26. [178]1 Cor 13:10. [179]Mt 25:31; Tit 2:13; Rom 11:25-26; 1 Cor 15:28. [180]Ezek 18:2-4. See Jerome *Comm. Ezech.* 18:1-4. [181]Ps 34:8. [182]Jn 6:50. [183]Aq gives the literalistic rendering, "I will cut" (Heb *crt*), but Jerome does not follow suit. [184]Heb *bryt* ("agreement, covenant," KB 157). Jerome uses the Latin *pactum*, and for the LXX he gives *testamentum*, which stands for the Greek *diathēkē* ("disposition [of property], testament, covenant," LSJ 394-95).

when I took them by the hand to bring them out of the land of Egypt, the pact"—or *"testament"*—*"that they made void, and I was Lord over them,"*—or *"and I was unconcerned for them"*[185]—*"says the Lord. But this is the pact"*—or *"testament"*—*"that I will make with the house of Israel after those days, says the Lord: I will put my law in their bowels,"*—or *"mind"*[186]—*"and I will write it on their hearts; and I will be their God, and they shall be my people. And no longer shall each man teach his neighbor and each his brother, saying, 'Know the Lord,' for they shall all know me, from the least of them to the greatest, says the Lord; for I will forgive their iniquity, and I will remember their sin no more."*

The apostle Paul—or whoever wrote the epistle to the Hebrews[187]—made use of this testimony, and thereafter all ecclesiastical men say that all these things were fulfilled in the first advent of the Savior and that the New Testament (that is, the Gospel) has succeeded the Old Testament. The law of the letter was replaced by the law of the spirit, so that everything—including the sacrifices, circumcision and the sabbath—was fulfilled spiritually.[188]

When Israel was brought out of the land of Egypt, their familiarity with God was so great that it says he took them by the hand and gave them a pact. But they made this pact void, and for this reason the Lord was unconcerned for them. But now in the Gospel—after the crucifixion, resurrection and ascension—he promises that he will put his pact "not on tablets of stone but on tablets of human hearts."[189] And when the testament of the Lord is written in the mind of those who believe, then he will be their God and they shall be his people, so that they shall no longer seek out Jewish teachers or human traditions and commandments,[190] but they shall be taught by the Holy Spirit, provided that they are worthy to hear: "You are God's temple, and God's spirit dwells in you."[191] Moreover, "The Spirit blows where he wills,"[192] and he holds a variety of gifts,[193] and to know the one God is to possess all of the virtues.[194] "And this shall come to pass," he says, "because I will forgive their iniquity, and I will remember their sin no more." From this it is clear, in agreement with our understanding of this pericope, that the above statements should be interpreted with reference to the first advent of the Savior, when both the people of Israel and the people of Judah were joined together.

Should anyone express uncertainty as to why it says, "I will establish a new pact (or "testament") with the house of Israel and the house of Judah, not like the pact that I made with their fathers," he should understand that the first church of Christ derived from the Jews, and our Lord and Savior went to them and said, "I have come only to the lost sheep of the house of Israel."[195] And the apostle affirms this very point: "It was necessary that the word of God should be spoken first to you; but since you thrust it from you, and judge yourselves unworthy of eternal life, behold, we turn to the Gentiles."[196] For it was not proper to give the children's bread to the dogs,[197] but since the children were unwilling to receive the bread when he came to his own, he gave to all who

---

[185]Heb (MT) *b'l* ("to rule over, to marry," KB 142). The LXX presupposes *bhl* ("to despise," KB 119). Jerome agrees with Aq. [186]Heb *qrb* ("entrails, inward parts," KB 1135). [187]Heb 8:8-12; 10:16-17. Jerome says that Hebrews is not considered to be one of Paul's letters because it differs from Paul's style, although the ideas may come from Paul. Some suggested Barnabas or Luke as the author, but Jerome favors Clement of Rome (*Vir. Ill.* 5.10; 15.2). [188]Rom 2:9; 7:6; 2 Cor 3:6; Gal 3:19-29; Col 2:11-12, 16-17; Heb 9:6–10:18, etc. [189]2 Cor 3:3. [190]Mk 7:8; Col 2:8. [191]1 Cor 3:16. [192]Jn 3:8. [193]1 Cor 12:4. [194]Cf. the Stoic doctrine that all of the virtues are linked together. Although distinct, the virtues are inseparable, and a person who has one virtue has them all (e.g., Plutarch *Stoic. Rep.* 1034C-E; 1046E-F). [195]Mt 15:24. [196]Acts 13:46. [197]Mt 15:26.

received him power to become children of God.[198]

31:35-36: *Thus says the Lord, who gives the sun for light by day and the order of the moon and the stars for light by night, who stirs up the sea and its waves roar—the Lord of Hosts is his name: "If those laws"—or "these statutes"*[199]*—"cease before me, says the Lord, then also the seed of Israel shall fail, so that they will not be a nation before me forever."*[200]

We read also at the beginning of Genesis that the sun was placed in heaven for light by day, and that the moon and stars likewise were placed for light by night.[201] And in the psalm we read, "Day to day announces speech, and night to night declares knowledge,"[202] because day and night come one after another in succession. He says, "Just as the order of things (especially the heavenly stars) cannot be changed, and the waves in the roaring seas roll toward the shore, and the terrible crashing of the deep and of the swelling waters is heard—and still they cannot go beyond what has been decreed by God's command, as it says, 'You set a bound that they do not pass, nor shall they return to cover the earth'[203]—in the very same way," he says, "the seed and race of Israel shall be eternal by the Lord's decision and shall never fail." The "laws" here are not to be understood as the Mosaic laws but as the set pattern and order of nature.

We may ask the Jews: "If the heavens will 'perish' and 'all wear out like a garment,' and it is said to God, 'But you are the same and your years do not fail,'[204] how can the seed of Israel be eternal?" For either as the heavens perish, the seed of Israel will also perish, or else if the

seed of Israel is eternal, then the heavens will not perish. But if Scripture cannot lie and the heavens are going to perish, then the seed of Israel will also perish—especially since Jacob says to his sons, "Come, and I will announce to you what will be in the last days."[205] When it says "in the last days," it suggests that the world will cease to be and another dispensation of things will come about. This is against them.

Otherwise, as it relates to us, the Gospel also shows that this world is not eternal, saying, "Heaven and earth will pass away,"[206] and, "Behold, I am with you always, to the close of the age."[207] We can also say this differently: as long as this world exists the seed of Israel and the Jewish nation shall remain, not among those who are presently unbelieving but among those who along with the apostles and through the apostles believe, so that the remnant might be saved.[208]

31:37: *Thus says the Lord: "If the heavens above could be measured and the foundations of the earth below be explored, then I would cast off all the seed of Israel for all that they have done, says the Lord."* LXX: *Thus says the Lord: "If heaven were raised up higher and if the base of the earth was lowered down, also I will not reject the race of Israel, says the Lord, because of all that they have done."*[209]

There is much in this passage where the Hebrew differs from the popular edition. Let us explain it first according to the Hebrew: "If the heavens above could be measured" and their altitude known, or "if the foundations of the earth below could be explored" and their lowest point comprehended by reason, "then,"

---

[198]Jn 1:11-12. [199]The first option is Jerome's IH edition, but it also matches the LXX. The identity of the second option is not known. Hexaplaric evidence is lacking. The Targ has "covenants." [200]Jerome's IH edition has "If those laws fail before me." Also, some MSS of the commentary lack the word *nation*. But it is supplied here in the lemma in accordance with the IH edition, a few MSS of the commentary and Jerome's discussion below (e.g., "the seed of Israel and the Jewish nation"). [201]Gen 1:14-18. [202]Ps 19:2. [203]Ps 104:9. [204]Ps 102:25-27. [205]Gen 49:1. [206]Mt 24:35; Mk 13:31; Lk 21:33. [207]Mt 28:20. [208]Rom 9:27; 11:5. [209]Jerome agrees with Aq and essentially matches MT. See also Origen *Fr. Jer.* 59.

he says, "I would cast off all the seed of Israel for all that they have done, says the Lord." Just as it is impossible for us to understand the highest reaches of the heavens and the foundations of the earth, so also it is impossible that "I would cast off all the seed of Israel." "But if I am going to cast off all the seed of Israel, then the high point of the heavens and the lowest point of the earth could be measured." This is a syllogism,[210] such as is constructed in the Gospel when the impossible is compared with the impossible: "It is easier for a camel to go through the eye of a needle than for a rich man to go into the kingdom of heaven."[211] For just as the one cannot possibly happen, so also the other cannot possibly happen. But if the first one were to take place, then the other one, which was thought to be impossible, could also take place. They are in error, therefore, who explain this passage differently by citing as testimony the fact that the Son could have petitioned the Father and summoned twelve legions of angels to his aid.[212]

The translation produced by the LXX is the exact opposite of the sense given above: "If heaven were raised up higher and the base of the earth was lowered down," he says, "also I will not reject the seed of Israel, says the Lord, on account of all that they have done." But if it is thus, then the nation of Israel is being rejected.[213] For just as heaven, being what it is, cannot be higher, nor can the earth, being what

it is, be made lower, so also the race of Israel cannot by any means find approval. If we see the Jews boasting in this testimony according to the Hebrew, we may agree with them that the whole seed of Israel was not cast aside, for not all were cast aside but only those who were unbelieving.

31:38-40: *"Behold, the days are coming, says the Lord, when the city shall be built for the Lord from the tower of Hananel to the Corner Gate. And the standard"*—or, according to Symmachus, *"line"*[214]—*"of measuring shall go out farther, facing it*[215] *over the hill Gareb, and it shall go around Goatha"*—or, according to the LXX, *"with choice stones."*[216] *"The whole valley of ruin"*—in place of which Theodotion put the Hebrew word itself, *"Phagarim"*[217]— *"and the ashes, and all Asaremoth"*—which we read better as *"Asademoth,"* which Aquila translated as *"suburbs"*[218]—*"as far as the torrent Kidron, to the corner of the Gate of Horses toward the east, shall be sacred to the Lord. It shall not be uprooted or overthrown until forever."*[219]

Those who accept a thousand-year reign of Christ in the land of Judea—namely, the Jews and our Judaizers—try to point to the tower of Hananel, the Corner Gate, the hill Gareb, Goatha, the valley of Phagarim, all Asademoth, the torrent Kidron and the corner of the

---

[210]The fourth-century rhetorician Julius Victor (*Art of Rhetoric* 9) defines a syllogism as "a form of argument that draws a probable conclusion from the content of the argument itself; once the conclusion has been set forth and examined by itself, it confirms itself by its own force and reasoning." See Cicero *Inv.* 1.57; cf. Aristotle *An. Pr.* 24b; 18-20. [211]Mt 19:24; Mk 10:25; Lk 18:25. [212]Mt 26:53. [213]The LXX, apparently misunderstanding the contrary-to-fact nature of this conditional sentence, added a negative to the apodosis and thereby said the opposite of what the verse intends. [214]The first option is Jerome, which matches Aq. [215]IH edition: "in his sight." Heb *ngdw*. Jerome is more literalistic here. [216]The first option, "it shall go around Goatha," matches Jerome's IH edition (but *circumibit* here instead of IH *circuibit*). The LXX reads, "It shall be surrounded all around with choice stones." The Hebrew verb *sbb* ("go around, surround") is Niphal, allowing either Jerome's middle sense or the LXX's passive. Jerome's "Goatha" agrees with Aq (= MT). [217]Heb *pgrym* ("corpses," KB 911). Jerome put "corpses" in the IH edition and "ruin" here, both of which are possible translations of Sym's *ptōma* (LSJ 1549). Th and Aq transliterate the word. The whole clause is absent from the LXX. [218]In MT, Ketiv = *hšrmwt*; Qere = *hšdmwt* (on the Ketiv and Qere, see the Introduction). The difference results from the confusion of the similar letters *dalet* and *resh* (cf. Jerome *Comm. Isa.* 8:9-10; 21:11-12; 28:9; 38:10-13; 44:24-28; *Comm. Ezech.* 27:15b-16; *Comm. Hos.* 2:10-12; 9:7; *Comm. Jer.* 15:12). The LXX transliterates the word with *resh*. Jerome's Hebrew text has *dalet*. In addition to Aq's rendering, Jerome also had Sym's "region of burials" (cf. IH: "region of death," as discussed below), and the Greek transliteration of "the Hebrew" in Eusebius (*Onom.* 38), *sadēmōth*. [219]IH edition: "any more forever" (= MT: *'wd l'wlm*). Here: "until forever" (=*'d l'wlm*).

Gate of Horses toward the east, and they say that in this place the sanctuary of the Lord—that is, the temple—will be established and will remain forever.[220] Since they cannot show that this took place after the captivity in the times of Zerubbabel and Ezra, they pass over to the times of Christ. They say that Christ will come at the consummation of the world, so that a golden and bejeweled Jerusalem may descend as in the Apocalype of John[221] and be built all around this plot of ground, that is, from this specific place to that one. And they grasp onto this slight breeze as hinting at their notion that the foundations of the city will be laid from the Tower of Anathoth (which today is called the tower of Jeremiah, located three thousand paces from Jerusalem),[222] to the torrent Kidron (which is mentioned in the Gospel and is in the valley of Jehoshaphat, where he had admonished them and where Judas the traitor also betrayed the Savior).[223] They say, "We are about to read in what follows that Hanamel the son of Shallum was Jeremiah's cousin, and Jeremiah buys his field.[224] This is the tower of Hananel!" Yet, they are ignorant of the Hebrew truth, for this is written according to the Hebrew: "from the tower of Hananel," that is, with a *nun* as the middle letter; whereas in the other passage it says, "Behold, Hanamel the son of Shallum, your cousin, will come to you,"[225] with "m" as the middle letter.

Therefore, calling on our Lord and Savior, "who has the key of David, who opens and no one shall shut, who shuts and no one opens,"[226] who also opened the sealed book of Isaiah and of all the prophets[227] and who was worshiped by the twenty-four elders holding

lutes since he alone was able to unlock the divine mysteries, let us approach the building of the city to which the prophetic word is directed: "Glorious things are spoken of you, O city of God,"[228] and "The rush of the river makes glad the city of God."[229] Accordingly, the church will be built from the tower of "obedience" or "the grace (and "gifts") of God"—for this is the interpretation of "Hananel"[230]—to the Corner Gate. Although this gate appears to have a lofty entrance, as long as we remain in this flesh we are not able to possess the straight line of truth, but we stand in the corner and in broken lines. And so the line of measuring goes out farther, facing it (that is, the Corner Gate) over the hill "Gareb," which translates into our language as "residing" or "skin rash,"[231] in order to teach us that we are strangers and foreigners with ears itching to give our ready consent to the novelty of wicked doctrines.[232]

He says, "And it shall go around Goatha," which the LXX translated as "all around with choice stones," which are built up on the land[233] and which are held together by the cornerstone,[234] as the apostle Peter says: "And like living stones be yourselves built into a spiritual house, to be a holy priesthood, to offer spiritual sacrifices acceptable to God through Jesus Christ."[235] And he says, "the whole valley of *Phagarim* (which means 'ruin'), and the ashes" (understand: "will go all around"), so that, even though it may seem to us that we are on high ground, we should always be afraid of falling into ruin, and we should consider the ashes and say penitently with David: "For I eat ashes like bread and mingle tears with my drink."[236] Thus it is said

---

[220]On Judaizers and the millennium, see Jer 19:10-11a; 31:27-30. [221]Rev 21:2, 10-21. [222]See Jer 11:21-23. [223]Jn 18:1-5. On the "valley of Jehoshaphat," see Joel 3:2, 12. [224]Jer 32:7-9. [225]Jer 32:7. [226]Rev 3:7. [227]Is 29:11. [228]Ps 87:3. [229]Ps 46:4 (LXX [45:5]). [230]Heb *ḥnn'l*. This could be read as *ḥēn* ("grace") and *'ēl* ("God"). The Latin *gratia* is used for both "grace" (Gk *charis*) and "gifts" (Gk *charisma*) as in 1 Cor 12:4, 9. In the *Nom. Hebr.*, Jerome gave "grace of God" for *Ananehel* (OS 52.30) and for *Ananahel* (OS 53.11); he also gave "one to whom God has given" for *Ananehel* (OS 53.10). The Greek onomastica gave "grace of God" for *anameēl* (OS 162.25; 186.20), as did Origen *Fr. Jer.* 60. The basis for the meaning "obedience" is not clear. [231]Heb *grb* ("festering rash," KB 201). Heb *gēr* means "sojourner, stranger." [232]2 Tim 4:3. [233]Zech 9:16 in the IH edition. [234]Eph 2:20; 1 Pet 2:6. [235]1 Pet 2:5. [236]Ps 102:9.

to those who lie low: "When people fall, do they not rise again? says the Lord."[237]

He says, "And all *Sademoth*," which we translate as "region of death," dividing the one name into two words: *sade*, which means "region," and *moth*, which means "death."[238] In place of this Aquila translated "suburbs," or "arable, country land."[239] Now the "region of death" is a region of sins, and the "suburbs" is a region of desires, which goes "as far as the torrent Kidron," which is interpreted as "darkness," where the Lord was betrayed.[240] See how many of these places the church has! And see how the apostolic saying, "that she may be without spot or wrinkle,"[241] is reserved for the future and the celestial realm. You hear of the corner, you hear of the skin rash, you hear of the ruin and the ashes and of the region of death and the darkness—and still you boast in your virtue and sinlessness![242]

And so he goes on: "to the corner of the Gate." It is a "corner," so as not to indicate any true righteousness or settled victory in this world. This is also a "corner gate;" although it is "toward the east," from where the light arises, it is nevertheless called a gate "of Horses," in order to teach us that we are required to race and to struggle, and in the end we may be worthy to hear together with the Lord: "You mounted up on your horses; your riding is salvation."[243] The sanctification of the Lord is in the eastern gate, in the gate of chariots, so that we may reckon ourselves as perfect only at that time when we have said to the Lord, "The chariot of God is ten thousandfold, thousands of those who rejoice; the Lord is among them."[244] A building of this kind, which is laid on the foundation of Christ and about which the apostle says, "Like a wise builder I laid a foundation,"[245] shall never be

overthrown but shall endure forever. Obscure and difficult matters should be discussed more extensively, so that we may touch more briefly on things that are clear.

32:1-3a: *The word that came to Jeremiah from the Lord in the tenth year of Zedekiah king of Judah; this was the eighteenth year of Nebuchadnezzar. At that time the army of the king of Babylon was besieging Jerusalem, and Jeremiah the prophet was shut up in the court of the guard that was in the house of the king of Judah. For Zedekiah king of Judah had imprisoned him, saying, "Why do you prophesy and say, 'Thus says the Lord'?"*

Not only the words but also the deeds of the prophets are to be examples of virtue for us. Jeremiah could have announced prosperity and made use of his friendship with King Zedekiah, but he preferred to obey God rather than human beings,[246] obeying him who is able to kill both body and soul in Gehenna rather than those who have power over the body alone.[247] And we should take note of this: it was the tenth year of the reign of Zedekiah, Jerusalem was already under siege, the city was being consumed by sword, famine and pestilence, and captivity was near. And still Zedekiah persisted in his decision! To some extent it was a demonstration of Zedekiah's clemency that he ordered Jeremiah to be confined not in prison but in "the court of the guard," that is, in free-moving confinement, so as to keep Jeremiah from being able to escape,[248] as if all Jerusalem were not a common prison for its inhabitants, shut in by its protective fortifications. This is the eighteenth year of the reign of Nebuchadnezzar, who came to power in the fourth year of King

---

[237]Jer 8:4. [238]Heb *śdh* ("field, land") and *mwt* ("death"). [239]Jerome is giving alternative Latin translations of Aq's Greek word, *proasteia*. [240]Heb *qdrwn* (cf. *qdr* ["to become dark" KB 1072]). See Jn 18:1-5. In the *Nom. Hebr.*, Jerome gave "severe sadness and grief" (OS 53.23) as the meaning of "Cedron." [241]Eph 5:27. [242]Cf. *Pelag.* 1.25; 3.4, etc. [243]Hab 3:8. [244]Ps 68:17 (LXX [67:18]). [245]1 Cor 3:10-11. [246]Acts 5:29. [247]Mt 10:28. [248]Jer 37:21; 38:13, 28.

Jehoiakim.[249] Now the whole basis for the king's anger is this: that the prophet speaks in the name of the Lord the things that were commanded to him.

32:3b-5: *"Behold, I am giving this city into the hand of the king of Babylon, and he shall take it; Zedekiah king of Judah shall not escape out of the hand of the Chaldeans but shall be given into the hand of the king of Babylon and shall speak with him face to face and see him eye to eye; and he shall lead Zedekiah to Babylon, and there he shall be until I visit him, says the Lord; but if you fight against the Chaldeans, you shall not have success."*

The reason for the king's anger was that the prophet preferred truth to falsehood and said that both the city of Jerusalem and King Zedekiah would be taken captive. Also, it is a grievous thing that he will see the face of the king of Babylon and that as a lowly captive he will speak with him out of his own folly as a powerless king. For it is a grievous terror to see the one whom you fear and to endure chastisement by words prior to the anguish of torture. He says, "And he shall lead Zedekiah to Babylon, and there he shall be," in place of which the LXX translated, "And Zedekiah shall enter Babylon,"[250] the one indicating that he was dragged unwilling, the other that he went by his own choice. "And there," he says, "he shall be"—he leaves the word ambiguous, so as not to appear to be prophesying torments and miseries. And that which follows, "until I visit him, says the Lord; but if you fight against the Chaldeans, you shall not have success," is not

found in the LXX. Prudently the prophet tempered his judgment, which as it is could be taken in either a good or bad sense. For "visitation," as I said above, can mean either "consolation" or "punishment."[251]

32:6-7: *Jeremiah said, "The word of the Lord came to me: Behold, Hanamel, the son of Shellum,"*—or *"Shalom"*[252]—*"your cousin,"*—which in Hebrew is *dodach*[253]—*"will come to you and say, 'Buy my field that is at Anathoth, for it is fitting for you to buy it in view of your kinship.' "*[254]

No one could have known that a secret word of God came to Jeremiah unless it was made known by the one to whom the word came. It is announced to Jeremiah that Hanamel his cousin is going to come to him and offer him possession of a field that had been his own. Moreover, this particular place in Anathoth was one of the local villas that had been given according to the Law to the priests throughout all of the individual tribes and cities.[255] It was not permitted for them to transfer possession from one tribe to another or from one family to another;[256] thus the daughters of Zelophehad received their assigned lot among their brothers.[257] And most importantly, the local villas of the priests were not to be sold to any other person even down to the year of remission, unless that person was of blood kinship.[258] Therefore Jeremiah's cousin, his near relation, comes to him and offers him the right of purchase, which was owed to him because of his kinship.

Hilkiah and Shellum were full brothers; Jeremiah was the son of Hilkiah, and Hanamel

---

[249]Jer 25:1. [250]Jerome's "lead" matches MT, which has the Hiphil of the verb *blk* and a direct object marker in front of "Zedekiah." The LXX presupposes the Qal of *blk* ("go") and takes "Zedekiah" as the subject. [251]See Jer 5:7-9; Jerome *Comm. Isa.* 24:21-23; *Comm. Ezech.* 9:1a; *Comm. Am.* 3:1-2. [252]Heb *šlm*, interpreted here as *šālōm* ("peace"; see Origen *Fr. Jer.* 60). At Jer 22:10-12, Jerome interpreted this name (vocalized as *šallum* in MT at Jer 22:11 and Jer 32:7) as "completion" (see KB 1533). [253]Heb *ddk* (MT: *dōdĕkā*; i.e., *dwd* ["beloved, father's brother," KB 215]) plus the second person masculine singular suffix. Jerome understands the word as referring to Hanamel, not Shellum. [254]The expression "to buy it" here is *emtio*, whereas in the IH edition Jerome used *ut emas*. [255]Num 35:2-3; Josh 21:1-42. [256]Num 36:7-9. [257]See Num 27:7; 36:10-12. [258]See Lev 25:34; Num 36:2-4.

was the son of Shellum. "Hilkiah" is interpreted as "portion of the Lord," and "Jeremiah" is interpreted as "loftiness of the Lord."[259] And rightly is the highness of the Lord born out of the Lord's portion. Now "Shellum" in our language is translated as "peace" or "peaceable," and Hanamel is "gift (or 'grace') of God."[260] We should not be surprised that "peace" is joined together with "grace," since this is also the opening of apostolic epistles: "Grace to you and peace."[261] First we obtain the peace of God; and after peace, grace is born to us, which is not by the will of the one who possesses it but by the will of the one who gives. The "grace of God" offers the right of purchase to him who converses in "lofty things," so that, although he may appear to be exalted, nevertheless he is needful of God's grace.

That which in the Song is often sung by the bride, "my nephew" (that is, *o adelphidos mou*), in Hebrew is *dodi*. Therefore, it should not be "nephew" but "father's brother's son," that is, "cousin."[262] Moreover, the introduction of this book bears witness that Jeremiah was the son of Hilkiah, one of the priests of Anathoth in the land of Benjamin.[263]

32:8a: *Then Hanamel, the son of my uncle, came to me in the court—or entryway[264]—of the guard, in accordance with the word of the Lord, and said to me, "Possess"—or "Buy"[265]—"my field that is at Anathoth in the land of Benjamin, for it is right for you to inherit it, and you are a relative, so that you may possess"—or "buy"—"it."*

That which the word of God announced to the prophet as going to happen in the future was fulfilled in deed immediately. He says, "Hanamel ('the grace of God'), the son of my uncle (that is, 'the son of peace'), came to me in the entryway of the guard and said to me the things that the Lord predicted he would say."[266] This priestly field, which was offered to Jeremiah to buy or possess, is at "Anathoth" in the land of "Benjamin," the first of which means "obedience," and the second means "son of the right hand."[267] And it is appropriate that he seeks to buy a field where "obedience" and the "strength" of the Lord dwell.[268] Instead of "relative," the LXX translated *presbyteron*, that is, "elder," which does not fit this passage.

32:8b-11: *Then I knew that this was the word of the Lord. And I bought the field at Anathoth from Hanamel, the son of my uncle, and weighed out the money to him, seven standard coins and ten silver coins. I wrote in a book, sealed it, brought witnesses and weighed the money on scales. Then I took the sealed book of possession, the stipulations fixed and sealed on the outside.*

Jeremiah had prophesied that Jerusalem was about to be captured and that everyone would be taken captive or else perish by sword, famine or pestilence. Therefore it was quite difficult, almost illogical and worthy of laughter for him to buy a field at Anathoth that he was not going to possess. "But I knew,"

[259]This interpretation of Hilkiah (*hlqyhw*) understands *hlq* ("portion") and the divine name (*yhw*); see Origen *Fr. Jer.* 60. On the meaning of Jeremiah, see Jer 1:10; 23:9b. [260]On Shellum, see n. 252. On Hanamel, see Jer 31:38-40. [261]Rom 1:7; 1 Cor 1:3; 2 Cor 1:2; Gal 1:3; Eph 1:2; Phil 1:2; Col 1:2; 1 Thess 1:1; 2 Thess 1:2; Philem 3; 1 Pet 1:2; 2 Pet 1:2; Rev 1:4. [262]Jerome interprets the Greek word *adelphidos* in the LXX at Song 1:13 as "nephew" and attempts to correct this by pointing out that the underlying Hebrew is the same as in this passage, *dwd*, which Jerome interprets as "cousin." What I have translated as "father's brother's son" is the Latin word *patradelfus*, which matches Aq (*patradelphos*) at Song 1:13. [263]Jer 1:1. [264]The first option matches Jerome's handling of the same phrase in Jer 32:2, whereas the second option reflects Jerome's IH rendering for this passage. [265]The first option ("possess") represents Jerome's IH edition and essentially represents the LXX and what is preserved for Th and Aq. The second option ("buy") matches the Targ (*tbwn*) and the Pesh (*zbn*). Heb *qnh* ("buy, acquire," KB 1112). The words are all close in meaning. [266]On Hanamel and Shellum (Jeremiah's uncle), see Jer 31:38-40; 32:6-7. [267]On Anathoth and Benjamin, see Jer 11:21-23; 6:1. [268]For "son of the right hand" (Benjamin) as "strength," see Jer 32:42-44.

he says, "that this was the word of the Lord and that my purchase by money was to be united with the Lord's prophecy. And so I agreed to the Lord's command that I should buy it. I knew that the word of the Lord would not come to me without good reason on a matter like this, so I weighed out ten silver coins and seven 'shekels' "—which we translated as "standard coins."[269] "And the shekel shall be twenty gerahs," as is written at the end of the book of Ezekiel.[270]

The prophet bought the field for seventeen shekels; by this number the Lord's servant David sang, "on the day when the Lord delivered him from the hand of all his enemies and from the hand of Saul."[271] "He said: I shall love you, O Lord, my strength. The Lord is my firmness, and my refuge and my deliverer; my God is my helper, and I shall hope in him; he is my protector and the horn of my salvation."[272] That the number of coins is mystical is shown by the Decalogue, which was written on tablets of stone by the finger of God,[273] and by the day of fasting and atonement in the seventh month.[274] We can confirm by many testimonies of Scripture the holiness of the number seven, in which there is true sabbath rest and repose.[275] In any case, I would have set down a few words about this were it not useless to teach things that are already well known. Therefore, by this number the right of possession was purchased by him who was priest and prophet. It was written in a book and sealed, witnesses were brought, and money was carefully weighed, so that all of the laws of buying and selling might be preserved and so that the act of possession might be confirmed, certified by stipulations and declarations. Let them hear this, who attempt to make legal claims through false wills, and sometimes even without wills, simply by bringing witnesses to testify for them!

32:12: *And I gave the book of possession to Baruch the son of Neriah son of Mahseiah, in the sight of Hanamel my cousin, in the sight of the witnesses who had been recorded in the book of purchase and in the sight of all the Jews who were sitting in the court of the guard.*

Although Jeremiah's possession of the field was going to be relinquished very soon—or rather, it was being purchased for future generations by him who had no sons, since he had not married[276]—nevertheless, in obedience to the Lord's command Jeremiah announced everything publicly in accordance with custom, and he gave the sealed book of possession to Baruch the son of Neriah son of Mahseiah. "Baruch" in our language means "blessed."[277] He was the son of "Neriah," which is translated as "my lamp,"[278] as the prophet says: "Your word is a lamp for my feet and a glowing light for my path."[279] Neriah, Baruch's father, is the son of "Mahseiah," that is, "creation (or 'work') of the Lord."[280] Therefore, let us take note of how many virtuous qualities Baruch the disciple had in

---

[269]From Heb *šeqel*. The LXX used *siklous* (Lat *siclos*) = "shekel." But Jerome translated with the word *stateres* ("standard coin"), which matches Aq and Sym (*statēras*). [270]Ezek 45:12. [271]Ps 18:1. This is Ps 17 according to the ancient Greek and Latin reckoning. Jerome sees an interpretive link between the seventeen shekels of Jer 32:9 and Ps 17. [272]Ps 18:1-2 (LXX [17:2-3]). [273]Ex 31:18; Deut 9:10. [274]Lev 16:29-34; 23:27-28; 25:9; Num 29:7; Zech 8:19. [275]Heb 4:9-10. [276]Jer 16:2. [277]Heb *bārûk* (passive participle of *brk*, "to bless"). This was a traditional Greek etymology found in the onomastica (OS 173.70; 185.79; 88.83; 201.56) and repeated by Jerome in the *Nom. Hebr.* (OS 53.19; cf. OS 160.27). [278]Heb *nryh*, which could be interpreted as *nēr* ("light, lamp") and *yh* ("of the Lord"). In the *Nom. Hebr.* Jerome gives "lamp of the Lord" as the meaning for *neria* (OS 55.1) in the section on Jeremiah. But here he transliterates the name as *neri* and interprets it to mean "my lamp" (i.e., *nēr* plus "*y*" the first-person singular suffix), either because the Hebrew text in front of him lacked the final "*h*" or because he was thinking of Neri in Lk 3:27 (see OS 65.15). In the Greek onomastica, *nēreus* was interpreted as "lamp of Christ" (OS 196.100). [279]Ps 119:105. [280]MT: *mhsyh* (perhaps, "refuge of the Lord"). Jerome's "creation" or "work of the Lord" reflects the consonants *m'syh*, which is found in a few Hebrew MSS (Kennicott 137). This is also the meaning given in the *Nom. Hebr.* (OS 54.24), which means that Jerome probably took it over from his Greek source.

---

ministering to Jeremiah; as David says, "He who walks in the way that is blameless shall minister to me."[281] So also Elisha, who ministered to Elijah, pleased God so much that after his master was carried away he was found worthy to receive a double share of his spirit.[282] I say this in order to admonish those who derive benefit from the ministries of bad people and are not bold enough to cast aside these bad people even though their guilty consciences know that they are joined to them with glue.

The book is handed over to Baruch, such a great man as this, in the sight of Hanamel, who had sold the field, and in the sight of the witnesses who had written in the book and whose names were being kept in the document of purchase. "And in the sight," he says, "of all the Jews who were sitting in the court of the guard," namely, those who came to comfort the prophet or who desired to hear the words of the Lord because of their earnest fear of God.

32:13-15: *"And I charged Baruch before them, saying, 'Thus says the Lord of hosts, the God of Israel: Take these books, both this sealed book of purchase and this book that is open, and put them in an earthenware vessel, that they may last for many days. For thus says the Lord of hosts, the God of Israel: Houses and fields and vineyards shall be possessed again in this land.'"*

Before all whom the previous narrative mentioned as present and watching,[283] he charges Baruch his servant and disciple, not simply with the words of a teacher but by the authority of God's command, that he should take

books, one sealed and the other open. This custom of purchasing is observed so that if anyone wants to read what is contained inside the book that is closed up by the seal, the open volume may be shown to him. He is to take both books and put them "in an earthenware vessel, that they may last for many days." Therefore, this right of possession was a sure thing and would take place after a long time, since it was preserved by this great protection. They did not want the books of possession to be left outside and exposed to plundering or stored in the ground to dissolve in the moisture of the earth. And this whole thing took place so that those who were watching would know that Jerusalem would again be inhabited and their fields possessed. Although they should have understood this on their own without the word of Jeremiah, they are reminded of this by the words of the Lord, and it is said to them: "Thus says the Lord of hosts, the God of Israel: Houses and fields and vineyards shall be possessed again in this land." This is what Jeremiah had said a short while ago: "Then I knew that this was the word of the Lord."[284] This is the reason why he bought a field that he was not going to possess.

32:16-19: *"And I prayed to the Lord after I had given the book of possession to Baruch the son of Neriah, saying, 'Ah, ah, ah, Lord God!'—or 'You who are, Lord God'[285]— 'Behold, you have made heaven and earth by your great power and by your outstretched'— or 'uplifted'[286]—'arm! No word is too difficult'—or 'impossible'—'for you,'—or according to the* LXX, *'nothing is hidden from you,'[287]*

[281]Ps 101:6. [282]2 Kings 2:9-11, 15. [283]Jer 32:12. [284]Jer 32:8. [285]In Hebrew, Jer 32:17 begins with the letters *'hh*, which Jerome takes to be an interjection (see KB 18, "alas") as do Aq and Sym ("O, Lord, Lord!"). Jerome repeats his interjection three times ("heu, heu, heu") for effect, or perhaps to match the three letters of the Hebrew word. The LXX, reading *'hh* as a form of the verb "to be" (*hyh*), translated "the one who is" (*o ōn*), which Jerome rendered into Latin as "you who are." [286]Jerome matches Aq and Sym (= MT). [287]Heb *pl'* (Niphal; "to be difficult, wonderful," KB 927). The first option is Jerome's IH translation, and the alternative ("impossible") is a literal rendering of Sym. Two readings are reported for Aq, "impossible" and "wondrous." The LXX, "nothing is hidden from you," is matched by the Targ and the Pesh.

'who shows mercy to thousands but renders the guilt of fathers to the bosom of their sons after them, O mighty, great and powerful'—which in Hebrew is *gibbor*[288]—*'the Lord of Armies'—or 'of Strength'*[289]—*'is your name! Great in counsel and incomprehensible in thought, whose eyes are open to all the ways of the sons of Adam'—or 'of humans'—'to render to every person according to his ways and according to the fruit of his doings.'"*

After the purchase of the field was publicly made known as required,[290] and after the Lord's statement in which he promised that houses, fields and vineyards would later be possessed,[291] the prophet prays to the Lord and expresses the grief of his heart in sighs, saying, "Ah, ah, ah, Lord God!" in place of which the LXX translated *o ōn*, that is, "you who are, Lord God," just as was said to Moses, "Go, say to the people Israel, 'The One Who Is has sent me.'"[292] It is not that no one else exists. But it is one thing to exist because of the graciousness of the Creator and another to exist because of an eternal nature. The prophet praises God, proclaiming the Creator on the basis of created things. First of all, the prophet extols God's power, mercy and justice toward the whole race of humans; then, passing on to Israel, he describes in majestic language what great deeds God performed for them. But even after such great blessings, he says that they were forgetful of his goodness and provoked his mildness to bitterness. As a result their city was besieged, and even before their enemies could break in against them, they were consumed by sword, famine and pestilence. Yet, God sent forth all these things so that afterwards he might introduce something that seems to put the divine decree to reproof: "Yet you, O Lord God, say to me, 'Buy the field for money and get witnesses, though the city is

given into the hand of the Chaldeans.'"[293] This is the content of this whole section of the passage;[294] let us now return to the individual details.

"You have made heaven and earth by your great power." John says concerning the Son, "All things were made through him, and without him was not anything made that was made."[295] For he is this "power" of the Lord, as the apostle confirms: "Christ the power of God and the wisdom of God."[296] "And by your outstretched (or 'uplifted') arm"—both of which signify striking. This is the arm about which Isaiah also speaks: "And to whom has the arm of the Lord been revealed?"[297] "No word is too difficult for you," since "what is impossible with people is possible with God."[298] Or, "Nothing is hidden from you," in accordance with what the psalmist says: "Since the darkness is not hidden from you, even the night is bright like the day."[299] "Who shows mercy to thousands but renders the guilt of fathers to the bosom of their sons after them." It is the great compassion of the Creator to extend his mercy to a thousand generations and to show his justice immediately in the next generation—justice that is itself mixed with mercy. For he does not immediately punish those who go astray, but he waits for their repentance, so that their punishment has been deferred for a long time before it is finally rendered—assuming that the children have imitated the sins of the parents. "O mighty, great and powerful, the Lord of Armies (or 'of Strength') is your name!" These names indicate the power of the Creator. Otherwise, the name of God properly speaking is Father, which is revealed in the Gospel when the Lord says, "Father . . . I have manifested your name to human beings."[300]

"Great in counsel"—and anyone dares to insert himself into the Lord's secrets and make

---

[288]Heb *gibbôr* ("manly, vigorous," KB 172). [289]See Jer 10:12-16. [290]Jer 32:12. [291]Jer 32:15. [292]Ex 3:14. [293]Jer 32:25. [294]Jer 32:16-25. [295]Jn 1:3. [296]1 Cor 1:24. [297]Is 53:1. [298]Lk 18:27; Mt 19:26. [299]Ps 139:12. [300]Jn 17:5-6.

determinations about his judgments! ". . . and incomprehensible in thought"—if thought does not comprehend him, how could speech possibly comprehend him? ". . . whose eyes are open to all the ways of the sons of Adam"—it is therefore pointless for a person to think that he can conceal anything from God's knowing. As for what he adds, "to render to every person according to his ways and according to the fruit of his doings," it signifies this: sometimes, because God's wisdom is beyond measure, his judgments may appear to be unjust. Paul explains this topic more fully to the Romans: "Do you not know that God's kindness is meant to lead you to repentance? But by your hard and impenitent heart you are storing up wrath for yourself on the day of wrath when God's righteous judgment will be revealed."[301] Therefore, the later in coming the punishment of sinners is, the more just God is. This is similar to Pharaoh, who was warned—not punished—by the ten plagues. But because he persisted in his hardness to the end he was buried in the waves of the Red Sea.[302]

32:20-23: *"You who set signs and wonders in the land of Egypt to this day in Israel and among humankind"—or "those born from the earth"*[303]*—"and made yourself a name, as at this day. You brought your people Israel out of the land of Egypt with signs and wonders, with a strong hand and outstretched arm and with great terror; and you gave them this land, which you swore to their fathers to give them, a land flowing with milk and honey; and they entered and took possession of it. But they did not obey your voice or walk in your law; all that you commanded them to do, they did not do. And so all this evil has come on them."*

Passing over from the general to the specific, he goes through in brief terms what exactly God accomplished for Israel. He says, "You who set signs and wonders in the land of Egypt"—with which he afflicted the Egyptians—"to this day in Israel and among humankind" (or "among those born from the earth"). This is what it means: "to this day" should be joined to what follows, so that we read, "even today your signs are being fulfilled both in Israel and among all human beings." Or, to put it differently: "Not only did you perform signs and wonders in Egypt, but even today the very same strength of your mercy saves your people, and in the power of the Creator you come to the aid of the whole race of humankind." And this should be noted: "Israel" is distinguished from "humankind" or "those born from the earth" in accordance with this testimony: "Israel is my firstborn son."[304] ". . . and made yourself a name, as at this day." He says, "Your praises are celebrated in the speech of the whole world."

"You brought your people Israel out of the land of Egypt." Beautifully he says "your people," for at the time when they were brought out, they were obedient to the Lord's commands. Moreover, "you brought them out with signs and wonders"—with which Egypt was afflicted—"with a strong hand and outstretched arm and with great terror"— when he provided a way for the people of Israel to pass through the Red Sea but crushed the army of the Egyptians.[305] "And you gave them this land, which you swore to their fathers"— namely, to Abraham, Isaac and Jacob—"to give them." Therefore, not by their own merit but by the virtues of their fathers did they receive the land of promise, "a land flowing with milk and honey." For they were not yet able to receive solid food,[306] but like infants they were nourished with milk and honey; or else the land flowed "with milk and honey," that is, richness and abundance in all things.

---

[301]Rom 2:4-5. [302]Ex 7:13, 14, 22; 8:15, 19, 32; 9:7, 34, 35; 14:27-28. [303]Heb *'dm* ("humankind"). Jerome matches all the hexaplaric versions. [304]Ex 4:22. [305]Ex 14:21-29. [306]Heb 5:11-14.

"And they entered and took possession of it." And right away there was no distinction between their possessing the land and their disobeying the Lord; for richness brought forth security, security brought forth negligence, and negligence brought forth contempt. "But they did not obey your voice," he says, "or walk in your law." Therefore, it was in vain that they promised in the desert: "All that the Lord has commanded we will do,"[307] for reward is not in the promising but in the doing. This should restrain the impudence of those who think that a person is able to fulfill all the things that he has promised to do. "All that you commanded them to do, they did not do"—although they certainly promised that they would do these things. "And so all this evil has come on them." What the Lord renders "to every person according to his ways"[308] is only "evil" to those who suffer it; otherwise, as a judgment of the Lord it is good.

32:24-25: *"Behold, siege works have been built up against the city to take it, and the city is given into the hands of the Chaldeans who are fighting against it, from the face of the sword and famine and pestilence. What you spoke has come to pass, and behold, you see it. Yet you, O Lord God, say to me, 'Buy the field for money and get witnesses, though the city is given into the hand of the Chaldeans.'"*

It was the tenth year of King Zedekiah; for thus it was written: "The word that came to Jeremiah from the Lord in the tenth year of Zedekiah king of Judah. At that time the army of the king of Babylon was besieging Jerusalem, and Jeremiah the prophet was shut up in the court of the guard."[309] So rightly it says here, "Behold, siege works have been built up against

the city to take it, and the city is given into the hands of the Chaldeans." The prophet says, "The Chaldeans do not have in their possession all those whom they have defeated but only those whom they have captured, since many have already been consumed by the sword, famine and pestilence. Indeed, we see that what you spoke about has come to pass. Therefore why, O Lord, do you say to me, 'Buy the field for money and get witnesses, though the city is given into the hand of the Chaldeans'?" Thus the prophet is not rebuking but asking, and he wants to learn the answer, not so much for himself as for the others "who were sitting in the court of the guard,"[310] since these others were perhaps silently finding fault with the fact that the same prophet—whom they believed to be announcing the truth—both says that the city is going to be captured and buys a field as if he were going to possess it.

32:26-29: *The word of the Lord came to Jeremiah: "Behold, I am the Lord, the God of all flesh; is any word too difficult"—or "impossible"—"for me?"—or else "Is any word hidden from me?"[311] "Therefore, thus says the Lord: Behold, I am giving this city into the hand of the Chaldeans and into the hand of Nebuchadnezzar king of Babylon, and he shall take it. And the Chaldeans who are fighting against this city shall come"—or "shall enter"[312]—"and set this city on fire and burn it, with the houses on whose roofs they offered sacrifices to Baal and poured out drink offerings to other gods, so as to provoke me to anger."*

He now adds pleasing statements to the harsh ones, promising to the people who were captured that after the city has been over-

---

[307]Ex 19:8. [308]Jer 32:19. [309]Jer 32:1-2. [310]Jer 32:12. [311]The first option ("difficult") is Jerome, the second ("impossible") is probably Sym, and the third ("hidden from me") is the LXX (agreeing with Targ and Pesh). See Jer 32:16-19. [312]The first option reflects Jerome's IH edition and the LXX; the second option is Aq, which Jerome gives in Greek below (Aq also matches Targ). Heb *bw'* ("come to, come in," KB 113). In the lemma, Jerome also provides the following alternate construal of the syntax: "And the Chaldeans, who are fighting, shall come against this city." On *bau*, see also Jer 31:9.

thrown they will return. But first he gives the reasons for God's offense and righteous anger, since however great the guilt of the sinners may be, the mercy of the Creator toward the sinners will be just as great. He says, "I am the Lord, the God of all flesh." He is not simply the God of all the nations, or the God of the people Israel or even, as is often said concerning the saints, "the God of Abraham, of Isaac and of Jacob,"[313] but he is "the God of all flesh," it says, so that it may be believed that he made both rational beings and brute beasts. For there are some who acknowledge the providence of the Creator as far as rational beings are concerned but claim that brute beasts live or die by chance happenings. But the prophetic word declares that there is nothing that escapes the providence and knowledge of God, since some things are made for their own sake and others are made to be used by people. "Is any word too difficult (or 'impossible') for me?"—or "Is any word hidden from me?" And as we said above, "What is impossible with human beings is possible with God."[314] Moreover, here and in many other passages we should understand "word" in the sense of "things."[315]

Why, then, was the word given? What came before, such that he used the causal conjunction "therefore," saying, "Therefore, thus says the Lord"? He says, "It is my responsibility to govern all things, to determine all things and to render to each one according to his ways; and for this reason "I am giving this city into the hand of the Chaldeans and into the hand of Nebuchadnezzar king of Babylon, and he shall take it." First the city was surrounded by the army, and then, with Nebuchadnezzar absent, Zedekiah was captured and led to Riblah, where he was

handed over to the king. "And the Chaldeans who are fighting against this city shall come." Better is Aquila, who instead of "shall come" translated *eiseleusontai*, that is, "shall enter" the city. For they were not far away, such that they should "come." In fact, they were already surrounding Jerusalem, as Scripture testifies: "At that time the army of the king of Babylon was besieging Jerusalem,"[316] and afterwards, "Siege works have been built up against the city to take it, and the city is given into the hands of the Chaldeans."[317] Therefore, if they are already present, how could they "come"? Rather, it says, "Those who are besieging the city shall enter, and they shall take it and set it on fire, and they shall burn it to the ground"—for the Hebrew word *bau* can mean both "to come to" and "to enter" in view of its ambiguity. He says, "with the houses on whose roofs they offered sacrifices to Baal"—an idol of the Sidonians[318]—"and poured out drink offerings to other gods, so as to provoke me to anger," so that they appear to be offending their Creator not simply out of religious error but out of a certain effort to do so. Moreover, just as it is written that the world will perish: "Heaven and earth will pass away," for it is "in the power of the evil one,"[319] so also the houses themselves and the places where the shameful acts were perpetrated are subject to God's anger.

There are some who stubbornly relate the verse, "where the Lord and Savior was crucified, which is spiritually called Gomorrah and Egypt,"[320] to this passage. But others think that the whole world is signified under the name of Egypt and Gomorrah.[321] For just as Gomorrah was wiped out by divine fire,[322] so also the world will be burned up by God's judgment.[323]

---

[313]E.g., Ex 3:16; Mt 22:32; Mk 12:26; Lk 20:37. [314]Lk 18:27; Mt 19:26. See Jer 32:16-19. [315]The Hebrew *dābār* can mean "word," "matter" or "thing" (KB 211). Jerome translates it with the Latin *verbum* ("word"), which does not normally have this range of meaning, so Jerome must explain the sense. Cf. RSV: "Is any*thing* too hard for me?" [316]Jer 32:2. [317]Jer 32:4. [318]1 Kings 16:31. [319]Mt 24:35; Mk 13:31; 1 Jn 5:19. [320]Rev 11:8. [321]Origen *Hom. Jer.* 9.2; *Hom. Exod.* 2.1; 3.3. [322]Gen 19:24-25. [323]2 Pet 3:7, 11-12.

32:30a: *"For the sons of Israel and the sons of Judah continually"—or "alone"—"have done evil in my eyes from their youth."*

The Hebrew word *ach* Aquila translated as *plēn*, which represents the conjunction "nevertheless." The first edition of Symmachus, the LXX and Theodotion translated it "alone." But the second edition of Symmachus translated it *diolou*, which we have followed in the present passage, so that we put "continually."[324] Therefore, let us first give the sense according to the Hebrew: "The sons of Israel and the sons of Judah continually have done evil." "Both the ten and the two tribes have done evil without ceasing, and they engaged in their wicked deeds with continuous persistence." But if this was continuous and always true for the whole people, where is eternal justice?[325]

Next, here is the sense according to the LXX, who said, "They alone have done evil." The question arises: Did not the other nations also do evil during that time when Israel and Judah were sinning? This is the solution: Only those who have a knowledge of God and then depart from it can "sin" in the eyes of God, whereas those who abide in unbelief merely "offend" God, since it is as if God were not watching or paying attention to them. Thus, after he had fallen into sin with Bathsheba the wife of Uriah,[326] the holy man David repents and says, "Against you only have I sinned and done what is evil before you,"[327] that is, "in your sight." Finally, he adds, "They alone have done evil in my eyes and in my sight from their youth." And that which follows:

32:30b: *"the sons of Israel, who even up to now provoke me to anger by the work of their*

hands, says the Lord" is not found in the LXX but was added from the Hebrew. So then, since from their youth up to the present day they have continually done wrong, the judgment of God is just, and with good reason Scripture continues:

32:31: *"This city has aroused my anger and wrath, from the day they built it to this day, on which I will remove it from my sight."*

From the time when the foundations of the city were laid, to the day on which it was captured, burned and removed from God's sight, this city was always given to vice and provoked God's wrath against itself. If this is so, then—as I have often said before[328]—where is the peaceful rest for sinners?

32:32: *"Because of the evil of the sons of Israel and the sons of Judah that they did to provoke me to anger—their kings and their princes, their priests and their prophets, the men of Judah and the inhabitants of Jerusalem."*

Since he said above, "This city has aroused my anger and wrath, from the day they built it to this day, on which I will remove it from my sight," pointing out generally that no one was without sin, he now specifies them individually: their kings, princes, priests and prophets; and then he includes everyone in one phrase, saying, "the men of Judah and the inhabitants of Jerusalem." Beautifully he did not say, "my kings, my princes, my priests and my prophets," but because they sinned he says, "their kings and their princes, their priests and their prophets."

32:33a: *"They have turned to me their back and not their face."*

---

[324]Heb *'ak* ("yea, surely," "only," "however, but," KB 45). On the "second edition" of Sym, see the Introduction. [325]Jerome asks this question of the Hebrew text, and he does not answer it until he returns to the Hebrew text with his discussion of Jer 32:30b. [326]2 Sam 11. [327]Ps 51:4. This verse would fit Jerome's point better if it said, "Against you I alone have sinned." [328]See Jer 17:15-17; *Comm. Isa.* 57:17-21.

This is like what is written elsewhere: "And they turned against me their shoulder, which was pulling away."[329] For a suppliant stretches out prostrate on the ground with his neck bent, but the one who turns his back indicates by this very gesture of the body that he has no regard for the one who is warning him. "And this," he says, "is what they were doing."

32:33b: *"Although I taught them at daybreak and I educated them, they have not listened so as to receive instruction."*

"Driving out the darkness of their error and all their worship of idols, I desired to enlighten their hearts daily and to teach them what is upright, thereby keeping my judgment in check." And so as to preserve free will, he goes on and says, "they have not listened so as to receive instruction."

32:34: *"They set up their idols in the house that is called by my name, to defile it."*

Not only in that time did Judah set up the statue of an idol in the temple of God (as we read about at the beginning of Ezekiel),[330] but even today in the house of God, which is interpreted as the church, an idol is set up in the heart or soul of believers when new doctrine is fabricated and worshiped in secret, as described in Deuteronomy.[331] "Do you not know that you are God's temple," it says, "and that God's Spirit dwells in you?"[332]

32:35a: *"They built the high places"*—or *"altars"*[333]—*"of Baal, which are in the valley of the son of Hinnom, to consecrate their sons*

and their daughters to Molech."

In place of "to consecrate," which in Hebrew is written *ebir*, Aquila and Symmachus translated "to lead through," and the LXX and Theodotion translated "to offer."[334] As for the "valley of the sons of Hinnom," which in Hebrew is said "Gehenna," we spoke about this above more fully.[335] It lies near to the springs of Siloam, and through its delights (since the place is well watered) the people were provoked to extravagance, which was followed by the worship of idols. And it should be noted that "altars" or "high places" in the Hebrew language are called *bamoth*.[336] I say this for the sake of those who are unsure about what this word means in the books of Samuel and Kings.[337] Molech, which is translated "king," is the idol of the Ammonites.[338] Furthermore, divine Scripture indicates that the people served not only the idol of Baal in this place but also all the demons of Moab.[339]

32:35b: *"Which I did not command them, nor did it enter into my mind, that they should do this abomination and lead Judah into sin."*

The tribes of Judah and Benjamin in particular worshiped the images of demons at the shrines of Baal and Molech. Moreover, it is clear that the ten tribes, which are called "Samaria," "Joseph" or "Ephraim," worshiped golden calves at Dan and Bethel.[340] The evil done by the people was so great that God declares that he never imagined such things, nor did it ever enter his mind that they were going to do

---

[329]Zech 7:11. [330]Ezek 8:3. [331]Deut 27:15. [332]1 Cor 3:16. [333]Jerome agrees with Aq; cf. Sym at Jer 7:31 and the asterisked reading at Jer 17:3. [334]Heb *'br* (Hiphil; "to cause to pass over," or KB 780, "to present offerings"). The Pesh translates "to burn," and the Targ uses the cognate Aramaic word (*'br*). Jerome's "to consecrate" is unique among the ancient versions. For the idea that "dedication" is the sense, see M. Weinfeld, "The Worship of Molech and of the Queen of Heaven and Its Background," *Ugarit-Forschungen* 4 (1972): 140-44, 154. [335]Heb *gy' bn hnm* (lit., "valley of the son of Hinnom"). See Jer 2:23a; 7:30-31; 19:1-3a, 6. [336]Heb *bāmôt* (singular *bāmâ* ["hill, high place, place of worship," KB 136]). Cf. Jer 7:30-31. [337]1 Sam 9:12-14, 19, 25; 10:5, 13; 1 Kings 3:2-4; 11:7; 12:31-32; 13:2, 32-33; 14:23; 15:14; 2 Kings 12:3; 14:4; 15:4, 35; 16:4; 17:9, 11, 29, 32; 18:4, 22; 21:3; 23:5, 8, 9, 13, 15, 19, 20. [338]MT: *mōlek* (cf. "king," *melek*). See 1 Kings 11:7; Jerome *Nom. Hebr.* (OS 46.17; 54.24; 70.5). [339]1 Kings 11:7; 2 Kings 23:13. [340]1 Kings 12:28-29.

them. These things are said anthropopathically.[341]

32:36: *"Now therefore thus says the Lord, the God of Israel, concerning this city of which you say, 'It is given into the hand of the king of Babylon by sword, by famine and by pestilence.'"*

To those hoping for aid and trusting in the strength of their defenses, he prophesies that Jerusalem is to be overthrown, the people are about to be captured, and prior to captivity many will die by sword, famine and pestilence. Conversely, to those in despair who have no hope of salvation after the overthrow of the city, he promises that he will aid them. Thus, confidence and pride earn just judgment, whereas despair and humility earn God's aid.

32:37-41: *"Behold, I will gather them from all lands to which I drove them in my anger and my wrath and in great indignation; I will bring them back to this place, and I will make them dwell securely. And they shall be my people, and I will be their God. I will give them one heart and one way, that they may fear me for all days, for their own good and the good of their children after them. I will make with them an everlasting pact"*—or *"I will establish with them an eternal testament"*[342]— *"that I will not cease from doing good to them; and I will put the fear of me in their hearts, that they may not turn from me. I will rejoice over them when I do them good,"*—or *"I will visit them in order to do them good"*[343]—*"and I will plant them in this land in truth"*—or *"in faithfulness"*[344]—*"with all my heart and all my soul."*

Many think that this was fulfilled in the time of Zerubbabel the son of Shealtiel and Jeshua the son of Jozadak the high priest, when Haggai and Zechariah prophesied under Ezra the priest, when the temple was rebuilt and when the walls surrounding the city were repaired under Nehemiah.[345] According to this view, the people who formerly were driven out of Jerusalem in God's anger, wrath and great indignation, being dispersed into the whole world, were afterwards to be brought back and made to dwell securely, so that they would be God's people and the Lord would be their God, as Scripture describes. Yet, although it is possible to fit this passage to those times, the phrases "I will make them dwell securely" and "I will make with them an everlasting pact" (or "I will establish with them an eternal testament") cannot be fully regarded as valid for them, since we have read (and sacred Scripture tells) how they were often conquered and made to serve not only the surrounding nations but also the Persians, the Macedonians, the Egyptians, and to this day, the Romans.

Therefore, all these things should be referred to the advent of the Savior, since we see that they are fulfilled in our time, which is the time of faith. As the apostle says, the elect remnant has been saved,[346] they dwell securely in Christ, and they have been given one heart, as it is written: "Now the company of those who believed were of one heart and soul."[347] He says, "And I will give them one way," namely, him who said, "I am the way, and the life and the truth."[348] ". . . that they may fear me for all days," for "The fear of the Lord is the beginning of wisdom."[349]

He says, "for all days." But if this does not fit the Jews, then it should be understood

---

[341]Jerome uses the Greek adverb *anthrōpopathōs* ("with human feelings"). See also Jer 14:8b-9a; 19:3b-5; 27:5. [342]See Jer 31:31-34. [343]Jerome's translation agrees with the hexaplaric versions (= MT). [344]Heb *'mt* ("trustworthiness, faithfulness, truth," KB 68-69). Jerome matches Aq and Sym. [345]Ezra 3:2, 8; 4:3; 5:1-2; 6:14; Neh 6:15; 12:1, 47; Hag 1:1, 12, 14; 2:2, 4, 21, 23; Zech 4:6-10; 6:11-13. Cf. Jer 16:14-15. [346]Rom 11:5. [347]Acts 4:32. [348]Jn 14:6. [349]Ps 111:10; Prov 9:10; 1:7; Sir 1:16.

with reference to our people, for whose good all of this was, is and will be—and not only for them but also "for their children after them." For with us he has drawn up an everlasting pact, and he will never cease to do us good. Regarding what follows, "And I will put the fear of me in their hearts, that they may not turn from me," he does allow for free will, but in such a way that the fear itself, which is given to us, remains by the grace of the giver. "And when I do them good," he says, "I will rejoice and be glad," namely, that his creatures are saved. This is like the joy of the angels in heaven over one sinner who repents.[350] He says, "And I will plant them in this land in truth"—or, as the LXX translated, "in faithfulness"—so that properly it signifies the Christian people, whose religion is faith. ". . . with all my heart and all my soul." If these are the words of the Lord and Savior, then rightly do we believe the heart and soul of him who says in the Gospel, "I have power to lay down my soul, and I have power to take it up again."[351] But if we take this as spoken out of the *persona* of God the Father, it should be understood according to this passage: "Your new moons, your sabbaths and your festival days my soul hates."[352]

32:42-44: *"For thus says the Lord: Just as I have brought all this great evil on this people, so I will bring on them all the good that I speak to them. Fields shall be possessed in this land, about which you are saying, 'It is a desolation, since no human or beast remains, and it is given into the hand of the Chaldeans.' Fields shall be bought for money, and they shall be recorded in a book, and the seal shall be imprinted, and the witness shall be summoned, in the land of Benjamin, in the places about Jerusalem and in the cities of Judah, in the cities of the hill country, in the cities of the flatlands"—or "the Shephelah"[353]—"and in the cities of the Negeb,"—that is, "in the South"[354]—"for I will restore their captivity, says the Lord."*

These things happened according to the letter as a type, after the return from Chaldea when the people were restored to Judea by command of Cyrus the king. Nevertheless, they were fulfilled spiritually in Christ and in the apostles more truly and more completely. Then, both humans and beasts were restored into the church in accordance with what is written: "O Lord, you save humans and beasts,"[355] all who are rational and simple. And then, fields were bought for money, so that we could make friends for ourselves by means of unrighteous mammon, so that they would receive us into the eternal habitations.[356] They were "recorded in a book"—no doubt, the "Book of Life,"[357] and the official "sign" was "imprinted"—the Lord's cross and his victory; and "witnesses" were "summoned"—the martyrs and the whole chorus of the saints.

"In the land of Benjamin," where the "fortitude" of the Lord is found.[358] "In the places about Jerusalem," where there is a "vision of peace" and eternal security.[359] "And in the cities of Judah," in which Christ is the true "confession."[360] And "in the cities of the hill country," about one of which he says, "A city set on a hill cannot be hid."[361] And "in the cities of the flatlands"—which in Hebrew is *sephela*—so that we may proceed from the

[350]Lk 15:7. [351]Jn 10:18. [352]Is 1:14. [353]The LXX transliterated "Shephelah" (*sephēla*) as a proper noun, whereas Jerome rendered it "flatlands," essentially matching Sym. [354]"Negeb" is the transliteration of the LXX (*nageb*), whereas "in the South" is Jerome, who agrees with Aq and Sym. [355]Ps 36:6. [356]Lk 16:9. [357]Ps 69:28; Phil 4:3; Rev 3:5; 13:8; 17:8; 20:12, 15; 21:27. Cf. Dan 7:10; Mal 3:16. [358]On "Benjamin," see Jer 6:1; 17:21-27; 20:1-2; 31:15; 32:8a. [359]The Hebrew *yrwšlm* is being read as from *rō'eh* ("vision") and *šālôm* ("peace"). This interpretation of "Jerusalem" was already found in Greek sources; see OS 169.66; 174.91; 203.99; Philo *Somn.* 2.250; Origen *Hom. Jer.* 28.2; *Fr. Jer.* 11. See Jer 3:17; 17:21-27. For a similar treatment in rabbinic midrash, see *Genesis Rabbah* 56.10. [360]On "Judah," see Jer 1:18-19; 3:6-10; 4:5. [361]Mt 5:14.

depths and recesses to the utmost heights.[362] "And in the cities in the South"—which the LXX translated as "Negeb"—where there is "midday" and the full light of truth.[363] And since all these things have taken place, the Scripture is fulfilled: "I will restore their captivity, says the Lord." Concerning this it is written, "Ascending on high, he led captivity captive; he received"—or, as the apostle says, "he gave"—"gifts to people."[364]

---

[362]Heb *šĕpēlâ* ("the low country on the western edge of the hills of Judaea," KB 1633). [363]Heb *negeb* ("arid terrain," "the South," KB 665). The Latin *meridies* ("midday") is another way to refer to "the South." [364]Eph 4:8; Ps 68:18. As Jerome points out, in the psalm he "receives" (Heb *lqh*) gifts, whereas in Paul's quotation he "gives" (*didōmi*) gifts.

BIBLIOGRAPHY

Studies:

Braverman, Jay. *Jerome's Commentary on Daniel: A Study of Comparative Jewish and Christian Interpretations of the Hebrew Bible.* Washington, DC: Catholic Biblical Association of America, 1978.

Cain, Andrew. *The Letters of Jerome.* Oxford: Oxford University Press, 2009.

Cain, Andrew, and Josef Lössl. *Jerome of Stridon: His Life, Writings and Legacy.* Farnham and Burlington: Ashgate, 2009.

Cavallera, Ferdinand. *Saint Jérôme. Sa vie et son oeuvre.* 2 vols. Louvain: Spicilegium Sacrum Lovaniense Bureaux, 1922.

Fürst, Alfons. *Hieronymus: Askese und Wissenschaft in der Spätantike.* Freiburg: Herder, 2003.

Graves, Michael. *Jerome's Hebrew Philology.* Leiden: Brill, 2007.

Kamesar, Adam. *Jerome, Greek Scholarship, and the Hebrew Bible: A Study of the* Quaestiones Hebraicae in Genesim. Oxford: Clarendon Press, 1993.

Kelly, J. N. D. *Jerome: His Life, Writings and Controversies.* London: Gerald Duckworth & Co., 1975.

Jay, Pierre. *L'exégèse de saint Jérôme d'après son "Commentaire sur Isaïe."* Paris: Études Augustiniennes, 1985.

Murphy, F. X., ed. *A Monument to St. Jerome.* New York: Sheed & Ward, 1952.

Penna, Angelo. *Principe e carattere dell'esegesi di S. Girolamo.* Rome: Pontifical Biblical Institute, 1950.

Rebenich, Stefan. *Jerome.* London: Routledge, 2002.

Rice, Eugene F., Jr. *Saint Jerome in the Renaissance.* Baltimore: Johns Hopkins University Press, 1985.

Steinmann, Jean. *Saint Jerome and His Times.* Translated by Ronald Matthews. Notre Dame, IN: Fides, 1959.

White, Carolinne. *The Correspondence (394-419) between Jerome and Augustine of Hippo.* Lewiston, NY: The Edwin Mellen Press, 1990.

Williams, Megan Hale. *The Monk and the Book: Jerome and the Making of Christian Scholarship.* Chicago: University of Chicago Press, 2006.

Translations:

Archer, Gleason L., Jr. *Jerome's Commentary on Daniel.* Grand Rapids: Baker, 1958.

Cain, Andrew. *St. Jerome: Commentary on Galatians.* FC 121. Washington, DC: Catholic University of America Press, 2010.

Donaldson, Malcom D. *A Translation of Jerome's* Chronicon *with Historical Commentary.* Lewiston, NY: Mellen University Press, 1996.

Ewald, Marie L. *The Homilies of Saint Jerome.* 2 vols. FC 48, 57. Washington, DC: Catholic University of America Press, 1964, 1966.

Freemantle, W. H. *The Principal Works of St. Jerome.* NPNF[2], 6. Grand Rapids: Eerdmans, 1954.

Halton, Thomas P. *St. Jerome: On Illustrious Men.* FC 100. Washington, DC: Catholic University of America Press, 1999.

Hayward, C. T. R. *Jerome's Hebrew Questions on Genesis: Translated with an Introduction and Commentary.* Oxford Early Christian Studies. Oxford: Clarendon Press, 1995.

Heine, Ronald E. *The Commentaries of Origen and Jerome on St. Paul's Epistle to the Ephesians.* Oxford Early Christian Studies. Oxford: Oxford University Press, 2002.

Hritzu, John N. *Saint Jerome: Dogmatic and Polemical Works.* FC 53. Washington, DC: Catholic University of America Press, 1965.

Scheck, Thomas P. *St. Jerome's Commentaries on Galatians, Titus and Philemon.* Notre Dame, IN: University of Notre Dame Press, 2010.

—————. *St. Jerome: Commentary on Matthew.* FC 117. Washington, DC: Catholic University of America Press, 2008.

Subject Index

Scripture Index